AN EXEGETICAL SUMMARY OF
REVELATION 1–11

AN EXEGETICAL SUMMARY OF REVELATION 1–11

Second Edition

Ronald L. Trail

SIL International

Second Edition
© 2003, 2008 by SIL International

Library of Congress Catalog Card Number: 2008923524
ISBN: 978-155671-198-5

Printed in the United States of America

All Rights Reserved
No part of this publication may be reproduced, stored in a retrieval system, or transmitted in any form or by any means without the express permission of SIL International. However, brief excerpts, generally understood to be within the limits of fair use, may be quoted without written permission.

Copies of this and other publications
of SIL International may be obtained from

International Academic Bookstore
SIL International
7500 West Camp Wisdom Road
Dallas, TX 75236-5699, USA

Voice: 972-708-7404
Fax: 972-708-7363
academic_books@sil.org
www.ethnologue.com

PREFACE

Exegesis is concerned with the interpretation of a text. Exegesis of the New Testament involves determining the meaning of the Greek text. Translators must be especially careful and thorough in their exegesis of the New Testament in order to accurately communicate its message in the vocabulary, grammar, and literary devices of another language. Questions occurring to translators as they study the Greek text are answered by summarizing how scholars have interpreted the text. This is information that should be considered by translators as they make their own exegetical decisions regarding the message they will communicate in their translations.

The Semi-Literal Translation

As a basis for discussion, a semi-literal translation of the Greek text is given so that the reasons for different interpretations can best be seen. When one Greek word is translated into English by several words, these words are joined by hyphens. There are a few times when clarity requires that a string of words joined by hyphens have a separate word, such as "not" (μή), inserted in their midst. In this case, the separate word is surrounded by spaces between the hyphens. When alternate translations of a Greek word are given, these are separated by slashes.

The Text

Variations in the Greek text are noted under the heading TEXT. The base text for the summary is the text of the fourth revised edition of *The Greek New Testament,* published by the United Bible Societies, which has the same text as the twenty-sixth edition of the *Novum Testamentum Graece* (Nestle-Aland). Dr. J. Harold Greenlee researched the variants and has written the notes for this part of the summary. The versions that follow different variations are listed without evaluating their choices.

The Lexicon

The meaning of a key word in context is the first question to be answered. Words marked with a raised letter in the semi-literal translation are treated separately under the heading LEXICON. First, the lexicon form of the Greek word is given. Within the parentheses following the Greek word is the location number where, in the author's judgment, this word is defined in the *Greek-English Lexicon of the New Testament Based on Semantic Domains* (Louw and Nida 1988). When a semantic domain includes a translation of the particular verse being treated, **LN** in bold type indicates that specific translation. If the specific reference for the verse is listed in *A Greek-English Lexicon of the New Testament and Other Early Christian Literature* (Bauer, Arndt, Gingrich, and Danker 1979), the outline location and page number is given. Then English equivalents of the Greek word are given to show how it is translated by commentators who offer their own translations of the whole text and, after a semicolon, all the versions in the list of abbreviations for translations. When reference is made to "all versions," it refers to only the versions in the list of translations. Sometimes further comments are made about the meaning of the word or the significance of a verb's tense, voice, or mood.

The Questions

Under the heading QUESTION, a question is asked that comes from examining the Greek text under consideration. Typical questions concern the identity of an implied actor or object of an event word, the antecedent of a pronominal reference, the connection indicated by a relational word, the meaning of a genitive construction, the meaning of figurative language, the function of a rhetorical question, the identification of an ambiguity, and the presence of implied information that is needed to understand the passage correctly. Background information is also considered for a proper understanding of a passage. Although not all implied information and background information is made explicit in a translation, it is important to consider it so that the translation will not be stated in such a way that prevents a reader from arriving at the proper interpretation. The question is answered with a summary of what commentators have said. If there are contrasting differences of opinion, the different interpretations are numbered and the commentaries that support each are listed. Differences that are not treated by many of the commentaries often are not numbered, but are introduced with a contrastive 'Or' at the beginning of the sentence. No attempt has been made to select which interpretation is best.

In listing support for various statements of interpretation, the author is often faced with the difficult task of matching the different terminologies used in commentaries with the terminology he has adopted. Sometimes he can only infer the position of a commentary from incidental remarks. This book, then, includes the author's interpretation of the views taken in the various commentaries. General statements are followed by specific statements, which indicate the author's understanding of the pertinent relationships, actors, events, and objects implied by that interpretation.

The Use of This Book

This book does not replace the commentaries that it summarizes. Commentaries contain much more information about the meaning of words and passages. They often contain arguments for the interpretations that are taken and they may have important discussions about the discourse features of the text. In addition, they have information about the historical, geographical, and cultural setting. Translators will want to refer to at least four commentaries as they exegete a passage. However, since no one commentary contains all the answers translators need, this book will be a valuable supplement. It makes more sources of exegetical help available than most translators have access to. Even if they had all the books available, few would have the time to search through all of them for the answers.

When many commentaries are studied, it soon becomes apparent that they frequently disagree in their interpretations. That is the reason why so many answers in this book are divided into two or more interpretations. The reader's initial reaction may be that all of these different interpretations complicate exegesis rather than help it. However, before translating a passage, a translator needs to know exactly where there is a problem of interpretation and what the exegetical options are.

Acknowledgments

This summary has been a team effort. Dr. Harold Greenlee prepared the Louw and Nida and Arndt and Gingrich lexicon readings as well as the textual questions. Richard Blight edited the final copy for its content and format, adding many valuable suggestions as well as the commentary by Thomas (EC). The author would like to express his sincere thanks to both of them.

ABBREVIATIONS

COMMENTARIES AND REFERENCE BOOKS

Alf   Alford, Henry. *Alford's Greek Testament, an Exegetical and Critical Commentary.* Vol. 4. 1875. Grand Rapids: Baker, 1980.

BAGD   Bauer, Walter. *A Greek-English Lexicon of the New Testament and Other Early Christian Literature.* Translated and adapted from the 5th ed., 1958 by William F. Arndt and F. Wilbur Gingrich. 2nd English ed. revised and augmented by F. Wilbur Gingrich and Frederick W. Danker. Chicago: University of Chicago Press, 1979.

BNTC   Caird, G. B. *A Commentary on the Revelation of St. John the Divine.* Black's New Testament Commentaries, edited by Henry Chadwick. London: Adam & Charles Black, 1966.

EC   Thomas, Robert L. *Revelation 1–7. Revelation 8–22.* An Exegetical Commentary. 2 vols. Chicago: Moody Press, 1992, 1995

ICC   Charles, R. H. *A Critical and Exegetical Commentary on The Revelation of St. John.* The International Critical Commentary. Edinburgh: T. & T. Clark, 1920.

Ld   Ladd, George Eldon. *A Commentary of the Revelation of John.* Grand Rapids: William B. Eerdmans, 1972.

LN   Louw, Johannes P., and Eugene A. Nida. *Greek-English Lexicon of the New Testament Based on Semantic Domains.* New York: United Bible Societies, 1988.

Lns   Lenski, R. C. H. *The Interpretation of St. John's Revelation.* Minneapolis: Augsburg, 1963.

NIC   Mounce, Robert H. *The Book of Revelation.* Revised ed. The New International Commentary on the New Testament, edited by F. F. Bruce and Gordon D. Fee. Grand Rapids: Eerdmans, 1977.

NIGTC   Beale, G. K. *The Book of Revelation, A Commentary on the Greek Text.* The New International Greek Testament Commentary. Grand Rapids: Eerdmans, 1999.

NTC   Bruce, F. F. *The Revelation to John.* A New Testament Commentary, edited by G. C. D. Howley. Grand Rapids: Zondervan, 1969.

Sw   Swete, Henry Barclay. *Commentary on Revelation.* Grand Rapids: Kregel Publications, 1977.

TH   Bratcher, Robert G. and Howard A. Hatton. *A Handbook on The Revelation to John.* New York: The United Bible Societies, 1993.

TNTC   Morris, Leon. *The Book of Revelation, an Introduction and Commentary.* Tyndale New Testament Commentaries. Revised Edition. Grand Rapids: Eerdmans, 1987.

TR   HE KAINE DIATHEKE, NOVUM TESTAMENTUM. Oxford: The Clarendon Press, 1891.

Wal	Walvoord, John F. *The Revelation of Jesus Christ*. Chicago: Moody, 1966.
WBC	Aune, David E. *Revelation*. Word Biblical Commentary, Vols. 52a and 52b, edited by Ralph p. Martin. Nashville: Thomas Nelson, 1997 and 1998.

GREEK TEXT AND TRANSLATIONS

GNT	The Greek New Testament. Edited by B. Aland, K. Aland, J. Karavidopoulos, C. Martini, and B. Metzger. 4th ed. London, New York: United Bible Societies, 1993.
CEV	The Holy Bible, Contemporary English Version. New York: American Bible Society, 1995.
KJV	The Holy Bible. Authorized (or King James) Version. 1611.
NAB	The New American Bible. New York: Catholic Book Publishing Co, 1970.
NET	The Net Bible. New English Translation, New Testament. Version 9.206. WWW.NETBIBLE.COM: Biblical Studies Press, 1999.
NIV	The Holy Bible, New International Version. Grand Rapids: Zondervan, 1984.
NLT	The Holy Bible, New Living Translation. Wheaton, Ill.: Tyndale House Publishers, 1996.
NRSV	The Holy Bible: New Revised Standard Version. New York: Oxford University Press, 1989.
REB	The Revised English Bible. Oxford: Oxford University Press and Cambridge University Press, 1989.
TEV	Good News Bible, Today's English Version. 2nd ed. New York: American Bible Society, 1992.
TNT	The Translator's New Testament. London: British and Foreign Bible Society, 1973.

GRAMMATICAL TERMS

act.	active		opt.	optative
fut.	future		pass.	passive
impera.	imperative		perf.	perfect
indic.	indicative		pres.	present
infin.	infinitive		subj.	subjunctive
mid.	middle			

MISCELLANEOUS

LXX	Septuagint		OT	Old Testament
TR	Textus Receptus		NT	New Testament

EXEGETICAL SUMMARY OF REVELATION

DISCOURSE UNIT: 1:1–20 [EC, NIC, NIGTC, TH, TNTC; NET, NLT]. The topic is prologue [NIC, NIGTC, TH, TNTC; NET], a prophecy from John [CEV], John's past vision [EC].

DISCOURSE UNIT: 1:1–8 [EC, GNT, Ld, NTC, WBC; CEV, TEV]. The topic is introduction and salutation [GNT], introduction [TEV], prologue [EC, Ld, NTC, WBC].

DISCOURSE UNIT: 1:1–3 [BNTC, ICC, NIC, NIGTC, NTC, Sw, TH, TNTC, Wal; NAB, NIV, NLT]. The topic is the title [BNTC], superscription [ICC, Ld, NIC], introduction [NIGTC, NTC, Sw, TH, TNTC, Wal; NAB, NIV].

1:1 (The) revelation[a] of-Jesus Christ that God gave him
LEXICON—a. ἀποκάλυψις (LN 28.38) (BAGD 2. p. 92): 'revelation' [BAGD, EC, LN, Lns, WBC; all versions except CEV, TEV, TNT], 'account of a revelation' [TNT], 'disclosure' [BAGD], 'Apocalypse' [BNTC]. This noun is also rendered as a clause or phrase: 'what God showed to Jesus Christ' [CEV], 'events that Jesus Christ revealed' [TEV]. Ἀποκάλυψις means something made known that could not have otherwise been discovered [Ld, Lns, TNTC].
QUESTION—How are the nouns related in the genitive construction ἀποκάλυψις Ἰησοῦ Χριστοῦ 'revelation of Jesus Christ'?
 1. It is a revelation from Jesus Christ [Alf, EC, ICC, Ld, NIC, Sw, TH, WBC; NLT, TEV; probably Lns, TNTC which say that it indicates possession]: this is what Jesus Christ revealed to people. God is the source of the revelation, but Jesus Christ is the agent who reveals it to people [NIC]. Christ is the revealer throughout the book, addressing the seven churches, opening the scroll, and disclosing its contents. This is the message that Jesus Christ was inspired by God to reveal to his servants [EC]. This interpretation is supported by the following context, 'that God gave to him' [EC, Lns].
 2. It is a revelation to Jesus Christ from God [CEV]: this is what God revealed to Jesus Christ.
 3. It means both that Jesus Christ is the one who is revealed and that it comes from him [NIGTC, Wal].

to-show[a] to-his servants[b] things-that must[c] happen[d] soon,[e]
LEXICON—a. aorist act. infin. of δείκνυμι (LN 28.47, 33.150) (BAGD 1.a. p. 172): 'to show' [BAGD, BNTC, EC, LN (28.47, 33.150), Lns; all versions except CEV, NLT], 'to reveal' [WBC], 'to make known' [BAGD, LN (28.47)], 'to tell (what happened)' [CEV], 'to share (the revelation)' [NLT], 'to point out' [BAGD], 'to explain, to make clear' [LN (33.150)].

b. δοῦλος (LN 87.76) (BAGD 4. p. 206): 'servant' [BNTC, WBC; all versions], 'bondservant' [LN], 'slave' [BAGD, EC, LN, Lns].
c. pres. act. indic. of impersonal verb δεῖ (LN 71.34) (BAGD 1. p. 172): 'must' [BAGD, EC, LN, Lns, WBC; all versions except NLT], '(events that) will (happen)' [NLT], 'to be bound to' [BNTC], 'to be necessary' [BAGD, LN]. The sense of obligation stems from God's purpose [Alf, ICC, NIC, TH].
d. aorist mid. (deponent = act.) infin. of γίνομαι (LN 13.107): 'to happen' [BNTC, EC, LN; CEV, NAB, NET, NLT, TEV], 'to take place' [NIV, NRSV, REB, TNT], 'to occur' [LN, Lns], 'to come to pass' [WBC; KJV].
e. τάχος (LN 67.56) (BAGD p. 807): 'speed, quickness, swiftness, haste' [BAGD]. The phrase ἐν τάχει is translated 'soon' [BAGD, BNTC, EC; CEV, NIV, NLT, NRSV, REB, TNT]; 'very soon' [NAB, NET, TEV]; 'shortly' [Lns; KJV]; 'quickly' [LN, WBC]; 'in a short time' [BAGD].

QUESTION—To whom does αὐτοῦ 'his' refer?
1. It refers to Jesus Christ [Alf, Lns]: Jesus Christ's servants.
2. It refers to God [EC, ICC, WBC; NLT]: God's servants. This interpretation is supported by a similar statement in 22:6 where only God is referred to [WBC].

QUESTION—To whom does τοῖς δοῦλος αὐτοῦ 'to his servants' refer?
1. It refers to believers [EC, NIGTC, TH, WBC]. This is supported by the fact that the revelation is for the ones who hear it read aloud [WBC]. The Christians in the seven churches are recipients of these words [EC].
2. It refers to Christian prophets [ICC, NIC]. The communication of a divine revelation is by means of a vision to a prophet [ICC].

QUESTION—What sense of ἐν τάχει 'soon' is being used here?
1. It does not strictly mean 'the near future' but 'soon' as viewed from certain perspectives [Alf, EC, Lns, NIC, NIGTC, TNTC]. It may not be 'soon' in human terms as much as in God's perspective where a thousand years with him is like a day [Alf, TNTC]. It means 'soon' in human terms, but it is relative to a similar phrase in Daniel 2:8 where Daniel saw these events as occurring in the latter days. What to Daniel was 'the latter days', to John, living in the latter days, was 'soon' [EC, NIGTC]. It means 'soon' in the prophetic perspective in which the prophets tended to blur the near and distant future into a single time period [Ld, NIC]. It indicates the imminence of the coming events without setting a time frame [EC, NIC].
2. It does not mean the near future but only that once the time comes, they will happen quickly [TNTC, Wal].
3. It means the near future [BNTC, NTC]. The events that will soon take place concern the persecution of the church, not the final consummation [BNTC].

and he-made-(it)-known[a] having-sent[b] (it) through[c] his angel[d] to-his servant John,

LEXICON—a. aorist act. indic. of σημαίνω (LN 33.153) (BAGD 1. p. 747): 'to make known' [BAGD, BNTC; NAB, NIV, NRSV, REB, TEV], 'to communicate' [BAGD], 'to indicate clearly' [LN], 'to make clear' [LN; NET], 'to signify' [EC, Lns; KJV], 'to inform' [TNT], 'to share' [NLT], not explicit [CEV]. The verb means to make known by means of signs [EC, NIC, TH, Wal, WBC]. This refers to the symbolic signs that make up much of the content of the book [EC]. This verb matches the visions which John saw [Lns].
- b. aorist act. participle of ἀποστέλλω (LN 15.67) (BAGD 1.d. p. 99): 'to send' [BNTC, EC, LN, WBC; all versions], 'to send word' [LN], 'to grant a commission' [Lns]. The phrase ἐσήμανεν ἀποστείλας 'he made it known having sent' is translated 'he had it made known' [BAGD], 'he sent with the message' [CEV].
- c. διά with genitive object (LN 90.4): 'through' [EC, LN, Lns], 'by' [LN; KJV], not explicit [all other versions]. Some versions render this word by making the angel the person who was sent [CEV, NLT, TNT]: he sent his angel. Others construe this preposition with the verb 'to send' [BNTC, WBC; NAB, NET, NIV, NRSV, REB, TEV]: by sending his angel.
- d. ἄγγελος (LN 12.28, 33.195): 'angel' [BNTC, LN (12.28), Lns, WBC; all versions], 'messenger' [LN (33.195)]. Ἄγγελος means 'messenger' but here has the sense of 'heavenly messenger' [TH].

QUESTION—Who is the implied actor of ἐσήμανεν 'he made known'?
1. The implied actor is Jesus Christ [Alf, EC, ICC, Lns, NIC, Sw, TH, WBC; CEV, REB]: Jesus Christ made known.
2. The implied actor is God [TNTC]: God made known. God is the actor of both 'made known' and 'having sent' [TNTC].

QUESTION—What relationship is indicated by the participle ἀποστείλας 'having sent'?
It expresses the means he used to make it known [NET, NIV, NRSV, REB, TEV]: he made it known *by* sending.

QUESTION—To whom does αὐτοῦ 'his' refer in the phrase 'his angel'?
It refers to Jesus Christ [Alf, EC, ICC, Lns, NIC, Sw, TH, WBC; CEV, REB]: the angel of Jesus Christ. This must be the angel referred to in 17:1, 7, 15, 19:9, 21:9 and 22:1, 6 [Alf, TH]. In 22:16 we read that Jesus says that he has sent his angel to give this testimony to the church [NIC]. Although at times Jesus dealt directly with John (6:9–17) he used angels at other times (e.g., 17:1; 21:9). Perhaps this also includes angelic beings such as the four living beings and twenty-four elders in chapter 4 [EC].

1:2 who testified-to[a] the word[b] of-God

LEXICON—a. aorist act. indic. of μαρτυρέω (LN 33.262) (BAGD 1.b. p. 493): 'to testify to' [EC, Lns; NET, NIV, NRSV], 'to tell' [CEV, REB, TEV], 'to tell...to openly declare' [TNT], 'to bear witness to' [BAGD, BNTC,

WBC], 'to witness' [LN], 'to bare record of' [KJV], 'to report' [NAB], 'to faithfully report' [NLT], 'to declare, to confirm' [BAGD]. The versions rendering this 'to tell' have 'all that he saw' as the object. The aorist tense does not refer to some testimony prior to what is written in this book [Lns, NIC]. Perhaps the prologue was written after having written the visions described in this book [NIC]. It is an epistolary aorist: John considers the moment when this book is read in the churches [EC, ICC, Lns].
   b. λόγος (LN 33.98, 33.100) (BAGD 1.b.β. p. 478): 'word' [LN (33.98); KJV, NAB, NET, NIV, NLT, NRSV, REB], 'Word' [EC, LN (33.100), Lns], 'message' [LN (33.98), WBC; CEV, TEV, TNT], 'Message' [LN (33.100)], 'purpose declared by God' [BNTC]. Λόγος refers to the divine revelation through Christ and his messengers [BAGD].

QUESTION—To whom does ὅς 'who' refer?
   It refers to John [EC, Lns, NIC, NTC, TH; all versions]: John bore witness. He testified by means of writing this book [Lns].

QUESTION—How are the nouns related in the genitive construction τὸν λόγον τοῦ θεοῦ 'the word of God'?
   1. The word is from God [BNTC, EC, ICC, Ld, NIC, Sw, TH, TNTC, Wal, WBC; CEV, TEV, TNT]. The word is the revelation that God gave in this book [ICC].
   2. The word is about God [Alf].
   3. The word is both from God and about Him [NIGTC].

and/even the testimony[a] of-Jesus Christ

LEXICON—a. μαρτυρία (LN 33.264) (BAGD 2.d.β. p. 493): 'testimony' [BAGD, EC, LN, Lns; all versions except CEV, TEV], 'witness' [LN, WBC], 'what Jesus Christ had said and done' [CEV], 'the truth revealed (by Jesus Christ)' [TEV]. This noun is also rendered as a verb: 'to be attested by' [BNTC].

QUESTION—How are the nouns related in the genitive construction τὴν μαρτυρίαν Ἰησοῦ Χριστοῦ 'the testimony of Jesus Christ'?
   1. Jesus Christ gave this testimony [BNTC, EC, ICC, Ld, NIC, TNTC, WBC; CEV, TEV, TNT]. He gave this testimony about the revelation in this book [EC, ICC].
   2. The testimony is about Jesus Christ [Alf, TH; NET].

QUESTION—What is the relationship between τὸν λόγον τοῦ θεοῦ 'the Word of God' and τὴν μαρτυρίαν Ἰησοῦ Χριστοῦ 'the testimony of Jesus Christ'?
   1. He bore witness both to the Word of God and to the testimony of Jesus Christ and these refer to the Book of Revelation he is now writing [Alf, ICC, Lns, NIC, Sw, TH, TNTC, Wal, WBC; all versions except TNT].
   2. He bore witness to the Word of God, *that is*, to the testimony of Jesus Christ [EC; TNT]. The καί 'even' is epexegetical, giving a fuller description of the Word of God [EC].

as-many-(things)-as[a] **he-saw.**

LEXICON—a. ὅσος (LN 59.7): 'as many as' [LN, Lns], 'as many things' [EC], 'everything' [CEV, NET, NIV, NLT, TNT], 'all the visions' [WBC], 'all things' [KJV], 'all' [BNTC; NAB, NRSV, REB, TEV].

QUESTION—To what does ὅσος εἶδεν 'as many (things) as he saw' refer?

It refers back to the Word of God and the testimony of Jesus Christ [EC, Lns, NIC, Wal; CEV, NET, NIV, NLT, NRSV, REB]: the Word of God and the testimony of Jesus Christ, that is, as many things as John saw. 'As many thing as he saw' refers to the visions he saw [TH]. The use of 'saw' indicates that the general character of the book is of prophetic vision [EC].

1:3 **Blessed**[a] **(are) the-one reading**[b] **and the-ones hearing**[c] **the words of-the prophecy**[d]

LEXICON—a. μακάριος (LN 25.119) (BAGD 1.b. p. 486): 'blessed' [BAGD, BNTC, EC, Lns; KJV, NET, NIV, NRSV], 'happy' [BAGD, LN; NAB, REB, TEV, TNT], 'fortunate' [BAGD, TH, WBC]. This noun is also rendered as a verb: '(God) will bless' [CEV, NLT]. Μακάριος 'blessed, happy, fortunate' refers to the condition of the one who is receiving God's favor [BAGD]. This is a promise of a special blessing to those who read and hear [EC].

b. ἀναγινώσκω (LN 33.68) (BAGD 1. p. 51): 'to read' [BNTC, EC, LN, Lns; KJV, NAB, NIV, NLT, TEV, TNT], 'to read aloud' [WBC; NET, NRSV, REB], 'to read to others' [CEV]. This normally carries the sense of being done aloud [Ld, LN, Sw, TH, TNTC, WBC; CEV, NET, NRSV, REB], and in public [Alf, BNTC, ICC, Ld, NIC, Sw, TH, TNTC]. The idea that the reading is done aloud or in public is supported by the following plural, 'those who hear' [ICC, Ld]. The present participle implies continued reading [Wal].

c. pres. act. participle of ἀκούω (LN 24.52, 31.56): 'to hear' EC, [LN (24.52), Lns, WBC; CEV, KJV, NAB, NET, NIV, NRSV], 'to listen (to)' [BNTC, LN (31.56); NLT, REB, TEV, TNT], 'to heed' [LN (31.56)]. The present participle implies continued hearing [Wal].

d. προφητεία (LN 33.460) (BAGD 3.b. p. 723): 'prophecy' [BAGD, BNTC, EC, LN, Lns; all versions except NAB, TEV], 'prophetic message' [NAB, TEV], 'prophetic words' [WBC], 'inspired utterance' [LN]. Prophecy is a message from God about present and/or future events but not exclusively future ones [EC, TH, TNTC]. It is primarily a message from God that requires compliance. It may also include prediction [NIGTC].

QUESTION—To what do τοὺς λόγους τῆς προφητείας 'the words of the prophecy' refer?

They refer to the book of Revelation that the author is writing [Ld, Lns, NIC, NTC, TH, TNTC, Wal, WBC; all versions except NRSV]: the words of this prophecy.

and keeping[a] the-things written in it,
LEXICON—a. pres. act. participle of τηρέω (LN 36.19, 13.32) (BAGD 5. p. 815): 'to keep' [BAGD, EC, LN (13.32), Lns; KJV, NRSV], 'to obey' [LN (36.19), NIC, TH, WBC; CEV, NET, NLT, TEV, TNT], 'to heed' [BNTC, TH; NAB], 'to take to heart' [NIV, REB], 'to observe' [BAGD, Wal], 'to keep commandments' [LN (36.19)], 'to pay attention to' [BAGD, TH, Wal], 'to retain' [LN (13.32)]. The present participle implies continued keeping [Wal]. It means to comply with the moral and ethical standards treated in the letter [EC]. This letter has many exhortations regarding faith, obedience, prayer, and watchfulness [Ld].
QUESTION—What is the function of the single article, οἱ 'the ones' modifying both '(the ones) hearing' and '(the ones) keeping'?
It joins the two classes of people into a single group [Alf, EC, NIGTC, Sw, TH; all versions]: those both hearing and keeping. It may emphasize obedience [NIGTC].

for the time[a] (is) near.[b]
LEXICON—a. καιρός (LN 67.1) (BAGD 3. p. 395): 'time' [EC, LN, WBC; all versions except NAB, REB, TNT], 'time of fulfillment' [NIC, Sw, TH, WBC; REB], 'appointed time' [NAB, TNT], 'crisis' [BNTC], 'period' [Lns], 'occasion' [LN]. The phrase ὁ καιρός 'the time' indicates 'the last times, the time of crisis' [BAGD]. It is the last of the critical periods foreordained by God [EC]. It is the time in which these things will occur [Lns, NIC].
b. ἐγγύς (LN 67.61) (BAGD 2.a. p. 214): 'near' [BAGD, BNTC, EC, LN, Lns, WBC; all versions except CEV, KJV], 'almost here' [CEV], 'at hand' [KJV].
QUESTION—What relationship is indicated by γάρ 'for'?
It indicates the grounds for saying they are blessed if they hear and keep the words of the prophecy [EC, Sw]: blessed are the ones hearing and keeping the prophecy *because* the time is near. It gives a reason they should heed those words [NIGTC, WBC].
QUESTION—In what respect was the time near?
The things that must happen were literally near in time as is seen in 1:1, they were to take place soon [NTC]. John is probably thinking that Jesus' death and resurrection mark the beginning of the end times [NIGTC]. This is stated from the perspective of prophetic anticipation [EC].

DISCOURSE UNIT: 1:4–3:22 [Alf; NAB, REB]. The topic is introduction to the prophecy [Alf], Christ's messages to the seven churches [REB], to the churches of Asia [NAB].

DISCOURSE UNIT: 1:4–8 [BNTC, ICC, Lns, NIC, NIGTC, Sw, TH, TNTC, Wal; NAB, NIV, NLT, TEV]. The topic is the address [BNTC, Lns], greetings [ICC, Sw, TH; NAB, TEV], greetings and doxology [NIV], salutation [NIGTC, TNTC, Wal], salutation and doxology [NIC].

DISCOURSE UNIT: 1:4–7 [NTC]. The topic is greetings and doxology.

DISCOURSE UNIT: 1:4–5a [Ld]. The topic is greeting and salutation.

1:4 John to-the seven[a] churches[b] the-ones in Asia:[c]

LEXICON—a. ἑπτά (LN 60.16): 'seven' [BNTC, EC, **LN**, Lns, WBC; all versions]. The number seven is used in Revelation to connote wholeness, completeness, or perfection [Alf, BNTC, Ld, NIGTC, Sw, TH, TNTC]. The reference to the *seven* churches is meant to allude to the universal church [Alf, BNTC, NIGTC, Sw]. John chose these seven churches because they were typical churches and represented the various spiritual situations of other churches at the time [EC, Ld]. They were probably the churches with whom John had the closest relationship [EC].
- b. ἐκκλησία (LN 11.32) (BAGD 4.b. p. 241): 'church' [BAGD, BNTC, EC, LN, Lns, WBC; all versions], 'congregation' [BAGD, LN]. This word in the NT primarily refers to a group of believers [TH].
- c. Ἀσία (LN 93.415) (BAGD p. 116): 'Asia' [BAGD, EC, LN, Lns, WBC; CEV, KJV, NET, NRSV, TNT], 'province of Asia' [BNTC; NAB, NIV, NLT, REB, TEV]. Asia was a Roman province ruled by proconsuls in western Asia Minor [BAGD]. This was located in the western part of present Turkey [LN].

QUESTION—What words are implied in this phrase?
The verb 'write' is implied [TH; TNT]: John *writes* to the seven churches. The word 'from' is implied [CEV, NET, NLT, TEV]: *from* John to the seven churches.

grace[a] to-you and peace[b] from the-one being[c] and the-one who-was and the-one coming[d]

LEXICON—a. χάρις (LN 88.66 25.89) (BAGD 2.c. p. 877): 'grace' [BAGD, BNTC, EC, LN (88.66), Lns, WBC; all versions except CEV], 'favor' [BAGD, ICC, LN (25.89)], 'kindness' [LN (88.66); CEV], 'goodwill' [BAGD, LN (25.89)]. Χάρις means God's constant love for his people [TH]. It indicates 'unearned favor' [Lns].
- b. εἰρήνη (LN 22.42, 25.248) (BAGD 2. p. 227): 'peace' [BNTC, EC, LN (22.42, 25.248), Lns, WBC; all versions], 'welfare, health' [BAGD]. Εἰρήνη indicates a sense of well-being, security, and wholeness as well as lack of hostility [TH]. It indicates spiritual well-being [NIC]. It indicates harmony between God and man [ICC].
- c. pres. participle of εἰμί (LN 13.1) (BAGD I.1. p. 223): 'to be' [BNTC, EC, LN, Lns, WBC; all versions]. The verbal phrase ὁ ὤ 'the one being' is translated 'the one who is' [EC; NLT], 'the One who is' [WBC], 'God, who is' [CEV, TEV, TNT], 'him who is' [KJV, NAB, NET, NIV, NRSV, REB], 'who is' [BNTC]. It refers to God's continuing existence in the present [EC].
- d. pres. mid. (deponent = act.) participle of ἔρχομαι (LN 13.50, 15.81) (BAGD I.1.b.β. p. 311): 'to come' [BAGD, BNTC, EC, LN (15.81), Lns,

WBC; all versions], 'to become' [LN (13.50)]. The participle here refers to time that is coming, or is future, or is imminent [BAGD].

QUESTION—What words are implied with χάρις ὑμῖν καὶ εἰρήνη 'grace to you and peace'?

The words 'may...be' or 'be' are implied [KJV, REB, TEV, TNT]: *May grace and peace be to you*. The words 'John wishes' are implied [NAB]: *John wishes you grace and peace*. The words 'I pray that (you) will be blessed with' are implied [CEV]: *I pray that you will be blessed with grace and peace*.

QUESTION—To whom does the phrase ὁ ὢν καὶ ὁ ἦν καὶ ὁ ἐρχόμενος 'the one being and the one who was and the one coming' refer?

It refers to God [EC, ICC, Ld, NIC, NIGTC, NTC, Sw, TH, TNTC, Wal, WBC; CEV, TEV, TNT]. It refers to God the Father [EC, Ld, Sw, TNTC, Wal]. This is probably a reference to God the Father because of the following references to the Holy Spirit and Jesus Christ [EC, Wal]. The three-fold participle indicates God's eternal nature [Ld, NTC, TNTC] and his unchanging character [TNTC]. It is John's way of expressing the name Yahweh that the Jews did not like to name [NTC].

QUESTION—Does the participial phrase ὁ ἐρχόμενος 'the one coming' indicate a physical act of coming or is it used for the future tense, 'the one who will be'?

1. It refers to a physical act of coming [EC, ICC, Lns, Sw, TH]: the one who will come. This refers to when God will come for the final judgment [Lns]. This interpretation is better because the purpose of Revelation is to show the coming of God into human history [Sw]. It refers to the Father although the Son's advent is in view. When the Son returns, he will come as representative of the Father and in that sense it will also be the advent of the Father [EC, ICC].
2. It is used for the future tense [Alf, BAGD]: the one who will be.

and from the seven spirits[a] that (are) before his throne

LEXICON—a. πνεῦμα (LN 12.33) (BAGD 4.b. p. 676): 'spirit' [BAGD, BNTC, EC, LN, Lns, WBC; all versions except KJV, NLT], 'Spirit' [KJV, NLT], 'spirit-being' [BAGD].

QUESTION—To whom does the phrase ἀπὸ τῶν ἑπτὰ πνευμάτων 'from the seven spirits' refer?

1. It refers to the Holy Spirit [Alf, BNTC, EC, Ld, Lns, NIGTC, NTC, Sw, TH, TNTC, Wal; NLT]. The position of this phrase between the Father and Jesus Christ argues for this meaning [Ld, NIGTC, Sw, TNTC]. It must refer to the Holy Spirit as grace and peace only come from God [EC, Lns]. The phrase 'seven spirits' is a figurative expression alluding to the effective operation of the Holy Spirit [NIGTC]. The word 'seven' indicates the fullness of the Holy Spirit [Alf, Ld], or the fullness of his kindness and power [NTC]. The expression has its origin in Zechariah 4:1–10 which speaks of seven lamps that are the eyes of the Lord [BNTC,

EC] and John identifies the seven lamps and seven eyes of Zechariah with the seven torches before the throne which are the seven spirits of the Lord (Rev. 4:5) [EC].
2. It refers to the seven archangels of God. These are the same as "the seven angels who stand before God" (see 8:2) [WBC].
3. It refers to seven spirits who are part of a heavenly retinue associated especially with the Lamb [NIC].

1:5 and from Jesus Christ, the faithful[a] witness,[b]
LEXICON—a. πιστός (LN 31.87) (BAGD 1.a.α. p. 664): 'faithful' [BAGD, BNTC, EC, LN; all versions], 'Faithful One' [Lns], 'reliable' [LN, TH, WBC], 'trustworthy' [BAGD, LN, WBC], 'dependable' [LN], 'true' [TH].
   b. μάρτυς (LN 20.67, 33.270) (BAGD 3. p. 494): 'witness' [BNTC, EC, LN (33.270), Lns, WBC; all versions except NLT], 'witness to these things' [NLT], 'martyr' [BAGD, LN (20.67)].
QUESTION—How are the two phrases ὁ μάρτυς, ὁ πιστός 'the witness, the faithful' related?
   The second phrase modifies the first [NTC, WBC; all versions]: the faithful witness. In this form, the adjective 'faithful' is as emphatic as the noun 'witness' [Lns].
QUESTION-- To what is Jesus Christ a faithful witness?
   1. He was a witness to the truth while he was on earth [Ld, Lns]. This is supported by John 18:37 where Jesus states to Pilate that he came to bear witness to the truth [Lns].
   2. He is a witness to the visions and statements of the book of Revelation [TH, TNTC, WBC; NLT].
   3. Both of the above are included [Alf, ICC, NIC, Sw]. Primarily it refers to mediating the revelation he received from God, but also to the larger purpose in his life to witness to God's truth [NIC].

the firstborn[a] of-the dead[b] and the ruler[a] of-the kings of-the earth.
LEXICON—a. πρωτότοκος (LN 10.43) (BAGD 2.a. p. 726): 'firstborn' [BAGD, BNTC, EC, LN, WBC; NAB, NET, NIV, NRSV, REB], 'Firstborn' [Lns], 'first-begotten' [KJV]. The phrase ὁ πρωτότοκος τῶν νεκρῶν 'the first born of the dead' is translated 'the first to conquer death' [CEV], 'the first to rise from the dead' [NLT, TNT], 'the first to be raised from death' [TEV].
   b. νεκρός (LN 23.121) (BAGD 2.a. p. 535): 'dead' [BAGD, BNTC, EC, LN, Lns, WBC; all versions except CEV, TEV, TNT], 'death' [CEV, TEV, TNT], 'lifeless' [LN]. This refers to the conglomerate of men who have died [Wal].
   c. ἄρχων (LN 37.56) (BAGD 1. p. 113): 'ruler' [BAGD, BNTC, EC, LN, Lns, WBC; all versions except KJV, NLT], 'prince' [KJV], 'commander' [NLT].

QUESTION—If the image is a baby being the first to be born in the family, and the topic is Jesus, what is the point of similarity?
1. The point of similarity is that as a firstborn baby is priority in time, that is, as a firstborn baby is the first to come out of the womb, so Jesus is the first to rise from the dead [Alf, BNTC, EC, Lns, TH, Wal, WBC; CEV, NLT, TEV, TNT]. The word 'first' implies that others will follow [TH]. Others were raised from the dead but subsequently died. Jesus is the first to rise and to receive a body that would not die Acts 26:23 [Wal].
2. The point of similarity is sovereignty, that is, as a firstborn child is in a position of authority over all subsequent children, so Christ being the first to rise from the dead is sovereign over the dead. This is supported by the following words that state he is the ruler of the living [ICC, Ld, NIGTC, NTC, Sw].
3. Both the concepts of being first to rise and being sovereign are in focus [NIC].

DISCOURSE UNIT—1:5b–6 [Ld]. The topic is a doxology to Christ.

To-the-one loving[a] us and having-freed[b] us from our sins by[c] his blood,[d]

TEXT—Instead of λύσαντι ἡμᾶς ἐκ 'having freed us from', some manuscripts have λούσαντι ἡμᾶς ἀπό 'having washed us from'. GNT selects the reading 'having freed us from' with an A rating, indicating that the text is certain. The reading 'having washed us from' is taken by KJV.

LEXICON—a. pres. act. participle of ἀγαπάω (LN 25.43): 'to love' [BNTC, EC, LN, Lns, WBC; all versions]. The significance of the present tense is that the loving is continuous [Alf, BNTC, EC, ICC, Ld, Lns, NIC, TH, Wal;]: keeps on loving.
  b. aorist act. participle of λύω (LN 37.127) (BAGD 2.b. p. 483): 'to free' [BAGD, WBC; NAB, NIV, NLT, NRSV, TEV, TNT], 'to set free' [LN; CEV, NET, REB], 'to release' [BNTC, LN], 'to loose' [EC, Lns]. The aorist tense signifies a single act completed in the past [Alf, ICC, Lns, Wal], and points to Jesus' sacrifice of himself [Alf]. This is a figure of Christ's action providing for our release from bondage to sin, which is pictured as a slave-master [EC].
  c. ἐν with dative object (LN 83.13, 90.10): 'by' [EC, LN (90.10), WBC; CEV, NAB, NIV, NRSV, TEV, TNT], 'by shedding' [NLT], 'at the cost of' [ICC, Ld, Sw; NET], 'with' [BNTC, LN (90.10); REB], 'in connection with' [Lns], 'in' [LN (83.13); KJV]. Ἐν indicates instrument [EC, NIGTC, TH]: he used his blood to free us. This involves a Hebrew idiom meaning 'he has freed us from our sins at the price of his blood' [Ld].
  d. αἷμα (LN 8.64, 23.107) (BAGD 2.b. p. 23): 'blood' [BAGD, EC, LN (8.64), Lns, WBC; all versions except TEV, TNT], 'sacrificial blood' [Wal], 'life blood' [BNTC], 'death' [LN (23.107); TNT], 'sacrificial death' [NIC, NIGTC, TH; TEV]. Here 'blood' is a figure for sacrificial death recalling the killing of the sacrificial lamb [Ld]. Blood is more than

death since death may occur without blood being shed. Here Jesus' blood was sacrificially shed to atone for sin [Lns, NIC].
QUESTION—Whom does the word ἡμᾶς 'us' include?
It includes all believers [EC, TH].
QUESTION—From what are people set free?
They are set free from: the power of sin [Alf, NIGTC, TH]; the bondage of sin [EC, Ld, NIC, WBC]; the penalty of sin [NIC]; the guilt of sin [Alf]; the domination of sin [TH]; the misery of sin [NIC].

1:6 and he-made[a] us (a) kingdom,[b]
TEXT—Instead of βασιλείαν 'kingdom', some manuscripts read βασιλείας καί 'kings and'. GNT does not mention this alternative. The reading 'kings and' is taken by KJV.
LEXICON—a. aorist act. indic. of ποιέω (LN 13.9) (BAGD I.1.b.ι. p. 682): 'to make' [BAGD, EC, LN, Lns, WBC; all versions except CEV, NET], 'to appoint' [BNTC; NET], 'to make to be' [Ld, LN], 'to cause to be' [LN]. The verb 'to make' has a double object indicating 'to make someone into something' [BAGD; NIV, NLT, NRSV, REB, TEV, TNT].
b. βασιλεία (LN 1.82) (BAGD 1. 134): 'kingdom' [BAGD, EC, LN, Lns, WBC; all versions except CEV, NAB, REB], 'royal house' [BNTC; REB], 'royal nation' [NAB]. The phrase ἐποίησεν ἡμᾶς βασιλείαν 'he made us a kingdom' is translated 'he lets us rule as kings' [CEV], 'he has appointed us as a kingdom' [NET]. Kingdom here does not indicate a realm with physical dimensions, but an entity composed of believers [TNTC]. God made the nation of Israel into a kingdom of priests at the Passover. See Exodus 19:6 [Ld] and 1 Peter 2:9 [Lns].
QUESTION—Is the kingdom a realm with only one king, or is it a realm in which all the members are kings?
1. It is a realm in which all the members are kings [Alf, BNTC, Ld, Lns, NIGTC, NTC, Wal, WBC; CEV, KJV]. Revelation 5:10 supports this alternative where it is explicitly stated that believers will reign on the earth [Alf, BNTC, Ld, Lns, WBC]. The two nouns, 'kingdom' and 'priests' are closely joined indicating that these are two separate roles and that they take effect together; if believers are priests now, they are also kings now [NIGTC]. Believers reign by using the Word of God. The word 'kingdom' is used instead of kings to stress the unity of believers, not everyone doing his own thing [Lns]. It is during the reign of Christ in the 1000 years that believers will reign. See Revelation 20:6, 22:5 [Ld].
2. It is a realm with only one king [EC, ICC, NIC, Sw, TH, TNTC; NAB, TEV, TNT]. The meaning is that believers are corporately a kingdom and individually priests [EC, ICC, NIC]. The second noun 'priests' is in apposition with the first, 'kingdom' indicating a priestly kingdom or a kingdom that consists of priests [Sw, TNTC].

priests[a] to-(the)-God and Father of-him;
LEXICON—a. ἱερεύς (LN 53.87) (BAGD 2.b. p. 372): 'priest' [BAGD, BNTC, EC, LN, Lns, WBC; all versions]. The phrase ἱερεῖς τῷ θεῷ 'priests to God' is translated making some form of the verb 'to serve' explicit [TH, TNTC; all versions except KJV]: priests to serve God. A priest is someone who goes to God in behalf of men, and to men on behalf of God [TNTC].

QUESTION—How do believers serve as priests?

They serve as priests by offering to God the sacrifices of obedience [BNTC], praise (Hebrews 13:15) [Ld, Lns], thanksgiving [Ld], worship [BNTC, Ld], their bodies (Romans 12:2) [Sw, TNTC]. They offer spiritual sacrifices to God (1 Peter 2:5) [Sw]. They are a faithful witness to the world of God's acts [NIGTC, TNTC]. They intercede for the world [NTC, TNTC, WBC].

QUESTION—To what is the pronoun αὐτοῦ 'of him' related in the phrase τῷ θεῷ καὶ πατρὶ αὐτοῦ 'to God and Father of him'?

1. It is related to both God and Father [BNTC, EC, ICC, Lns, Sw, WBC; NAB, NET, NIV, NRSV, REB, TEV, TNT]: to *his* God and Father. Since Jesus is willing to call men his brothers as seen in Hebrews 2:11, he is also willing to call the Father his God [Sw]. God is Jesus' God according to his humanity and his Father according to his divinity [Lns].
2. It is related to Father only [Alf; CEV, KJV, NLT]: to God and *his* Father. Note that otherwise, John's typical style is to repeat the possessive genitive after each noun to which it applies. See especially John 2:12 [Alf].

to-him (be) the glory[a] and the power[b] into the ages[c] of-the ages;[c] amen.[d]
TEXT—Following εἰς τοὺς αἰῶνας 'into the ages', some manuscripts omit τῶν αἰώνων 'of the ages'. It is included by GNT in brackets with a C rating, indicating difficulty in deciding whether or not to include it in the text. It appears to be included by all versions except perhaps WBC and REB.
LEXICON—a. δόξα (LN 33.357, 87.4, 87.23): 'glory' [BNTC, EC, LN, Lns, WBC; all versions except NLT], 'everlasting glory' [NLT], 'praise' [LN (33.357), NIC], 'honor' [LN, NIC, TH], 'greatness' [LN, TH], 'fame' [TH]. Δόξα denotes the shining light of God's presence revealed especially in God's works in his people's behalf [TH]. Glory here is defined by the qualities of God's character [Lns].
  b. κράτος (LN 76.6) (BAGD 4. p. 449): 'power' [BAGD, LN, WBC; all versions except KJV, NRSV, REB], 'dominion' [BNTC; KJV, NRSV, REB], 'might' [LN, Lns], 'strength' [EC], 'rule, sovereignty' [BAGD]. This noun is also translated as a verb 'to rule' [NLT].
  c. αἰών (LN 67.95, 67.143) (BAGD 1.b. p. 27): 'age' [LN], 'era' [LN], 'eon' [Lns]. The phrase εἰς τοὺς αἰῶνας τῶν αἰώνων 'into the ages of the ages' is translated 'forever and ever' [BNTC, EC, LN (67.95); all versions except REB], 'forever' [WBC; REB], 'for evermore' [BAGD].

d. ἀμήν (LN 72.6) (BAGD 1. p. 45): 'amen' [BAGD, BNTC, EC; all versions], 'truly' [BAGD, LN], 'indeed' [LN], 'let it be so' [BAGD], not explicit [WBC]. Ἀμήν is a transliteration of the Hebrew word for 'verity' or 'truth' [Lns].

QUESTION—To whom does the pronoun αὐτῷ 'to him' refer?

It refers to Jesus Christ [ICC, Lns, NIC, Sw, TH, TNTC, Wal, WBC; TEV].
It refers to God [NIGTC].

QUESTION—What verb should be supplied between 'him' and 'glory'?

The verb 'be' should be supplied [Alf; all versions except NLT]: to him *be* glory. The verb 'let be' should be supplied [EC]: let glory and strength be to him. The verb 'is' should be supplied [Alf]: to him *is* glory. The verb 'belongs' should be supplied [Alf]: to him *belongs* glory. The verb 'give' should be supplied [NLT]: *give* him glory.

DISCOURSE UNIT: 1:7 [Ld]. The topic the theme of the book.1:7

1:7 Look[a] he-comes with[b] the clouds,[c] and every eye[d] will-see him

LEXICON—a. ἰδού (LN 91.13, 91.10) (BAGD 1.a p. 370): 'look' [BAGD, LN (91.13); CEV, NET, NIV, NLT, NRSV, REB, TEV], 'lo' [Lns], 'see' [BAGD; NAB], 'behold' [BAGD, BNTC, EC; KJV], 'pay attention' [LN (91.13), TH], 'indeed' [LN (91.10), WBC], 'listen, come now, then.' [LN (91.13)], 'certainly, at all, at least, in any event' [LN (91.10)], not explicit [TNT]. Ἰδού functions to arouse the attention of the listeners [BAGD (91.13), LN] and to emphasize the following statement [LN (91.13)]. It serves to affirm the truth of the coming of Jesus that follows [WBC].

b. μετά with genitive object (LN 89.108) (BAGD A.I. p. 508): 'with' [BNTC, EC, LN, WBC; all versions except NAB, TEV], 'together with' [LN], 'in company with' [Lns], ' in the company of' [LN], 'amid' [NAB], 'on' [TEV], 'in the midst of' [BAGD].

c. νεφέλη (LN 1.34) (BAGD p. 536): 'cloud' [BAGD, BNTC, EC, LN, Lns, WBC; all versions except NLT], 'cloud of heaven' [NLT]. 'Clouds' connoted majesty and power, see Matthew 24:30 and Luke 21.27 [Lns]. In Hebrew thinking, clouds indicated God's presence [NIC, TNTC], see Exodus 13:21 and 16:10 [NIC], and Numbers 11:25, Psalms 104:3 and Isaiah 19:1 [TNTC]. Jesus comes riding on the clouds [Lns, TH; TEV]. The clouds are probably not to be thought of as Jesus' means of conveyance [NIC]. Jesus returns in a cloud as he was taken away from his disciples (Acts 1:9). In 14:14 the Son of Man is seen to be sitting on a cloud [Wal].

d. ὀφθαλμός (LN 8.23) (BAGD 1. p. 599): 'eye' [BAGD, BNTC, EC, LN, Lns, WBC; KJV, NAB, NET, NIV, NRSV]. The phrase πᾶς ὀφθαλμός 'every eye' is translated 'everyone' [CEV, NLT, REB, TEV, TNT]. 'Eye' here is used figuratively to refer to the whole person [Alf].

QUESTION—What other Scriptures describe a similar event to the one described in this verse?
    Zechariah 12:10, Daniel 7:13 and Matthew 24:30 all describe a similar event [Ld]. Matthew 26:64 describes the Son of Man's coming in the clouds [Alf].
QUESTION—To whom does the pronoun 'he' in ἔρχεται 'he comes' refer?
    It refers to Jesus Christ [Alf, EC, Ld, NIC, TH]. It naturally refers to the person last referred to in 1:6 [Alf].
QUESTION—What is the significance of the present tense ἔρχεται 'he comes'?
    It serves to emphasize the fact of Jesus' coming [Wal]: he definitely will come.

even/and[a] they-who pierced[b] him,
LEXICON—a. καί (LN 89.92, 89.93): 'even' [EC, LN (89.93); CEV, NAB, NET, NIV, NLT, NRSV], 'including' [Sw, WBC; REB, TEV], 'among them' [Alf], 'and also' [LN (89.93); KJV], 'and' [LN (89.92), Lns], 'also, in addition' [LN (89.93)], not explicit [BNTC; TNT]. Καί here indicates an explanation, pointing out one group in particular, namely, those who pierced him [TH].
    b. aorist act. indic. of ἐκκεντέω (LN 19.14) (BAGD p. 240): 'to pierce' [BAGD, BNTC, EC, LN, Lns, WBC; all versions except CEV], 'to stick a sword through' [CEV]. The meaning of 'pierce' here is to kill [BAGD, TH] by the thrust of a sword or spear [TH]. The piercing referred to here, is that which occurred on Calvary, see John 19:37 [Lns].
QUESTION—To whom does the pronoun οἵτινες 'they who' refer?
    1. It refers only to those who actually put Jesus to death [Alf, EC, TH]. It refers to the Jewish leaders who had Jesus crucified and probably to the Romans who actually carried out the crucifixion [Alf, EC, TH]. 'Even those who pierced him' makes this a prominent class within the larger group of 'every eye' [EC]. If it referred to all people who rejected him, there is no point in making this a separate class from the class of the preceding clause that includes all people [Alf].
    2. It refers to all people who by rejecting Jesus in effect 'pierced' him [ICC, Ld, Lns, NIC, NIGTC, Sw]. This does not refer so much to those who actually carried out the crucifixion as to people in every age who, in effect, by their enmity and apathy have joined in the act of His crucifixion [Sw]. It refers specifically to the unbelieving Jews but also includes all unbelievers who by their unbelief belong to that class [Lns].

and all the peoples[a] of-the earth will-mourn[b] over[c] him.
LEXICON—a. φυλή (LN 10.2, 11.56) (BAGD 2. p. 869): 'peoples' [BAGD, LN (11.56); CEV, NAB, NIV, REB, TEV], 'family' [EC], 'tribe' [BNTC, LN (10.2), Lns, WBC; NET, NRSV], 'nation' [BAGD, LN (11.56); NLT, TNT], 'kindred' [KJV].
    b. fut. mid. indic. of κόπτω (BAGD 2. p. 444): 'to mourn' [BAGD, EC, Lns; NET, NIV, TEV], 'to wail' [WBC; KJV, NRSV], 'to weep' [CEV, NLT], 'to lament' [BNTC], 'to lament bitterly' [NAB], 'to lament in remorse'

[REB], 'to be filled with sorrow' [TNT]. Κόπτω means 'to weep loudly' [TH]. It means to beat one's breast in grief [Lns].
  c. ἐπί with accusative object (LN 89.27) (BAGD III.1.b.ε. p. 289): 'over' [EC, Lns; TEV], 'because of' [LN; CEV, KJV, NET, NIV, NLT, TNT], 'on account of' [WBC; NRSV], 'on the basis of' [LN], 'for' [BAGD, BNTC], not explicit [NAB, REB].

QUESTION—To whom does πᾶσαι αἱ πυλαὶ τῆς γῆς 'all the tribes of the earth' refer?

It refers to all unbelieving peoples [EC, NIC]. It refers to all the people of the world [TH, WBC]. It refers to all the ethnic peoples of the world including the nation of Israel [Wal].

QUESTION—Is the 'mourning' due to repentance or to fear of judgment?
  1. It is a mourning of regret and possible repentance [BNTC, NIGTC; REB, TNT]. Since the people do not mourn over themselves, but over Jesus, it probably indicates repentance on their part [NIGTC]. That they mourn over Jesus rather than themselves at least indicates that they feel guilty. But we cannot be sure that it causes them to repent because that is not John's focus here [BNTC]
  2. It is a mourning of despair and fear of judgment [Alf, EC, Ld, Lns, NIC, TH]. This interpretation is supported by similar references in 18:9 and Matthew 24:30 [TH]. Their mourning is out of fear of the one coming and the consequences it will have [Alf]. It is not Him they are mourning, but He is the cause of their mourning in view of the judgment he will bring [Ld].

Yes,^a amen.

LEXICON—a. ναί (LN 69.1) (BAGD 4. p. 533): 'yes' [EC, LN; NLT], 'yea' [Lns], 'so it shall be' [NIV, REB, TEV], 'so it is to be' [BAGD; NAB, NRSV], 'it is so' [ICC], 'so be it' [BNTC; TNT], 'yes, it will happen' [CEV], 'this will certainly come to pass' [NET], 'assuredly' [WBC], 'even so' [KJV], 'yes it is true that, yes it is so, sure, indeed' [LN]. Ναί emphatically affirms a statement [WBC].

QUESTION—What is the significance of the combination of the Greek ναί 'yes', and the Hebrew ἀμήν 'so be it'?

It forms an expression of enthusiastic approval [NIC, TNTC]. It shows John's exuberance over the return of the Lord [TNTC]. It is a double affirmation that the prophecy will be fulfilled [EC].

DISCOURSE UNIT: 1:8 [Ld, NTC]. The topic is the divine authentication.

1:8 I am the Alpha^a and the Omega,^b says the Lord God,

TEXT—Following ˀΩ 'Omega' some manuscripts include ἀρχὴ καὶ τέλος 'beginning and end'. They are omitted by GNT with an A rating, indicating that the text is certain. The words 'beginning and end' are included by KJV.

TEXT—Instead of κύριος ὁ θεός 'the Lord God' some manuscripts possibly have ὁ κύριος 'the Lord'. GNT does not mention this variant. The reading 'the Lord' is taken by the TR. It is also taken by KJV.

LEXICON—a. Ἄλφα (LN **61.7**)(BAGD p. 41): 'Alpha' [BNTC, EC, Lns, WBC; all versions except TEV], 'alpha' [BAGD, LN], 'first' [LN; TEV], 'beginning' [LN]. Ἄλφα carries the sense of significance or importance [LN].

b. Ὦ (LN **61.18**) (BAGD p. 895): 'Omega' [BNTC, EC, Lns, WBC; all versions except TEV], 'last' [LN; TEV], 'omega' [BAGD, **LN**], 'end' [LN]. Used with ἄλφα it implies a high status and authority over everything [LN].

QUESTION—To whom does ἐγώ 'I' refer?

1. It refers to God [Alf, BNTC, EC, ICC, Ld, NIC, NIGTC, Sw, TH, TNTC, WBC]. This interpretation is supported by the words κύριος ὁ θεός 'the Lord God' identifying the speaker [Sw]. A similar reference in which God speaks in Revelation is in 21:6 [Alf, NIC, TH]. The word 'Lord' most frequently refers to the Father in Revelation, as it does here. Elsewhere in the NT it refers most often to Christ [TNTC]. This same reference to being the 'Alpha and Omega' refers to Jesus Christ in 22:13 [TH].
2. It refers to Christ [Lns, Wal]. 'I' is emphatic here. Jesus is speaking both here and in 21.6. The references to Alpha and Omega refer to Jesus as being God's revelation to men in written form. Jesus is also spoken of as the Word of God (19:13). It is the Scriptures that bear witness to Christ (John 5:39) [Lns].

QUESTION—What is the meaning of the figure τὸ Ἄλφα καὶ τὸ Ὦ 'the Alpha and the Omega'?

The figure is known as a *merism* in which the beginning and the end of a series are named with the purpose of emphasizing all that comes in between [NIGTC]. It indicates God's control over all history [Ld, NIC, NIGTC]. It is a reference to everything in between these letters [NIC, Sw] and indicates totality [Alf, ICC, Sw]. It indicates God's sovereignty [TH, WBC]. It indicates God's eternal existence [TH, Wal].

the-one being and the-one who-was and the-one coming, the Almighty.[a]

LEXICON—a. παντοκράτωρ (LN 12.7) (BAGD p. 609): 'Almighty' [BAGD, EC, LN, Lns, WBC; KJV, NAB, NIV, NRSV, TEV, TNT], 'Almighty One' [NLT], 'All-Powerful' [BAGD; CEV, NET], 'sovereign Lord of all' [REB], 'All-Ruler' [Ld], 'Omnipotent' [BNTC], 'Omnipotent One' [BAGD], 'the one who has all power' [LN].

DISCOURSE UNIT: 1:9–3:22 [Ld, WBC]. The topic is the first vision [Ld], John's vision and commission [WBC].

DISCOURSE UNIT: 1:9–20 [Alf, EC, GNT, ICC, Ld, Lns, NIC, NIGTC, NTC, Sw, TH, WBC; CEV, NAB, NIV, NLT, TEV]. The topic is a vision of Christ [GNT, Lns, Sw, WBC; CEV, TEV], a vision of the Son of Man [WBC;

NIV, NLT], the first vision [NIC, NTC, TH, TNTC; NAB], John's call and commission [ICC], John's commission to write [EC], the glorified Christ [Ld].

DISCOURSE UNIT: 1:9–18 [Wal]. The topic is a vision of Christ.

DISCOURSE UNIT: 1:9–11 [BNTC, EC, NIGTC, TNTC]. The topic is the exile [BNTC], John's commission to write [NIGTC, TNTC], John's first commission to write [EC].

1:9 I John, your brother[a] and partner[b] in the suffering[c] and kingdom[d] and endurance[e] in[f] Jesus,

TEXT—Some manuscripts include ἐν τῇ 'in the' before βασιλείᾳ 'kingdom'. GNT does not mention this alternative. The words 'in the' are included by KJV.

TEXT—Instead of ἐν Ἰησοῦ 'in Jesus' some manuscripts have Ἰησοῦ Χριστοῦ 'of Jesus Christ'. GNT does not mention this alternative. The reading 'of Jesus Christ' is taken by KJV.

LEXICON—a. ἀδελφός (LN 11.23) (BAGD 2. p. 16): 'brother' [BAGD, BNTC, EC, Lns, WBC; all versions except CEV], 'Christian brother, fellow believer' [LN], 'follower' [CEV]. Ἀδελφός here refers to a 'fellow believer' in contrast to a blood relation [BAGD, Lns, NIC, TH; CEV].

b. συγκοινωνός (LN 34.6, 57.10) (BAGD p. 774): 'partner' [BNTC, LN (34.6, 57.10); NLT, TEV], 'companion' [KJV, NIV], 'fellow participant' [WBC], 'fellow-partaker' [EC], 'fellowshipper' [Lns], 'sharer' [BAGD, LN (57.10)], 'associate, one who joins in with' [LN (34.6)], 'one who shares in' [LN (57.10)]. This noun is also translated as a clause: 'who share(s) with you' [NAB, NET, NRSV, REB, TNT], 'I am your partner' [TEV]. The phrase ὁ ἀδελφὸς ὑμῶν καὶ συγκοινωνός 'your brother and partner' is translated 'a follower together with all of you' [CEV].

c. θλῖψις (LN 22.2) (BAGD 1. p. 362): 'suffering' [LN; NIV, NLT, REB, TEV], 'persecution' [LN; NET, NRSV, TNT], 'tribulation' [BAGD, Lns, WBC; KJV], 'distress' [NAB], 'ordeal' [BNTC], 'affliction' [BAGD, EC], 'oppression' [BAGD], 'trouble and suffering' [LN]. This noun is also translated as a verb: 'to suffer' [CEV]. It refers to distress brought about by outward circumstances [BAGD].

d. βασιλεία (See this word at 1:6): 'kingdom' [EC, Lns; KJV, NET, NIV, NRSV], 'Kingdom' [NLT, TEV], 'kingship' [WBC], 'king' [CEV], 'royal status' [TNT], 'kingly reign' [NAB], 'sovereignty' [BNTC; REB]. Kingdom for believers means to belong to God's Kingdom or to have Him rule over them [TH].

e. ὑπομονή (LN 25.174) (BAGD 2. p. 846): 'endurance' [BNTC, EC, LN, Lns, WBC; NAB, NET, REB], 'patient endurance' [NIV, NLT, NRSV], 'patience' [KJV], 'courage' [TNT], 'patient expectation' [BAGD], 'strength to endure' [CEV], 'being able to endure' [LN]. This noun is also

translated as a verb: 'to patiently endure' [TEV]. Ὑπομονή is not an act of resignation, but an active courageous kind of activity [TNTC].
f. ἐν with dative object (LN 89.119): 'in' [BNTC, EC, LN, WBC; NET, NLT, NRSV, REB], 'in union with, one with, joined closely to' [LN], 'in connection with' [Lns], 'as (a Christian/follower)' [TH; TEV, TNT], not explicit [CEV]. This preposition is also translated as a clause '(that) are ours in (Jesus)' [BNTC; NIV], 'we have in (Jesus)' [NAB]. The phrase ἐν τῇ θλίψει καὶ βασιλείᾳ καὶ ὑπομονῇ ἐν Ἰησοῦ 'in the suffering and kingdom and endurance in Jesus' is translated 'we suffer because Jesus is our king, but he gives us the strength to endure' [CEV], 'as a follower of Jesus…patiently enduring the suffering that comes to those that belong to his Kingdom' [TEV]. 'In Christ' means to be in spiritual union with Christ [Ld].

QUESTION—To whom does ὑμῶν 'your (brother)' refer?
It includes all to whom this book was being written [TH].

QUESTION—What is the significance of a single article preceding the two nouns 'brother' and 'partner'?
It indicates that the two should be taken closely together [ICC, Lns, WBC]. The two are in apposition to 'John' and both modify him [WBC].

QUESTION—What is the significance of a single article preceding the three nouns suffering, kingdom, and endurance?
It indicates that the three together form a unity [Lns], or refer to a single person [WBC]. It shows that the three are in some way related [EC, TNTC].

QUESTION—How are the nouns θλίψις, βασιλεία, and ὑπομονή 'suffering', 'kingdom,' and 'endurance' related?
Believers enter the Kingdom through suffering (see Acts 14:22) [Alf, Ld, NTC], but then, since the Kingdom is not fully realized, endurance is required [Alf]. Affliction is the central thought, and it is connected with the kingdom and it requires endurance [EC]. Suffering requires endurance [Ld]. Believers, like Jesus, reign through suffering [BNTC, NIGTC] while endurance changes suffering into dignity [BNTC, ICC]. The suffering is the Great Tribulation spoken of in 3:10 and 7:14 that precedes the Millennial Kingdom, and endurance is required in order to have a part in the Kingdom [ICC]. Believers suffer now before they enter the Kingdom in the future, so endurance is required [NIC, TH]. Suffering comes because believers are part of the Kingdom, but through the powers of the Kingdom believers have the strength to endure [Lns]. The three nouns function to mutually interpret each other. Endurance through suffering is the means by which a believer reigns with Jesus [NIGTC].

QUESTION—What is the function of the phrase ἐν Ἰησοῦ 'in Jesus'?
1. It should be construed with all three preceding nouns [Lns, NIC, NIGTC, Sw, TH]: suffering and kingdom and endurance *in Jesus*. Because believers are a part of Christ's body they experience suffering, have strength to endure it, and rule as kings [NIGTC]. The Christian life is

suffering, reigning, and waiting and this is accomplished by being united with the life of Jesus [Sw].
2. It should be taken with the final two nouns, 'endurance and kingdom' [WBC]: endurance and kingdom *in Jesus*.
3. It should only be construed with the final noun 'endurance' [ICC]: endurance *in Jesus*. A person can only endure in partnership with Jesus.

QUESTION—To what does θλίψις 'suffering' refer?
1. It refers to the great tribulation mentioned in 3:10 and 7:14 [ICC].
2. It refers to general suffering and persecution of the Christian life [BNTC, EC, Lns, Sw, TH]. The hostility of the world results in pressure on believers [Lns]. It refers to a persecution that is soon about to occur to the church [BNTC].
3. It refers to both of the above [Ld, NIC, NIGTC]. Godly living produces suffering (see John 16:33 and 2 Timothy 3:12). But the great tribulation is also part of this suffering [NIC].

QUESTION—To what does βασιλεία 'kingdom' refer?
1. It refers to the millennial reign of Christ [EC, ICC, TH]. The believer must patiently suffer in order to be a part of the Kingdom [ICC]. This is a time during which God and Jesus will reign over the world (see 11:15, 12:10) [TH].
2. It refers to the reigning that Christians do as being part of God's kingdom [Sw].
3. It refers to both of the above [Ld, Lns, NIGTC]. Verse 5 states that Christ has made us a kingdom indicating that the kingdom is both present and future [Lns]. As Jesus reigned on earth by enduring suffering so that he could achieve his heavenly rule, so believers reign by enduring suffering until the time when Jesus returns and they are exalted over their enemies [NIGTC].

was[a] on the island called Patmos[b]

LEXICON—a. aorist mid. (deponent = act.) indic. of γίνομαι (LN 85.7) (BAGD II.4.a. p. 160): 'to be' [BAGD, BNTC, Lns, WBC; KJV, NET, NIV, NRSV, REB, TNT], 'to be sent (to)' [CEV], 'to find oneself' [NAB], 'to be exiled (to)' [NLT], 'to be put (on)' [TEV], 'to come to be' [EC, LN].

b. Πάτμος (LN 93.548): 'Patmos' [BNTC, EC, LN, Lns, WBC; all versions]. It was a small rocky island [ICC, Ld, LN]. It was roughly 10 miles long by 5 miles wide [ICC, Ld, NIC, Wal]. It was crescent-shaped [Sw, TNTC]. It was one of the Sporades Islands [BNTC, ICC, NIGTC, WBC], or one of the Dodecanese Islands [EC, TNTC]. It was located in the Aegean Sea [LN, NIC, TH, Wal], about forty miles southwest of Miletus [NIC, Sw, WBC]. It may have been a Roman penal colony [BNTC, EC, ICC, Ld, Lns, NIC, TH].

because-of[a] the word[b] of-God and the testimony[a] of-Jesus.

TEXT—Some manuscripts include διά 'because of' before τὴν μαρτυρίαν 'testimony'. GNT does not mention this alternative. The words 'because of' are included by KJV.

LEXICON—a. διά with accusative object (LN 90.44): 'because of' [BNTC, EC, LN, Lns, WBC; NET, NIV, NRSV], 'because' [CEV, REB, TEV, TNT], 'for' [KJV, NLT], 'on account of, for this reason' [LN], 'for' [NLT]. The phrase διὰ τὸν λόγον τοῦ θεοῦ 'because of the word of God' is translated 'because I had preached God's word/message' [CEV, REB, TNT], 'because I proclaimed God's word' [NAB, TEV], 'for preaching the word of God' [NLT].

b. λόγος (LN 33.100, 33.260): 'word' [BNTC, WBC; all versions except CEV, TNT], 'Word' [EC, LN (33.100), Lns], 'message' [CEV, TNT] 'Message' [LN (33.100)], 'Christian message' [BAGD], 'gospel' [BAGD, LN (33.260)], 'what is preached' [LN (33.260)]. See this word also at 1:2.

c. μαρτυρία (See this word at 1:2): 'testimony' [EC, LN (33.264), Lns; KJV, NET, NIV, NRSV], 'my witness' [WBC]. The phrase τὴν μαρτυρίαν Ἰησοῦ 'the witness of Jesus' is translated '(I)…had told about Jesus' [CEV], '(I) bore witness to Jesus' [NAB], 'speaking about Jesus' [NLT], '(I had) publicly spoken about Jesus' [TNT], '(I had) borne my testimony to Jesus' [REB], 'the truth that Jesus revealed' [TEV], 'attested by Jesus' [BNTC].

QUESTION—Why was John on Patmos?

He was there because he had been sent there in exile [Alf, BNTC, EC, Ld, Lns, NIC, NIGTC, NTC, Sw, Wal, WBC; NLT, TEV]. There is much agreement that John had been exiled to Patmos by the Roman authorities [WBC].

QUESTION—What was the cause of John's exile?

He had been exiled for preaching the Word of God and bearing witness about Jesus [Alf, EC, ICC, Ld, Lns, NIC, NIGTC, Sw, TH, Wal, WBC]. The preposition διά with the accusative can mean either 'because of' or 'for the purpose of' but similar references such as 6:9 and 20:4 suggest that 'because of' should be chosen here [Sw, WBC]. The fact that John calls himself a partner in suffering supports this view plus the fact that this is a nearly unanimous opinion of the early church [Sw].

QUESTION—How are the nouns related in the genitive construction τὴν μαρτυρίαν Ἰησοῦ 'the testimony of Jesus'?

1. The testimony is about Jesus [Alf, Ld, Lns, NTC, WBC; CEV, NAB, NET, NLT, REB, TNT]. The Word of God and the testimony of Jesus tell us the content of John's preaching [Alf, ICC, Lns]. The Word of God refers to the oral tradition of the gospel [Ld].
2. Jesus himself gave this testimony [BNTC, EC; TEV]: the truth that Jesus revealed [TEV]. With καί meaning 'even', this refers to the gospel that John preached as being the Word of God, specifically defined as being the testimony that Jesus bore through John's preaching [EC].

3. Both of the above are true [NIGTC].

1:10 **I-was in spirit[a] on the Lord's[b] day**

LEXICON—a. πνεῦμα (BAGD I.5.d. p. 260, 6.e., p. 677): 'spirit' [Lns], 'the spirit' [EC; NRSV], 'the Spirit' [KJV, NET, NIV], 'a state of inspiration' [BAGD]. The phrase ἐγενόμην ἐν πνεύματι 'I was in spirit' is translated 'the Spirit took control of me' [CEV, TEV], 'the Spirit came upon me' [REB, TNT], 'I fell into a trance' [BNTC, Ld], 'I fell into a prophetic trance' [WBC], 'I was caught up in ecstasy' [Ld; NAB], 'I was worshiping in the Spirit' [NLT]. This refers to the author's state of mind [BAGD].

b. κυριακός (LN 12.10) (BAGD p. 458): 'Lord's' [BAGD, BNTC, EC, LN, Lns, WBC; all versions], 'belonging to the Lord' [BAGD, LN]. The phrase τῇ κυριακῇ ἡμέρᾳ 'the Lord's day' certainly means 'Sunday' [BAGD].

QUESTION—What is the meaning of ἐγενόμην 'I was'?
1. It implies a change of state [Alf, BNTC EC, ICC, Ld, NTC, TNTC, Wal, WBC; CEV, NAB, REB, TEV, TNT]: I became.
2. It implies that he was in such a state [Lns; NLT]: I was.

QUESTION—What is the meaning of being ἐν πνεύματι 'in spirit'?
1. This refers to being in the Holy Spirit [Alf, BAGD, NIC, Sw, TH, TNTC; CEV, KJV, NET, NIV, NLT, REB, TEV, TNT]. It indicates that John was under the control of God's Spirit [CEV, TEV]; that the Spirit came on him [REB, TNT]; that he was possessed by God's Spirit [TH]; that he was being inspired by the Spirit [Alf, BAGD, Sw]; that the Spirit was enabling him to worship [NLT]. The Spirit caused him to be in a trance [NIC].
2. This refers to a special state of John's own spirit [BNTC, EC, Ld, Lns, Wal, WBC; NAB, NRSV]. It means that he was: in a state of ecstasy [Alf, EC, Ld, NTC; NAB]; in a trance [Alf, BNTC, ICC, Ld, NIC, TNTC, WBC]; in an attitude of worship [NIGTC]. It indicates a state in which John was supernaturally able to see things of the world of spirit [Alf, Lns, Wal]. He was in a state of being open to God's Spirit and able to see visions [TNTC]. What John experienced was not in the body, but in the spirit, that is in a vision trance [WBC].

QUESTION—To what does τῇ κυριακῇ ἡμέρᾳ 'the Lord's day' refer?
1. It refers to the first day of the week, Sunday [Alf, BAGD, EC, ICC, Ld, Lns, NIC, NIGTC, NTC, Sw, TH, TNTC, WBC; NET]. This was the day that the early church set aside to celebrate the resurrection of the Lord [Alf, ICC, Ld, Lns, NIC, Sw, TH, TNTC]. Both the resurrection of Jesus Christ and the day of Pentecost fell on the first day of the week, warranting that it be called the Lord's day [Lns]. It means, 'the day consecrated to the Lord' [ICC, Sw]. Acts 20:7 and 1 Corinthians 16:2 indicated that this was a day on which the early Christians met to break bread and to offer love gifts [Ld, TH, TNTC]. This is the first place in

Christian literature where this phrase is used [ICC]. See also John 20:19 [TNTC].

2. It refers to the Day of the Lord as used in the Old Testament to refer to the Last Days [Wal]. This was the day of God's judgment and sovereign rule over the world and John was put forward into this time. It is true that the term κυριακῇ 'Lord's' does not occur in the Septuagint, but this was only because at that time no adjectival term existed in Greek and therefore the phrase τοῦ κυρίου 'of the Lord' was used [Wal].

and I-heard (a) loud[a] voice[b] behind me like[c] (a)-trumpet[d]

LEXICON—a. μέγας (LN 78.2) (BAGD 2.a.γ. p. 497): 'loud' [BAGD, EC, WBC; all versions except KJV, NAB], 'piercing' [NAB], 'great' [BNTC, LN, Lns; KJV], 'intense, terrible' [LN].

b. φωνή (LN 14.74, 33.103): 'voice' [BNTC, LN (33.103), Lns; all versions], 'sound' [EC, LN (14.74), WBC]. The sound was a voice [EC].

c. ὡς (LN 64.12) (BAGD II.3.b. p. 897): 'like' [BAGD, BNTC, LN; NAB, NET, NIV, NRSV, TEV], 'like the sound of' [WBC; REB, TNT], 'that sounded like' [CEV, NLT], 'as' [EC, LN, Lns; KJV].

d. σάλπιγξ (LN 6.89, 6.93) (BAGD 1. p. 741): 'trumpet' [BAGD, BNTC, EC, LN (6.89), Lns, WBC; all versions except NAB, NLT], 'trumpet sound' [LN (6.93); NAB], 'trumpet blast' [LN (6.93); NLT]. It refers to the instrument itself [BAGD]. In the OT the σάλπιγξ was a ram's horn. In the NT it is probably a metal instrument like a modern trumpet. If necessary, an animal horn could be substituted or any musical instrument that is similarly loud [TH]. Josephus describes a trumpet as being a metal tube about eighteen inches long with a mouthpiece on one end and a bell on the other (Ant. 3.291) [NIC].

QUESTION—What is the point of similarity between a trumpet and the sound?

It was *loud* like a trumpet [Alf, ICC, Lns, TH, WBC]. It was *clear* like a trumpet [Alf, EC, ICC, NIC]. It was *pulsing and penetrating* like a trumpet [Lns]. The trumpet was used to announce festivities [Alf]. Like a trumpet, it signaled the necessity to submit to whatever it commanded [EC].

QUESTION—Whose sound or voice did John hear?

1. It was the voice of Jesus Christ [EC, ICC, Lns, NIC, Wal]. In 1:17–19 it is Christ who commanded John to write and it is to be assumed that here it is Christ speaking also [NIC].
2. It was the voice of an angel or some other being [Alf, Ld, NIGTC, NTC, Sw, WBC]. Verse 1:1 supports this view in which Jesus sends his angel to John [Sw]. Verse 4:1 supports this view in which John identifies the voice he had heard at first [Ld].

1:11 saying, "Write what you-see in (a) book[a]

TEXT—Some manuscripts include the words Ἐγώ εἰμι τὸ Α καὶ τὸ Ω, ὁ πρῶτος καὶ ὁ ἔσχατος καί, 'I am the Alpha and the Omega, the first and the last; and' following λεγούσης 'saying'. GNT does not mention this alternative. These words are included by KJV and seem to be supported by Sw as well.

LEXICON—a. βιβλίον (LN 6.64) (BAGD 1. p. 141): 'book' [BAGD, LN, Lns, WBC; CEV, KJV, NET, NRSV, REB, TEV, TNT], 'scroll' [BAGD, BNTC, EC, LN; NAB, NIV], 'roll' [LN], not explicit [NLT]. A βιβλίον was literally a scroll [BAGD, BNTC, Ld, LN, NIC, Sw, TH; NAB, NIV], a roll of papyrus or coarse writing material [EC, Sw, TH].

and send (it) to-the seven churches, to Ephesus and to Smyrna and to Pergamum and to Thyatira and to Sardis and to Philadelphia and to Laodicea."

TEXT—Some manuscripts possibly include ταῖς ἐν 'Ασίᾳ 'to the (ones) in Asia' following ταῖς ἑπτὰ ἐκκλησίαις 'to the seven churches', although GNT does not mention this alternative. The reading 'to the (ones) in Asia' is included by the TR. It is also included by KJV.

QUESTION—Is there any significance to the order of the cities?

The order may indicate the route taken by the messenger who was to carry the book [EC, Sw, TH, TNTC]. All seven letters were to be read at each church [NIC]. The seven churches were apparently churches with the most representative spiritual situations [EC].

1:12 **And I turned to-see the voice that was-speaking with me,**

TEXT—Instead of the imperfect tense ἐλάλει 'was speaking' some manuscripts have the aorist tense ἐλάλησε 'spoke'. GNT does not mention this alternative. The reading 'spoke' is taken by KJV.

QUESTION—Does John really intend to *see* τὴν φωνήν 'the voice'?

'The voice' stands for the person who was speaking [Alf, BNTC, EC, ICC, Ld, Lns, TH, TNTC, Wal, WBC; all versions except KJV, NIV]: I turned to see who was speaking to me.

and having-turned I-saw seven golden lampstands[a]

LEXICON—a. λυχνία (LN 6.105) (BAGD p. 483): 'lampstand' [BAGD, EC, LN; all versions except KJV, TNT], 'lamp' [BNTC; TNT], 'candlestick' [KJV], 'pedestal lamp' [Lns], 'manorah' [WBC]. The λυχνία was a holder for an oil lamp that was composed of a clay bowl filled with oil and a wick that extended from the oil out onto the lip of the bowl [TH]. This does not refer to a candelabrum, but to seven separate stands for lamps [Alf, BNTC, EC, ICC, Ld, Lns, NIC, NTC, Wal, WBC], arranged in a circle [Lns, Wal].

QUESTION—What does a lamp or lampstand symbolize?

It is a symbol of being a witness (see John 5:35 and Philippians 2:15) [NTC]. Each of the seven churches has the function of embodying and giving forth the light of God on the earth [EC, ICC]. Here it is a symbol of God's presence with the Church (see 11:4) [NIGTC].

1:13 and in (the) middle[a] of-the lampstands (one) like[b] (the/a) son-of-man[c]

LEXICON—a. μέσος (LN 83.9, 83.10) (BAGD 2. p. 507): 'middle' [BAGD, EC, LN (83.10); NLT], 'midst' [LN (83.10), Lns, WBC; KJV, NET, NRSV], The phrase ἐν μέσῳ 'in (the) middle' is translated as a preposition: 'among' [BNTC, LN (83.9); NAB, NIV, REB, TEV, TNT], 'with' [LN (83.9); CEV].

 b. ὅμοιος (LN 64.1) (BAGD 3. p. 567): 'like' [BAGD, BNTC, EC, LN, Lns, WBC; KJV, NAB, NET, NIV, NRSV, REB, TNT], 'like, such as, similar' [LN], not explicit [NLT]. This word is also translated as a clause: 'who seemed to be' [CEV], 'what looked like' [TEV].

 c. υἱὸς ἀνθρώπου (LN 9.3): 'a son of man' [BNTC, WBC; NET, NIV], 'the Son of man' [EC, Lns; CEV, KJV, NLT, NRSV], 'a Son of man' [NAB], 'a man' [REB, TNT], 'a human being' [TEV], 'Son of man' [LN].

QUESTION—To what does the phrase to υἱὸν ἀνθρώπου 'son of man' refer?

 1. It indicates one who is like a 'man' or a 'human being' [Ld, Sw, TH, WBC; REB, TEV, TNT]: one like a man. Here it means 'a human being' with a possible allusion to the messianic title in Daniel, but it is not equivalent to the full title with the articles ὁ υἱὸς τοῦ ἀνθρωπού 'the son of man' as used in the Gospels [Sw]. The phrase suggests the title 'son of man' as used in Daniel 7:13 so that even though the person is like a man, he is more than a man, he is a supernatural being [Ld].

 2. It is a messianic title for Christ [Alf, EC, Lns, NIGTC, NTC, TNTC, Wal; probably CEV, KJV, NLT, NRSV]: one like the Son of Man. The comparison is dropped in some versions: 'There with the lampstands was someone who seemed to be the Son of Man' [CEV], 'standing in the middle of the lampstands was the Son of Man' [NLT]. While it is true that there is no article ('the') in the title, there are none in the Daniel reference nor in the phrase πνεῦμα θεοῦ 'spirit of God', the latter of which would hardly indicate 'a spirit of God' [Alf]. The title refers to both his humanity and his messianic role [Wal].

 3. It indicates an angel [ICC]: one like an angel. Both Ezekiel and Enoch (I Enoch 37–71) use the term 'man' to mean angel. Since this being *is*, not *like*, the Son of Man, he is here 'like a son of man' meaning 'like an angel' [ICC].

dressed-in[a] (a) long-robe[b] and wrapped-around[c] at the chest[d] (with a) golden[e] band.[f]

LEXICON—a. perf. mid. participle of ἐνδύω (LN 49.1) (BAGD 2.a. p. 264): 'to be dressed (in)' [BNTC, LN; NET, NIV], 'to be clothed (with)' [LN, Lns; KJV, NRSV], 'to clothe oneself in' [BAGD], 'to wear' [BAGD, WBC; CEV, NAB, NLT, TEV, TNT], 'to put on' [BAGD, LN]. This verb is also translated as a preposition: 'in (a robe)' [REB].

 b. ποδήρης (LN **6.175**) (BAGD p. 680): 'long robe' [BNTC, LN, WBC; NLT, NRSV], 'robe reaching to the feet' [BAGD, **LN**; CEV, NET, NIV,

REB, TEV, TNT], 'garment down to the foot' [KJV], '(clothed) to the foot' [Lns], '(clothed) down to the foot' [EC], 'ankle-length robe' [NAB].
c. perf. mid. participle of περιζώννυμι (LN **49.15**) (BAGD 1., 2.b., p. 647): 'to be wrapped around' [CEV], 'to wear...around' [NET], 'to be girt about' [KJV], 'to be girded around' [**LN**], 'to be girded' [EC], 'to be girdled' [Lns], 'to gird oneself' [BAGD, LN], 'to bind (something) about oneself' [BAGD], 'to be tied around' [LN]. This verb is also translated as a discontinuous phrase: 'with...around' [BAGD; NIV], 'with...round' [BNTC; REB, TNT], 'with...about' [NAB], 'and...around' [TEV], 'with...encircling' [WBC], 'with...across' [NLT, NRSV].
d. μαστός (LN **8.37**) (BAGD 1. p. 495): 'breast' [LN], 'pap' [Lns; KJV]. This plural noun is translated as a singular: 'breast' [BAGD, BNTC, EC, **LN**; NAB, REB, TNT]. 'chest' [LN, WBC; CEV, NET, NIV, NLT, NRSV, TEV].
e. χρυσοῦς (LN 2.50) (BAGD p. 888): 'golden' [BAGD, EC, LN, Lns, WBC; KJV, NET, NIV, NRSV, REB, TNT], 'gold' [BNTC; CEV, NAB, NLT, TEV], 'made of gold' [LN]. It means made of or adorned with gold [BAGD]. Χρυσοῦς can either mean made of gold or made with interwoven golden thread [TH]. It means made of gold [EC, Wal]. Josephus says that the priest's sash was interwoven with gold [NIC].
f. ζώνη (LN 6.178) (BAGD p. 341): 'band' [TEV, TNT], 'sash' [WBC; NAB, NIV, NLT, NRSV], 'wide belt' [NET], 'belt' [BAGD, LN], 'girdle' [BAGD, BNTC, EC, LN, Lns; KJV, REB], 'cloth' [CEV].

QUESTION—What is the significance of the ποδήρης 'long robe' and the ζώνη 'golden sash'?

They signify the dress of a priest [BNTC, NIC, NIGTC, NTC, Wal]. They are not necessarily intended to signify the dress of a priest [TNTC, WBC]. The long robe signifies dignity and high rank [Alf, EC, ICC, Ld, Sw, TH, TNTC]. The high position of the golden sash signifies dignity [NIC].

1:14 And his head and hair (were) white like white wool like snow

QUESTION—Were both his head and his hair white?

The wording means that only his hair was white [BNTC, Lns, NIC, TH, WBC; NAB, REB, TEV, TNT]. The second καί 'and' is an explanatory use of this word [NIC, WBC]: and his head, *namely*, his hair was white.

QUESTION—What is the significance of white hair?

It signifies wisdom and dignity [NIC, TNTC, WBC]; purity [Sw, Wal], purity and glory [Alf]; holiness [Lns]; and eternity [Wal]. It associates this person with the "Ancient of Days" described in Daniel 7:9 and so ascribes to him the attributes of deity [EC, ICC, Ld, NIC, NTC, Wal].

and his eyes (were) like (a) flame of-fire

QUESTION—What is the significance of having eyes like a flame of fire?

This signifies: energy [Alf, TNTC]; fierce opposition to enemies [TH]; authoritative presence [Alf]; anger [Ld, Sw]; judgment [NIGTC, Wal];

penetrating insight [EC, Lns, NIC]; intelligence [Sw];, and omniscience [Ld].

QUESTION—What reference in the Old Testament does this resemble?

It is similar to Daniel's vision of the heavenly being in Daniel 10:6 [EC, ICC, Lns, NIC, NIGTC, Sw, TH, TNTC, WBC].

1:15 and his feet (were) like bronze[a] as heated[b] in (a) furnace[c]

TEXT—Instead of the genitive participle πεπυρωμένης 'of heated' (which may mean 'of something heated', or it may be merely an ungrammatical form for 'heated') some manuscripts read the dative participle πεπυρωμένῳ 'heated', agreeing with the dative noun χαλκολιβάνῳ 'bronze'. Other manuscripts read the nominative plural πεπυρωμένοι 'heated', agreeing with πόδες 'feet'. GNT reads πεπυρωμένης 'of heated' with a C rating, indicating difficulty in deciding which variant to place in the text.

LEXICON—a. χαλκολίβανον (LN 2.57) (BAGD p. 875): 'bronze' [WBC; CEV, NIV, NLT], 'pure bronze' [BNTC], 'fine bronze' [BAGD, LN], 'polished bronze' [NET], 'gleaming bronze' [EC], 'burnished bronze' [NRSV, REB], 'brass' [TEV], 'fine brass' [BAGD, LN; KJV], 'polished brass' [BNTC; TEV], 'gold-bronze' [Lns], 'precious metal' [TNT], 'precious metal, bright and flashing' [Sw], 'gold ore' [BAGD]. This word only occurs in Revelation and is an unknown metal or alloy. It is something like gold ore, fine brass, or fine bronze [BAGD]. Although this word is unknown, since χαλκός means 'copper', it suggests that it is some kind of alloy of copper [TNTC]. It may be an alloy of gold [NIC]. Bronze is an alloy of copper and tin while brass is an alloy of copper and zinc [WBC]. Here the stress is on the shining appearance of the metal. A good translation may be: 'bright bronze' or 'shining metal' [LN].

b. perf. pass. participle of πυρόω (LN 79.72) (BAGD 2. p. 731): 'to be heated' [LN; CEV], 'to be refined' [NAB, NET, NLT, NRSV, REB, TEV, TNT], 'to be made fiery hot' [**LN**], 'to be made red hot, to be caused to glow, to be heated thoroughly' [BAGD], 'to be fired', [LN], 'to burn' [KJV], 'to be smelted' [WBC], 'to be aglow' [EC], not explicit [NIV]. This verb is also translated as an adjective: 'fired (furnace)' [Lns]. This verb is also translated as an adjective: 'fresh (from the furnace)' [BNTC]. This participle adds the sense that the metal was glowing [Alf, EC, Lns].

c. κάμινος (LN 7.73) (BAGD p. 402): 'furnace' [BAGD, BNTC, EC, **LN**, Lns, WBC; all versions except TEV], 'kiln' [LN], 'oven' [BAGD], not explicit [TEV].

QUESTION—What relationship is indicated by the genitive participle πεπυρωμένης 'heated'?

It modifies χαλκολιβάνῳ 'bronze' although it does not agree in case with it [BNTC, WBC; all versions]: heated bronze.

QUESTION—What is the point of similarity between his feet and heated bronze?

The point of similarity is the shining or glowing quality of the bronze [Alf, BNTC, EC, LN, Lns, TH; CEV, NAB, NIV, NLT]: his feet were glowing like bronze. The stress is on the lustrous appearance of the metal 'shining metal, bright bronze' [LN].

QUESTION—What does bronze symbolize here?

It symbolizes strength and stability [NIC, Sw], judgment [Wal], moral purity [NIGTC], or consuming anger against one's enemies [Lns].

and his voice as (the) sound of-many waters,

QUESTION—To what does the phrase 'sound of many waters' refer, and what is the point of similarity?

It refers to: the sound of a waterfall [NIC, TH; CEV, TEV]; the sound of rushing waters [NTC; NAB, NIV]; the sound of cascading water [WBC]; the sound of ocean waves [EC, TH; NLT]; the sound of a mighty torrent [REB]. The point of similarity is: loudness [TH]; strength or power [EC, Ld, Lns, Wal]; or majesty [Wal].

1:16 and having in his right hand seven stars[a] and (a) sharp[b] two-edged[c] sword[d] coming-out[e] of his mouth

LEXICON—a. ἀστήρ (LN 1.30) (BAGD p.117): 'star' [BAGD, BNTC, EC, LN, Lns, WBC; all versions], 'planet' [LN].

b. ὀξύς (LN **79.95**) (BAGD 1. p. 574): 'sharp' [BAGD, BNTC, EC, **LN**, Lns, WBC; all versions].

c. δίστομος (LN **79.94**) (BAGD p. 200): 'two-edged' [BNTC, EC, **LN**, Lns; KJV, NAB, NLT, NRSV, REB, TEV, TNT], 'double-edged' [BAGD, LN, WBC; CEV, NET, NIV].

d. ῥομφαία (LN 6.32) (BAGD p. 737): 'sword' [BAGD, BNTC, LN, WBC; all versions], 'great sword' [Lns]. The ῥομφαία was a large, broad sword [BAGD, LN] used for cutting and piercing [LN]. It was heavy and nearly as tall as a man and was wielded with both hands [Lns].

e. pres. mid. (deponent = act.) participle of ἐκπορεύομαι (LN 15.40) (BAGD 2. p. 244): 'to come out' [BAGD, BNTC; all versions except KJV, NET], 'to go out', [BAGD; KJV], 'to go forth' [Lns], 'to project (from)' [BAGD, WBC], 'to proceed from' [EC], 'to extend out' [NET], 'to go out of, to depart out of, to leave from within' [LN].

QUESTION—What is indicated by the location of the stars in his right hand?

It indicates: that he protects them (see John 10:28) [Alf, EC, Ld, NIC, TNTC, Wal]; that he has sovereign control over them [EC, ICC, Lns, NIC, NTC, Wal]; that he possesses them [Alf, Wal]; that he provides for them [Alf, Ld]; or that he favors them [TNTC].

QUESTION—What is indicated by the image of the sword coming out of his mouth?

The sword indicates the word of God or Christ [Alf, Ld, NTC, TH]. It indicates speaking words of comfort and reprimand with those under his care

[Alf]. It represents the sword of the Spirit that is the Word of God (Ephesians 6:17). This word is irresistible and accomplishes all that he wills (Hebrews 4:12) [Ld]. It indicates God's judgment [EC, ICC, NIC, NIGTC, Wal, WBC]. See 2:16 where Christ threatens to fight Pergamum with the sword of his mouth [NIC, NIGTC, WBC] and 19:15, 21 where he strikes down the nations with the sword coming from his mouth [NIC, NIGTC, Wal, WBC]. It represents decisive action against one's enemies [TNTC, Wal]. It indicates Christ's unlimited power and sovereignty [Wal]. The sword is both the Good News and judgment on those who disobey [NTC]. The sharpness indicates the power and effectiveness of his words [WBC].

and his face[a] (was) like the sun shines[b] in its strength.[c]
LEXICON—a. ὄψις (LN **8.18**, 30.14) (BAGD 2. p. 601; 3. p. 602): 'face' [BAGD (3), BNTC, **LN**, WBC; all versions except KJV], 'countenance' [BAGD (3); KJV], 'appearance' [EC, Lns], 'outward appearance' [BAGD (2), LN (30.14)], 'external form' [LN (30.14)], 'aspect' [BAGD (2)].
  b. pres. act. indic. of φαίνω (LN 14.37) (BAGD 1. p. 851): 'to shine' [BAGD, BNTC, EC, LN, Lns, WBC; all versions except NLT, TEV], 'to give light' [BAGD, LN], 'to be bright' [BAGD], 'to bring light' [LN]. This verb is also translated as an adjective: '(as) bright (as)' [NLT, TEV].
  c. δύναμις (LN 76.1): 'strength' [BNTC, EC, WBC; KJV, NET, REB], 'brilliance' [NIV, NLT], 'power' [LN, Lns], 'force' [NRSV]. The phrase ἐν τῇ δυνάμει αὐτοῦ 'in its strength', is translated 'as bright as (the sun) at noon' [CEV, TEV], 'at/in full strength' [WBC; NET, REB], 'with full force' [NRSV], 'at mid-day' [TNT], 'at its brightest' [NAB].
QUESTION—What is indicated by this description of his face?
It indicates the glory [EC, Ld, Lns], power [Ld], and majesty of Christ [Lns].

1:17 **And when I-saw him, I-fell[a] at his feet as dead,[b] and he-placed[c] his right-hand[d] on me saying,**
TEXT—Some manuscripts possibly include μοι 'to me' after λέγων 'saying', although GNT does not mention this alternative. The reading 'to me' is included by the TR and KJV.
LEXICON—a. aorist act. indic. of πίπτω (LN 17.22) (BAGD 1.b.α. p. 659): 'to fall' [BAGD, BNTC, EC, Lns; all versions except NAB, NET, TEV], 'to fall down (before)' [LN, WBC; NAB, NET, TEV], 'to prostrate oneself before' [LN], 'to fall to the ground, to fall down' [BAGD].
  b. νεκρός (See this word at 1:5): 'dead' [EC, Lns, WBC; KJV, NAB, NET, NIV, NLT, NRSV, REB], 'lifeless' [LN]. The phrase ὡς νεκρός 'as dead' is translated 'like a dead man' [BNTC; CEV, TEV, TNT], 'as a dead one' [EC], 'as though I were dead' [NET, REB]. This indicates his motionless appearance in his stupefaction [EC].
  c. aorist act. indic. of τίθημι (LN 85.32) (BAGD I.1.a.β. p. 816): 'to place' [BNTC, EC, LN; NET, NIV, NRSV, TEV], 'to lay' [Lns, WBC; KJV, NLT, REB, TNT], 'to put' [BAGD, LN; CEV], 'to touch' [NAB].

d. δεξιός (LN 82.8) (BAGD 2. p.174): 'right hand' [BAGD, BNTC, EC, Lns, WBC; all versions], 'right' [BAGD, LN], 'right side' [LN].

QUESTION—Does πίπτω 'to fall' indicate an active or a passive action?

1. It indicates the passive action of a person overcome by what he has seen [Alf, BNTC, EC, Ld, Lns, TNTC, WBC]. John reacts with fear to what he sees and falls as though dead [WBC]. This was a death-like swoon [BNTC, Lns]. The phrase 'as though dead' shows that it was not a conscious act of prostrating oneself [TNTC].
2. It indicates an active act of reverence and worship [NIC, TH]. Πίπτω here has the active meaning of prostrating oneself in an act of worship with both body and forehead touching the ground, rather than passively falling from the force of gravity [TH]. To stand in the presence of such majesty would have been the same as blasphemy [NIC].

"Do-not be-afraid;^{a} I am the first^b and the last^c

LEXICON—a. pres. act. impera. of φοβέομαι (LN 25.252): 'to be afraid' [BNTC, LN, WBC; all versions except KJV, NAB], 'to fear' [EC, LN, Lns; KJV, NAB].

b. πρῶτος (LN 60.46) (BAGD 1.a. p. 725): 'first' [BAGD, BNTC, EC, LN; all versions except NAB, NIV, NLT], 'First' [Lns, WBC; NAB, NIV, NLT].

c. ἔσχατος (LN **61.13**) (BAGD 3.b. p. 314): 'last' [BAGD, BNTC, EC, **LN**; all versions except NAB, NIV, NLT], 'Last' [Lns, WBC; NAB, NIV, NLT].

QUESTION—What is indicated by the present tense imperative μὴ φοβοῦ 'do not be afraid'?

It indicates that the action was already going on [EC, Lns, TH, TNTC, WBC]: stop being afraid.

QUESTION—What is meant by the statement ἐγώ εἰμι ὁ πρῶτος καὶ ὁ ἔσχατος 'I am the first and the last'?

It has the effect of ascribing to Christ the attributes of God as seen in similar statements about God in 1:8 and Isaiah 41:4, 44:6, and 48:12 [Alf, NIC, NIGTC, NTC, Sw, TNTC, WBC; probably NAB, NIV, NLT]. 'First and last' refer to the eternity of God [Alf, EC, TH, Wal] and his sovereignty [TH].

QUESTION—What is the purpose of laying the right hand on John?

It reassures him that he has nothing to fear [BNTC, EC, TNTC, Wal, WBC]. It strengthens or revives him [Ld, NIC]. It blesses him [Lns, NIC]. It invests him with authority or power [WBC].

1:18 and^a the living-one,^{b} and was^c dead

LEXICON—a. καί (LN 89.92): 'and' [EC, LN, Lns; CEV, NAB, NRSV, REB], 'even' [WBC], 'namely' [NET], 'that is' [NIC, NIGTC], not explicit [BNTC; KJV, NIV, NLT, TEV, TNT].

b. pres. act. participle of ζάω (LN 23.88): 'to live' [BNTC, LN, Lns, WBC; all versions], 'to be alive' [LN]. This participle is translated 'living one'

[BNTC, EC; CEV, NLT, NRSV, TEV, TNT], 'Living One' [WBC; NIV], 'living One' [REB], 'One who lives' [NAB]. The present tense indicates that this state is continuous [Wal].

c. aorist mid. (deponent = act.) indic. of γίνομαι (LN 13.3, 13.48): 'to be' [BNTC, LN (13.3), Lns, WBC; KJV, NAB, NET, NIV, REB, TEV], 'to become' [Alf, LN (13.48), Wal], 'to come to be' [EC]. The phrase ἐγενόμην νεκρὸς 'I became dead' is translated 'I died' [CEV, NLT, TNT]. The aorist tense indicates that an event has occurred some time in the past [Lns].

QUESTION—What relationship is indicated by καί 'and/even' before 'the living one'?

1. It relates the phrase ὁ ζῶν, 'the living one' to the previous phrase 'the first and the last' by explaining it [NIC, NIGTC, WBC; NET]: the first and the last, *that is*, the living one. Καί functions here as an explanatory conjunction to enlarge on the preceding statement that Jesus is the first and the last [NIC, NIGTC]. This title proves that Christ is the first and the last [NIGTC].
2. It relates this verse to the preceding verse in a conjoining relationship [EC, ICC, NTC; CEV, NAB, NRSV, REB]: I am the first and the last *and* the living one.

QUESTION—What is implied by the phrase ὁ ζῶν 'the living one'?

It implies that life is an essential possession of Christ and contrasts with the non-living gods of paganism [NIC]. It is a divine title [Alf, EC, Sw, TH, TNTC] also used of God the Father (see Joshua 3:10; Psalms 42:2; Daniel 12:7; Matthew 16:16; Acts 14:15; Romans 9:26) [NIC, Sw, TNTC]. He has life in his essential nature [EC].

and behold[a] I-am living[b] forever-and-ever[c]

LEXICON—a. ἰδού (See this word at 1:7): 'behold' [EC, WBC; KJV, NIV], 'lo' [Lns], 'look' [NET, NLT], 'see' [NRSV], 'now' [BNTC; CEV, NAB, REB, TEV, TNT]. This word emphasizes the words that follow [Lns, TH, WBC]. It draws attention to the Christ's state of life following his resurrection [EC].

b. pres. act. participle of ζάω (LN 23.93): 'to live' [EC, Lns, WBC; TNT], 'to be alive' [BNTC; all versions except TNT], 'to come back to life, to live again, to rise to life again' [LN]. This participle modifies the subject, stating that he is marked as one who lives [Lns]. See this word also in this verse just above.

c. αἰών (LN 67.95, 67.143): 'age, era' [LN], 'eon' [Lns]. The phrase εἰς τοὺς αἰῶνας τῶν αἰώνων 'into the ages of the ages' is translated 'forever and ever' [EC, LN, WBC; NAB NET, NIV, NLT, TEV, TNT], 'forevermore' [BAGD; CEV, KJV, NAB, REB], 'forever' [BNTC], 'for the eons of the eons' [Lns]. See this phrase at 1:6.

QUESTION—What is the significance of the combination of the verb εἰμι 'I am' with the participle ζῶν 'living'?
   It functions to emphasize the fact of Jesus' life more than the simple verb (I live) would [Alf]. It forms the periphrastic present and as such contrasts with the temporal state of having been dead [WBC]. It focuses on the fullness of his present life [EC].

and I-have[a] the keys[b] of death[c] and of Hades.[d]
TEXT—Instead of τοῦ θανάτου καὶ τοῦ ᾅδου 'of death and of Hades' some manuscripts transpose the two nouns to read τοῦ ᾅδου καὶ τοῦ θανάτου 'of Hades and of death'. GNT does not mention this alternative. The reading 'of Hades and of death' is taken by KJV.
LEXICON—a. pres. act. participle of ἔχω (LN 57.1) (BAGD I.2.h. p. 333): 'to have' [BAGD, EC, LN, Lns; CEV, KJV, NRSV, TNT], 'to hold' [BNTC, WBC; NAB, NET, NIV, NLT, REB], 'to have/hold in one's charge, to have/hold in one's keeping' [BAGD], 'to own, to possess' [LN]. The phrase ἔχω τὰς κλεῖς 'I have the keys' is translated 'I have authority (over)' [TEV].
   b. κλείς (LN 6.220) (BAGD 1. p. 434): 'key' [BAGD, BNTC, EC, LN, Lns, WBC; all versions except TEV]. The phrase ἔχω τὰς κλεῖς 'I have the keys' is translated 'I have authority over' [TEV].
   c. θάνατος (LN 23.99) (BAGD 1.f. p. 351): 'death' [BAGD, BNTC, EC, LN, Lns; all versions except NRSV], 'Death' [WBC; NRSV]. Θάνατος is personified here [BAGD]. This draws attention to the state of death [EC].
   d. ᾅδης (LN 1.19) (BAGD 1. p. 17): 'Hades' [BAGD, EC, LN, WBC; NET, NIV, NRSV, REB, TNT], 'Hell' [KJV], 'hades' [Lns], 'the world of the dead' [LN; CEV, TEV], 'the grave' [BNTC; NLT], 'the nether world' [NAB], 'the underworld' [BAGD]. Hades to the Greeks and Sheol to the Jews meant the grave [BNTC]. It is the place of the unbelieving dead [ICC, Lns] as seen in Luke 16:23 where it is contrasted with Paradise [ICC]. It is the intermediate state of the dead [Ld, Wal]. It is the place where departed spirits live [NIC, TNTC]. This clause implies that death and Hades are locked [BAGD]. This draws attention to the place of death [EC].
QUESTION—If the image is a person with keys to open doors and the topic is Jesus and his relationship to Hades and death, what is the point of similarity?
   The point of similarity is: access to these places to do as one wills [Alf]; authority over someone or thing [BNTC, EC, ICC, Ld, Lns, NIC, NIGTC, NTC, Sw, TH, TNTC, Wal]; authority to free the occupants of these places [BNTC, Ld]; double power both to open these and to rescue the repentant from them or to consign the unrepentant there [EC, Lns, NIGTC, TH, TNTC].

1:19 Therefore[a] write the-things-that you saw and/even[b] the-things-that are and the-things-that are-about[c] to-happen after these-things.
LEXICON—a. οὖν (LN 89.50): 'therefore' [BNTC, LN, WBC; NAB, NET, NIV, REB], 'so' [LN; TNT], 'then' [EC, LN, Lns; TEV], 'now' [NRSV], 'consequently, accordingly, so then' [LN], not explicit [CEV, KJV, NLT].
  b. καί (LN 89.92, 89.93): 'and' [EC, LN (89.92), Lns; CEV, KJV, NAB], 'and also, even' [LN (89.93)], 'both...and' [NLT, TEV], 'that is' [WBC], not explicit [BNTC; NET, NIV, NRSV, REB, TNT].
  c. pres. act. indic. of μέλλω (LN 67.62, 71.36) (BAGD 1.c.δ. p. 501): 'to be about to' [LN (67.62), Lns], 'must' [BAGD], 'must be, has to be' [LN (71.36)], 'is destined, will certainly' [BAGD]. The phrase μέλλει γενέσθαι 'about to happen' is translated 'will happen' [EC, WBC; CEV, NLT, TEV], 'is to happen' [BNTC], 'shall be' [KJV], 'will be' [NET], 'will take place' [NIV], 'are to take place' [NRSV, REB, TNT], '(you) will see' [NAB].
QUESTION—What relationship is indicated by οὖν 'therefore'?
  1. It indicates that John should write as the consequence of his vision of Christ [Alf, Lns, NIGTC, WBC; NAB, NET, NIV, REB, TNT]: I have the keys, therefore write. Who Christ is and what he has done constitute the reason for John to write [NIGTC].
  2. It resumes the command from 1:11 to write what he would see [EC, ICC, NIC, Sw; probably NRSV]: write what you see in a book...*now* write. It resumes the command from 1:11 and strengthens it with the fact of Christ's conquest over death [Sw].
QUESTION—What is the function of the first καί 'and/even'?
  1. It functions to conjoin what John saw with the things that are and the things that are about to happen [Alf, ICC, Ld, Sw, TNTC, Wal; CEV, KJV, NAB; probably NET, NIV, NRSV, REB, TNT]: write what you saw *and* the things that are and the things that are about to happen. What John saw refers to the vision he had just seen of Jesus. The things that are refer to the present state of the church (chapters 2 and 3). The things that are about to happen refer to the whole book of Revelation [EC, Wal], or to what is described beginning at chapter 4 [ICC, Sw, TNTC], or to what is described beginning at the seven seals of chapter 6 [Ld]. The words 'the things that are' mean 'the things that John's vision *signified*'. The things that are about to happen refer to what will *occur* and this begins with chapter 4 [Alf].
  2. It indicates the explanation of what John saw [BNTC, NIC, NTC, TH, WBC; NLT, TEV]: write what you saw (or 'see' [TEV], 'will see' [WBC]), *that is, both* what is *and* what will be. The verb εἶδες 'you saw' is an epistolary aorist and the visions John was yet to see would be in the past from the standpoint of the reader. This means that John is to write what was yet to be seen by him, namely, present and future events [TH, WBC]. What John saw refers to the whole book of Revelation as it

includes things that are past, present, and future [BNTC]. The interplay of present and future is seen throughout Revelation [NIC].

1:20 The mystery[a] of-the seven stars that you-saw on[b] my right-side[c] and the seven golden lampstands:

LEXICON—a. μυστήριον (LN 28.77) (BAGD 3. p. 530): 'mystery' [BAGD, EC, LN, Lns; CEV, KJV, NET, NIV, NRSV], 'secret meaning' [ICC, TH, WBC; NAB, REB, TEV], 'secret' [BNTC, LN; TNT], 'meaning' [TNTC; NLT], 'allegorical significance' [BAGD]. A μυστήριον is a concept that is not understood by human reasoning but is revealed by God [EC, TH, TNTC]. It is the underlying meaning of a symbolic vision [EC, NIC, Sw].
  b. ἐπί with genitive object (LN 83.23, 83.46): 'on' [EC, LN (83.46), Lns], 'at' [LN (83.23); CEV], 'in' [BNTC, WBC; all versions except CEV], 'by' [LN (83.23)], 'upon' [LN (83.46)]. In 1:16 the seven stars are said to be ἐν 'in' his right hand and all versions except CEV continue to have the stars 'in' his right hand. The stars that were seen *in* his right hand are now seen to be resting *upon* his open right hand [EC, Sw].
  c. δεξιός (See this word at 1:17): 'right side' [CEV], 'right hand' [BNTC, EC, Lns, WBC; all versions except CEV].

QUESTION—How are the nouns related in the genitive construction τὸ μυστήριον τῶν ἑπτὰ ἀστέρων 'the mystery of the seven stars'?
  The 'mystery' is *about* the seven stars [TH].

QUESTION—How should the accusative cases of τὸ μυστήριον 'the mystery' and τὰς ἑπτὰ λυχνίας 'the seven lampstands' be translated?
  The accusative case is unusual here and should be translated: 'As for the secret of the seven stars…and the seven lampstands' [ICC, Sw, WBC; NRSV], or 'I will explain the mystery of the seven stars…and the seven lampstands' [CEV].

the seven stars are angels[a] of-the seven churches

LEXICON—a. ἄγγελος (BAGD 2.a. p. 7): 'angel' [BAGD, BNTC, Lns, WBC; all versions except NAB], 'presiding spirits' [NAB], 'messenger' [EC]. An angel is a messenger of God [BAGD]. See this word also at 1:1.

QUESTION—What does ἄγγελος 'angel' refer to?
  1. It refers to angels or heavenly guardians of the churches [Alf, BAGD, NIGTC, NTC, TH; all versions except NAB]. As there are representatives or guardians of nations (Daniel 10:13, 20; 12:1) and of people (Matthew 18:10; Acts 12:15), so there are representatives of churches [NTC, TH]. The word ἄγγελος is used elsewhere in Revelation only to refer to actual angels [Alf].
  2. It refers to the churches themselves [ICC, Ld, NIC, Sw, TNTC]. 'Angel' here refers to the spirit of the church, that is, to the church itself [Sw]. 'Angel' personifies the prevailing spirit of the church [NIC]. It is a symbol that represents the heavenly character of the church [Ld].
  3. It refers to human messengers to the churches [EC, Lns, Wal]. Probably pastors or prophets to the churches is indicated [Wal]. This may refer to

the bishop or the entire eldership of the church [Lns]. It is probable that they were not the leaders of the churches, but were representatives from the churches who were sent to assist John in his exile. They will be bringing messages back to their churches [EC].

4. It refers to spirits [NAB]: the seven stars are the presiding spirits.

and the seven lampstands are the seven churches.
TEXT—Some manuscripts include ἅς εἶδες 'that you saw' before ἑπτὰ ἐκκλησίαι 'seven churches'. GNT does not mention this alternative. The words 'that you saw' are included by KJV.

DISCOURSE UNIT: 2:1–3:22 [Alf, EC, ICC, Ld, Lns, NIC, NIGTC, NTC, TH, TNTC, WBC]. The topic is the letters to the seven churches.

DISCOURSE UNIT: 2:1–7 [Alf, BNTC, EC, GNT, ICC, Ld, Lns, NIC, NIGTC, NTC, Sw, TH, TNTC, Wal, WBC; CEV, NAB, NET, NIV, NLT, NRSV, TEV]. The topic is the message to Ephesus.

2:1 **Write to the angel[a] of the church in Ephesus:[b]**
TEXT—Instead of ἐν Ἐφέσῳ 'in Ephesus' some manuscripts possibly read Ἐφεσίνης 'Ephesian', although GNT does not mention this alternative. The reading 'Ephesian' is taken by the TR. It is also taken by KJV.
LEXICON—a. ἄγγελος: 'angel'. This word is applied to each of the seven churches. See 1:20 for the various views of what this means.
  b. Ἔφεσος (LN 93.471): 'Ephesus' [BAGD, BNTC, EC, LN, WBC; all versions]. Ephesus was a major seaport city of the Roman province of Asia and was the center of the worship of the goddess Artemis [TH]. From Ephesus the Romans administered all of Asia [ICC]. It was the center of control of the magical arts that were widely practiced in Asia Minor [Sw]. It was the location of the most important church of Asia [Ld].

'These-things[a] says the-one holding[b] the seven stars in his right-hand,
LEXICON—a. ὅδε (LN 92.32) (BAGD 1. p. 553): 'these things' [EC, Lns; KJV], 'these (are the words)' [NIV, NRSV, REB, TNT], 'this' [BAGD, BNTC, LN; CEV, NAB, NET, NLT, TEV], 'thus' [WBC].
  b. pres. act. participle of κρατέω (LN 18.6) (BAGD 2.b. p. 448): 'to hold' [BAGD, BNTC, **LN**, Lns, WBC; all versions except NET], 'to hold fast' [EC], 'to have a firm grasp on' [NET], 'to hold on to, to retain in one's hand, to seize' [LN]. Κρατέω denotes a firm grip [TNTC; NET].
QUESTION—What is implied by his 'holding' the stars?
  The slight change from 'having' the seven stars in his right hand to 'holding' them in his right hand draws attention to Christ's majestic activity in having absolute control of the angels [EC]. It implies that they are in his strong possession [Ld, Sw]; that he controls them [NIC, Wal]; that he protects them [Wal]. The right hand implies that he is almighty and majestic [Lns].

the-one walking[a] **in the-midst of-the seven golden lampstands:**
LEXICON—a. pres. act. participle of περιπατέω (LN 15.227, 41.11) (BAGD 1.a. p. 649): 'to walk' [BNTC, EC, LN (15.227), Lns, WBC; all versions], 'to walk around, to go about' [BAGD], 'to live' [LN (41.11)].

QUESTION—What is implied by his 'walking in the midst of the lampstands'?
It implies: his presence among the churches [NIC, NIGTC, Sw, TNTC, WBC]; his presence not being localized at one church [Sw]; his personal concern and care for the churches [TH, TNTC]; his vigilance over the churches [ICC, Ld, Sw]; his availability to the churches [Sw]; his awareness of their situation [EC, NIC, NIGTC, NTC]; his royal activity among them [Lns]; that since he walks among them, his vigilance extends to all the churches [ICC].

2:2 I-know your works[a] **and/even the labor**[b] **and the endurance**[c] **of-you**
LEXICON—a. ἔργον (LN 42.11, 42.42) (BAGD 1.c.β., 2. p. 308): 'work' [BAGD (2), EC, LN (42.42); KJV, NET, NRSV], 'deed' [BAGD (1), LN (42.11), WBC; NAB, NIV], 'act' [LN (42.11)], 'action' [BAGD (1)], 'task' [BAGD (2), LN (42.42)], 'accomplishment' [BAGD]. The plural of this word is translated 'everything you have done' [CEV], 'what you have done' [BNTC; TEV], 'all the things you do' [NLT], 'what you are doing' [REB], 'all about you' [TNT]. The plural 'works' here refers to conduct or way of life [BNTC, EC, Ld, NIC, TH; NLT, REB, TEV, TNT].

b. κόπος (LN 42.47) (BAGD 2. p. 443): 'labor' [BAGD, EC; KJV, NAB, NET], 'hard work' [BNTC; CEV, NIV, NLT], 'toil' [BAGD, LN; NRSV], 'work' [BAGD], 'effort' [WBC]. This noun is also translated as a verb: 'to toil' [REB], 'to toil hard' [TNT], 'to work hard' [TEV]. Κόπος indicates effort [ICC, WBC], or labor to the extent of weariness [TNTC]. It refers to how hard they have worked in their Christian duties [Sw, TH].

c. ὑπομονή (BAGD 1. p. 846): 'endurance' [BAGD, BNTC, EC, WBC], 'patient endurance' [NAB, NLT, NRSV], 'steadfast endurance' [NET], 'patience' [BAGD; KJV], 'perseverance' [BAGD; NIV], 'steadfastness, fortitude' [BAGD]. This noun is also translated as a verb: 'to endure' [CEV, REB], 'to bravely endure' [TNT], 'to be patient' [TEV]. Ὑπομονή has reference to endurance against opposition that a Christian faces in the world [ICC] or against suffering and persecution [TH]. See this word also at 1.9.

QUESTION—What is the significance of the singular pronoun σου 'your'?
Being singular it refers to the angel, but it refers to the believers as well and translators must decide how they will translate it [TH].

QUESTION—What is the relationship between the three nouns ἔργα 'works', κόπον 'labor', and ὑπομονήν 'endurance'?
1. The nouns 'labor' and 'endurance' explain 'works' [Alf, EC, Ld, NIC, Sw, WBC; CEV]: your deeds, *that is*, your labor and endurance. The word καί 'even' after 'deeds' is explanatory [Alf, WBC]. Their moral conduct

(works) is exemplified by their outward activity of labor and inward disposition of endurance [EC].
2. All three nouns are coordinate [ICC; KJV, NAB, NET, NIV, NLT, NRSV, TEV, TNT]: your works and labor and endurance.

QUESTION—What is the significance of the single possessive pronoun in the phrase τὸν κόπον καὶ τὴν ὑπομονήν σου 'the labor and the endurance of you'?

It joins the two nouns together in a single unit governed by the pronoun [Alf, EC, ICC, Lns, Sw, TH, WBC; all versions]: your labor and endurance. It indicates that they are two aspects of a single feature [TH].

and that not you-can[a] not tolerate[b] evils/evil-people,[c]

LEXICON—a. pres. mid. (deponent = act.) indic. of δύναμαι (LN 74.5): 'can' [BNTC, EC, LN, WBC; all versions except CEV, NLT], 'to be able, to be able to' [LN], not explicit [CEV, NLT].
  b. aorist act. infin. of βαστάζω (LN 25.177) (BAGD 2.b.β. p. 137): 'to tolerate' [BNTC; NAB, NET, NIV, NLT, NRSV, TEV], 'to bear' [BAGD, EC, WBC; KJV, TNT], 'to bear up under' [LN], 'to endure' [BAGD, LN], 'to put up with' [CEV], 'to abide' [REB].
  c. κακός (LN 88.106) (BAGD 1.a. p. 397): 'evil' [BAGD, LN; NET], 'bad' [BAGD, LN]. This plural adjective is also rendered as a noun phrase: 'wicked men' [NAB, NIV], 'evil men' [BNTC; TNT], 'wicked people' [WBC; REB], 'evil people' [NLT, TEV], 'evil ones' [EC], 'anyone who is evil' [CEV], 'them that are evil' [KJV], 'evildoers' [NRSV]. Κακός indicates bad in a moral sense from a Christian perspective, a disgraceful church member [Lns]. The plural here refers to false teachers among them [Ld] or false brothers [Sw]. It referred to men and women alike [TH]. These are the 'savage wolves' about whom Paul warned the Ephesian elders in Acts 20:29 [TNTC]. In 2:6 they are identified as the Nicolaitans [EC].

and you-tested[a] the-ones calling[b] themselves apostles[c] and they-are not

LEXICON—a. aorist act. indic. of πειράζω (LN 27.46) (BAGD 2.a. p. 640): 'to test' [BNTC, EC, LN, WBC; CEV, NAB, NIV, NRSV, TEV, TNT], 'to put to the test' [BAGD, LN; NET, REB], 'to try' [BAGD; KJV], 'to examine the claims of' [NLT], 'to make trial of' [BAGD]. The aorist tense indicates a definite time in the past when this action occurred [Alf, ICC].
  b. pres. act. participle of λέγω (LN 33.131): 'to call' [EC, LN, WBC; TNT], 'to say' [KJV, NLT, TEV], 'to pretend to be' [CEV], 'to refer to' [NET], 'to claim (to be)' [BNTC; NIV, NRSV, REB]. This verb is also translated as an adjective: 'self-styled (apostles)' [NAB].
  c. ἀπόστολος (LN 53.74) (BAGD 2. p. 99): 'apostle' [BAGD, BNTC, EC, LN, WBC; all versions]. It refers to a messenger of God [BAGD]. The reference here is not to the original twelve, but to a wider group of apostles [BNTC, EC, Ld, Lns, NIGTC, Sw, TNTC]. This group would include such men as James, Silas, Barnabas, Junias [BNTC, EC, Ld,

NIGTC], Paul and Barnabas [BNTC, Ld]. See Acts 14:14, Romans 16:7, 1 Corinthians 15:7 and Galatians 1:19 [BNTC, Ld, NIGTC]. These would be men who were sent by Jesus Christ [Lns, TH], and who taught the true Gospel [Lns]. They were an authoritative group and the Twelve were a special segment within that group because they had been the original apostles [EC]. They were itinerant teachers ranking above local church officials [Sw].

QUESTION—How did the Ephesian believers 'test' these men?

They watched them to see if they lived up to their claims [BNTC, NIGTC, Sw, TH, TNTC], or if their teaching matched that of known truth [NIGTC]. They watched them to see if they behaved like Christ [ICC, NIC]. This was the test recommended in the Didache [ICC, NIC, NIGTC, WBC]. They may have requested information about them from other churches [TH].

QUESTION—What is the significance of the clause καὶ οὐκ εἰσίν 'and they are not'?

This is a parenthetical insertion [NET] by John into Christ's message to the church [EC, Lns]. Other commentaries and versions do not mark this as being parenthetical.

and you-found[a] them (to be) false,[b]

LEXICON—a. aorist act. indic. of εὑρίσκω (LN 27.1) (BAGD 2. p. 325): 'to find' [BAGD, BNTC, EC, WBC; KJV, NIV, NRSV, REB, TNT], 'to find out' [LN; CEV, TEV], 'to discover' [BAGD, LN; NAB, NET, NLT], 'to learn' [LN]. The aorist tense points to an event of the past [WBC].

b. ψευδής (LN **33.255**) (BAGD 1. p. 891): 'false' [BAGD; NET, NIV, NRSV, REB], 'lying' [BAGD]. This adjective is also translated as a noun: 'liar' [BNTC, EC, **LN**, WBC; CEV, KJV, NLT, TEV, TNT], 'imposter' [NAB]. These were deceivers, not merely self-deceived men [Sw, TNTC].

2:3 and you-have endurance and you-endured-hardship[a] for-the-sake-of[b] my name[c] and not you-have-given-up.[d]

TEXT—Instead of ὑπομονὴν ἔχεις καὶ ἐβάστασας 'you have endurance and endured hardship' some manuscripts transpose these words to ἐβάστασας καὶ ὑπομονὴν ἔχεις 'you endured hardship and you have endurance'. GNT does not mention this alternative. The reading 'you endured hardship and you have endurance' is followed by KJV.

TEXT—Instead of διὰ τὸ ὄνομά μου καί 'for the sake of my name and' some manuscripts possibly read καὶ διὰ τὸ ὄνομά μου 'and for the sake of my name', although GNT does not mention this alternative. The reading 'and for the sake of my name' is taken by TR. It is also taken by KJV.

TEXT—Instead of οὐ κεκοπίακες 'you have not given up' some manuscripts possibly read κεκοπίακας καὶ οὐ κέκμηκας 'you have toiled and have not given up', although GNT does not mention this alternative. The reading 'you have toiled and have not become weary' is taken by TR. It is also taken by KJV.

LEXICON—a. aorist act. infin. of βαστάζω (LN 25.177) (BAGD 2.b.β. p. 137): 'to endure hardship' [NAB, NIV], 'to endure' [LN; NET], 'to go through hard times' [CEV], 'to suffer' [TEV], 'to have patience' [KJV], 'to bear patiently' [BAGD, WBC], 'to bear up' [EC; NRSV, REB], 'to bear up under' [LN], 'to bear much' [TNT], 'to bear a burden' [BNTC], 'to put up with' [BAGD]. The phrase ὑπομονὴν ἔχεις καὶ ἐβάστασας 'you have endurance and endured hardship' is translated 'you have patiently suffered' [NLT]. The aorist tense points to some particular event in the past [ICC, Lns, WBC], or to several [Lns]. This is the same word in 2:2 that was there translated 'tolerate' [TNTC]. They have put up with their labor of resisting the false prophets and endured their taunts [EC, Sw]. This word has a different sense than its use in 2:2 and is practically synonymous with ὑπομονή 'endurance' [TH].
  b. διά with accusative object (LN 89.26): 'for the sake of' [KJV, NET, NRSV, TEV, TNT], 'for' [NAB, NIV, NLT], 'because of' [EC, LN, WBC; CEV], 'on account of, by reason of' [LN], 'in' [REB], 'of' [BNTC]. See this word also at 1:9.
  c. ὄνομα (LN 33.126) (BAGD I.4.c.α. p. 572): 'name' [EC, LN, WBC; KJV, NET, NIV, NRSV, TNT], 'cause' [BNTC; NAB, REB], 'name's sake' [BAGD]. Ὄνομα 'name' is also translated as the person himself: 'me' [CEV, NLT], 'my (sake)' [TEV]. This is a case of metonymy in which a personís name is used for the person himself [NIC, TH, WBC; CEV, NLT, TEV].
  d. perf. act. indic. of κοπιάω (LN 23.78, **25.289**) (BAGD 1. p. 443): 'to give up' [**LN** (25.289); CEV, TEV], 'to lose heart' [LN (25.289)], 'to quit' [NLT], 'to flag' [BNTC], 'to faint' [KJV], 'to become discouraged' [NAB], 'to grow weary' [EC; NET, NIV, NRSV, TNT], 'to become weary' [BAGD, WBC; REB], 'to be weary, to be tired' [LN (23.78)], 'to become tired' [BAGD]. Κοπιάω 'to grow weary' is related to the word κόπος 'labor' of 2:2 [TNTC]. The perfect tense indicates a past event, the effect of which continues into the present [Lns, Sw, WBC]. They had not given up their faith [Ld, TH]. They had not grown weary, never entertaining the thought of giving up resisting the false teachers [EC].
QUESTION—What kind of things did those at Ephesus 'endure'?
  The kind of things they 'endured' would be: suffering from persecution [Sw, TH]; hardship [Lns, NIC; NAB, NIV]; difficulties and trials [LN]; evil [BAGD]; burdens [Lns, Wal]. The rest of the verse elaborates their endurance [EC].

2:4 But[a] I-have (this) against[b] you that[c] you-left[d] your first[e] love.[f]
LEXICON—a. ἀλλά (LN 89.125): 'but' [BNTC, EC, LN, WBC; CEV, NET, NLT, NRSV, TEV, TNT], 'nevertheless' [KJV], 'yet' [NIV], 'however' [REB], 'though' [NAB], 'instead, on the contrary' [LN]. Ἀλλά is a marker of emphatic contrast [LN].

b. κατά with genitive object (LN 90.31) (BAGD I.2.b.β. p. 405): 'against' [BAGD, EC, LN; all versions], 'in opposition to, in conflict with' [LN].
c. ὅτι (LN **90.21**): 'that' [EC, LN], 'the fact that' [**LN**]. Ὅτι is also translated 'something…and it is this' [CEV], 'somewhat…because' [KJV], 'this (against you)' [BNTC; NAB, NET, NIV, REB], 'this (against you) that' [WBC; NRSV, TNT], 'this complaint (against you)' [NLT], 'this is what (I have against you)' [TEV]. Ὅτι here indicates 'something…namely that' [WBC].
d. aorist act. indic. of ἀφίημι (LN **68.43**) (BAGD 3.b. p. 126): 'to leave' [EC; KJV], 'to depart from' [NET], 'to forsake' [NIV], 'to give up' [BAGD, LN], 'to abandon' [BAGD; NRSV], 'to lose' [BNTC, WBC; REB, TNT], 'to turn aside from' [NAB]. The phrase τὴν ἀγάπην σου τὴν πρώτην ἀφῆκες 'your love the first you have left' is translated 'you have stopped loving me as you did at first' [**LN**], 'you don't have as much love as you used to' [CEV], 'you don't love me or each other as you did at first' [NLT], 'you do not love me now as you did at first' [TEV].
e. πρῶτος (LN 60.46): 'first' [EC, WBC; KJV, NET, NIV], 'early' [NAB]. It is also translated as an adverbial phrase or clause: 'at first' [BNTC, LN; NLT, NRSV, REB, TEV, TNT], 'as you used to' [CEV]. 'First love' refers back to the time of Paul's ministry among them (see Acts 20:37) [Sw]. 'First' refers to the time when they first became believers [EC, TH]. See this word also at 1:17.
f. ἀγάπη (LN 25.43) (BAGD I.1.a. p. 5): 'love' [BAGD, BNTC, EC, LN; all versions except CEV, NLT, TEV]. This noun is also translated as a verb 'to love' [NLT, TEV], 'to have love' [BNTC; CEV].

QUESTION—Who is the implied object of ἀγάπη 'love'?
1. The object is Jesus Christ (or God) [EC, NIGTC, Sw, Wal; TEV]: love for me. The point is that they no longer expressed their keen love for Christ by maintaining a strong witness to the world [NIGTC]. Jeremiah 2:2 and Ezekiel 16:8ff probably show the kind of initial love for God that the Ephesian believers had lost [Sw].
2. The object is other believers [ICC, Ld, NTC]: love for each other. It may be that the Ephesian intolerance for and struggles against false teaching had resulted in bad attitudes toward each other [ICC, Ld, NIC, Sw]. Their initial love 'for all the saints' had declined (see Ephesians 1:15) [NTC].
3. The object is both Christ (or God) and other believers [Lns, NIC, TH; NLT]. While it mainly refers to brotherly love, love for God is also included [NIC]. 1 John 4:20 shows that love for Christ and love for one's brother are inseparable [Lns].
4. The object is Christ (or God), other believers, and unbelievers [BNTC, TNTC]. The Ephesian church's zeal for truth had blinded them to the fact that God is love [BNTC].

QUESTION—What does the Greek word order indicate in the phrase τὴν ἀγάπην σου τὴν πρώτην ἀφῆκες 'your love the first you left'?
The object 'your first love' is emphasized, being fronted to a position before the verb [Wal]. The word 'first' is emphatic, 'you have left your love, at least the love of the first days' [Sw].

2:5 Remember[a] therefore from-where[b] you-have-fallen[c]
LEXICON—a. pres. act. impera. of μνημονεύω (LN 29.7) (BAGD 1.c. p. 525): 'to remember' [BAGD, BNTC, EC, LN, WBC; KJV, NET, NIV, NRSV, TNT], 'to recall' [LN], 'to think about' [CEV], 'to think' [REB, TEV], 'to look' [NLT], 'to keep firmly in mind' [NAB]. The present imperative indicates continuous action [EC, Lns, NIC, TH, TNTC]: keep on remembering.
  b. πόθεν (LN 84.6) (BAGD 1. p. 680): 'from where' [BAGD, LN; CEV, TNT], 'from whence' [KJV], 'whence' [BAGD, EC, LN], 'from what' [NRSV], 'from what state' [BAGD], 'from what high state' [NET], 'the height(s) from which' [NAB, NIV, REB], 'how far' [BNTC, WBC; TEV], 'how far…from your first love' [NLT]. The place from which they had fallen was the ardor of their initial love [Alf].
  c. perf. act. indic. of πίπτω (LN **13.59**) (BAGD p. 659; 2.a.β. p. 660): 'to fall' [BAGD, BNTC, EC, **LN** (13.59), WBC; all versions], 'to worsen' [LN], 'to be completely ruined, to go astray morally' [BAGD]. Πίπτω here indicates a change for the worse with particular focus on the suddenness and the extent [LN]. It indicates a moral fall [BAGD, Sw]. See Romans 11:11 and 1 Corinthians 10:12 [Sw]. The perfect tense indicates completeness [TNTC]. It indicates that its results continue into the present [EC, Lns].
QUESTION—What relationship is indicated by the conjunction οὖν 'therefore'?
It indicates an exhortation based on the reprimand expressed in 2:4 [EC, Lns]: You have left your first love. *Therefore*, remember from where you have fallen.
QUESTION—What are the Ephesians encouraged to 'remember'?
They are to remember: the times when love was in great supply among them [NIC]; how strong their desire was to serve the Lord when they first became Christians [Ld].

and repent[a] and do the first[b] works;[c]
LEXICON—a. aorist act. impera. of μετανοέω (LN 41.52) (BAGD p. 512): 'to repent' [BAGD, BNTC, EC, LN, WBC; KJV, NAB, NET, NIV, NRSV, REB, TNT], 'to change one's way' [LN], 'to turn back' [CEV], 'to turn from one's sins' [TEV], 'turn back to me again' [NLT]. Μετανοέω ινδιχατεσ to change one's way of life as the result of a complete change of thought with regard to sin and truth [LN]. The aorist imperative indicates a decisive action [Alf, NIC, TH, TNTC].

b. πρῶτος (LN 60.46, 67.18): 'first' [BAGD, EC, LN (60.46); KJV, NET], 'former' [LN (67.18); NAB], 'formerly' [WBC], 'earlier' [BAGD], 'before' [BNTC]. The phrase τὰ πρῶτα ἔργα 'the first works' is translated 'as/what you did at first' [BNTC; CEV, NIV, NRSV, TEV, TNT], 'as you once did' [REB], 'work as you did at first' [NLT]. See this word also at 2:4.

c. ἔργον (See this word at 2:2): 'work' [EC; KJV, NRSV], 'deed' [WBC; NAB, NET], 'thing' [NIV], not explicit [BNTC; CEV, REB, TEV, TNT]. This noun is also translated as a verb: 'to work' [NLT]. 'Works' here refers to their way of life [TH].

QUESTION—What is the significance of the twice repeated word 'repent'?

It serves to emphasize the word [TH].

QUESTION—What is indicated by the phrase τὰ πρῶτα ἔργα ποιήσον 'do the first works'?

It indicates that they should return to doing things out of love [Alf, ICC, Ld, NIC, NTC, TH, TNTC], particularly by loving each other [NIC]. It indicates that they should return to their love for God and the works that such a love produced [Wal]. It indicates that they should resume their role as a dependable witness. A lamp is a symbol of light, that is, a witness to unbelievers [NIGTC].

but if not, I-am-coming to-you and I-will-remove[a] your lampstand from its place,[b] unless you-repent.

TEXT—Some manuscripts include τάχυ 'quickly' following σοι 'to you'. GNT does not mention this alternative. It is included by KJV.

LEXICON—a. fut. act. indic. of κινέω (LN **15.3**) (BAGD 1. p. 432): 'to remove' [BAGD, EC, **LN**, WBC; KJV, NAB, NET, NIV, NLT, NRSV, REB, TNT], 'to take away' [**LN**; CEV], 'to take' [TEV], 'to move' [BNTC, LN].

b. τόπος (LN 80.1) (BAGD 1.f. p. 823): 'place' [BAGD, BNTC, EC, LN, WBC; all versions except CEV, NLT], 'place among the churches' [NLT], not explicit [CEV].

QUESTION—What is the significance of the present tense ἔρχομαι 'I am coming'?

It is being used in a quasi-future sense [BNTC, EC, Lns, Sw, WBC; all versions]: I will come. John uses the present tense as though he were seeing it happen [TNTC]. The present tense stresses the nearness of the coming [NIC].

QUESTION—What particular 'coming' is referred to?

1. The 'coming' of Christ refers here to a special coming to the Ephesian church in judgment and not to his Second Coming [Alf, BNTC, ICC, Ld, NIC, Wal, WBC]. However, reference to the Second Coming may also be indicated [ICC].

2. This refers to the Second Coming [EC, Sw]. The condition is to be taken as "I will remove your lampstand when I come, if you shall not have repented before that coming" [EC].

QUESTION—What is indicated by κινήσω 'I will remove'?

It may indicate the end of their existence as a community of believers [ICC, Ld, Lns, TH, TNTC, WBC].

QUESTION—Did the Ephesian church obey this command?

Yes, since in a later letter to Ephesus, Ignatius commends them on their love [ICC, NIC, NTC, Sw].

2:6 But[a] you-have[b] this, that you-hate[c] the works of-the Nicolaitans,[d] that I-also hate.

LEXICON—a. ἀλλά (See this word at 2:4): 'but' [EC, WBC; CEV, KJV, NAB, NET, NIV, NLT, TEV], 'yet' [BNTC; NRSV, REB, TNT].

b. pres. act. indic. of ἔχω (LN 57.1) (BAGD I.7.b. p. 333): 'to have' [BAGD, EC, LN; KJV], 'to possess' [LN]. The phrase τοῦτο ἔχεις 'you have this' is also translated: 'you have this in your favor' [BAGD, WBC; NIV, TEV], 'you have this much in your favor' [NAB, REB], 'you do have this going for you' [NET], 'there is one thing you are doing right' [CEV], 'there is this about you that is good' [NLT], 'you have this to your credit' [BNTC], 'this is to your credit' [NRSV], 'this is in your favor' [TNT].

c. pres. act. indic. of μισέω (LN 88.198) (BAGD 2. p. 522): 'to hate' [BAGD, EC, LN; all versions except NAB, REB], 'to detest' [BAGD, LN; NAB, REB], 'to despise' [WBC], 'to abhor' [BAGD].

d. Νικολαΐτης (LN 93.282) (BAGD p. 539): 'Nicolaitan' [BAGD, BNTC, EC, LN, WBC; all versions except NLT], 'immoral Nicolaitan' [NLT]. A Nicolaitan was a follower of Nicolaus [BAGD, EC, LN]. Irenaeus, and the other early church fathers held that Nicolaus was the convert to Judaism from Antioch mentioned in Acts 6:5 [Alf, EC, Wal]. It is wrong to assume that the Nicolaus of Acts was the founder of this sect since there is no dependable evidence of this [Lns].

QUESTION—Who were the Nicolaitans?

They may have been Gnostics [Lns], who separated the material from the spiritual dimension and taught that immoral living does not affect one's spiritual life [TH]. They may have been related to the Baalamites and the followers of Jezebel and claimed their goal was not to destroy Christianity, but to improve it [TNTC]. They may have taught that the commands of Acts 15:20 and 29, concerning the eating of food offered to idols and sexual immorality, were no longer binding [ICC, NIC, NTC]. They taught that it was permissible to some degree to participate in the idolatrous activity of Ephesus [NIGTC]. In general they taught a compromise between Christianity and pagan society [NIC].

2:7 **The-one having (an) ear**[a] **let-him-hear**[b] **what the Spirit says to-the churches.**

LEXICON—a. οὖς (LN 24.59, 8.24) (BAGD 2. p. 595): 'ear' [BAGD, BNTC, LN (8.24), WBC; all versions except NLT]. The phrase ὁ ἔχων οὖς 'the one having an ear' is translated 'if you can hear' [LN (**24.59**)], 'anyone who is willing to hear' [NLT], 'you have ears' [REB]. The phrase is idiomatic of 'being able to hear' and implies that people should be able to hear and pay attention [LN (24.59)]. The phrase is a call to attention [TNTC].

b. aorist act. impera. of ἀκούω (LN 24.52, 31.56) (BAGD 1.a. p. 31): 'to hear' [BAGD, BNTC, EC, LN (24.52), WBC; KJV, NET, NIV, REB, TNT], 'to listen to' [LN (31.56); CEV, NRSV, TEV], 'to listen and understand' [NLT], 'to heed' [LN (31.56); NAB], 'to accept, to listen and respond, to pay attention and respond' [LN (31.56)]. It means to effectively hear [Lns].

QUESTION—What is the significance of the plural ταῖς ἐκκλησίαις 'the churches'?

It shows that the message is addressed not only to the believers at Ephesus, but to all seven churches [TH], and not only to the seven but to the entire body of believers [EC, ICC, Ld, Lns]. It shows that the message was intended for anyone who wanted to hear it [TNTC].

QUESTION—To what do the words τί τὸ πνεῦμα λέγει ταῖς ἐκκλησίαις 'what the Spirit says to the churches' refer?

The words refer to giving heed to what is said to each church [EC]. The words comprise the whole book of Revelation [Alf, TH], including these seven letters [TH].

QUESTION—Who is τὸ πνεῦμα 'the Spirit'?

It is the Spirit of God [Alf, BNTC, Lns, TH, WBC; probably all versions], Jesus does not say, "I say." The Spirit is named because it is he who effects faith by hearing [Lns]. It is the Spirit of God speaking through Jesus [Alf, TH]. It is the Spirit of Christ [Sw, TNTC]. It is the Spirit of Christ since Christ is the speaker (see 2:1) [EC, ICC]. Christ speaks through the Spirit and so the voice of Christ is the voice of the Spirit [Ld].

To-the-one-who conquers[a] **I-will-give**[b] **to-him to-eat from**[c] **the tree**[d] **of-life,**

LEXICON—a. pres. act. participle of νικάω (LN 39.57) (BAGD 1.a. p. 539): 'to conquer' [BAGD, LN, WBC; NET, NRSV, TNT], 'to be victorious' [BAGD; NLT, REB], 'to win the victory' [CEV, TEV], 'to overcome' [EC; KJV, NIV], 'to be victorious over' [LN], 'to be (a) victor' [BAGD, LN], 'to prevail' [BAGD]. This verb is also translated as a noun: 'the victor' [NAB], 'the conqueror' [BNTC].

b. fut. act. indic. of δίδωμι (LN 13.142, 57.71): 'to give' [LN (57.71); KJV], 'to give the right' [BNTC; NIV, REB, TEV, TNT], 'to give permission' [TH; NRSV], 'to permit' [Alf; NET], 'to grant (the opportunity)' [EC, LN

(13.142)], 'to allow' [LN (13.142), WBC], 'to let' [CEV], 'to see to it' [NAB], not explicit [NLT].
   c. ἐκ with genitive object (LN 63.20, 90.16) (BAGD 4.a.ε. p. 236): 'from' [BAGD, BNTC, EC, LN (90.16); all versions except TEV, TNT]. 'a part of' [BAGD, LN (63.20)], not explicit [WBC; TEV, TNT].
   d. ξύλον (LN **3.4**) (BAGD 3. p. 549): 'tree' [BAGD, LN]. The phrase ξύλον τῆς ζωῆς 'tree of life' is translated 'tree of life' [BAGD, BNTC, EC, **LN**; all versions except CEV, TEV, TNT]; 'life-giving tree' [CEV]; 'the fruit of the tree of life' [Alf, Lns, WBC; TEV, TNT]. Since a person does not eat a tree, it may be necessary to translate, 'eat of the fruit of the tree that causes life' [**LN**].

QUESTION—What is the implied object of νικῶντι 'conquering', and what does 'conquering' mean?

The object is: evil forces [Ld, TH]; the unbelief and sin of the world (see 1 John 5:5) [Wal]; sin and evil [ICC]; the sin of failing to testify about Christ to people since the function of a lamp is to be a light [NIGTC]. 'Conquering' indicates: remaining faithful to Christ to the end [BNTC, ICC, Ld, Lns, NIC, TNTC]; being faithful to Christ to the extent of martyrdom [BNTC, ICC, Ld].

QUESTION—How are the nouns related in the genitive construction τοῦ ξύλου τῆς ζωῆς 'the tree of life'?
   1. Life modifies tree [Lns]: the living tree.
   2. The tree gives or causes life [TH; CEV]: the life-giving tree.

QUESTION—What is the significance of 'to eat from the tree of life'?

'To eat from the tree of life' means: to have eternal life [ICC, Ld, Lns, NIC, NTC, Sw, TH, Wal]; to have immortality in the new Jerusalem [EC]; to be forgiven and to enjoy the life-giving presence of God [NIGTC]; to enjoy all that life in Heaven holds in store for believers [Sw, Wal]. It is to realize God's original intention for man when he offered the Tree of Life to Adam and Eve in the garden of Eden [WBC].

that is in the paradise[a] of God'.

TEXT—Instead of τῷ παραδείσῳ 'the paradise' some manuscripts read μέσῳ τοῦ παραδείσου 'midst of the paradise'. GNT does not mention this alternative. It is followed by KJV.

LEXICON—a. παράδεισος (LN **1.14**) (BAGD 2. p. 614): 'paradise' [BAGD, LN; KJV, NET, NIV, NLT, NRSV], 'Paradise' [EC, WBC; TNT], 'garden' [NAB, REB], 'Garden' [BNTC; TEV], 'wonderful garden' [CEV].

QUESTION—What is the meaning of παράδεισος 'paradise'?

Παράδεισος is a Persian word that means: 'garden' [TH, WBC]; 'pleasure garden' [EC, NIC]; 'park' [EC, TNTC, WBC]; 'beautiful park' [Lns]; 'fruit orchard' [TH]. It is the dwelling place of believers who have died (see Luke 23:43) [ICC, LN, Lns]. It is the same as heaven [LN, TH]. It is the same as the Heavenly Jerusalem that will descend to earth as described in Revelation

21 and 22 [ICC, Ld]. This word refers to the third heaven or part of it (see 2 Corinthians 12:2–4) [ICC, Ld]. It is a name for the dwelling place of God [EC, Ld]. It refers to a place of blessedness above the earth [BAGD]. It is a place of joy where believers revel in the presence of God and Christ [Sw, TNTC].

DISCOURSE UNIT: 2:8–11 [Alf, BNTC, EC, GNT, ICC, Ld, Lns, NIC, NIGTC, NTC, Sw, TH, TNTC, Wal, WBC; all versions except REB, TNT]. The topic is the letter to Smyrna.

2:8 **And write to-the angel of-the church in Smyrna:**
LEXICON—a. Σμύρνα (LN 93.583) (BAGD p. 759): 'Smyrna' [BAGD, EC, LN; all versions]. Smyrna was a prosperous commercial city on the west coast of Asia Minor [BAGD]. It had been destroyed in 627 B.C. by the Lydians and rebuilt in 290 B.C. by Lysimiachus [NTC]. It was 35 miles north of Ephesus and vied with Ephesus for being the most important city of Asia Minor. It had a temple to Roma, the goddess of Rome and one to the Roman Emperor Tiberius. It had many Jews who were hostile to Christianity [Ld]. The founding of the church is a mystery [EC]. It is modern day Izmir [NIC].

'These things says the First and the Last, who was dead and came-to-life:[a]
LEXICON—a. aorist act. indic. of ζάω (LN 23.88, 23.93) (BAGD 1.a.β. p. 336): 'to come to life' [BNTC, WBC; NET, NRSV], 'to come to life again' [NIV, REB, TNT], 'to be alive' [LN (23.88); CEV, KJV, NLT], 'to live again' [LN (23.93); TEV], 'to live' [EC, LN (23.88); NAB], 'to come back to life' [LN (23.93)], 'to become alive again' [BAGD], 'to be resurrected' [LN (23.93)]. The two aorist tenses 'was dead' and 'came to life' are historical and point to Calvary and the Resurrection [Lns]. The aorist is ingressive, meaning Christ 'began to live' after death [EC].

QUESTION—What is the significance of Jesus' description of himself in this way?

It is significant in the light the suffering that some of the believers in Smyrna will have to undergo. It would be encouraging to them to keep in mind that Jesus himself is sovereign has conquered death and that their faithfulness would be rewarded with eternal life [NIC]. As a living Savior, he is able to keep his promises [EC].

2:9 **I-know your affliction**[a] **and poverty,**[b] **but you-are rich,**[c]
TEXT—Some manuscripts include τὰ ἔργα καί 'the works and' before τὴν θλῖψιν 'the tribulation'. GNT does not mention this alternative. It is included by KJV.

LEXICON—a. θλῖψις (See this word at 1:9): 'affliction' [EC; NIV, NRSV, TNT], 'tribulation' [WBC; KJV, NAB], 'suffering' [BNTC, LN; NLT], 'trouble' [TEV], 'distress you are suffering' [NET]. This noun is also translated: 'how much (you) suffer' [CEV], 'how hard-pressed (you are)' [REB]. Even though this noun is singular, it refers to many kinds of

trouble [NIC], and is translated in the plural [TH; NIV, TEV]. This could have been caused by persecution [NET], or, taking καί 'and' as 'even', be defined by 'poverty' and 'slander' [EC].
- b. πτωχεία (LN 57.52) (BAGD p. 728): 'poverty' [BNTC, EC, LN, WBC; all versions except CEV, REB, TEV], 'extreme poverty' [BAGD, TNTC], 'abject poverty' [Wal], 'stark poverty' [NIC], 'destitution' [LN]. This noun is also translated as an adjective: 'poor' [TEV]; and as an adjective phrase: 'how poor' [CEV, REB]. Πτωχεία literally means 'beggarliness' [BAGD]. Literal or material poverty is indicated here [Alf, BNTC, ICC, Ld, Lns, NIC, Sw, TH, TNTC, Wal, WBC].
- c. πλούσιος (LN 57.26) (BAGD 2. p. 673): 'rich' [BAGD, BNTC, EC, LN, WBC; all versions], 'wealthy' [BAGD, LN], 'well-to-do' [LN].

QUESTION—Why were the believers at Smyrna poor?

Since the word poverty is linked with affliction, it may have been due to persecution [Alf, EC, Ld, Lns, Wal]. It may have been due to the looting of their property by mobs (see Hebrews 10:34) [Alf, BNTC, ICC, Ld, Lns, NIC, Sw, TNTC, Wal]. It may have been due to the difficulties of earning a living as committed believers in a hostile environment [BNTC, Ld, Lns, NIC, WBC]. Their goods may have been confiscated by the authorities [TH]. The believers may have been from a poor class of society [Sw].

QUESTION—In what way were the believers at Smyrna rich?

They were spiritually rich [Alf, BAGD, ICC, Ld, Lns, NIC, TH, TNTC, Wal, WBC]. They were rich in faith (see James 2.5 and 2 Corinthians 6:10) [NIC, Wal].

and the slander[a] of the-ones saying[b] themselves to-be Jews and they-are not,

LEXICON—a. βλασθημία (LN 33.400, 33.401) (BAGD 2.a.α. p. 143): 'slander' [BAGD, BNTC, EC, WBC; NIV, NLT, NRSV, TNT], 'slander against you' [NET], 'slander you endure' [NAB], 'blasphemy' [LN (33.401); KJV], 'cruel things being said about you' [CEV], 'evil things said against you' [TEV], 'reviling, defamation, false witness' [LN (33.400)], 'serious insult' [LN (33.401)]. This noun is also translated as a verb: 'to be slandered' [REB]. Βλασθημία means to speak against someone so as to harm her or his reputation [LN (33.400)].
- b. pres. act. participle of λέγω (LN 33.69, 33.131): 'to say' [EC, LN (33.69); KJV, NIV, NLT, NRSV, TNT], 'to call' [LN (33.131), WBC; NET]. The phrase λεγόντων ἑαυτούς 'saying themselves' is translated 'to claim' [BNTC; CEV, REB, TEV]. It is also translated as an adjective phrase: 'self-styled (Jews)' [NAB].

QUESTION—In what ways are these people who claim to be Jews, not Jews?

They are not Jews because they are only Jews by physical not spiritual birth (see Romans 2:28, Matthew 3:9, John 8:31ff, 2 Corinthians 11:22, Philippians 3.4ff, Galatians 6:15) [Alf, ICC, Ld, Lns, NIC, Sw, TH, TNTC, Wal]. They are not Jews because they have rejected the Messiah [BNTC,

ICC, Ld], and attacked his followers [BNTC]. A true Jew is one who is committed to doing the will of God and these people did not qualify in this sense to be Jews [WBC].

QUESTION—Were these men Jews by birth then?

Yes, they were physically Jews who were slandering the believers [Alf, BNTC, EC, ICC, Ld, Lns, NIC, NIGTC, NTC, Sw, TH, TNTC, Wal, WBC]. The Jews of Smyrna and took an active part in the martyrdom of Polycarp, Bishop of Smyrna [Alf, ICC, Lns, NIC, NTC, Sw].

but (they are a) synagogue[a] of Satan.[b]

LEXICON—a. συναγωγή (LN 7.20, **11.44**) (BAGD 2. p. 782; 4. p. 783): 'synagogue' [BAGD (4), BNTC, EC, LN (7.20), WBC; KJV, NET, NIV, NLT, NRSV, REB, TNT], 'a group that belongs to (Satan)' [CEV, TEV], 'members of (Satan's) assembly' [NAB], 'congregation' [**LN** (11.44)], 'assembly' [LN (11.44)], 'place of assembly' [BAGD (2)].

b. Σατανᾶς (LN 12.34, 93.330) (BAGD p. 744): 'Satan' [BAGD, BNTC, EC, LN, WBC; all versions], 'Devil' [LN (12.34)], 'Adversary' [BAGD]. Σατανᾶς literally means 'adversary'. He is the principle supernatural evil being [LN (12.34)]. He is the ruler of all evil spiritual forces [TH].

QUESTION—How are the nouns related in the genitive construction συναγωγὴ τοῦ Σατανᾶ 'synagogue of Satan'?

These were people who belonged to or served Satan [TH; CEV, NAB, TEV]. Synagogue indicates a group or gathering of Jews, not a building [EC, TH, WBC].

QUESTION—What action(s) qualified these people to be a 'synagogue of Satan'?

They accused and slandered believers and became Satan's agents (see 12:10, 13:1, 5–6; 17:3–6; John 8:44) [BNTC, EC, Lns, NIC, NIGTC]. The Jews rejected the Messiah and so became a synagogue of Satan [Ld].

2:10 **Fear not the-things you-are-about-to[a] suffer.[b]**

LEXICON—a. pres. act. indic. of μέλλω (See this word at 1:19): 'to be about to' [BNTC, EC; NET, NIV, NLT, NRSV, TEV], 'to be going to' [TNT], 'will' [WBC; CEV], 'shalt' [KJV]. This word is also translated '(sufferings) to come' [NAB, REB].

b. pres. act. infin. of πάσχω (LN 24.78, **90.66**) (BAGD 3.b. p. 634): 'to suffer' [BNTC, EC, **LN** (90.66, 24.78), WBC; all versions except NAB, REB], 'to experience' [**LN** (90.66)], 'to endure, undergo' [BAGD]. This verb is also translated as a noun: 'sufferings' [NAB, REB].

QUESTION—What is the significance of the present tense of μηδὲν φοβοῦ 'fear not'?

It indicates that the action was already going on [EC, Lns, NIC, Wal]: Stop being afraid! It may indicate that there was a general feeling of fear among the believers there [NIC]. Already persecuted, they expected worse things to happen [EC].

Behold[a] the Devil[b] is-about-to to-throw[c] some-of[d] you into prison[e]

LEXICON—a. ἰδού (See this word at 1:7): 'behold' [EC, WBC; KJV], 'I tell you' [NIV], 'beware' [NRSV], 'listen' [TEV], 'indeed' [BNTC; NAB], not explicit [CEV, NET, NLT, REB, TNT]. This directs special attention to the announcement [EC].

b. διάβολος (LN 12.34) (BAGD 2. p. 182): 'Devil' [BNTC, LN, WBC; NLT, TEV], 'devil' [BAGD, EC; CEV, KJV, NAB, NET, NIV, NRSV, REB, TNT], 'Satan' [LN], 'the slanderer' [BAGD]. Διάβολος literally means 'slanderer' [LN]. This is Satan, the ruler of the forces of evil [TH].

c. pres. act. infin. of βάλλω (LN 15.215) (BAGD 1.b. p. 131): 'to throw' [BAGD, BNTC, LN; all versions except KJV, NAB, NIV], 'to cast' [EC, WBC; KJV, NAB], 'to put' [NIV]. This would not be done personally, but he would cause them to be thrown into prison [TH].

d. ἐκ with genitive object (LN 63.20): 'some of', [BNTC, EC, WBC; all versions], 'one of, a part of, one among' [LN].

e. φυλακή (LN 7.24) (BAGD 3. p. 867): 'prison' [BAGD, BNTC, EC, LN, WBC; all versions except CEV], 'jail' [CEV].

QUESTION—In what way is the devil involved in casting them into prison?

The devil will work through his servants the Jews and Romans to persecute the Christians [EC, Ld, Lns]. The devil will cause their enemies to do this [TH].

so-that[a] you-may-be-tested[b] and you-will-have affliction (for) ten days.

LEXICON—a. ἵνα (LN 89.59) (BAGD p. 379): 'so that' [LN, WBC; NRSV], 'so' [NET], 'that' [BAGD, EC; KJV, TNT], 'in order that' [BAGD], 'to' [BNTC; NAB, NIV, REB], 'and' [CEV, NLT], 'in order to, for the purpose of' [LN], not explicit [TEV].

b. aorist pass. subj. of πειράζω (LN 27.46, 88.308) (BAGD 2.d. p. 640): 'to be tested', [EC, LN (27.46), WBC; CEV, NET, NRSV, TNT], 'to be tried' [KJV], 'to be trapped' [LN (88.308)], 'to be tempted' [BAGD, LN (88.308)], 'to be led into temptation' [LN (88.308)]. 'to be examined' [LN (27.46)], 'to be put to the test' [LN (27.46); REB]. This passive voice is also translated actively: 'to put to the test' [BNTC; NAB, NLT, TEV], 'to test' [NIV]. A trial of a person's faith is indicated here [BNTC, Ld, Lns, Sw, TH]. The testing here referred to is persecution [ICC]. The testing was in the temptation to abandon their faith, not to prove them [Alf].

QUESTION—Who is the implied actor of πειράζω 'to test'?

1. The implied actor is the Devil [Alf, EC, Ld, NIC, Sw]: so that the Devil may test you. The conjunction ἵνα 'so that' indicates the purpose of the one mentioned in the preceding clause [Alf]. This was intended to prove the genuineness of a person's faith [Ld, Sw]. The devil was not interested in showing their faith to be real but in enticing them to give up their faith [EC].

2. The actor is God [BNTC, Lns, NIGTC, TH]: so that God may test you. The believers were not to fear this persecution [NIGTC] because it was God's test to distinguish true believers from false [NIGTC, TH].
3. Both of the above are true because what the Devil intends as a temptation, God intends as a test of one's faith [BNTC].

QUESTION—What does the phrase ἡμερῶν δέκα 'ten days' imply?

It refers to a limited period of time of exactly ten days [EC]. It refers to a limited period of time [NIGTC, TNTC, Wal]. It refers to a long but limited period [NIC, NTC, Sw]. It implies a short period of time [Alf, BNTC, ICC, Ld, TH, WBC]. It refers to a period of time long enough to complete God's purpose and may have included the martyrdom of Polycarp about 60 years later [Lns].

Be faithful[b] until[c] death,[d]

LEXICON—a. πιστός (See this word at 1:5): 'faithful' [EC, WBC; all versions except TEV], 'faithful to me' [TEV], 'loyal' [BNTC]. Πιστός refers to being loyal to their Christian commitment [TH].
  b. ἄχρι with genitive object (LN 67.119, 84.19) (BAGD 1.c. p. 129): 'until' [LN (67.119); CEV, NAB, NRSV], 'till' [REB], 'up to' [LN (84.19)], 'even to' [TNT], 'even to the point of' [Alf; NET, NIV], 'even when facing' [NLT], 'even if it means' [TEV], 'even if you (die) for it' [BNTC], 'to' [EC, LN (67.119, 84.19)], 'unto' [BAGD, WBC; KJV], 'as far as' [LN (84.19)]. This does not focus on the duration of their faithfulness but the extent: be faithful even to death [EC].
  c. θάνατος (BAGD 1.a. p. 350): 'death' [BAGD, EC, LN, WBC; all versions except CEV]. This noun is also translated as a verb: 'to die' [BNTC; CEV]. Θάνατος here refers to death by persecution, not death by normal processes [EC, TH]. Not everyone in the church would face death as a martyr, but each one there should be willing to be killed for their faith [EC, Lns]. See this word also at 1:18.

and I-will-give you the crown[a] of life.

LEXICON—a. στέφανος (LN 6.192, **57.121**) (BAGD 2.a. p. 767): 'crown' [BNTC, EC, LN (6.192); all versions except CEV, TEV, TNT], 'wreath' [LN (6.192), WBC], 'prize' [BAGD, **LN** (57.121)], 'crown of victory' [TNT], 'prize of victory' [TEV], 'reward' [BAGD, LN (57.121)]. This noun is also translated as an adjective: 'glorious (life)' [CEV]. The στέφανος was a wreath of foliage or precious metals formed to resemble foliage and was worn as a symbol of honor, victory, or as a badge of high office [LN (6.192)]. It may have been braided oak, ivy, parsley, myrtle, or olive branches [Lns]. It was a wreath made of laurel leaves [TH]. Its value was not in itself but in what it symbolized [NIC].

QUESTION—What does the image of a στέφανος 'crown/wreath' symbolize.
  1. It symbolizes a prize that a person receives for winning an athletic event [EC, ICC, Ld, LN, Lns, NIC, NTC, TH, TNTC, WBC; TEV, TNT]. The focus is not on the athletic part of the image but on victory over evil [EC].

2. It symbolizes royalty, being the crown a king would wear [Alf, NIGTC]. The crown here symbolizes Christ's victorious rule [NIGTC].

QUESTION—How are the nouns related in the genitive construction τὸν στέφανον τῆς ζωῆς 'the crown of life'?

1. The genitive 'of life' is in apposition to or defines 'crown' [Alf, EC, Ld, LN, Lns, NIC, NIGTC, NTC, Sw, TH, TNTC, WBC; NET, TEV, TNT]: the crown that is life. 'Life' here indicates 'eternal life' [ICC, Ld, NIGTC, NTC, TH, TNTC, Wal]. The article with 'life' (τῆς ζωῆς) indicates 'eternal life' [TNTC]. Faithfulness is not a means of earning eternal life, but perseverance through suffering provides tangible assurance they will receive this life through their faith in Christ [EC].
2. They indicate a crown that belongs to eternal life being symbolical of the full realization of that life [ICC].

2:11 The-one having an-ear let-him-hear what the spirit says to-the churches. The-one-who conquers[a] never[b] will-be-hurt[c] by[d] the second death.'

LEXICON—a. pres. act. participle of νικάω (See this word at 2:7): 'to conquer' [WBC; NET, NRSV, TNT], 'to be victorious' [NLT, REB], 'to win the victory' [CEV, TEV], 'to overcome' [EC; KJV, NIV]. This verb is also translated as a noun: 'the victor' [NAB], 'the Conqueror' [BNTC]. The direct object would be the forces of evil [TH].

b. οὐ μή (LN 69.5) (BAGD D.1.a. p. 517): 'never' [BAGD; NAB], 'certainly not' [BAGD, BNTC, LN; CEV, KJV, NLT, NRSV, REB, TEV, TNT], 'by no means' [LN], 'in no way' [NET], 'absolutely not' [WBC], 'in not wise' [Sw], 'not at all' [NIV]. Οὐ μή is a marker of emphatic negation [BAGD, LN]. The two negatives together are the most forceful way to negate a future action [BAGD, EC, ICC].

c. aorist pass. subj. of ἀδικέω (LN 20.25) (BAGD 2.b. p. 17): 'to be hurt' [EC, LN; CEV, KJV, NIV, NLT, TEV], 'to be harmed' [BAGD, BNTC, LN, WBC; NAB, NET, NRSV, REB, TNT]. Ἀδικέω here comes close to meaning 'will not be affected by' [TH].

d. ἐκ with genitive object (LN 89.77, 89.25, 90.12) (BAGD 3.e.α. p. 235): 'by' [BAGD, BNTC, EC, LN (90.12), WBC; all versions except KJV], 'of' [KJV], 'by means of' [LN (89.77)], 'because of' [BAGD, LN (89.25)], 'from' [LN (89.77)]. Ἐκ indicates the source [Lns], or the agent or instrument of the hurt [EC, ICC].

QUESTION—What is indicated by the phrase τοῦ θανάτου τοῦ δευτέρου 'the second death'?

The second death is defined in 20:6, 14 and 21:8 as the lake of fire [Alf, BNTC, GNT, ICC, Ld, Lns, NIC, NIGTC, NTC, Sw, TH, TNTC, Wal, WBC]. It is the place of the destruction of the soul (see Matthew 10:28) [BNTC, Ld]. It is the place of eternal damnation in the lake of fire [Lns]. The second death is a spiritual death as opposed to natural physical death [TH]. It refers to eternal punishment [NIGTC, TNTC]. It is the place of final judgment [NIGTC, NTC]. It is the judgment at the great white throne (see 20:11–15) [Wal].

DISCOURSE UNIT: 2:12–17 [Alf, BNTC, EC, GNT, ICC, Ld, Lns, NIC, NIGTC, NTC, Sw, TH, TNTC, Wal, WBC; all versions except REB, TNT]. The topic is the letter to Pergamum.

2:12 And write to-the angel of-the church in Pergamum:[a] 'These things says the-one having the sharp two-edged sword:[b]
LEXICON—a. Πέργαμος (LN 93.550) (BAGD): 'Pergamum' [BAGD, BNTC, EC; all versions], 'Pergamon' [WBC].
  b. ῥομφαία (LN **6.32**): 'sword' [BNTC, **LN**, WBC; all versions]. See this word also at 1:16.
QUESTION—What was Pergamum noted for?
Pergamum was the capital city of the Roman province of Asia and home of the temple dedicated to the worship of the Roman Emperor Augustus and the goddess Roma [BNTC, ICC, Ld, Lns, NIC, NIGTC, Sw, TH, TNTC]. It was located about 15–20 miles from the sea [ICC, Sw, TNTC, Wal, WBC]. It was the center for the worship of Asclepias, the Greek god of healing [BNTC, Ld, Lns, NIC, NIGTC, TH, Wal], whose symbol is a serpent [BNTC, Lns, NIGTC]. Other Greek deities worshiped there were Zeus Soter, Dionysos Nikephoros, and Athene [NIC, Sw, TNTC, Wal]. It housed a library of 200,000 volumes [TNTC, Wal]. Its being the center of the worship of the Roman Emperor put pressure on the believers there, since refusal to worship the Emperor would be looked on as treason [EC, ICC, Ld, NIGTC].
QUESTION—What significance is there in Christ's reminder of his having a sword?
The Roman governor of Pergamum had the *ius gladii* 'the right of the sword' over its inhabitants meaning that he could have anyone put to death at will. Christ's word to the believers was meant to reassure them that even though Rome had a temporal sword, he held ultimate power over Rome [NIC, NIGTC, TNTC]. The sword may have been a symbol of judgment to the believers in Pergamum who had become slack in their attitude toward pagan activities [Ld]. It was a symbol of Christ's judicial authority and indicated his defeat of enemies and pronouncing judgment upon them [EC].

2:13 I-know where you live,[a] where Satan's throne[b] (is),
TEXT—Some manuscripts include τὰ ἔργα σου καί 'your works and' before ποῦ 'where'. GNT does not mention this alternative. It is included by KJ.V
LEXICON—a. pres. act. indic. of κατοικέω (LN 85.69) (BAGD 1.a. p. 424): 'to live' [BAGD, BNTC, LN, WBC; CEV, NAB, NIV, NLT, NRSV, REB, TEV, TNT], 'to dwell' [BAGD, EC, LN; KJV], 'to reside' [BAGD, LN; NET].
  b. θρόνος (LN 6.112, **37.72**) (BAGD 1.e. p. 364): 'throne' [BAGD, BNTC, EC, LN (6.112, 37.72), WBC; all versions except NLT], 'great throne' [NLT], 'seat' [KJV], 'rule' [**LN** (37.72)], 'place of authority, place of

ruling' [LN (37.72)]. This noun is also translated as a verb: 'to be enthroned' [REB]. A θρόνος is a rather large, ornate seat on which a ruler sits to enact his kingly responsibilities [LN (6.112)]. Since the statement 'where Satan's throne is' may indicate only its location, it may be better to translate: 'where Satan rules' or 'where Satan is king' [TH].

QUESTION—What made Pergamum the throne of Satan?

1. It was probably a reference to the fact that Pergamum was the center for the worship of the Roman Emperor [BNTC, EC, ICC, Ld, NIC, NTC, Sw, TNTC]. Rome was the most recent and most powerful agent of Satan because of its demands for absolute allegiance [BNTC, EC].
2. It was probably a reference to the presence of the altar to the Greek god Zeus on a cliff above the city [TH]. This altar was throne-like [NIC, NTC].
3. It was probably a reference to Pergamum's evil character shown by the persecution of Christians there and especially seen in the worship of the Greek god of healing, Asclepius, the serpent god [Wal].
4. It was probably a reference to the fact that Pergamum was a center of Roman persecution of Christians as seen in the death of Antipas [WBC].
5. It was a reference to the general pagan environment of Pergamum due to the worship of the Roman Emperor and the Greek gods [NIGTC].

yet/and[a] you-hold-fast-to[b] my name and you-denied[c] not the faith[d] of-me

LEXICON—a. καί (LN 91.12): 'yet' [LN; NET, NIV, NRSV, REB], 'and yet' [BNTC, EC; NLT], 'but' [CEV, TNT], 'and' [KJV, NAB], not explicit [WBC; TEV].

b. pres. act. indic. of κρατέω (LN 13.34) (BAGD 2.e.β. p. 448): 'to hold fast (to)' [BAGD, EC; KJV, NAB, NRSV, REB, TNT], 'to hold' [LN, WBC], 'to keep true to' [CEV], 'to remain true to' [NIV], 'to be true to' [BNTC; TEV], 'to remain loyal to' [NLT], 'to continue to cling to' [NET], 'to keep, to cause to continue' [LN]. Κρατέω implies that they remain closely united to him [BAGD].

c. aorist act. indic. of ἀρνέομαι (LN 33.277, 34.48, 36.43) (BAGD 3.d. p. 108): 'to deny' [BAGD, BNTC, EC, LN (33.277, 34.48); KJV, NAB, NET, NLT, NRSV, REB], 'to renounce' [WBC; NIV], 'to abandon' [TEV], 'to disown' [BAGD; TNT], 'to give up' [CEV], 'to refuse to follow, to refuse to obey' [LN (36.43)], 'to reject' [BAGD, LN (36.43)], 'to repudiate' [BAGD], 'To refuse, to decline' [BAGD]. The aorist tense indicates a definite instance when this occurred, not to a continuing action [ICC, Ld, Lns, TNTC]. Ἀρνέομαι means to state that one has no knowledge of or relationship to a person, or to refuse them as a leader [LN (33.277, 34.48, 36.43)].

d. πίστις (LN 31.85, 31.102) (BAGD 2.b.β. p. 663): 'faith' [BAGD, BNTC, EC, LN (31.85), WBC; all versions except NLT], 'trust' [LN (31.85)], 'Christian faith' [LN (31.102)], not explicit [NLT].

QUESTION—How is τὸ ὄνομά μου 'my name' used here?

'Name' refers to the person himself [Ld, TH; NLT, TEV]: you hold fast to me. 'My name' here is used of Christ's cause [BNTC; REB]: you hold fast to my cause. 'To hold fast to Christ's name' is to be his loyal follower [TH]. 'Name' indicates the believers' profession of faith in Christ [Alf]. 'Name' indicates Christ's self-revelation to the believers [Lns].

QUESTION—How are the nouns related in the genitive construction τὴν πίστιν μου 'the faith of me'?

1. The pronoun 'me' is the object of 'faith' [BNTC, EC, ICC, Ld, NIGTC, Sw, TH, WBC; all versions except KJV]: deny your faith in me.
2. 'Faith' refers to the body of Christian truth about Christ [Lns, Wal]: deny what is true about me.

QUESTION—What is the relationship between the two clauses κρατεῖς τὸ ὄνομά μου 'you hold fast to my name', and οὐκ ἠρνήσω τὴν πίτιν μου 'you did not deny my faith'?

The second clause restates the first in a negative manner [TH, WBC] and so emphasizes it [WBC].

even[a] in the days of-Antipas the faithful witness[b] of-me, who was-killed[c] among[d] you, where Satan lives.

TEXT—Some manuscripts include ἐν αἷς 'in which' before Ἀντιπᾶς 'of Antipas'. GNT does not mention this alternative. It is included by KJV.

LEXICON—a. καί (LN 89.93): 'even' [BNTC, EC, LN, WBC; all versions].

   b. μάρτυς (See this word at 1:5): 'witness' [BNTC, EC, WBC; all versions except KJV], 'martyr' [KJV].

   c. aorist pass. indic. of ἀποκτείνω (LN 20.61): 'to be killed' [BNTC, EC, LN; NET, NRSV, TEV, TNT], 'to be martyred' [NAB, NLT], 'to be slain' [KJV], 'to be put to death' [NIV, REB], 'to be taken (from you) and put to death' [CEV], 'to be (publicly) executed' [WBC]. Here a deliberate action is implied rather than that he merely got killed. So 'was executed' or 'was put to death' are more to the point [TH].

   d. παρά with dative case (LN 83.9) (BAGD II.1.b.β. p. 610): 'among' [EC, LN; KJV, NLT, NRSV, TNT], 'from (you)' [CEV], 'with' [LN], not explicit [WBC]. The phrase παρ' ὑμῖν 'among you' is translated 'in your city' [BAGD, BNTC; NAB, NET, NIV, REB], 'there (where Satan lives)' [TEV], 'publicly' [WBC].

QUESTION—How are the nouns related in the genitive construction ὁ μάρτυς μου 'the witness of-me'?

The pronoun 'me' is the object of the 'witness' [NIGTC, Sw, TH]: he witnessed about me.

QUESTION—What is meant by μάρτυς 'witness' here?

1. It is being used in its original meaning of 'witness' [BNTC, Lns, NTC, Sw, TH TNTC, WBC; all versions except KJV]. It originally indicated a witness in a court and only after that did it come to mean someone who witnessed about his faith and was put to death for it [WBC].

2. It includes the meaning 'martyr' [EC, ICC, Ld, Sw, Wal; KJV]. While μάρτυς denotes 'witness' and only later came to mean a 'witness about Christ who was faithful to death', John may be using it with this meaning here [ICC, Ld]. Acts 22:20 is an instance where μάρτυς was used to mean 'martyr' [ICC]. The meaning martyr is intended and clarifies that Antipas had been killed, probably because of his faith [EC].

2:14 But[a] I-have a-few-things[b] against you that you-have there ones-holding-to[c] the teaching[d] of-Balaam,

LEXICON—a. ἀλλά (See this word at 2:4): 'but' [BNTC, EC, WBC; KJV, NET, NRSV, REB, TEV, TNT], 'nevertheless' [NAB, NIV], 'and yet' [NLT], not explicit [CEV].

b. ὀλίγος (LN 59.3) (BAGD 1.b. p. 563): 'a few things' [BAGD, EC; all versions except NAB, NLT, REB], 'a few complaints' [NLT], 'a few matters' [NAB, REB], 'one or two things' [BNTC], 'a minor matter' [WBC], 'few' [BAGD, LN]. The fact that they were few does not indicate that they were not serious [EC, Lns]. Here ὀλίγος indicates a single matter, not several [Alf, ICC, TH, WBC]. The plural is explained by there being two groups of heretics [EC].

c. pres. act. participle of κρατέω (LN 18.6) (BAGD 2.e.β. p. 448): 'to hold to' [NIV, NRSV, REB], 'to hold' [EC, WBC; KJV, TNT], 'to follow' [Alf, TH; CEV, NAB, NET, TEV], 'to hold on to' [LN], 'to hold fast to' [BAGD]. This verb is also translated as a noun: 'adherent' [BNTC]. The phrase κρατοῦντασ τὴν διδαχὴν Βαλαάμ 'ones holding the teaching of Balaam' is translated 'some...who are like Balaam' [NLT]. See this word also at 2:13.

d. διδαχή (LN 33.224, 33.236) (BAGD 2. p. 192): 'teaching' [BAGD, BNTC, EC, LN (33.224, 33.236), WBC; all versions except KJV, NLT], 'doctrine' [LN (33.236); KJV], 'what is taught' [BAGD, LN (33.236)], not explicit [NLT].

QUESTION—What particular event is referred to here about Balaam?

The Scripture referred to is Numbers 22:5–25 and 31:8, 16. Here Balaam, by his advice to Balak, is depicted as causing Israel to be led into idol worship and sexual immorality [NIGTC].

who was-teaching Balak to-put (a) trap[a] before the sons-of-Israel[b]

LEXICON—a. σκάνδαλον (LN 6.25, 88.306) (BAGD 2. p. 753): 'trap', [LN (6.25); TNT], 'stumbling block' [EC, WBC; KJV, NAB, NET, NRSV], 'pitfall' [BNTC], 'that which causes someone to sin' [LN (88.306)], 'temptation to sin, enticement to apostasy' [BAGD], not explicit [CEV]. The phrase βαλεῖν σκάνδαλον 'ἐνώπιον 'to put a trap before' is translated 'to entice to sin' [BAGD; NIV], 'to trip up' [NLT], 'to put temptation in the way of' [REB], 'to lead...into sin' [TEV], 'to throw a stumbling block in the way...by tempting' [NAB], 'to set a pitfall for...He tempted' [BNTC]. A σκάνδαλον was a type of trap involving a stick that acted as a trigger causing the trap to shut when touched by an animal [LN, Lns, TH, TNTC]. It indicates any object in the way that will trip up a person who is walking carelessly [Sw].

b. υἱοὶ Ἰσραήλ (LN 11.58): 'the sons of Israel' [WBC], 'the people of Israel' [LN; CEV, NET, NLT, NRSV, TEV], 'the Israelites' [BNTC; NAB, NIV, REB, TNT], 'the children of Israel' [EC; KJV], 'the nation of Israel' [LN].

QUESTION—If a trap to catch an animal is the image and Balaam's teaching to the believers in Pergamum is the topic, what is the point of similarity?

The point of similarity is entrapment or trouble [TNTC]. The point of similarity is enticement to do something [BAGD, BNTC; NIV, TEV].

QUESTION—If an object that one trips over is the image and Balaam's teaching to the believers in Pergamum is the topic, what is the point of similarity?

The point of similarity is that both cause a person to fall [WBC; KJV, NAB, NET, NLT, NRSV, REB].

to-eat food-sacrificed-to-idols[a] and to-commit-fornication.[b]

LEXICON—a. εἰδωλόθυτος (LN 5.15) (BAGD p. 221): 'food sacrificed to idols' [NAB, NET, NIV, NRSV, REB], 'food offered to idols' [CEV, NLT, TEV, TNT], 'meat offered to an idol' [BAGD], 'meat sacrificed to idols' [BNTC], 'things sacrificed to idols' [EC; KJV], 'sacrificial meat' [LN, WBC], 'meat of animals sacrificed to an idol' [LN]. Part of this sacrificial meat was burned on the altar, part was eaten at a formal meal in the temple, and part was sold in the market [BAGD].

b. aorist act. infin. of πορνεύω (LN 88.271) (BAGD 1. p. 693): 'to commit fornication' [BNTC, EC, LN, WBC; KJV, REB], 'to practice fornication' [NAB, NRSV], 'to practice sexual immorality' [BAGD; TEV], 'to commit sexual immorality' [NET, NIV], 'to commit sexual sin' [NLT], 'to practice sexual vice' [TNT], 'to be immoral' [CEV], 'to practice prostitution, to prostitute' [BAGD], 'to engage in illicit sex' [LN]. This involved illicit sex with temple prostitutes [Lns].

QUESTION—What relationship is indicated by the infinitive φαγεῖν 'to eat'?

1. It indicates result [TH]: to put a trap before the sons of Israel *with the result that* they ate.
2. It indicates an explanatory relationship [EC, Lns]: to put a trap before the sons of Israel, *that is*, they ate.
3. It indicates why he enticed them to eat [Alf]: to put a trap before the sons of Israel *in order to* get them to eat.

QUESTION—To what does φαγεῖν ιδωλόθτα 'to eat food sacrificed to idols' refer?

1. It refers literally to meat that had been offered to an idol and was sold in the market place [NTC, TH]. While this is definitely indicated it may include a token participation in idol worship as well [NTC].
2. It refers to taking part in a feast in honor of an idol [EC, Ld, Lns, NIC, NIGTC, Sw, TNTC, WBC]. Paul had argued in 1 Corinthians 7:1–13 that

food in itself is neither clean nor unclean if a man could eat it in good conscience. At the same time he argues in 1 Corinthians 10:21 that it is impossible to drink of the cup of the Lord and the cup of demons. Here then eating such food must refer to actual participation in the temple feasts in honor of an idol [Ld].
   3. It refers to both 1 and 2 [ICC, Wal]. It includes both participation in the ritual banquets and buying sacrificial meat and eating it at home [ICC].
QUESTION—To what does πορνεῦσαι 'to commit fornication' refer?
   1. It refers literally to unlawful sexual relations between men and women [EC, Ld, Lns, NIC, NTC, Sw, TH, TNTC, Wal, WBC]. This was part of the pagan festivities [NIC]. Idol worship usually included both the eating of sacrificial food and immoral activities [TNTC].
   2. It refers figuratively to spiritual infidelity to God [BNTC, NIGTC]. Since John uses this verb figuratively in all but one case, it is best to conclude that he is using it so here [BNTC]. It has a broader sense here because this is how it is commonly used in Revelation and because sexual immorality was not the only form of compromise that the believers there were guilty of [NIGTC].

2:15 In-the-same-way[a] also you-have ones-holding the teaching of-the Nicolaitans likewise.[b]
TEXT—Instead of ὁμοίως 'likewise' some manuscripts read ὃ μισῶ 'which I hate'. GNT does not mention this alternative. It is followed by KJV.
LEXICON—a. οὕτως (LN 61.9): 'in the same way' [BNTC; NET, NLT, REB, TEV], 'so' [LN; KJV, NRSV, TNT], 'likewise' [NIV], 'thus' [EC, LN, WBC], 'yes' [NAB], 'now' [CEV].
   b. ὁμοίως (LN 64.1): 'likewise' [LN], 'as well' [WBC], 'similarly' [LN, Lns], 'also' [EC], not explicit [BNTC; all versions except TNT]. This word is also translated as an adjective: 'similar (teaching)' [TNT]. See this word also at 1:13.
QUESTION—What is the function of οὕτως 'in the same way'?
   It connects with the preceding verse by way of explanation or interpretation [WBC]: ones holding the teaching of Balaam...*that is*, you also have.... It points to a comparison with 2:14 [Sw, TNTC]. The phrase 'likewise you also' indicates that the situation of the believers in Pergamum was like that of the ancient Israelis of 2:14 [NIC, TH].
QUESTION—What is the function of the phrase καὶ σὺ 'you also'?
   It indicates 'you also' (in addition to the Ephesians as mentioned in 2:6) [ICC, WBC]. The phrase is emphatic and indicates 'you also, (in addition to others things)' [TNTC]. The phrase emphasizes the comparison between the ancient Israelis and the believers at Pergamum [Alf, NIC, TH].
QUESTION—Does this verse indicate a different group than the one mentioned in 2:14 or are they the same?
   1. It indicates that the two groups of people mentioned were really the same [BNTC, ICC, Ld, Lns, NIC]. The verse suggests that 2:15 further defines

the teaching of Balaam [Ld]. The teaching of Balaam in the OT was the teaching of the Nicolaitans in the NT [BNTC].
2. It indicates that there were two groups: the ones who held to the teaching of Balaam and the Nicolaitans who taught the same thing [EC, NIGTC].

QUESTION—What did the Nicolaitans teach?
They taught laxity towards pagan practices [BNTC, Sw].

QUESTION—What is the function of ὁμοίως 'likewise'?
1. It functions to emphasize οὕτως 'in the same way' [Sw; probably all versions except KJV, TNT].
2. It functions to continue the comparison of the believers at Pergamum with those at Ephesus [ICC, WBC].
3. Both οὕτως 'in the same way' and ὁμοίως 'likewise' indicated that those in Pergamum who follow the teaching of Nicolaitans are those referred to in 2:14 [Lns].

2:16 Therefore repent;[a] but if not, I-will-come to-you soon[b]

LEXICON—a. aorist act. impera. of μετανοέω (See this word at 2:5): to 'repent' [BNTC, EC, LN, WBC; all versions except CEV, TEV], 'to turn from one's sins' [TEV], 'to turn back' [CEV].
  b. ταχύ (LN 67.56, 67.110) (BAGD 2.b. p. 807): 'soon' [BNTC, EC, LN (67.56); NAB, NIV, NRSV, TEV, TNT], 'quickly' [BAGD, LN (67.110), WBC; CEV, KJV, NET, REB], 'suddenly' [NLT], 'very soon' [LN (67.56)], 'hurriedly' [LN (67.110)], 'without delay, at once' [BAGD].

QUESTION—To whom was this command given?
It was given to all the believers in Pergamum to discipline the followers of the teaching of the Nicolaitans [Alf, BNTC, EC, ICC, Ld, Lns, NIC, NIGTC]. The church was guilty of unjustified tolerance [EC]. The believers should expel the Nicolaitans from their fellowship [ICC].

QUESTION—To what does ἔρχομαι 'I come' refer?
The present tense of 'come' here is a vivid present tense in which John sees Christ actually coming [TNTC].
1. It refers to a coming of Christ in judgment to those in Pergamum and not to his final coming [BNTC, Ld, Lns, NIC, TH, WBC].
2. It refers to Christ's Second Coming [EC]. This coming is imminent and is the same coming as in 2:5 [EC].

and I-will-fight[a] against[b] them with[c] the sword of my mouth.

LEXICON—a. fut. act. indic. of πολεμέω (LN 39.26, 55.5) (BAGD 1.a. p. 685): 'to fight' [LN (39.26), WBC; CEV, KJV, NAB, NIV, NLT, TEV, TNT], 'to make war' [BNTC, EC; NET, NRSV, REB], 'to war' [BAGD], 'to wage war' [LN (55.5)], 'to war against' [LN (39.26)].
  b. μετά with genitive object (LN **90.32**) (BAGD A.II.3.a. p. 509): 'against' [BAGD, EC, **LN**; all versions except REB, TNT], 'with' [BAGD, WBC], 'on' [BNTC; REB], not explicit [TNT].
  c. ἐν with dative object (LN 90.10): 'with' [BNTC, EC, LN, WBC; all versions except CEV], 'by' [LN], not explicit [CEV].

QUESTION—To whom does 'them' refer?
It refers to those who follow the teaching of the Nicolaitans [Sw, TH] and of Balaam [NET]. It refers to those who are enemies [Lns]. It refers to the corrupt teachers [ICC]. It refers to the Nicolaitans [Alf]. It refers to the whole church since being tolerant of the Nicolaitans makes the church as guilty as those who follow the false teaching. The change from singular 'you' to plural 'them' is a Hebraism and the two pronouns refer to the same group [EC].

QUESTION—How are the nouns related in the genitive construction τῇ ῥομφαίᾳ τοῦ στόματός μου 'the sword of my mouth'?
'My mouth' explains 'the sword' [WBC]: with the sword, that is, my mouth. The sword is a figure of the tongue [WBC], and refers to the word that Christ will speak [TNTC, WBC]. 'The sword' is the word of Christ and comes *out of* his mouth (see 1:16) [Sw, TH]. Christ will strike those who hold the teaching of the Nicolaitans with the destructive power of his Word [Lns]. His words will cut like a sword [CEV]. The figure is kept in most translations: 'the sword that comes out of my mouth' [TEV].

2:17 The-one having an-ear let-him-hear what the spirit says to-the churches. To-the-one-who conquers I-will-give of-the hidden[a] manna[b]

LEXICON—a. perf. pass. participle of κρύπτω (LN 24.29, 28.79) (BAGD 1.a. p. 454): 'to be hidden' [BAGD, BNTC, EC, LN (24.29, 28.79), WBC; all versions except NLT], 'to be hidden away in heaven' [NLT], 'to be concealed' [LN (28.79)], 'to be kept secret' [LN (28.79)], 'to be made invisible, to be made hidden and safe' [LN (24.30)]. This refers to hidden manna that is concealed from human eyes being laid up in heaven [BAGD].

b. μάννα (LN 5.22) (BAGD 2. p. 491): 'manna' [BAGD, BNTC, EC, LN, WBC; all versions except CEV], 'food' [CEV]. Μάννα here contrasts with the food offered to idols referred to in 2:14 [Alf, ICC].

QUESTION—What is the function of the genitive in the phrase δώσω αὐτῷ τοῦ μάννα 'I will give *of-the manna* to him'?
It is a partitive genitive and indicates 'some of' or 'a share of' [BNTC, ICC, Lns, Sw, WBC; all versions except KJV, NAB, NLT]: I will give him *some of the* manna.

QUESTION—To what does τοῦ μάννα τοῦ κεκρυμμένου 'the hidden manna' refer?
It may refer to the manna in the golden jar inside the Ark of the Covenant. It was believed that Jeremiah hid the Ark in a cave on Mt. Nebo at the destruction of Solomon's temple in 586 B.C. The Jews believed that it would remain there until the Messianic age when God would again feed his people with it (see 2 Maccabees 2:4–8) [Ld, NIC, Sw, TH]. It refers to eternal life [NTC]. The figure means that the conquering believer will receive eternal life and enjoy fellowship with God [WBC]. Hidden manna refers to fellowship with Christ and the spiritual strength it gives [NIGTC, Wal].

Hidden manna probably refers to heavenly food that a believer would receive [ICC, NIC, TNTC]. It refers to spiritual gifts that believers will receive in their intimate relationship with Christ [ICC]. It signifies the life-sustaining power of the believer as his/her life is hid with Christ in God (Colossians 3:3) [Sw]. It signifies admission to the marriage supper of the Lamb (19:9) [Ld]. It comprises more than adequate compensation for the sacrifice of abstaining from food offered to idols [NTC]. The fact that it is hidden means that it is something that will be revealed to believers at the end of time [NIGTC].

and I-will-give him a-white[a] stone,[b] and on the stone (a) new[c] name written

LEXICON—a. λευκός (LN 79.27) (BAGD 2. p. 472): 'white' [BAGD, BNTC, EC, LN, WBC; all versions], 'light color' [LN]. White symbolized victory [Alf, BNTC, TH]. White symbolized holiness [Lns].

b. ψῆφος (LN **2.27**) (BAGD 2. p. 892): 'stone' [BNTC, EC, **LN**, WBC; all versions except TNT], 'pebble' [BAGD, LN; TNT], 'small stone' [LN].

c. καινός (LN 28.33) (BAGD 2. p. 394): 'new' [BNTC, EC, LN, WBC; all versions], 'unknown' [BAGD], 'previously unknown, previously unheard of' [LN], 'strange, remarkable' [BAGD]. Καινός means new in quality [EC, NIC], one that is fitting to eternity [NIC], not new in the sense of recent [EC]. Καινός carries the sense of 'marvelous' or 'unheard of' [BAGD].

QUESTION—What does ψῆφον λευκήν 'white stone' symbolize?

Pebbles were used as an admission to public events. Here the white stone was a pass admitting the victor to the heavenly feast [BAGD, BNTC, EC, Ld, NIC, NTC, TH], of hidden manna [EC, NIC]. It symbolizes a kind of charm or amulet to which mysterious powers were attached [ICC, Sw, WBC]. The magic of God and Christ was given in place of the magic of pagan powers [Sw]. Since a white stone symbolized a vote of acquittal in a law court (black was a guilty vote), the white stone here symbolized Jesus' vote of approval of the believer in the face of his/her condemnation in the Roman law court and so constituted an invitation to Jesus' supper (see 19:9) [NIGTC]. It signified that the person receiving the stone had been favored by Christ, though rejected by the pagan world [Wal]. It is a reward for endurance and represents permanent protection for the possessor [WBC].

QUESTION—Whose name would be written and what did the name signify?

1. It was a name of God or Christ [BNTC, ICC, NTC, Sw, WBC]. Only a person who shared Christ's sufferings could learn this secret name (see 3:12 and 14.3) [BNTC]. Knowing this name would give the believer supernatural power [ICC, NTC]. It signified the favor of God and gave him/her an intimate knowledge of God and Christ that only he/she could understand [Sw].

2. It was a name of the person receiving the stone [Alf, EC, Lns, NIC, TH, TNTC]. This name would reveal the person's eternal character [Alf,

TNTC]. The name would give the highest honor to the recipient [Lns]. It indicates his status as belonging to Christ [EC].
3. Either of the above could be true [Ld, Wal]. It signified entrance into the heavenly banquet [Ld]. It symbolized the believer's eternal salvation and his share in the riches of Heaven [Wal].

which no-one knows[a] except the-one receiving[b] (it).'
LEXICON—a. perf. act. ind. of οἶδα (LN 28.1, 32.4): 'to know' [BNTC, EC, LN (28.1), WBC; all versions except NET], 'to understand' [LN (32.4); NET], 'to know about, to have knowledge of' [LN (28.1)], 'to comprehend' [LN (32.4)].
b. pres. act. participle of λαμβάνω (LN 57.125): 'to receive' [BNTC, EC, LN; all versions except CEV]. It is also translated as a noun: 'recipient' [WBC]. This word is also translated by its reciprocal: 'to be given (the stone)' [CEV]. The sense is that the knowledge pertains to the new name, but the reception of 'it' includes receiving both the stone and the name upon it [EC].

QUESTION—What was the significance of the name being secret?
The new name would give the believer power that only he would possess. If the name were known by others, it would diminish that power [ICC]. People who made amulets knew that it was essential that a name be kept secret to retain its power [NTC]. The secret name was known only to God and the believer and was therefore precious to the believer [TNTC].

DISCOURSE UNIT: 2:18–29 [Alf, BNTC, EC, GNT, ICC, Ld, Lns, NIC, NIGTC, NTC, Sw, TH, TNTC, Wal, WBC; all versions except REB, TNT]. The topic is the letter to Thyatira.

2:18 And write to-the angel of-the church in Thyatira:[a] 'These-things says the Son of God, the-one having eyes as a-flame of-fire and his feet like bronze:
LEXICON—a. Θυάτειρα (LN 93.476) (BAGD p. 364): 'Thyatira' [BAGD, BNTC, LN, WBC; all versions]. Θυάτειρα is modern day Ahisar [WBC]. It was a center of manufacturing and trade and was the home of many trade guilds [NIC]. It was almost imperative for a person in a trade to be a member of the appropriate trade guild. The trade guilds probably were dedicated to some pagan deity and so it was difficult for Christian believers who were part of the guild [Ld]. It was famous for the manufacture of purple dye [Wal]. It was the home of Lydia, the woman who sold purple (see Acts 14:16) [NTC]. The Greek god Apollo Tyrimnos was worshiped there. His worship was merged with the worship of the Roman emperor as both were considered sons of Zeus [NIC]. There were temples there dedicated to Apollo Tyrimnaios and Artemis [ICC]. It was located about 35 miles inland between Pergamum and Sardis [WBC].

QUESTION—What is the significance of Jesus' eyes being like a flame of fire?
They signify: anger [Ld, Sw, Wal]; the ability to penetrate into the falsehood of Jezebel [Lns, NIC]; the ability to see far and into dark places [TH]; the ability to see all [TNTC]; the ability to probe the inner man [EC]; judgment [Wal]. See 1:14 for a more complete answer.

QUESTION—What is the significance of Jesus' feet being like bronze?
They signify: that he will trample down his enemies [Ld, Lns, Sw, TH, TNTC]; strength and majesty [NIC]. See 1:15 for a more complete answer.

2:19 I-know your works[a] and/even love[b] and faith/faithfulness[c] and service[d] and endurance[e] of-you,

LEXICON—a. ἔργον (See this word at 2:2): 'work' [EC, WBC; KJV, NRSV], 'deed' [NAB, NET, NIV], not explicit [CEV]. This noun is also translated: 'what you do' [BNTC; NLT, REB, TEV], 'all about you' [CEV, TNT].

b. ἀγάπη (See this word at 2:4): 'love' [BNTC, EC, WBC; all versions except KJV], 'charity' [KJV]. 'Love' here is probably for fellow believers [TH]. It is for God and man [Alf, EC].

c. πίστις (See this word at 2:13): 'faith' [EC, WBC; all versions except REB, TEV, TNT], 'faithfulness' [WBC; REB, TEV], 'fidelity' [TNT], 'loyalty' [BNTC].

d. διακονία (LN **35.19**, 35.21) (BAGD 1. p. 184): 'service' [BAGD, BNTC, EC, LN (35.19), WBC; all versions], 'ministry' [LN (35.21)]. This service is directed to fellow believers [Lns, TH], or to all who are in need [Alf].

e. ὑπομονή (See this word at 1:9): 'endurance' [EC, WBC; REB], 'patient endurance' [NAB, NLT, NRSV], 'steadfast endurance' [NET], 'patience' [KJV, TEV], 'perseverance' [NIV], 'steadfastness' [TNT], 'fortitude' [BNTC]. This noun is also translated as a verb: 'to endure' [CEV]. Ὑπομονή is used in reference to the adversity they faced [Ld, Lns].

QUESTION—What is the relationship of 'your works' with '*and* the love and the faith and the service and the endurance of you'?

1. The καί 'and' which follows 'works' is explanatory [Alf, EC, ICC, Ld, NIC, TNTC, WBC; NET, NLT, NRSV; probably TEV, TNT]: 'your works, *namely* your love and faith and service and endurance' or 'your works, *including* your love and faith and service and endurance' [CEV]. The single σου 'of you' preceding τὰ ἔργα 'the works', coupled with a single σου 'of you' following the four nouns indicates that the four qualities further delineate 'works' [NIC, TNTC].

2. The καί 'and' which follows 'works' is translated consecutively [Lns; KJV, NAB, NIV, REB]: 'your works and your love and faith and service and endurance'.

QUESTION—What is meant by πίστις 'faith/faithfulness'?

1. It refers to their personal faith [EC, Ld, Lns, NIC; all versions except REB, TEV, TNT]. Faith is a firm persuasion which has as its object God, Christ, or spiritual things [EC]. The motive forces of their deeds are love

and faith [NIC]. Their faith has led them to endurance when confronted by their pagan environment [Ld].
2. It refers to their faithfulness or loyalty [BNTC, TH, WBC; REB, TEV].

and (I know that) your last works (are) more-than^a the first.

LEXICON—a. πλείων (LN 78.28) (BAGD II.1.a. p. 689): 'more than' [LN; CEV, KJV, NIV, TEV], 'greater than' [BAGD, EC; NAB, NET, NRSV], 'better than' [BNTC, WBC; REB, TNT], 'more' [LN], 'to a greater degree, even more' [LN]. This adjective is also translated: 'constant improvement (in all these things)' [NLT].

QUESTION—Does πλείων 'more than' refer to quantity or quality?
1. It refers to quantity [Lns, Sw, TH, TNTC]: more works than the first.
2. It refers to quality [BNTC, ICC, WBC; REB, TNT]: better works than the first.
3. It may refer to both one and two [Alf, EC]: more works and more important works than the first.

QUESTION—To what does τῶν πρώτων 'the first' refer?
It refers to when they first became Christians [TH].

2:20 But^a I-have against you that you tolerate^b the woman Jezebel, the-one calling herself (a) prophetess,^c

TEXT: Some manuscripts include σου 'your' following γυναῖκα 'woman'. GNT omits this word with a B rating, indicating that the text is almost certain. The evidence for including σου 'your' is convincing [Alf].

LEXICON—a. ἀλλά (See this word at 2:4): 'but' [BNTC, EC, WBC; CEV, NET, NLT, NRSV, REB, TEV, TNT], 'nevertheless' [KJV, NAB, NIV].
  b. pres. act. indic. of ἀφίημι (LN **13.140**) (BAGD 4. p. 126): 'to tolerate' [BAGD, BNTC, EC, WBC; all versions except CEV, KJV, NLT], 'to let' [**LN**; CEV], 'to permit' [NLT], 'to allow' [LN], 'to suffer' [KJV]. Ἀφίημι 'to tolerate' indicates that the believers recognized the evil of this woman's teaching, but they permitted it to continue [Ld].
  c. προφῆτις (LN 53.80) (BAGD p. 724): 'prophetess' [BAGD, BNTC, EC, LN, WBC; KJV, NAB, NET, NIV, REB, TNT], 'prophet' [CEV, NLT, NRSV], 'messenger of God' [TEV]. A προφῆτις was a woman who proclaimed inspired messages from God [LN]. This woman said that she had special revelations from God and this qualified her to be a teacher in the church [EC].

QUESTION—Who was Jezebel and was this the real name of the woman at Thyatira?
Jezebel was the name of the daughter of Ethbaal, King of Sidon, and wife of King Ahab. She tried to unite the worship of the god Baal with the worship of God (1 Kings 16.29–31; 18.4, 19; 2 Kings 9.22) [TH, Wal]. She was a member of the church in Thyatira [EC, Ld, Lns, NIC, Sw] and she claimed to be a prophetess [EC]. What Jezebel was to King Ahab (1 Kings 21:25), this woman was to the believers at Thyatira [Alf, EC]. The name Jezebel is being used symbolically of someone who was like the Jezebel of Jewish

history [Alf, BNTC, EC, ICC, Ld, Lns, NTC, TH, TNTC, Wal; NAB, NLT, REB].

and she-teaches and misleads[a] my servants to-commit-fornication[b] and to-eat food-sacrificed-to-idols.[c]

LEXICON—a. pres. act. indic. of πλανάω (LN 31.8) (BAGD 1.b. p. 665): 'to mislead' [BAGD, BNTC, LN, WBC; CEV, NIV, TEV], 'to lead astray' [NLT, TNT], 'to deceive' [BAGD, EC, LN; NET], 'to seduce' [KJV, NAB], 'to beguile' [NRSV], 'to lure' [REB], 'to cause to be mistaken' [LN]. This states the consequences of her teaching [EC].
- b. aorist act. infin. of πορνεύω (See this word at 2:14): 'to commit fornication' [EC; KJV], 'to fornicate' [WBC], 'to practice fornication' [NRSV], 'to practice sexual immorality' [TEV], 'to commit sexual immorality' [NET], 'to do immoral things' [CEV], 'to commit sexual sin' [NLT], 'to practice sexual vice' [TNT], 'to practice lewdness' [NAB]. This verb is also translated as a noun: 'sexual immorality' [NIV], 'fornication' [BNTC; REB].
- c. εἰδωλόθυτος (See this word at 2:14): 'food sacrificed to idols' [NAB, NET, NIV, NRSV, REB], 'food offered to idols' [CEV, NLT, TEV, TNT], 'things sacrificed to idols' [EC; KJV], 'meat sacrificed to idols' [BNTC, WBC].

QUESTION—How did the situation at Thyatira lend itself to the acceptance of Jezebel's teaching?

There were many trade guilds at Thyatira each of which was dedicated to the worship of a deity. Membership in a guild required participation in the guild feasts and these were often accompanied by immoral behavior. Any Christian who was a member of a trade guild therefore would be under great pressure to participate. To fail to do so could mean social and economic isolation [NIGTC]. It was difficult to earn a living without being a member of a trade guild [TNTC]. The reason the believers tolerated this teaching was that it excused their membership and participation in the activity of the trade guilds. It amounted to tolerance of fornication [ICC].

QUESTION—Should 'commit fornication' here be understood literally or figuratively?
1. It should be understood literally [BAGD, EC, ICC, Ld, Lns, NIC, NIGTC, TH, TNTC, Wal; probably all versions]. Probably the argument was that men and women believers know that the flesh cannot defile the spirit and they need not separate themselves from pagan immorality and sacrificial practices [EC].
2. It should be understood figuratively as referring to apostasy from God [WBC].

2:21 And I-gave her time[a] that[b] she-might-repent,[c]

LEXICON—a. χρόνος (LN 67.78) (BAGD p. 888): 'time' [BAGD, BNTC, EC, LN, WBC; all versions except CEV, KJV, NAB], 'a chance' [CEV, NAB], 'space' [KJV], 'period of time' [LN]. Χρόνος indicates that some

time had elapsed since Jezebel had been warned about this [EC, ICC, Ld, Lns, NIGTC, Sw, TH, TNTC].
  b. ἵνα (LN 90.22) (BAGD II.1.d. p. 377): 'that' [EC, LN], 'for' [BNTC]. Ἵνα is used as a substitute for an infinitive [BAGD, Lns, WBC; all versions]: to repent. See this word also at 2:10.
  c. aorist act. subj. of μετανοέω (See this word at 2:5): 'to repent' [BAGD, EC, LN, WBC; all versions except CEV, TEV], 'to repent of her sins' [TEV], 'to turn from sin' [CEV]. This is verb is also translated as a noun: 'repentance' [BNTC].

but/and[a] not she-is-willing[b] to-repent of her fornication.[c]
LEXICON—a. καί (See this word at 2:13): 'but' [BNTC, WBC; all versions except KJV], 'and' [EC; KJV].
  b. pres. act. indic. of θέλω (LN 25.1): 'to be willing' [NET, NIV, NLT], 'to want' [LN, WBC; CEV, TEV], 'to wish' [LN], 'to desire' [EC, LN], not explicit [KJV]. The phrase οὐ θέλει 'she is not willing' is translated 'she refuses' [BNTC; NAB, NRSV, TNT].
  c. πορνεία (LN 88.271) (BAGD 2. p. 693): 'fornication' [BNTC, EC, LN; KJV, NRSV], 'immorality' [BAGD, WBC; NIV, NLT, TEV], 'sexual immorality' [LN; NET], 'vice' [TNT], 'lewdness' [NAB], 'prostitution' [LN]. This noun is also translated as a verb: 'to do immoral things' [CEV].

QUESTION—Should πορνεία 'fornication' be taken literally or figuratively?
  1. It should be taken figuratively [BAGD, NIC, WBC]. It is figurative for apostasy [BAGD], or religious infidelity [NIC]. Most of the occurrences of words beginning with *porn-* in Revelation are figurative. If they are meant literally they are usually included in a list of other vices [WBC]. Jezebel's sin was compromise with the pagan environment of Thyatira [NIC].
  2. It should be taken literally [Alf, EC, Lns]. It should be taken inclusively to include her teaching and other deeds [Lns]. The literal sense of this noun in 2:20 is reason to take that sense here [EC].

2:22 Behold,[a] I-am-throwing[b] her on (a) bed[c]
TEXT: Instead of κλίνην 'bed', one early manuscript reads φυλακήν 'prison'. GNT reads κλίνην 'bed' with an A rating, indicating that the text is certain.
LEXICON—a. ἰδού (See this word at 1:7): 'behold' [EC, WBC; KJV], 'lo' [Lns], 'look out' [NET], 'beware' [NRSV], 'so' [BNTC; NIV, REB, TEV], 'therefore' [NLT], not explicit [CEV, NAB, TNT]. Ἰδού functions to attract attention and indicates that her refusal to repent is something unexpected and terrible [Alf, EC].
  b. pres. act. indic. of βάλλω (See this word at 2:10): 'to throw' [Lns, WBC; NET, NLT, NRSV, REB, TEV], 'to cast' [EC; KJV, NIV], 'to cast down' [NAB], 'to consign someone to' [TNT], 'to make someone take to (one's bed)' [BNTC], not explicit [CEV]. The present tense here should be taken

as a future [ICC, NIC, Sw, TH, Wal]: I will throw. It indicates an emphatic future [NIC, Wal]. It indicates that the action is imminent [NIC, Sw]: I am about to throw. It indicates that the action is certain [NIC].
- c. κλινή (LN 6.106, **23.152**) (BAGD p. 436): 'bed' [BNTC, EC, LN, Lns; KJV, NRSV], 'bed of sickness' [TNT], 'bed of violent illness' [NET], 'bed of suffering' [NIV], 'bed of pain' [NAB, REB], 'bed where (she)…will suffer terribly' [TEV], 'sickbed' [BAGD, WBC; NLT], 'couch, cot, stretcher, bier' [LN (6.106)], not explicit [CEV]. The phrase βάλλω αὐτὴν εἰς κλίνην 'I am throwing her on a bed' is translated 'I will make her sick' [**LN** (23.152)], 'I am going to strike down Jezebel' [CEV], 'strike her with an illness' [BAGD].

QUESTION—What is implied by κλινή 'bed'?

It implies a 'sickbed' or 'bed of suffering' [Alf, BAGD, ICC, NIC, NIGTC, Sw, TH, TNTC, WBC; NAB, NET, NLT, REB, TEV, TNT]. 'To throw into bed' was a Hebrew idiom indicating 'to cause someone to be sick' [ICC, WBC].

and the-ones committing-adultery[a] with her into[b] great suffering,[c]

LEXICON—a. pres. act. participle of μοιχεύω (LN 88.276) (BAGD 2.c. p. 526): 'to commit adultery' [BAGD, EC, LN, Lns; all versions except CEV, NAB, REB], 'to commit fornication' [WBC], 'to do immoral things' [CEV]. The phrase τοὺς μοιχεύοντας μετ' αὐτῆς 'the ones committing adultery with her' is translated 'her lovers' [BNTC; REB], 'her companions in sin' [NAB]. Μοιχεύω means for a man to have sexual intercourse with another man's wife [LN]. It is a general term that includes both 'fornication' and 'eating food offered to idols' [Alf].
- b. εἰς with accusative object (LN 84.22) (BAGD 4.a. p.229): 'into' [EC, LN; KJV, NAB, NET, NRSV, REB], 'to' [TNT], 'for' [Lns], not explicit [BNTC, WBC; CEV, NIV, NLT, TEV].
- c. θλῖψις (See this word at 1:9): 'suffering' [NAB, NET, REB], 'distress' [NRSV], 'affliction' [TNT], 'tribulation' [BAGD, EC, Lns, WBC; KJV], 'pain' [BNTC]. This noun is also translated as a verb: 'to suffer' [LN (23.152); NIV, NLT, TEV]. The phrase εἰς θλῖψιν μεγάλην 'into great suffering' is translated '(they)…will also be punished' [CEV].

QUESTION—Should 'commit adultery' be taken literally or figuratively?
1. It is literal [EC, TH]. Verse 2:20 is to be taken as literal fornication and therefore this should be taken literally also. 'With her' means that they participated by tolerating her adultery or even followed her example [EC]. It may be figurative but should be translated literally [TH].
2. It is figurative of spiritual infidelity [BNTC, Sw, WBC]. It should be taken both literally and figuratively [Lns]. It is close to a figurative meaning [BAGD].

QUESTION—What words are implied before εἰς θλῖψιν μεγάην 'into great suffering'?

The implied words are: *I will throw* into great suffering [Ld, Lns, NIGTC, TH, Wal, WBC; NAB, NRSV]; *I will cause* great suffering [WBC; NIV]; *I will bring* great suffering [BNTC]; *I am consigning* to great suffering [TNT]. This is a form of Hebrew parallelism in which the second part matches the first [Ld, WBC]: (1) I will throw her on a bed and (2) those committing adultery with her *I will throw* into great suffering.

QUESTION—Are the punishments the same or different?

Both Jezebel and those who committed adultery with her receive the same punishment [Ld, Lns, NTC]. The Hebrew parallelism indicates that the punishments are the same [Ld]. The 'great suffering' of her followers is a similar punishment to her bed of suffering [NIGTC]. It is possible that the punishment was the same [TH].

unless they-repent of her works,

TEXT: Instead of αὐτῆς 'her', some manuscripts read αὐτῶν 'their'. GNT reads αὐτῆς 'her' with an A rating, indicating that the text is certain. The reading 'their' is taken by KJV, NAB, NLT, and TEV translate: 'their sins with her'. They must repent of the works have sprung from Jezebel's influence. Even though committed by others, they are still her works since she led them astray [EC].

2:23 and I-will-kill[a] her children[b] with death.[c]

LEXICON—a. fut. act. indic. of ἀποκτείνω (See this word at 2:13): 'to kill' [EC, LN, Lns, WBC; CEV, KJV, REB, TEV], 'to strike' [NET, NIV, NLT, NRSV], 'to strike dead' [BNTC]. The phrase ἀποκτενῶ ἐν θανάτῳ 'to kill with death' is translated 'to utterly destroy' [TNT], 'to put to death' [NAB]. The phrase 'to kill with death' is very strong and implies swift and merciless action [TH].

b. τέκνον (LN 10.36, 36.40) (BAGD 2.b. p. 808): 'child' [BAGD, BNTC, LN (10.36), Lns, WBC; all versions except CEV, NET, TEV], 'disciple' [LN (36.40)], 'follower' [CEV, NET, TEV], 'offspring' [LN (10.36)]. Τέκνον is used figuratively here of adherents of Jezebel's teaching [Alf, BAGD, BNTC, ICC, Ld, Lns, NIC, NIGTC, Sw, TH, TNTC, WBC; CEV, NET, TEV].

c. θάνατος (BAGD 1.e. p. 351): 'death' [Lns; KJV, NAB], 'fatal illness' [BAGD; NET], 'pestilence' [BAGD, EC, ICC, NTC, Sw, TNTC; REB], 'plague' [BNTC, WBC], not explicit [CEV, TEV, TNT]. This noun is also translated as an adjective: '(to strike) dead' [NIV, NLT, NRSV]. Θάνατος is frequently used to indicate 'pestilence' in the Septuagint [TNTC]. In 6.8 the 2nd use of 'death' is used with this sense [ICC, NTC, Sw]. See this word also at 1:18.

QUESTION—Are the τέκνα 'children' of this verse, the same or different from τοὺς μοιχεύοντας μετ' αὐτῆς 'the ones committing adultery with her' of 2:22?
1. They are a different group [Alf, ICC, Ld, Lns, Sw, TH, TNTC]. The object, τὰ τέκνα αὐτῆς 'her children', is emphatically fore fronted in the verse and so distinguished from those just mentioned in 2:23 [Alf]. The 'children' were followers of Jezebel's teaching while 'those committing adultery with her' were her colleagues [TH]. The 'adulterers' of 2:22 are those who were trying to combine loyalty to Christ with participation in the obligations of the trade guilds, while the 'children' were those who had committed themselves completely to the teachings of Jezebel [ICC, Ld]. The 'children' are perhaps more intimate than those referred to in 2:22 [TNTC]. The children are a future generation of followers who remained after the first generation has been punished [Lns].
2. They are the same group [BNTC, EC, NIC, NIGTC]. Both are those who unreservedly followed Jezebel's teachings [BNTC, NIC].

And all the churches will-know that I am the-one searching[a] (the) minds[b] and hearts,[c]
LEXICON—a. pres. act. participle of ἐραυνάω (LN 27.34) (BAGD p. 306): 'to search' [BAGD, BNTC, EC, LN, Lns, WBC; all versions except CEV, NLT, TEV], 'to search out' [NLT], 'to examine' [BAGD], 'to know' [CEV, TEV], 'to try to learn, to try to find out, to seek information' [LN]. Ἐραυνάω implies that nothing can be hidden from him [TNTC].
b. νεφρός (LN **26.11**) (BAGD p. 537): 'mind' [BAGD, BNTC, WBC; NAB, NET, NIV, NRSV, REB, TNT], 'thought' [CEV, NLT, TEV], 'feelings and desires' [**LN**], 'heart, kidney' [LN], 'reins' [EC, Lns; KJV]. Νεφρός 'kidney' connotes: the center of the emotions [EC, ICC, TNTC]; affections [ICC]; the will and affections [EC, NIC, Sw]; the most secret thoughts [TH]; the innermost being [Lns, Wal].
c. καρδία (LN 26.3) (BAGD 1.b.α. p. 403): 'heart' [BAGD, BNTC, EC, LN, Lns, WBC; all versions except CEV, NLT, TEV], 'feeling' [CEV], 'intention' [NLT], 'wish' [TEV], 'mind, inner self' [LN]. Καρδία 'heart' connotes: the center of one's thoughts [ICC, Lns, NIC, Sw, TNTC]; the center of the will [Lns]; the most secret desires [TH]; the center of the complete inner life, the thinking, feeling and will [BAGD].

and I-will-give to-you each according-to[a] your works.
LEXICON—a. κατά with accusative object (LN 89.8) (BAGD II.5.a.β. p. 407): 'according to' [BAGD, EC, Lns; KJV, NIV, TEV, TNT], 'in accordance with' [BAGD, LN, WBC], 'corresponding to, in conformity with' [BAGD], 'in relation to' [LN]. The phrase κατὰ τὰ ἔργα ὑμῶν 'according to your works', is translated 'as you deserve' [CEV], 'what your deeds deserve' [BNTC; NAB, NET, NLT, NRSV, REB].

QUESTION—Does 'give' imply reward or punishment?
It implies punishment [NIGTC, TH]. It includes the possibility of both reward and punishment [EC, Lns].

2:24 But I-say to-you the rest^a to-the-ones in Thyatira, as-many-as have^b not this teaching,

LEXICON—a. λοιπός (LN 63.21) (BAGD 2.b.α. p. 480): 'rest' [BAGD, BNTC, EC, LN, Lns, WBC; all versions except CEV, NAB], 'remaining' [LN], 'some' [CEV], 'other' [BAGD; NAB]. Λοιπός refers to the part of a whole that remains after some has been eliminated [LN]. It does not necessarily indicate that the remnant is a minority and the praise for the church in 2:19 hints that they are a majority [EC].

b. pres. act. indic. of ἔχω (See this word at 2:6): 'to have' [EC, Lns; KJV]. The phrase οὐκ ἔχουσιν τὴν διδαχὴν ταύτην 'they have not this teaching' is translated 'they hold not this teaching' [WBC; NET, NIV, NRSV, TNT], 'they follow not this teaching' [CEV, NLT, TEV], 'they accept not this teaching' [BNTC; REB], 'they uphold not this teaching' [NAB].

who not did-know^a the-deep-things^b of Satan as they-say;

TEXT—Instead of βαθέα 'deep', some manuscripts have βάθη 'depths'. GNT does not mention this alternative. The reading 'depths' is taken by KJV.

LEXICON—a. aorist act. indic. of γινώσκω (LN 28.1): 'to know' [EC, LN, WBC; KJV, NAB], 'to know about' [LN; CEV], 'to get to know' [Lns], 'to have knowledge of' [LN; TNT], 'to learn' [NET, NIV, NRSV, TEV], 'to have experience of' [BNTC; REB], 'to be acquainted with' [LN], not explicit [NLT]. Γινώσκω may refer here to experiential knowing [EC, Lns, TH].

b. βαθύς (LN 81.10, **28.76**) (BAGD 2. p. 130): 'deep' [LN (81.10)]. The phrase τὰ βαθέα 'deep things' is translated 'deep things' [EC, Lns, WBC; NRSV, TNT], 'deep secrets' [**LN** (28.76); CEV, NAB, NET, NIV, REB, TEV], 'deeper truths' [NLT], 'profundities' [BNTC], 'secrets difficult to find out about' [LN], 'depths' [BAGD; KJV]. This plural phrase is a figurative use of βαθύς 'deep' [LN (81.10)].

QUESTION—How are the nouns related in the genitive construction τὰ βαθέα τοῦ Σατανᾶ 'the deep things of Satan'?
1. Satan reveals these deep things [TH]: the deep things revealed by Satan.
2. The deep things are Satanic [NIGTC]: Satanic depths.

QUESTION—Are the words 'of Satan' part of an actual quote, or are they an evaluation of what was said?
1. They are Jesus' or John's evaluation of what was said [Alf, Ld, Sw]. The heretics claimed their teaching included deep things. But Christ substitutes the words 'of Satan' where the words 'of God' would normally have followed (see 1 Corinthians 2:10) [Alf]. John is speaking ironically and changing Jezebel's claim to agree with reality [Ld]. The heretics

blamed the believers for not knowing their deep teachings, and John adds the words 'of Satan' [Sw].
2. They are an actual quote of the heretics [EC, Lns, NIC, TNTC]. The heretics taught that by indulging the flesh (eating at the feasts and engaging in sexual immorality) a Christian could destroy the flesh. It was only weak Christians who could not do this [Lns]. The teaching that what a person did with his body did not affect his/her spirit, gave Jezebel the basis to argue that participation in the idol feasts was permissible and showed the power of God's love and kindness over evil. It was taught that a person could not know God's grace fully until he/she had known the deep things of Satan [NIC]. They could venture into Satan's strongholds to show that Satan had no power over them or to learn firsthand the real nature of sin [EC].
3. They are either an actual quote of the heretics or an evaluation of what was said [BNTC, ICC, NIGTC, WBC]. If they are taken as a quote by the heretics, they taught that it was necessary to know the deep things of Satan and to take part in the sacrificial feasts and immorality. By doing this, and remaining pure spiritually, the spiritual man could show his superiority over these things. If they are an evaluation of what was said, it was John's editing of the original quote [BNTC, ICC].

QUESTION—Who is the antecedent of 'they'?
1. It is the adherents of the teaching of Jezebel or Jezebel herself [Alf, BNTC, ICC, Ld, Lns, NIC, NIGTC, Sw, TH, TNTC, WBC]. Jezebel claimed that her teaching would acquaint her followers with the deep thing of God (1 Corinthians 2:10; Romans 11:33; Ephesians 3:18) [Ld].
2. It is either the adherents of Jezebel's teaching or the believers at Thyatira [NIGTC].

not I-am-putting[a] on you another burden,[b]

LEXICON—a. pres. act. indic. of βάλλω (LN 85.34) (BAGD 2.b. p. 131, 1. p. 134): 'to put' [BAGD (p. 131), LN, WBC; KJV, NET, TEV], 'to impose' [BAGD (p. 134); NIV, REB], 'to lay' [BNTC; NRSV, TNT], 'to place' [NAB], 'to throw' [Lns], 'to cast' [EC]. The phrase ὀυ βάλλω ἐφ' ὑμᾶς ἄλλο βάρος 'I am not putting another burden on you', is translated 'I won't burden you down with any other commands' [CEV], 'I will ask nothing more of you' [NLT]. See this word also at 2:10.

b. βάρος (LN 22.4) (BAGD 1. p. 134): 'burden' [BAGD, BNTC, EC, LN, Lns, WBC; all versions except NLT], 'hardship' [LN], not explicit [NLT].

QUESTION—What was the burden that Christ had already put on them that he would not give them 'another' one?
1. The burden is stated in 2:5 [EC, Lns, NIC, TH, Wal]: I am not putting another burden on you *besides this, that* you hold what you have until I come. The opposition that the believers at Thyatira were enduring was a burden against which they were being encouraged to hold fast [Lns]. They are to resist Jezebel [EC].

2. The burden he had already given him was that stated in the Jerusalem Council of Acts 15:28 [Alf, ICC, Ld, NIGTC, NTC, Sw, TNTC]: I am not putting another burden on you *in addition to* keeping yourself from meat offered to idols, from blood, from strangled meat, and from fornication.

2:25 Only,[a] hold what you-have until when ever I-come.
LEXICON—a. πλήν (LN 89.130) (BAGD 1.c. p. 669): 'only' [BAGD, BNTC, LN, WBC; NIV, NRSV, REB], 'but' [BAGD, LN, Lns; CEV, KJV, TEV, TNT], 'except' [LN, NIC; NLT], 'other than this' [EC], 'in any case' [BAGD; NAB], 'however' [BAGD; NET], 'nevertheless' [LN].

QUESTION—To what things are the believers 'to hold'?
They are to hold to their 'good works, love, faith, service, and endurance' as stated in 2:19 [Sw]. They are to continue to believe in Christ [Ld, TH]. They are hold to the works that Christ commended them for (2:19) and their separation from defilement (2:14) [EC]. They are to continue to refrain from attending the idol feasts and participating in the immorality that goes with them [ICC].

QUESTION—To what specific coming does ἥξω 'I come' refer?
It refers to Jesus' Second Coming [EC, TH, TNTC, Wal, WBC].

2:26 And the-one conquering[a] and the-one keeping[b] my works until (the) end,[c]
LEXICON—a. pres. act. participle of νικάω (See this word at 2:7): 'to conquer' [BNTC, Lns, WBC; NET, NRSV, TNT], 'to win the victory' [CEV, NAB, TEV], 'to overcome' [EC; KJV, NIV], 'to be victorious' [NLT, REB],
b. pres. act. participle of τηρέω (See this word at 1:3): 'to keep' [EC, Lns, WBC; KJV, NAB], 'to continue in' [NET], 'to do' [TH; NRSV]. The phrase τηρῶν...τὰ ἔργα μου 'keeping...my works' is translated 'to do my will' [NIV, REB, TEV], 'to perform what I require' [TNT], 'to obey me' [CEV, NLT], 'to persevere at work' [BNTC]. The present tense indicates on-going activity [BNTC; CEV, NRSV, REB, TEV, TNT]: keeps on keeping.
c. τέλος (LN 67.66) (BAGD 1.d.β. p. 812): 'end' [BAGD, BNTC, EC, LN, Lns, WBC; all versions except NLT], 'very end' [NLT], 'last' [BAGD].

QUESTION—What is the function of the second καί 'and'?
It is an explanatory καί [EC, NIC]: And the one conquering, *namely*, the one keeping my works. The second phrase further specifies the first [BNTC, WBC].

QUESTION—What is the function of the repetition of the article in ὁ νικῶν καὶ ὁ τηρῶν...τὰ ἔργα μου 'the one conquering and the one keeping...my works'?
It indicates that 'the one conquering' and 'the one keeping' are the same person [ICC, Lns]. It functions to emphasize the two means of success [Sw].

QUESTION—What is implied by τὰ ἔργα μου 'my works'?
It implies Christ's commands [EC, Ld, TH, WBC; CEV, NLT]. It is the concrete expression of keeping his commands and is in contrast to 'her works' (2:22) [EC]. It implies Christ's will [NIV, REB, TEV, TNT].

QUESTION—To what does τέλος 'end' refer?
It refers to the Second Coming of Christ [BAGD, EC, TH]. It refers to the end of a person's life [Lns]. It refers either to the Second Coming or to the end of a person's life [NIGTC].

I-will-give him authority[a] over the nations[b]

LEXICON—a. ἐξουσία (LN 37.35, 37.36) (BAGD 3. p. 278): 'authority' [BAGD, BNTC, EC, Lns, WBC; all versions except CEV, KJV], 'authority to rule' [LN (37.55), TH], 'power' [CEV, KJV], 'right to control' [LN (37.35)], 'jurisdiction' [LN (37.36)], 'absolute power, warrant' [BAGD].

b. ἔθνος (LN 11.55): 'nation' [BNTC, EC, LN, Lns, WBC; all versions], 'people' [LN].

QUESTION—Does αὐτῷ 'to him' only refer to men?
It refers to whoever conquers, both to men and to women [WBC].

QUESTION—To what Scripture is this clause similar?
It is similar to Psalms 2:8, 9 where Christ is promised authority over the nations by God [EC, Ld, Lns, NIC, NIGTC, TH, WBC].

2:27 and he-will-rule[a] them with (an) iron[b] rod[c]

LEXICON—a. fut. act. indic. of ποιμαίνω (LN **37.57**, 44.3) (BAGD 2.a.γ. p. 683): 'to rule' [BAGD, **LN** (37.57); all versions], 'to drive' [WBC], 'to smash' [BNTC], 'to destroy' [EC], 'to shepherd' [LN (44.3), Lns], 'to tend, to take care of, to pasture' [LN (44.3)], 'to govern' [BAGD, LN (37.57)], 'to lead, to guide' [BAGD].

b. σιδηροῦς (LN 2.59) (BAGD p. 750): 'iron' [BNTC, EC, Lns, WBC; all versions], 'made of iron' [BAGD, LN].

c. ῥάβδος (LN 6.218, 37.53) (BAGD p. 733): 'rod' [BAGD, EC, LN (6.218), Lns; all versions except NIV], 'scepter' [LN (37.53), WBC; NIV], 'bar' [BNTC], 'staff' [BAGD], 'stick' [BAGD, LN (6.218)], 'rule, governing' [LN (37.53)].

QUESTION—What is the form of the 'iron rod' and what does it symbolize?
It is in the form of a shepherd's rod [NIC, Sw]. It was a wooden club, possibly oak, that was capped with iron [NIC, Sw, TH, TNTC]. It symbolizes a royal scepter [EC].

as the clay[a] pots[b] are-shattered,[c]

LEXICON—a. κεραμικός (LN **2.19**) (BAGD p. 428): 'clay' [**LN**; CEV, NET, NLT, NRSV, TEV], 'made of clay' [BAGD, LN], 'earthen' [TNT], 'earthenware' [BNTC], 'ceramic' [Lns, WBC], 'of a potter' [EC; KJV], 'belonging to the potter' [BAGD]. The phrase τὰ σκεύη τὰ κεραμικά

'vessels of clay' is translated 'pottery' [NIV], 'earthenware' [REB], 'crockery' [NAB].
   b. σκεῦος (LN **6.118**) (BAGD 1.b. p. 754): 'pot' [**LN**; CEV, NLT, NRSV, TEV, TNT], 'jar' [BAGD, BNTC, WBC; NET], 'vessel' [BAGD, EC, LN, Lns; KJV], 'dish' [BAGD], 'container' [LN], not explicit [NAB, NIV, REB].
   c. pres. pass. indic. of συντρίβω (LN 19.39) (BAGD 1.a. p. 793): 'to be shattered' [BAGD, LN, Lns, WBC; NAB, NRSV], 'to be broken into pieces' [LN; NET, TEV], 'to be smashed' [BAGD; NLT, TNT], 'to be smashed to pieces' [CEV, REB], 'to be dashed to pieces' [EC; NIV], 'to be broken to shivers' [KJV], 'to be broken' [BAGD, BNTC], 'to be crushed' [BAGD].

QUESTION—What is the meaning of the figure 'to rule with an iron rod as clay pots are shattered'?

It means to rule completely, without mercy, riding roughshod over the opposition [TH]. It symbolizes the destruction of the nations [ICC, Ld, Lns]. It symbolizes absolute power over disobedient nations [NIC, TNTC]. Not only the execution of judgment is implied, but also kindness and guidance [Wal]. The iron rod symbolizes the death of Christ and his saints which will mean victory over heathen resistance [BNTC].

QUESTION—To whom else was this kind of action attributed?

Ruling with an iron rod was also a function of Christ himself (see 12:5 and 19:15) [Ld, NIC].

2:28 As I-also[a] have-received from my Father, and[b] I-will-give him the morning[c] star.

LEXICON—a. κἀγώ (BAGD 3. p. 386): 'I also' [BAGD, EC, Lns; NRSV], 'I too' [BAGD; TNT], 'even I' [KJV], 'and I' [BAGD], 'I' [BNTC, WBC; NAB, NET, NIV, NLT, REB, TEV], 'me' [CEV]. Κἀγώ is a contraction of καί 'and' plus ἐγώ 'I' [LN].
   b. καί (See this word at 1:7): 'and' [BNTC, EC, Lns, WBC; KJV, NAB, NET, REB, TNT], 'also' [CEV, NIV, NRSV, TEV], 'and…also' [NLT].
   c. πρωϊνός (LN **67.188, 1.33**) (BAGD p. 725): 'morning' [BAGD, EC, **LN** (1.33), Lns, WBC; all versions except REB], 'of dawn' [REB], 'early morning' [**LN** (67.188)], 'of the early morning' [LN]. The phrase ἀστὴρ πρωϊνός 'morning star' is translated 'bright star in the morning sky' [LN (1.33)]. The 'morning star' is the brightest object in the sky after the sun and the moon [WBC].

QUESTION—Does the first clause refer to the word 'authority' of 2:26, or to 'the morning star' of this verse?

It refers to 'authority' of 2:26 [BNTC, EC, NIC, Sw, TH, TNTC, WBC; all versions]: I will give him *authority* over the nations…as I also have received authority from my Father. Note: Some versions either put the first clause of this verse, back with 2:26 where 'authority' is mentioned, or repeat the word 'authority' in this clause.

QUESTION—What is the significance of 'the morning star'?
1. It symbolizes the presence of Christ [BNTC, ICC, Lns, NTC, Sw, TNTC, Wal, WBC]. In 22.16 Christ is called 'the morning star', so it is probable that Christ is promising to give his own presence to the conqueror [TNTC]. The believer possesses Christ [Sw]. Christ shares his own rank with the conqueror [WBC]. This gift causes the conqueror to be like Christ in kingly glory [Lns]. Christ will return in the time preceding the dawn of his millennial kingdom [Wal].
2. It symbolizes victory or messianic reign [EC, NIGTC, TH]. Roman generals built temples to honor Venus and the sign of Venus was on the standards of the Roman legions [NIGTC, TH]. It indicates that the conqueror will participate in Christ's reign [NIGTC]. The statement distinguishes between Christ and the gift of the morning star that he gives, so this is a promise that the righteous will shine as stars. In symbolic form this refers to ruling with the Messiah after his second coming [EC].
3. It symbolizes honor or glory to be given to the conqueror [Ld]. Daniel 12:3 states that "those who turn many to righteousness" will shine "like the stars for ever and ever." [Ld].

2:29 The-one having an-ear let-him-hear what the spirit says to-the churches.'
QUESTION—Where is this phrase discussed?
It is discussed at 2:7.

DISCOURSE UNIT: 3:1–6 [Alf, BNTC, EC, GNT, ICC, Ld, Lns, NIC, NIGTC, NTC, Sw, TH, TNTC, Wal, WBC; CEV, KJV, NAB, NET, NIV, NLT, TEV]. The topic is the message to Sardis.

3:1 And to-the angel of-the church in Sardis[a] write: 'These-things says the-one having the seven spirits of-God and the seven stars:
LEXICON—a. Σάρδεις (LN 93.573) (BAGD p. 742): 'Sardis' [BAGD, BNTC, EC, LN, Lns, WBC; all versions]. Sardis was located about 30 miles southeast of Thyatira [ICC, Wal, WBC], and 50 miles east of Ephesus [NIC]. It was the ancient capital of the kingdom of Lydia under the wealthy King Croesus in the Sixth Century B.C. [ICC]. Sardis was thought to be virtually unapproachable as the fortified upper part was guarded on three sides by almost vertical 1500-foot high walls [NIC]. It was a prosperous center of trade [BNTC]. It was famous for its woolen manufacture and dyeing industry [ICC, Ld, Sw, TH]. The mother goddess Cybele was worshipped there [Wal]. The goddess Cybele was identified with the Greek goddess Artemis [NIC]. She was associated by Greeks with Persephone or with Demeter (Mother Earth) [BNTC]. Emperor worship was also present [Ld]. It was noted for its luxury and loose living [ICC, Ld, Sw]. It was known for its glorious past and current decline [ICC]. Sardis is now the modern town of Sart [Sw, Wal].

QUESTION—Who are the 'seven spirits of God'? (See this question also at 1:4.)
1. The seven spirits of God are the Holy Spirit [Alf, BNTC, EC, Ld, Lns, Sw, TH, TNTC, Wal]. The seven spirits of God indicates the fullness of the Holy Spirit [Alf, BNTC, Ld]. The number seven refers to the seven-fold character of the Holy Spirit [Wal].
2. The seven spirits of God are the seven angels who stand before God as depicted in 8:2 [WBC].
3. The seven spirits of God represent the full implementation of God's power among the churches [NIC].

QUESTION—In what sense did Christ 'have' the seven spirits?
Christ had the seven spirits of God in the sense that when he was exalted he received the Holy Spirit to give to the church (see Acts 2:33) [Lns, Sw]. That Christ 'has' the seven spirits, indicates that he gives the Spirit [TNTC]. It indicates that he had authority over the seven spirits [TH].

QUESTION—Who are the 'seven stars'? (See this question also at 1:16 and 20.)
1. The seven stars are the angels of the churches [Alf, EC, NIC, TNTC, Wal]. The stars are identified with the angels of the churches in 1:20 [NIC, Wal].
2. The seven stars are the same as the seven spirits of God [BNTC, WBC]. The καί 'and' joining these two phrases is explanatory [WBC]: the seven spirits of God, *that is*, the seven stars.

QUESTION—In what sense does Christ 'have' the seven stars?
Christ has the seven stars in the sense that He controls them [EC, TNTC]. It indicates that He cares for the churches [Ld]. It indicates that they belong to and are responsible to Christ [Wal]. It indicates that he possesses them [Ld]. See similar questions at 1:16 and 2:1.

I-know your works that you-have (a) name[a] that you-are-alive,[b] but/and[c] you-are dead.

LEXICON—a. ὄνομα (LN **33.265**, 33.126) (BAGD IV. p. 573): 'name' [BNTC, EC, LN (33.126), Lns; KJV, NRSV, TNT], 'reputation' [BAGD, **LN**, TH, WBC; NAB, NET, NIV, NLT, TEV], 'well-known name' [BAGD], 'fame' [BAGD, TH]. The clause ὄνομα ἔχεις ὅτι ζῇς 'you have a name that you are alive' is translated 'everyone may think you are alive' [CEV], 'people say you are alive' [REB]. To 'have a name to be alive' indicates to be Christian in name only [Alf, NTC]. It indicates that its dying condition was not apparent to the casual observer [BNTC]. 'Name' refers to either the reputation of the church as a body or of its members individually [EC].

b. pres. act. indic. of ζάω (BAGD 2.a. p. 336): 'to be alive' [BNTC, WBC; all versions except KJV], 'to live' [BAGD, EC; KJV], 'to be living' [Lns]. Ζάω is used here of spiritual life [EC, Ld, Lns, NIGTC, TH]. See this word also at 2:8.

c. καί (See this word at 2:13): 'but' [TH, WBC; CEV, NIV, NLT, NRSV, TNT], 'but, in fact' [REB], 'but in reality' [NET], 'though' [BNTC], 'even though' [TEV], 'when in fact' [NAB], 'and' [Alf; KJV], 'and yet' [EC, Lns]. The καί here is adversative, being placed between two opposites [EC, WBC]. The word 'and' carries the contrast more intensely than the word 'yet' [Alf].

QUESTION—In what sense is the word νεκρός 'dead' used?

It indicates that they were spiritually dead [Alf, EC, Ld, NIC, NIGTC, Sw, TH]. Because they are commanded to 'strengthen', the word 'dead' is not used in an absolute sense. They did not have real vitality and genuine fruitfulness, yet there is hope that that they might arouse themselves to living activity [EC].

3:2 Be watchful^a and strengthen^b the remaining-things that are-about^c to-die,^d

TEXT—Instead of the imperfect ἔμελλον 'were about', some manuscripts possibly have μέλλει 'are about', although GNT does not mention this alternative. The reading 'are about' is taken by TR and is so translated by BNTC, WBC; KJV, NIV, NLT, NRSV.

LEXICON—a. pres. act. participle of γρηγορέω (LN 23.72, 23.97, 27.56) (BAGD 2. p. 167): 'to be watchful' [BAGD, EC, LN (23.72, 27.56); KJV], 'to be alert' [LN (27.56)], 'to be vigilant' [LN (27.56), WBC], 'to be on the alert' [BAGD], 'to be awake' [Lns], 'to stay awake' [LN (23.72)], 'to be/remain alive' [LN (23.97)]. The phrase γίνου γρεγορῶ 'be watchful' is translated 'Wake up!' [BNTC; all versions except KJV]. Γρηγορέω literally means 'to be or keep awake'. Here it is used figuratively of 'to be alert' or idiomatically 'to keep one's eyes open' [BAGD]. It means to be spiritually alert [Ld, NIGTC, TNTC]. It means to begin living as Christians again [TH]. The present imperative indicates a state that continues on [Lns, TNTC]: keep on being watchful. It is 'become watchful' with the sense 'wake up and keep on watching' [Alf, EC].

b. aorist act. impera. of στηρίζω (LN 74.19) (BAGD 2. p. 768): 'to strengthen' [BAGD, BNTC, LN, WBC; all versions except CEV, REB], 'to put strength into' [BNTC; REB], 'to try to become stronger' [CEV], 'to make firm' [Lns], 'to make more firm' [LN], 'to establish' [BAGD, EC], 'to confirm' [BAGD]. Στηρίζω indicates 'to invigorate' [TH]. The aorist imperative indicates decisive and effective action [Lns].

c. imperf. act. indic. of μέλλω (BAGD 1.b.α. p. 501): 'to be about to' [BAGD, EC, Lns; NET, NIV], 'to be ready to' [KJV], 'to be on the point of' [BAGD; NLT, NRSV], 'to be likely to' [BNTC], 'must' [LN; REB], 'to have to' [LN], not explicit [CEV]. The phrase ἔμελλον ἀποθανεῖ 'to be about to die' is translated 'before it dies' [NAB, TEV, TNT], '(your strength) is almost gone' [CEV]. See this word also at 1:19.

d. aorist act. infin. of ἀποθνῄσκω (LN 23.99) (BAGD 1.b.α. p. 91): 'to die' [BAGD, EC, LN, Lns; all versions except CEV, KJV, NRSV], 'to be gone' [CEV]. This verb is also translated as a noun: 'death' [WBC; NLT, NRSV]. It is used here figuratively of losing eternal life [BAGD].

QUESTION—What is meant by γίνου γρηγορῶν 'be watchful'?
1. It means 'to wake up' [BNTC, Ld; all versions except KJV]. The call was to awaken from spiritual stupor [Ld]. It means 'to wake up from death', 'to begin living as Christians again' [TH].
2. It means 'to be alert' [BAGD, EC, NIC; KJV]. They must be alert and not allow themselves to blend into their non-Christian surroundings [EC].
3. It means to wake up and be alert. A good translation would be 'awake and watch' [Alf].

QUESTION—Why was this warning especially relevant to the church at Sardis? Two times in the history of Sardis it had fallen to its enemies because of lack of being alert and watchful [Ld, Wal], once in 549 B.C. when the Persian King Cyrus conquered it, and once in 214 B.C. when Antiochus the Great did so [Wal].

QUESTION—Does the neuter phrase τὰ λοιπά 'the remaining things' refer to persons or to things?
1. It refers to things [Alf, BNTC, NIGTC, TH; KJV]: strengthen *the things* that remain. The reference to some other persons in 3:4 shows that this reference is to things rather than persons [Alf]. Here it refers to virtues that lacked spiritual vitality [Alf, TH]. The remaining things pertained to their conduct as Christians that was in question [NIGTC, TH].
2. It refers to persons: [WBC]: strengthen *those* who remain. 1 Corinthians 1:27, 28 and Hebrews 7:7 are two other instances where a neuter pronoun is used to refer to people. Here some in the congregation were not dead but were on the point of it [WBC].
3. It refers to both persons and things [EC, ICC, Sw]. It refers to persons and whatever else remained that was salvageable [ICC]. It refers to things like faith, love and good works and includes persons as well [EC, Sw].

for not I-have-found[a] your works completed[b] in-the-sight-of[c] my God.

TEXT—Some manuscripts do not include μου 'my' with θεοῦ 'God'. GNT does not mention this alternative. The reading 'my' is omitted by KJV.

LEXICON—a. perf. act. indic. of εὑρίσκω (See this word at 2:2): 'to find' [BNTC, EC, Lns, WBC; all versions]. Here εὑρίσκω is language of the law court and refers to the process of determining a person's innocence or guilt [WBC]. The perfect tense indicates that the search is not complete yet [Sw].

b. perf. pass. participle of πληρόω (LN 59.33, 68.26) (BAGD 3. p. 671): 'to be completed' [BNTC, LN (68.26); TNT], 'to be brought to completion' [BAGD; REB], 'to be fulfilled' [EC], 'to be filled full' [Lns], 'to be made complete' [LN (59.33)], 'to be finished' [BAGD, LN (68.26)]. This verb is also translated as an adjective: 'perfect' [WBC; KJV, NRSV, TEV], 'complete' [NAB, NET, NIV]. The phrase οὐ σου τὰ ἔργα πεπληρωμένα ἐνώπιον τοῦ θεοῦ μου 'your works completed before my God' is translated 'you are not completely obeying God' [CEV], 'your deeds are far from right in the sight of God' [NLT]. Πληρόω indicates reaching a certain standard [Alf, TH]. It means that their works were not being done in the power of the Holy Spirit [Ld, Sw]. This refers to the quality of their works; they must be motivated by a living faith [EC]

c. ἐνώπιον with genitive object (LN 83.33, 90.20) (BAGD 3. p. 270): 'in the sight of' [Ld, LN (90.20), Lns, WBC; NAB, NET, NIV, NLT, NRSV, REB, TEV], 'in the eyes of' [BNTC], 'in the opinion of, in the judgment of' [BAGD, LN (90.20)], 'before' [EC, LN (83.33); KJV], 'in front of' [LN (83.33)], not explicit [CEV]. The phrase ἐνώπιον τοῦ θεοῦ μου 'before my God' is translated 'as my God sees (your actions)' [TNT]. Here ἐνώπιον means 'from God's viewpoint' [TH]. In the opinion of the Christian church, Sardis had a reputation for good works, but not before God [ICC].

QUESTION—How are the nouns related in the genitive construction θεοῦ μου 'my God'?

It means 'the God whom I serve or worship' [TH].

3:3 Remember[a] therefore[b] how[c] you-have-received and heard and keep[d] (it) and repent.

LEXICON—a. pres. act. impera. of μνημονεύω (LN 29.16): 'to remember' [BNTC, EC, LN, Lns, WBC; all versions except NAB, NLT], 'to call to mind' [NAB], 'to recall' [LN], 'to go back to' [NLT]. The present imperative indicates an action that continues [EC, Lns, NIC, TNTC]: keep remembering or bear in mind. See this word also at 2:5.

b. οὖν (See this word at 1:19): 'therefore' [EC, Lns, WBC; KJV, NET, NIV, REB], 'then' [NRSV, TEV], 'so' [BNTC], not explicit [CEV, NAB, NLT, TNT]. This occurrence of οὖν indicates a resumptive and coordinating relationship [Sw]: so.

c. πῶς (LN 92.16) (BAGD 2.a. p. 732): 'how' [BAGD, EC, LN, Lns; KJV, NAB], 'what' [NIC, WBC; NET, NIV, NLT, NRSV, TEV, TNT], 'in what way' [BAGD], 'by what means' [LN], 'after what sort' [Alf], not explicit [BNTC; CEV, REB]. Since τηρέω requires an object, it is best to translate πῶς 'what', not 'how' [NIC].

d. pres. act. impera. of τηρέω (See this word at 1:3): 'to keep' [EC, Lns], 'to obey' [TH, WBC; NET, NIV, NRSV, TEV], 'to observe' [REB, TNT], 'to heed' [BNTC], 'to keep to' [NAB], 'to hold firmly to' [CEV, NLT], 'to hold fast' [KJV]. The present imperative indicates an action that continues [Alf, Lns, TNTC]: continue to keep.

QUESTION—What is the implied direct object of 'receive, hear, and keep'?

The implied object of all three verbs is: 'the teaching' [CEV, REB]; Christian traditions [BNTC, WBC]; what they had been taught [NIC, TH]; the truth they had heard [Wal]; the Good News [ICC, Ld]. 'Keep' has the sense of obeying what they had been taught [NET]. It has the sense of holding fast to what they had received and heard [ICC]. There are two steps to restoration: remember how you received and heard the gospel and keep strengthening what remains. They are to keep on giving attention to the need to strengthen the remaining vitality they have [EC].

If therefore[a] you-watch[b] not, I-will-come[c] as (a) thief,[d]

TEXT—Some manuscripts include ἐπί σε 'on you' after ἥξω 'I will come'. GNT does not mention this alternative. The reading 'on you' is taken by KJV.

LEXICON—a. οὖν (See this word at 1:19): 'therefore' [EC, Lns, WBC; KJV], not explicit [BNTC; all versions except KJV]. This occurrence of οὖν indicates a resumptive relationship referring back to the command 'wake up' of 3:2 [Sw].

b. aorist act. subj. of γρηγορέω (See this word at 3:2): 'to watch' [EC, WBC; KJV], 'to wake up' [BNTC; CEV, NET, NIV, NRSV, REB, TEV], 'to be awake' [TNT], 'to awaken' [Lns], 'to rouse oneself' [NAB], 'to go back' [NLT]. The aorist tense indicates a single act of awakening [Lns].

c. fut. act. indic. of ἥκω (LN 15.84) (BAGD 1.c. p. 344): 'to come' [BNTC, EC, Lns, WBC; all versions], 'to come to, to arrive, to reach' [LN], 'to have come, to be present' [BAGD].

d. κλέπτης (LN 57.233) (BAGD p. 434): 'thief' [BAGD, BNTC, EC, LN, Lns, WBC; all versions].

QUESTION—Does 'I will come' refer to Christ's Second Coming or to another coming in judgment?

    1. It refers to some other coming in judgment on Sardis [Alf, BNTC, Ld, Lns, NIC, NIGTC, NTC, TH, Wal, WBC]. Since this coming is dependent on the repentance of the church in Sardis, it does not refer to the Second Coming of Christ [BNTC, Ld, NIC].

    2. It refers to the Second Coming of Christ [EC, ICC]. This warning is similar to Matthew 24:43, Luke 12:39, and Mark 13:35 where the Second Coming of Christ is indicated [EC, ICC]. This is based on the prospect of the imminence of Christ's coming [EC].

QUESTION—If the image is the way a thief comes, and the topic is the way the Lord will come, and what is the point of similarity?

The point of similarity is that both come: unexpectedly [BAGD, EC, ICC, Ld, NIC, NIGTC, Sw, TH, TNTC, Wal]; unpredictably [BNTC, ICC, NTC, Wal]; quickly [NIC, Sw]; secretly [Sw]; suddenly [BAGD]. Twice before in history Sardis had been caught off guard, once by Cyrus and again by Antiochus [NIGTC].

and never[a] would-you-know at-what hour I-will-come on you.

LEXICON—a. οὐ μή (See this phrase at 2:11): 'never' [NET], 'not' [BNTC, Lns, WBC; KJV, NIV, NRSV, REB, TNT], 'by no means' [LN], 'in no way' [EC], 'certainly not' [LN], 'can not' [NAB], 'not even' [TEV], not explicit [CEV, NLT]. This is a strong negative that emphasizes the certainty of their not knowing [Alf].

3:4 But[a] you-have (a) few names[b] in Sardis who not have-soiled[c] their clothes,[d]

TEXT—Instead of ἀλλὰ ἔχεις ὀλίγα ὀνόματα 'but you have a few names' some manuscripts possibly read ἔχεις ὀλίγα ὀνόματα καί 'you have a few names even', although GNT does not mention this alternative. The reading 'you have a few names even' is taken by TR and KJV.

LEXICON—a. ἀλλά (See this word at 2:4): 'but' [EC, WBC; NET, TEV, TNT], 'yet' [BNTC; NIV, NLT, NRSV, REB], 'nevertheless' [Lns], not explicit [CEV, KJV]. This conjunction is also translated as a clause: 'I realize that...' [NAB].
- b. ὄνομα (LN 9.19) (BAGD III. p. 573): 'name' [EC, Lns; KJV], 'person' [BAGD, ICC, LN, Lns, NIC; NAB, NRSV, TNT], 'individual' [Sw, WBC; NET], 'some' [NLT], '(a few of) you' [BNTC; CEV, TEV]. The plural of this noun is translated 'people' [BAGD; NIV, REB]. See this word also at 2:3.
- c. aorist act. indic. of μολύνω (LN 53.34, **79.56**) (BAGD 1. p. 527): 'to soil' [BAGD, **LN** (79.56), WBC; NAB, NET, NIV, NRSV], 'to soil with evil deeds' [NLT], 'to defile' [BAGD, EC, LN (53.34); KJV, TNT], 'to dirty with sin' [CEV], 'to pollute' [REB], 'to befoul' [Lns], 'to stain' [BAGD, BNTC, LN (53.34)], 'to make dirty' [LN (79.56)], 'to make impure' [BAGD]. The phrase οὐκ ἐμόλυναν 'not soiled' is translated 'kept (your clothes) clean' [TEV].
- d. ἱμάτιον (LN 6.162): 'clothes' [BNTC, WBC; CEV, NET, NIV, NRSV, TEV], 'garment' [EC; KJV, NAB, NLT, TNT], 'clothing' [LN; REB], 'apparel' [LN], 'robes' [Lns].

QUESTION—What does the figure of 'soiling' symbolize?

It symbolizes sinning in general [Alf, EC, Lns, Sw, TH; CEV, NLT]. It symbolizes idol worship [NIGTC]. It symbolizes compromising one's Christian behavior with the pagan society around them [Ld, NIC]. It symbolizes especially fornication (see 14:4) [ICC].

QUESTION—What are 'clothes' a symbol of?

Clothes symbolize a person's moral and spiritual condition [WBC]. They symbolizes a person's behavior or conduct [BAGD, TH]. They symbolize the commitment a person makes in baptism [Sw].

and they-will-walk[a] with me in white, because they-are-worthy.[b]

LEXICON—a. fut. act. indic. of περιπατέω (BAGD 1.b. p. 649): 'to walk' [BNTC, EC, Lns, WBC; all versions], 'to go about' [BAGD]. See this word also at 2:1.
- b. ἄξιος (LN 65.17) (BAGD 2.a. p. 78): 'worthy' [BAGD, EC, LN, Lns; all versions except REB, TEV], 'fit' [BAGD]. Ἄξιος has to do with having a relatively high degree of comparable merit or value [LN]. The clause ἄξιοί εἰσιν 'they are worthy' is translated 'they deserve to' [BAGD,

BNTC, TH; REB, TEV]. They are worthy not by merit [Alf] but by the love and kindness of Jesus [Lns]. They are worthy by withstanding the pressure to compromise with their pagan environment [NIC]. They are worthy because following Jesus' example, they suffered for their faithful testimony [NIGTC].

QUESTION—What is symbolized by 'walking with someone'?
It symbolizes a close relationship with that person [EC, Ld, Lns, NIGTC, NTC, TH, WBC]. It symbolizes identification with that person [NIGTC]. It may symbolize being a disciple of that person [TH].

QUESTION—What is implied in the phrase ἐν λευκοῖς 'in white'?
The words 'dressed' or 'clothed' are implied [ICC, NIC; NET, NIV, NRSV, TEV]: *dressed* in white. The white clothing here refers to spiritual bodies a believer will receive in Heaven [ICC].

QUESTION—What is symbolized by λευκός 'white'?
It symbolizes: purity [BNTC, EC, Ld, NIGTC]; victory [Alf, BNTC, Ld]; holiness [EC, Lns]; justification [NIC, TNTC]. It symbolizes the fact that God accepts them and recognizes their role as his priests [Wal]. They walk with Christ as justified people. The fact that their names are in the book of life supports this interpretation (see 3:5) [TNTC]. The person is pure because of remaining true though tested by painful trials [NIGTC].

3:5 The-one conquering like-this[a] will-be-clothed[b] in white clothes

TEXT—Instead of οὕτως 'thus' some manuscripts have οὗτος 'this one'. GNT selects the reading οὕτως 'thus' with a B rating, indicating that the text is almost certain. It seems to be taken by KJV.

LEXICON—a. οὕτως (See this word at 2.15): 'like this' [TEV], 'thus' [EC, Lns, WBC], 'like them' [BNTC; NET, NIV, NRSV, REB, TNT], 'the same' [KJV], not explicit [CEV, NAB, NLT].
b. fut. mid. indic. of περιβάλλω (LN 49.3) (BAGD 1.b.γ. p. 646): 'to be clothed' [EC, WBC; KJV, NLT, NRSV, TEV, TNT], 'to go clothed' [NAB], 'to be dressed' [NET, NIV], 'to be robed' [BNTC; REB], 'to wear' [CEV], 'to be enveloped' [Lns], 'to clothe (oneself)' [BAGD, LN]. The verb is in middle voice and so means 'will clothe themselves' [BAGD, TH]. The middle means 'to have himself clothed' presumably by Christ [EC].

QUESTION—To what does οὕτως 'like this' refer?
It refers to the group just mentioned in 3:4 [Alf, BNTC, Lns, Sw, TH; NET, NIV, NRSV, REB, TNT]: like those who walk with me in white. Οὕτως means 'in the same manner' and refers to the action of continuing not soiling their garments of 3:4 [NIGTC].

QUESTION—What do 'white clothes' symbolize here?
They symbolize: moral purity [EC, NIGTC, Sw, WBC]; heavenly holiness [Lns]; festivity and victory [NIGTC, Sw]; heavenly life [Sw]; the justified condition of believers whose robes have been washed in the blood of the Lamb (see 7:14) [NIC]; the spiritual bodies that will clothe believers in the

resurrection (see 2 Corinthians 5:1, 4) [ICC]; a non-compromising spirit seen in contrast to those who have stained their clothing [NIGTC]; the glory of the resurrected body [Sw].

and never[a] will-I-erase[b] his name from the book[c] of-life

LEXICON—a. οὐ μή (See this phrase at 2:11): 'never' [BNTC; NAB, NET, NIV, NLT, REB], 'in no way' [EC], 'in no wise' [Lns], 'not' [WBC; CEV, KJV, NRSV, TEV, TNT].

b. fut. act. indic. of ἐξαλείφω (LN 13.102, 47.18) (BAGD 1.b. p. 272): 'to erase' [BAGD, Lns, WBC; CEV, NAB, NET, NLT], 'to wipe out' [BAGD, EC, LN (13.102); TNT], 'to blot out' [KJV, NIV, NRSV], 'to remove' [TEV], 'to strike from' [BNTC], 'to strike off' [REB], 'to wipe away' [LN (47.18)], 'to eliminate, to do away with' [LN (13.102)].

c. βίβλος (BAGD 2. p. 141): 'book' [BAGD]. The phrase βίβλος τῆς ζωῆς 'book of life' is translated 'book of life' [BAGD, BNTC, EC, WBC; all versions except NAB, REB, TEV], 'roll of the living' [REB], 'book of the living' [NAB, TEV], 'Book of the Life' [Lns].

QUESTION—What is meant by erasing names from the book of life?

1. The book contains the names of all people who potentially have a share in eternal life [BNTC, EC, Wal]. All people potentially have a share since Christ died for all [BNTC]. Eternal life becomes actual when appropriated by trusting in Christ [EC, Wal]. When a person dies without having shown by an enduring loyalty that his faith is genuine, his name is erased from the book of life [EC]. To have one's name erased refers to forfeiting a conditional predestination [BNTC].

2. The book contains the names of all believers who have been given spiritual life [Lns, TNTC]. This serves as warning and exhortation to the saved to make them examine their lives and amend them and does not imply that any could lose their salvation [NIGTC]. Since only the eternally saved are in the book of life, this is a *litotes* and indicates positively that their names will remain in the book of life permanently [Lns].

QUESTION—What other Scripture references speak about a book of life or something similar?

Other references to a book of life are found in Exodus 32:32; Psalms 69:28; Isaiah 4:3; Daniel 12:1; Luke 10:20; Philippians 4:3; Hebrews 12:23; Revelation 13:8; 17:8; 20:12, 15; and 21:27 [Alf, BNTC, ICC, Ld, Lns, NIC, NIGTC, NTC, Sw, TH].

and I-will-confess[a] his name before my Father and before his angels.

LEXICON—a. fut. act. indic. of ὁμολογέω (LN 33.274) (BAGD 4. p. 568): 'to confess' [BAGD, EC, LN, Lns; KJV, NRSV], 'to acknowledge' [BAGD, WBC; NIV, TNT], 'to declare' [NET], 'to declare publicly' [BAGD], 'to profess' [LN]. The phrase ὁμολογήσω τὸ ὄνομα αὐτοῦ 'I will confess his name' is translated 'I will tell that they are my followers' [CEV], 'I will announce that they are mine' [NLT], 'I shall acknowledge him as mine' [REB], 'I will declare openly that they belong to me' [TEV], 'I will acknowledge him' [BNTC; NAB]. Ὁμολογέω indicates to openly declare one's commitment to a person [LN].

QUESTION—What does the action of confessing someone's name before a person mean?

It means: that Christ will acknowledge that the names written in the book of life are the names of those who belong to him [Alf, EC, TH]; that these persons are Jesus' followers [BNTC, TH]. It means to vouch for that person [TNTC].

QUESTION—What other Scripture references speak about Jesus confessing a believer's name or something similar?

Other references similar to this kind of action may be Matthew 10:32, Luke 12:8, and Mark 8:38 [Alf, BNTC, Ld, Lns, NIC, NIGTC, NTC, TH].

3:6 **The-one having an-ear let-him-hear what the spirit says to-the churches.'**

QUESTION—Where is this phrase discussed?

It is discussed first at 2:7.

DISCOURSE UNIT: 3:7–13 [Alf, BNTC, EC, GNT, ICC, Ld, Lns, NIC, NIGTC, NTC, Sw, TH, TNTC, Wal, WBC; CEV, KJV, NAB, NET, NIV, NLT, TEV]. The topic is the message to Philadelphia.

3:7 **And to-the angel of the church in Philadelphia[a] write:**

LEXICON—a. Φιλαδέλφεια (LN 93.603) (BAGD p. 858): 'Philadelphia' [BNTC, Lns, WBC; all versions]. Philadelphia is located 28–30 miles southeast of Sardis [ICC, NIC, Sw, Wal]. It was the home of the pagan cult of the Greek god Dionysus [ICC, Ld, NIC, Sw, TNTC], and had temples to other gods as well [NIC, TNTC]. It was a commercial center [NIC, TH]. It is modern day Alashehir [NIC, Sw, Wal].

'These‑things says the Holy-One,[a] the True-One,[b] the-one having[c] the key[d] of-David,

LEXICON—a. ἅγιος (LN 88.24) (BAGD 2.c.β. p. 10): 'Holy One' [BAGD, BNTC, Lns, WBC; NAB, NET, REB], 'holy one' [EC; NRSV, TNT], 'holy' [LN; CEV, KJV, NIV, NLT, TEV], 'pure, divine' [LN], 'genuine' [Lns]. Ἅγιος means being in possession of divine and superior moral qualities [LN].

b. ἀληθινός (LN 70.3, 72.1, 73.2) (BAGD 1. p. 37): 'True One' [WBC; NET, REB], 'true one' [EC; NRSV, TNT], 'Genuine One' [Lns], 'genuine, sincere' [LN (73.2)], 'true' [BAGD, BNTC, LN (70.3, 72.1, 73.2); CEV, KJV, NAB, NIV, NLT, TEV], 'dependable' [BAGD], 'real' [LN (70.3, 73.2)]. Ἀληθινός indicates either the quality of being historically reliable, the quality of being real as contrasted with being imaginary, or the quality of being what it claims to be [LN].

c. pres. act. participle of ἔχω (See this word at 1:18): 'to have' [EC, Lns; CEV, KJV, NLT, NRSV, REB, TEV, TNT], 'to hold' [BNTC; NET,

NIV], 'to wield' [NAB]. This verb is also translated as a preposition: '(the one) with (the key)' [WBC].

d. κλείς (See this word at 1:18): 'key' [BNTC, EC, Lns, WBC; all versions]. The phrase τὴν κλεῖν Δαυίδ 'the key of David' is translated 'the key(s) that belonged to David' [CEV, TEV], 'David's key' [NAB, REB].

QUESTION—What is implied by the titles ὁ ἅγιος 'the Holy One' and ὁ ἀληθινός 'the True One'?

These were titles used of God in 6:10 and are here used of Christ [ICC, Ld, NIC, NIGTC, NTC, TH, TNTC], suggesting the deity of Christ [NIGTC]. The term 'the Holy One' was a Jewish title for God (see Isaiah 40:25 and Habakkuk 3:3) [ICC, NIC]. The title 'the Holy One of God' was a title of the Messiah (see Mark 1:24; Luke 4:34; John 6:69; 1 John 2:20) [Ld, Lns, NIGTC].

QUESTION—What sense of ἅγιος 'holy' is indicated here?

The focus is not on his sinlessness but on his being especially set apart and belonging exclusively to God [EC]. The sense of Christ's being completely dedicated to God is indicated [Ld]. The senses of being morally pure, separate from sin, unique and Godly are indicated [TH]. The sense of connection with deity is indicated [TNTC].

QUESTION—What sense of ἀληθινός 'true' is indicated here?

1. The Greek sense of 'genuine, real' is indicated [EC, Lns, NIGTC]. The sense of being genuine as opposed to counterfeit is in focus [Lns]. Jesus is the real Messiah and not a pretender as the Jews claim [NIGTC].
2. The Hebrew sense of 'reliable, dependable' is indicated [ICC, Ld, TNTC]. In Hebrew thinking, when God is described as 'true' it means that he is faithful to keep his promises (see Exodus 34:6) [Ld].
3. It could have either the Greek or the Hebrew sense [NIC, TH]. If taken to mean 'genuine' it would be being used in contrast to the Jewish claim that Jesus was a false Messiah. If used in the sense of 'reliable' it is being used to assure the believers there that Christ can be counted on to complete his Messianic work [NIC].

QUESTION—What is meant by Christ ἔχων τὴν κλεῖν Δαυίδ 'having the key of David'?

It refers to Christ's complete authority to admit or prohibit entrance into the city of David, the New Jerusalem [ICC, NIC, TNTC]. Here it refers to Christ's authority to permit access to God's Kingdom or the Kingdom of the Messiah [Alf, EC, Ld, Lns, NIGTC, TH]. A key is a symbol of complete control over access to a place, power to allow entrance or to disallow it [BNTC, ICC, Ld, Lns, NIC, NIGTC, Sw, TH]. The key symbolized authority to enforce the laws of the kingdom [TH]. Christ having the key of David and being the one who shuts and opens is parallel to Isaiah 22:22 where Eliakim was given the key to the house of David so that he could shut and open [Alf, BNTC, GNT, ICC, Ld, Lns, NIC, NIGTC, NTC, Sw, TH, TNTC, Wal, WBC].

QUESTION—To what does the phrase 'of David' refer in the phrase 'key of David'?
It refers to David's Kingdom or House, the Messianic Kingdom [Ld, Lns, NTC, TH, WBC]. It refers to the city of David, the New Jerusalem [ICC, NIC, TNTC]. It refers to the House of David, the church [Alf].

the-one opening[a] and no-one will-shut[b] and shutting and no-one opens:
TEXT—Instead of the future indicative κλείσει 'will shut', some manuscripts have the present indicative κλείει 'shuts'. GNT does not mention this alternative. The present indicative 'shuts' is followed by KJV, TNT. However, only NRSV translates: 'will shut'. WBC; CEV, NAB, NET, NIV, NLT, REB, TEV translate: 'can shut'.
LEXICON—a. pres. act. participle of ἀνοίγω (LN 79.110) (BAGD 1.a. p. 71): 'to open' [BAGD, BNTC, EC, LN, Lns, WBC; all versions], 'to make open' [LN].
b. fut. act. indic. of κλείω (LN 79.112) (BAGD 1. p. 434): 'to shut' [BAGD, BNTC, EC, LN, WBC; all versions except CEV, NAB, TEV] 'to close' [LN; CEV, NAB, TEV], 'to lock' [BAGD, Lns], 'to bar' [BAGD], 'to make shut' [LN].

3:8 **I-know your works, look[a] I-have-placed[b] before you (an) opened door,[c] that no-one is-able to-shut,**
LEXICON—a. ἰδού (See this word at 1:7): 'look' [NET, NRSV], 'see' [BNTC; NIV], 'behold' [EC, WBC; KJV], 'lo' [Lns], not explicit [CEV, NAB, NLT, REB, TEV, TNT]. Ἰδού calls attention to what follows [TH].
b. perf. act. indic. of δίδωμι (LN 85.33): 'to place' [WBC; CEV, NIV], 'to set' [ICC; KJV, NRSV, REB, TNT], 'to put' [LN; NET], 'to leave' [NAB], 'to give' [EC, Lns]. The clause δέδωκα ἐνώπιόν σου θύραν ἠνεῳγμένην 'I have placed before you an opened door' is translated 'I have opened a door for you' [BNTC; NLT, TEV].
c. θύρα (LN 7.49) (BAGD 2.b., c. p. 366): 'door' [BAGD, BNTC, EC, LN, Lns, WBC; all versions], 'gate' [LN]. Here it is used figuratively to indicate 'the door to the kingdom of heaven'. Or the opening of a door indicates something being made possible or feasible [BAGD].
QUESTION—What does the figure of an 'open door' symbolize?
1. It symbolizes an opportunity for spreading the Good News [Alf, BNTC, ICC, Lns, NIC, NTC, Sw, TH, Wal, WBC]. In this context it indicates an opportunity to the believers in Philadelphia for the conversion of the Jews [BNTC]. Note 1 Corinthians 6:9, 2 Corinthians 2:12 and Colossians 4:3 where Paul uses this figure to indicate an opportunity for proclaiming the Good News. The following verse also supports this interpretation [Alf]. It symbolizes an opportunity for service [TH].
2. It symbolizes free access into God's Kingdom [EC, Ld, NIC, TNTC]. The believers in Philadelphia may have been excluded from the local synagogue but Christ had opened the door to his eternal Kingdom to them [NIC].

3. It symbolizes both access into God's Kingdom and opportunity for witness [NIGTC].

that/because^a you-have little^b strength^c yet^d you-have-kept^e my word^f

LEXICON—ὅτι (See this word at 2:4): 'that' [EC, Ld, NIGTC, Sw, TH; NAB, NET, NIV, NRSV, REB, TEV, TNT], 'because' [Lns, WBC], 'for' [TNTC; KJV], not explicit [BNTC; CEV, NLT].
- b. μικρός (LN 59.15, **78.9**) (BAGD 2.c. p. 521): 'little' [EC, **LN** (59.15, 78.9); NET, NIV, NLT, TNT], 'but little' [NRSV], 'limited' [WBC; NAB], 'a little' [KJV, TEV], 'small' [BAGD, BNTC; REB], 'a small' [Lns], 'insignificant' [BAGD], 'very little' [LN (78.9)], 'limited amount of' [LN (59.15)]. The phrase μικρὰν ἔχεις δύναμιν 'you have little strength' is translated 'you were not very strong' [CEV].
- c. δύναμις (LN 74.1) (BAGD 5. p. 208): 'strength' [BNTC, WBC; KJV, NAB, NET, NIV, NLT, REB], 'power' [EC, Lns; NRSV, TEV, TNT], 'ability, capability' [LN], 'resources' [BAGD]. This noun is also translated as an adjective: 'strong' [CEV]. See this word also at 1:16.
- d. καί (See this word at 2:13): 'yet' [WBC; NAB, NIV, NLT, REB], 'and yet' [EC, ICC; NRSV], 'but' [CEV, NET, TNT], 'though' [BNTC], 'and' [Alf, Lns; KJV], not explicit [TEV].
- e. aorist act. indic. of τηρέω (See this word at 1:3): 'to keep' [BNTC, EC, Lns; KJV, NIV, NRSV, TNT], 'to obey' [WBC; CEV, NET, NLT], 'to observe' [REB], 'to follow' [TEV], 'to hold fast to' [NAB]. The aorist tense points to a definite time in the past when this occurred [Alf, NIC, Sw].
- f. λόγος (See this word at 1:2): 'word' [BNTC, EC, Lns; KJV, NAB, NET, NIV, NLT, NRSV, TNT], 'command' [WBC; REB], 'message' [CEV], 'teaching' [TEV]. It refers here to the divine revelation through Christ and his messengers [BAGD].

QUESTION—What relationship is indicated by ὅτι 'that/because'?
1. It indicates the object of the verb 'I know' [EC, ICC, Ld, NIC, NIGTC, Sw, TH, TNTC; NAB, NET, NIV, NRSV, REB, TEV, TNT]: I know...*that* you have little strength. This indicates that the clause, 'Look I have placed before you an opened door, that no one is able to shut' is parenthetical [EC, ICC, NIGTC, Sw, TH]. A similar construction in which ὅτι 'that' follows the words, 'I know your works' occurs in 3:2 and 3:15 [NIGTC].
2. It reason [Alf, Lns, WBC; KJV]: I have placed before you an open door...*because* you have little strength. Christ placed an open door before them because they had little strength to open it themselves [Alf, WBC].

QUESTION—Does the phrase μικρὰν δύναμιν 'little strength' mean 'a little strength' or 'little strength'?
1. It means 'little strength' and has a negative implication [BAGD, BNTC, EC, ICC, Ld, LN, NIC, TNTC; CEV, NAB, NET, NIV, NLT, NRSV, REB, TNT]: you do not have much strength.

2. It means 'a little strength' and has a positive implication [Lns, Wal; KJV, TEV]: you do have a little strength. Although short of a full compliment, it indicates that Christ recognizes that the believers have a significant amount of spiritual power [Wal].

QUESTION—What is being specifically referred to by μικρὰν δύναμιν 'little strength'?

It may specifically refer: to the small number of believers in the church in Philadelphia [Alf, EC, Lns, TH]; to the low status of the church in society [EC, Lns, NIGTC, TH]; to the poverty of the believers in contrast to the wealth of those in the world around them [Alf]; to the relative ineffectiveness of the witness of the believers [NIGTC].

and not you-have-denied[a] my name.[b]

LEXICON—a. aorist mid. (deponent = act.) indic. of ἀρνέομαι (See this word at 2:13): 'to deny' [EC, Lns, WBC; all versions except REB, TEV, TNT], 'to disown' [BNTC; REB, TNT], not explicit [TEV]. Aorist tense points to a definite time in the past when this occurred [Alf, EC, NIC, Sw]. This action is a negative restatement of the clause 'you kept my word' [WBC].

b. ὄνομα (See this word at 2:3): 'name' [BNTC, EC, WBC; KJV, NAB, NET, NIV, NRSV, REB, TNT]. The phrase οὐκ ἠρνήσω τὸ ὄνομά μου 'you did not deny my name' is translated 'you did not deny that you are my followers' [CEV], 'you did not deny me' [NLT], 'you have been faithful to me' [TEV].

QUESTION—What is meant by οὐκ ἠρνήσω τὸ ὄνομά μου 'you did not deny my name'?

Probably the Jews had tried to force them to disregard Christ's teachings and deny him [EC]. It is a *litotes* and means that 'you confessed my name' [Lns].

3:9 Look, I-make[a] some-of[b] the synagogue[c] of Satan the-ones declaring themselves to-be Jews, and they-are not but they-are-lying.[d]

LEXICON—a. pres. act. indic. of δίδωμι (LN 90.51): 'to make' [KJV, NAB, NIV, NRSV, REB, TEV], 'to cause' [BNTC, LN, WBC; NET], 'to force' [NLT], 'to bring about, to produce' [LN], 'to give' [EC, Lns], not explicit [TNT]. This verb is also translated: '(you will see) what I will do with' [CEV]. This indicates that the homage of these Jews will come as a gift from Christ [EC]. It has the same meaning as ποιέω 'to cause, to make' in the next clause [NET].

b. ἐκ with genitive object (See this word at 2:10): 'some of' [EC, Lns; NAB], 'them of' [KJV], 'of' [NIV], 'those (who are) of' [WBC; NIV, NRSV, REB], 'those people from' [NET], 'men from' [BNTC], 'those who belong to' [CEV, NLT], 'that group that belongs' [TEV], 'some who belong to' [TNT].

c. συναγωγή (See this word at 2:9): 'synagogue' [BNTC, EC, Lns, WBC; KJV, NET, NIV, NRSV, REB, TNT], 'assembly' [NAB], 'group' [CEV, TEV], not explicit [NLT].

d. pres. mid. (deponent = act.) indic. of ψεύδομαι (LN 33.253) (BAGD 1. p. 891): 'to lie' [BAGD, EC, LN, Lns, WBC; KJV, NET, NRSV, TNT], 'to falsely claim' [REB], 'to tell falsehoods' [BAGD, LN]. This verb is also translated as a noun: 'liar' [BNTC; CEV, NIV, NLT, TEV], 'fraud' [NAB].

QUESTION—What is meant by διδῶ 'I make'?

1. It used in the same sense as ποιήσω 'I will make' in the following clause [Lns, NIGTC, WBC; NET; and the versions which translate the same in both clauses: KJV, NAB, NIV, NRSV; and the versions which use but one verb for both clauses: NLT, REB, TEV, TNT]. This is not a complete sentence since it lacks an infinitive to complete it, so in the next clause he resumes the thought by switching to a verb which has the same sense [WBC]. The second clause picks up the first part of the first and restates it [NIGTC]. The sense of 'I am giving' is the same as 'I shall make' in the following clause which repeats and explains the first [Lns]. Having virtually the same meaning, the change of verbs is stylistic variation [NET].
2. It is used in a different sense than ποιήσω 'I will make' in the following clause [EC, NIC]. It means 'I give to you those of the synagogue of Satan' and 'given' is to be taken as meaning that they will come to realize that the church is God's beloved people [NIC]. The meaning is 'I am giving some of the synagogue as your converts…I will make them come and do homage' [EC].

QUESTION—In what way were those who declared themselves to be Jews, lying?

They were lying in that they were only Jews from an outward perspective and not an inward one in which a true Jew is one from the heart (see Romans 2:28, 29) [Alf, EC, Ld, NIC, TNTC]. By this criterion Christians were the true Jews [EC, NIC, TNTC].

Look, I-will-make[a] them that they-will-come and they-will-bow-down[b] before your feet and they-will-know that I loved you.

LEXICON—a. fut. act. indic. of ποιέω (BAGD I.1.b.θ. p. 681): 'to make' [BAGD, BNTC, EC, Lns; CEV, KJV, NET, NIV, NRSV, REB, TEV], 'to force' [WBC; NLT], 'to cause' [BAGD; NET, TNT], 'to bring it about that' [BAGD], not explicit [NAB]. See this word also at 1:6.

b. fut. act. indic. of προσκυνέω (LN **17.21**) (BAGD 1. p. 716): 'to bow down' [EC; NET, NLT, NRSV, TEV], 'to prostrate oneself' [BAGD, LN; TNT], 'to kneel down' [CEV], 'to worship' [KJV], 'to fall' [REB], 'to fall down' [NAB, NIV], 'to do homage' [BNTC], 'to do obeisance' [Lns], 'to grovel' [WBC], 'to fall down and worship, to do obeisance to, to do reverence to, to welcome respectfully' [BAGD].

QUESTION—To what does the act of 'bowing down before your feet' refer?

1. It refers to the conversion of some of the Jews of Philadelphia to Christianity due to the witness of believers there [Alf, BNTC, Lns,

NIGTC, WBC]. It does not refer to the conversion of Israel since this promise is addressed only to the church at Philadelphia. Also, the word ἐκ 'of' with the genitive, indicates 'some of' not all [WBC].
2. It refers to the final conversion of the Jewish nation as depicted in Romans 11 [EC, Ld, NIC]. The passages, Isaiah 45:14, 60:14, 49:23, Ezekiel 37:28, and 36:23, show that the Jews expected the Gentiles to finally acknowledge that the Jews were in fact God's people. Here this is reversed and the Jews will acknowledge that Christians are the true people of God. This looks forward to the final conversion of the Jewish nation [Ld].

3:10 Because you-kept[a] the word of endurance[b] of-me, I-also will-keep[c] you from[d] the hour[e] of testing[f]

LEXICON—a. aorist act. indic. of τηρέω (See this word at 1:3): 'to keep' [BNTC, EC, Lns; all versions except CEV, NAB, NLT], 'to obey' [WBC; CEV, NAB, NLT]. The aorist tense points to an historical event [Lns].
   b. ὑπομονή (See this word also at 1:9 and 2:2): 'endurance' [BNTC, EC, Lns], 'patience' [KJV], 'patient endurance' [NRSV]. This noun is also translated as a verb: 'to endure' [WBC; CEV, TEV], 'to endure steadfastly' [NET], 'to endure patiently' [NIV], 'to stand firm' [REB], 'to stand fast' [NAB], 'to persevere' [NLT], 'to be steadfast' [TNT].
   c. fut. act. indic. of τηρέω (LN 37.122) (BAGD 4. p. 815): 'to keep' [BAGD, EC, Lns; KJV, NET, NIV, NRSV, REB, TNT], 'to keep safe' [BNTC; NAB, TEV], 'to protect' [BAGD; CEV], 'to preserve' [WBC], 'to guard, to keep watch' [LN]. See this word also at 1:3.
   d. ἐκ with genitive object (LN 89.121) (BAGD 1.c. p. 234): 'from' [BAGD, EC, LN, WBC; all versions except TNT], 'out of' [Lns], 'in' [NAB, TNT], 'through' [BNTC], 'separate from' [LN], 'free from, apart from' [LN].
   e. ὥρα (LN 67.1) (BAGD 3. p. 896): 'hour' [BNTC, EC, Lns; KJV, NET, NIV, NRSV], 'time' [BAGD, LN, WBC; CEV, NAB, TEV, TNT], 'great time' [NLT], 'occasion' [LN], not explicit [REB].
   f. πειρασμός (LN 27.46, 88.308) (BAGD 2.b. p. 641): 'testing' [LN (27.46); CEV, NET, NLT], 'trial' [EC, Lns; NAB, NIV, NRSV, TNT], 'trouble' [TEV], 'affliction' [WBC], 'temptation' [BAGD, LN (88.308); KJV], 'ordeal' [BNTC; REB], 'examination' [LN (27.46)].

QUESTION—In the phrase τὸν λόγον τῆς ὑπομονῆς μου 'the word of endurance of me ', does the pronoun 'of me' modify 'word' or 'endurance' and what does it mean?
   1. It modifies 'word' [BNTC, NIC, NTC, TH, WBC; CEV, NAB, NET, NIV, NLT, NRSV, REB, TEV, TNT]: you kept my word of endurance, i.e., you kept my command to you to endure. The general statement that the believers had kept his word in 3:8 is made more specific here showing that his word was his command to endure [NTC]. The following versions support this interpretation as follows: 'my command to endure' [WBC;,

TEV], 'my admonition to endure steadfastly' [NET], 'my command to endure patiently' [NIV], 'my command to stand firm' [REB], 'my plea to stand fast' [NAB], 'my command to be steadfast' [TNT], 'my command to persevere' [NLT], 'my call to endurance' [BNTC], '(you obeyed) my message and endured' [CEV].

2. It modifies 'endurance' [Alf, EC, ICC, Ld, Lns, NIGTC, Sw, TNTC]: you kept the word of my endurance. It means that believers both share and imitate the endurance of Christ [EC, Ld]. It means the gospel of the endurance that Christ practiced [ICC]. It means the teaching of which his endurance was an example [TNTC]. It was a teaching that focused on Christ's endurance [Sw].

QUESTION—To what does τῆς ὥρας τοῦ πειρασμοῦ 'the hour of testing' refer?

1. It refers to the time of tribulation before the return of Christ [Alf, ICC, Ld, NIC, NTC, Sw, TH, Wal]. This refers to the miseries that will happen preceding the Second Coming of Christ (see Daniel 12:2; Mark 13:14; 2 Thessalonians 2:1–12, Matt 24.21). It has two aspects: the persecution of the church by the Antichrist (Revelation 13:7, 8), and the God's judgments on unbelievers [Ld]. While it refers to the time of trouble preceding the Second Coming of Christ it was an assurance to the church in Philadelphia of safekeeping in any such trial [Sw]. It refers to the three and a half years during which the Antichrist rules (Revelation 13:5–10) [NIC] and in general to all the judgments from 6:1 on to the end [NIC, NTC]. It refers to the time of trouble described in 6–19 [Wal].

2. It refers to some other time of testing in the experience of the church in Philadelphia [BNTC, Lns, WBC]. It could not refer to the Second Coming because it was written to the church in Philadelphia in Asia Minor. It refers to the persecutions beginning with the Emperor Trajan in 98 A.D. [Lns]. It refers to all the trials preceding the Second Coming of Christ and not specifically to the woes described in 9:3–21 [WBC].

3. It may refer to both 1 or 2 [NIGTC]. It may refer to a final period of tribulation against the church as depicted in 11:7ff and 20:8ff, or to the judgment of unbelievers at Christ's Second Coming, or to a trial soon to come on all in Asia Minor [NIGTC].

QUESTION—What is meant by πειρασμός ἀτεστινγᾷ in this context?

1. It means trouble, disaster, or affliction that God uses to test people [Alf, BNTC, EC, Ld, Lns, NIC, NIGTC, NTC, Sw, TH, WBC; CEV, NAB, NET, NIV, NLT, NRSV, REB, TEV, TNT]. This period of testing is the same as that spoken of in Matthew 24:21ff. that will come on the earth before the Second Coming [Alf, Ld, Sw, TH]. It will reveal the loyalty of believers, but will further set unbelievers in their rejection of God [Alf]. This testing will entail the persecution of the Antichrist (Revelation 13:7–8) as well as God's judgments against unbelievers [Ld]. This trial came on the Philadelphia church alone and was the siege of Jerusalem in 70 A.D. [Lns]. This is the three-and-a-half-year rule of the Antichrist

(13:5–10; see also Daniel 12:2; Mark 13:19; 2 Thessalonians 2:1–12) [NIC]. It is directed against unbelievers [NIC, NIGTC, NTC]. It refers specifically to the judgments described from 6:1 and following [NTC].
2. It means temptation by which a person is enticed to sin [KJV].
3. It means both affliction and temptation and will badly affect only unbelievers. This is the activity of demons (see 9:1–21) [ICC].

QUESTION—Does the promise to be kept from the hour of testing mean that the believers will be taken away *from* the testing or kept *though* it?
  1. It indicates that they will be kept *through* the testing [Alf, BNTC, ICC, Ld, NIC, NIGTC, NTC, TH, WBC]. The only other occurrence of τηρέω 'to keep' with ἐκ 'from' is in John 17:15 where Christ prays that the Father would not take his followers out of the world, but that He would *keep* them *from* the evil. This supports the view that the believers in Philadelphia would be kept from the testing while having to go through it [ICC, NIC, NIGTC, TH, WBC]. The testing only affects those who do not have the seal of God on their foreheads (see 7:3 and 9:4) [Alf, ICC, Ld, NTC]. It is important to note the testing from which they are to be kept. It is not from persecution, but from God's judgment on the ungodly [Ld, NTC]. In John 17 Jesus prayed that his disciples be kept from the evil influence of Satan, not from physical evils. The same kind of spiritual protection is indicated here [ICC]. It is not bodily removal that is indicated but spiritual protection from the forces of evil [NIC].
  2. It indicates that they will be kept *from* the testing [EC, Lns, Wal]. The fact that the promise is not only to keep them from the testing but also from the hour of testing indicates that believers will not have to go through this testing [Wal]. This promise refers to removal from the earth by means of the rapture for the period of time of the trial [EC]. It means that they will be kept 'untouched' from the trial, not that the Lord will keep them from being overwhelmed by it [Lns].

the-one about to-come on all the world[a] to-test[b] the-ones living[c] on the earth.

LEXICON—a. οἰκουμένη (LN 1.39, 9.22) (BAGD 1.a. p. 561): 'world' [BAGD, LN (1.39); all versions except CEV], 'earth' [BNTC, LN (1.39), Lns, WBC], 'inhabited earth' [BAGD, EC, LN (9.22)], 'all mankind, people' [LN (9.22)], not explicit [CEV].
  b. aorist act. infin. of πειράζω (BAGD 2.b. p. 640): 'to test' [BNTC; all versions except CEV, KJV, TNT], 'to put to the test' [BAGD; TNT], 'to try' [BAGD, EC, Lns; KJV], 'to afflict' [WBC], 'to go through testing' [CEV], 'to make a trial of' [BAGD]. It refers to testing in a good sense, to enable people to prove themselves genuine [BAGD]. See this word also at 2:10.
  c. pres. act. participle of κατοικέω (See this word at 2:13): 'to live' [NET, NIV], 'to dwell' [EC, Lns; KJV], 'to belong to' [NLT], not explicit [CEV,

NAB, TEV]. This verb is also translated as a noun: 'inhabitant' [BNTC, WBC; NRSV, REB, TNT].

QUESTION—Who are those indicated by the phrase τοὺς κατοικοῦντας ἐπὶ τῆς γῆς 'the ones living on the earth'?
1. It indicates those who are not believers in Christ [ICC, Ld, Lns, NIC, NIGTC, NTC, Sw, TNTC, WBC]. This phrase is always used to refer to the unbelieving world in Revelation (see 6:10; 8:13; 11:10; 13:8, 14; 17:8) [Ld, NIC, NIGTC, WBC].
2. It indicates absolutely all the people on the earth. Here it refers to all people since the previous clause indicates this [TH].

3:11 I-am-coming soon;^a hold-on-to^b what you-have,

TEXT—Some manuscripts include ἰδού 'behold' before ἔρχομαι 'I am coming'. GNT does not mention this alternative. The reading 'behold' is included by KJV, NLT.

LEXICON—a. ταχύ (See this word at 2:16): 'soon' [BNTC, EC, WBC; all versions except KJV, NLT], 'quickly' [Lns; KJV, NLT].
   b. pres. act. impera. of κρατέω (BAGD 2.e.γ. p. 448): 'to hold on to' [NET, NIV, NLT], 'to hold fast (to)' [BAGD, EC, Lns; KJV, NAB, NRSV, REB, TNT], 'to hold firmly' [CEV], 'to keep safe' [TEV], 'to keep' [BNTC, WBC], 'to keep hold of' [BAGD]. The present imperative indicates a continuing aspect [TNTC]: keep on holding on to. See this word also at 2.13.

QUESTION—Does this coming refer to Christ's Second Coming or to other comings?
1. It refers to Christ's Second Coming [ICC, Ld, NIC, Sw, TH].
2. It refers to the Rapture of the Church, not to the establishment of Christ's kingdom on earth [EC, Wal].
3. It refers to other comings including his Second Coming [Lns, NIGTC].

QUESTION—What is indicated by ταχύ 'soon'?
It means: imminently [EC, NIGTC, Wal, WBC]; without delay [Lns, NIC]; at any time [Lns]; unexpectedly, without announcement [Wal].

QUESTION—What is indicated by the words ὃ ἔχεις 'what you have'?
The things that they are to hold on to are: their faith in Christ [Ld, Lns, NIC, NIGTC, NTC, TH, Wal]; his Word [Lns]; obedience to his word [NIC]; witness about Christ to others [NIGTC]; loving ways [Ld]; inheritance [ICC]; spiritual growth already gained [Alf, EC, Lns].

so-that^a no-one may-take-away^b your crown.^c

LEXICON—a. ἵνα (See this word at 2:10): 'so that' [NET, NIV, NLT, NRSV, TEV], 'that' [EC, WBC; KJV, TNT], 'in order that' [Lns], 'lest' [NAB], 'and' [BNTC; CEV, REB].
   b. aorist act. subj. of λαμβάνω (LN 18.1) (BAGD 1.b. p. 464): 'to take away' [BAGD, WBC; CEV, NET, NLT], 'to take' [EC, Lns; KJV, NIV, TNT], 'to seize' [NRSV], 'to rob (one) of' [NAB, REB, TEV], 'to deprive

(one) of' [BNTC], 'to take hold of' [LN], 'to grasp, to grab' [LN], 'to remove' [BAGD].

c. στέφανος (See this word at 2:10): 'crown' [BNTC, EC, Lns; all versions except CEV, TEV], 'victory prize' [TEV], 'wreath' [WBC]. This noun is also translated as a clause: 'the crown that will be given as your reward' [CEV].

QUESTION—What is symbolized by στέφανος 'crown'?

It symbolizes: a reward [NIC, Sw, TH, Wal]; life or eternal salvation (see 2:10) [Lns]; victory [TNTC]. See this question also at 2:10.

3:12 **The-one conquering I-will-make him (a) pillar[a] in the temple[b] of-my God**

LEXICON—a. στῦλος (LN **7.45**, 36.7) (BAGD p. 772): 'pillar' [BAGD, BNTC, EC, **LN** (7.45), Lns, WBC; all versions], 'column' [BAGD, LN (7.45)], 'leader' [LN (36.7)]. A στῦλος is a post of wood or stone that supports a building [TH].

b. ναός (LN 7.15) (BAGD 1.b. p. 533): 'temple' [BAGD, BNTC, EC, LN, WBC; all versions except NLT], 'Temple' [NLT], 'sanctuary' [LN, Lns]. The ναός is the central room where God lives [Lns].

QUESTION—What is the thrust of this verse?

The four promises (made a pillar; the written name of God; the written name of the city of God; the written Christ's new name) are different aspects of one promise. That promise is that the person who conquers will receive as a reward at the end: fellowship and identification with Christ [NIGTC].

QUESTION—If the image is a pillar in a temple and the topic is the person who conquers being in a certain place and what is the point of similarity?

The point of similarity is: permanence in that place [Alf, BNTC, EC, Lns, NIC, NIGTC, NTC, TH, TNTC, Wal, WBC]; importance in that place [Alf, TH]; assurance of being a part of the finished place [Ld]. The pillar will last as long as the building [TH].

QUESTION—What does the temple of God symbolize?

It symbolizes: the presence of God [BNTC, EC, ICC, Lns, Wal]; the kingdom of God [Ld, TH]; ultimate salvation [WBC]; the heavenly city [Wal]. This temple is a heavenly temple [Ld, Lns, WBC]. Since 'pillar' is figurative, this requires that 'temple' should also be figurative. This latter fact removes any conflict between this verse and 21:22 where it is stated that there is no temple in the New Jerusalem [EC, ICC]. The temple here is made up of believers themselves [BNTC].

QUESTION—How are the nouns related in the genitive construction τοῦ θεοῦ μου 'the God of me'?

It means 'the God whom I serve' [TH].

and never[a] will-he-go[b] out[c] again[d]

LEXICON—a. οὐ μή (See this phrase at 2:11): 'never' [BNTC, WBC; NAB, NET, NIV, NLT, NRSV, TEV], 'not' [Lns], 'not possibly' [EC]. The clause ἔξω οὐ μὴ ἐξέλθῃ ἔτι 'never will he go out anymore' is translated

'they will stay there forever' [CEV, REB, TNT]. The phrase οὐ μή...ἔτι 'never...again' is translated 'no more' [KJV].
   b. aorist act. subj. of ἐξέρχομαι (LN 15.40) (BAGD 1.a.β. p. 274): 'to go' [EC; KJV, NRSV], 'to go out' [LN, Lns], 'to depart out of, to leave from within.' [LN], 'to go away, to get out of, to disembark' [BAGD], not explicit [CEV, REB, TNT]. The phrase ἔξω...ἔξω 'he will go out' is translated 'to depart' [NET], 'to leave' [BNTC, WBC; NAB, NIV, NLT, TEV].
   c. ἔξω (LN 83.20, 84.27) (BAGD 1.b. p. 279): 'out' [BAGD, LN (84.27); KJV, NRSV], 'outside' [BAGD, EC, LN (83.20, 84.27), Lns], 'away' [LN (84.27)], 'apart from' [LN (83.20)], not explicit [BNTC, WBC; all versions except KJV, NRSV].
   d. ἔτι (LN 67.128): 'again' [Lns; NIV], 'any longer' [EC], '(no) more' [KJV], 'ever' [WBC], 'still, yet' [LN], not explicit [BNTC; all versions except KJV, NIV].

and I-will-write on him the name of-my God and the name of-the city of-my God, the new[a] Jerusalem the-one coming-down[b] out-of heaven[c] from my God, and my new name.
LEXICON—a. καινός (LN 58.71, 67.115): 'new' [BNTC, EC, LN (58.71, 67.115), Lns, WBC; all versions], 'recent' [LN (67.115)]. See this word also at 2:17.
   b. pres. act. participle of καταβαίνω (LN 15.107) (BAGD 1.b. p. 408): 'to come down' [BAGD, BNTC, LN, Lns; KJV, NET, NIV, NLT, NRSV, REB, TEV, TNT], 'to descend' [EC, LN, WBC], 'to move down, to go down' [LN]. This verb is also translated: '(God) will send down' [CEV, NAB].
   c. οὐρανός (LN 1.11) (BAGD 2.d. p. 595): 'heaven' [BAGD, EC, LN, Lns; all versions]. Οὐρανός is the place where God lives [BAGD, LN, TH].
QUESTION—Who or what is the antecedent of ἐπ' αὐτόν 'on him/it'?
   The antecedent is the conqueror, 'on him' [Alf, ICC, Lns, NIC, NIGTC, TH, TNTC, WBC]. The antecedent is ambiguous, but since the pillar is the conqueror it makes no difference [NIGTC]. The preceding clause is, 'he will never go out again' so the proper antecedent is the subject of that clause [Lns, NIC]. It is better 'on him' since 14:1 and 22:4 state that God's name is written on the foreheads of believers [ICC, NIGTC, TNTC, WBC].
QUESTION—What is the significance of writing the name of God on someone?
   It signifies: that the person belongs to God [Alf, EC, ICC, Ld, Lns, NIC, NTC, TH, TNTC, WBC]; that the person's life is dedicated to the service of God [Sw, WBC].
QUESTION—What is the significance of writing the name of a city on a person?
   It signifies that the person is a citizen of that city [Alf, EC, ICC, Ld, NIC, NTC, Sw, TH, TNTC, WBC].

QUESTION—What is the significance of writing the new name of Christ on a person?
It signifies that: the person belongs to Christ [Alf]; the person has a special relationship to Christ [NIC]; the person will share Christ's glory and majesty [Ld]. The new name might be: 'The Word of God' (19:12–13); 'King of kings and Lord of lords' (19:16); or 'the Lamb' (5:6) [TH]. Christ's new name will reveal more fully his character [EC, NIC, Sw].

3:13 The-one having an-ear let-him-hear what the Spirit says to-the churches.'
QUESTION—Where is this phrase discussed?
It is discussed at 2:7.

DISCOURSE UNIT: 3:14–22 [Alf, BNTC, EC, GNT, ICC, Ld, Lns, NIC, NIGTC, NTC, Sw, TH, TNTC, Wal, WBC; CEV, KJV, NAB, NET, NIV, NLT, TEV]. The topic is the message to Laodicea.

3:14 And to-the angel of the church in Laodicea^a write:
TEXT—Instead of ἐν Λαοδικείᾳ 'in Laodicea' some manuscripts possibly read Λαοδικέων 'of Laodiceans', although GNT does not mention this alternative. The reading 'of Laodiceans' is taken by TR and KJV.
LEXICON—a. Λαοδίκεια (LN 93.514) (BAGD p. 466): Laodicea [BAGD, BNTC, EC, LN, Lns, WBC; all versions]. Λαοδίκεια was a city in Phrygia in Asia Minor [BAGD, LN]. It was located 40 miles southeast of Philadelphia [Sw]. It was founded by Antiochus II in the 3rd Century B.C. and was named in honor of his wife Laodice [ICC, NIC, Sw, Wal]. It was a wealthy city [NIC, TH, TNTC]. It was a center for banking [BNTC, ICC, Ld, NIC, TH TNTC]. It was famous for the production of black wool for making clothing and carpets [BNTC, ICC, Ld, Sw]. It was a center for the worship of Asclepius, the god of healing [TH]. It had an important medical school [BNTC, ICC, Ld, NIC, TNTC]. It was noted for the production of an ear ointment and eye salve made from 'Phrygian powder' [BNTC, Ld, NIC]. It is modern day Iski Hisar [NIC].

'These (things) says the Amen,^a the faithful^b and true^c Witness,^d
LEXICON—a. ἀμήν (BAGD 4. p. 46): 'Amen' [BNTC, EC, Lns, WBC; all versions], 'amen' [BAGD], 'truly' [LN]. Ἀμήν indicates strong affirmation [WBC]. See this word also at 1:6.
  b. πιστός (See this word at 1:5): 'faithful' [BNTC, EC, Lns, WBC; all versions except TNT], 'trustworthy' [TNT]. Christ can be trusted never to misrepresent his message [EC].
  c. ἀληθινός (See this word at 3:7): 'true' [BNTC, EC, WBC; all versions], 'Genuine' [Lns]. His truthfulness extends not only to his character, but also to his message [EC].
  d. μάρτυς (See this word at 1:5): 'Witness' [Lns, WBC; NAB], 'witness' [BNTC, EC; all versions except NAB]. Christ is a witness to every divine revelation [EC, ICC].

QUESTION—What sense is indicated by the title ἀμήν 'Amen' for Christ?
It indicates that Jesus is the certainty of the fulfillment of God's promises (see 2 Corinthians 1:20) [ICC, TH, Wal]. It indicates Christ's sovereignty [Wal]. It indicates a title associated only with God (see Isaiah 65:16) [WBC]. It indicates that the truth of his word is guaranteed by his character [Ld, Sw]. It indicates that in him there is perfect agreement with reality [NIC]. It indicates that Christ is absolute verity personified [EC, Ld, Lns].

the origin[a] of-the creation[b] of God:
LEXICON—a. ἀρχή (LN 37.56, **89.16**) (BAGD 2. p. 112): 'origin' [**LN** (89.16); NRSV, TEV, TNT], 'Origin' [WBC], 'source' [CEV, REB], 'Source' [NAB], 'originator' [NET], 'first cause' [BAGD, LN (89.16)], 'ruler' [LN (37.56); NIV, NLT], 'beginning' [BNTC, EC, Lns; KJV], 'governor' [LN (37.56)].
  b. κτίσις (LN 42.35) (BAGD 1.b.β. p. 456): 'creation' [BAGD, EC, LN, Lns; all versions except TEV], 'world' [BAGD]. This noun is also translated as a verb: 'to create' [TEV].
QUESTION—What is meant by ἀρχή here?
  1. It indicates the originator, source or first cause of creation [Alf, EC, ICC, Ld, LN, Lns, NIC, Sw, TH, Wal, WBC; CEV, NAB, NET, REB]. Christ is the agent of creation (see John 1:3 and 1 Corinthians 8:6) [Ld].
  2. It indicates the ruler of creation [TNTC; NIV, NLT]. Both the idea of ruler of God's creation and the originator of it are present (see John 1:3; Colossians 1:15–18) [NIC].
  3. It indicates the beginning in the sense of being temporally prior to all creation [Lns, WBC; KJV]. John 1:2 says that, 'He was in the beginning (ἐν ἀρχῇ John 1:2) with God' [WBC].
  4. It indicates the first creature of God's creation [BNTC].

3:15 I-know your works that you-are neither cold[a] nor hot.[b]
LEXICON—a. ψυχρός (LN **79.77**) (BAGD 2. p. 894): 'cold' [BAGD, BNTC, EC, **LN**, WBC; all versions], 'icy cold' [Sw], 'cool' [BAGD]. Ψυχρός indicates lack of enthusiasm [BAGD, TH].
  b. ζεστός (LN **79.71**) (BAGD p. 337): 'hot' [BAGD, BNTC, EC, **LN**, WBC; all versions]. Ζεστός figuratively indicates a favorable attitude towards something [LN].
QUESTION—What is symbolized by ψυχρός 'cold' here?
  1. It symbolizes the state of being unconverted [Alf, BNTC, EC, ICC, Ld, Lns, TH, Wal, WBC]. It symbolizes opposition to Christ [Alf, BNTC, Ld, WBC]. It refers to unbelievers who openly rejected the gospel [EC, Lns]. It symbolizes that they were out of fellowship with Christ (see 3:20) [ICC]. It symbolizes that they were part of the world around them, without spiritual life, without relationship to Christ's church, and actively opposed to it [Alf]. It symbolizes that they were dead and had never really converted [Lns].

2. It symbolizes the state of being refreshing to people like cold water is [NIC, NTC]. The cold waters of the city of nearby Colossae refreshed those who drank. Compared with this, the Laodiceans were not giving spiritual refreshment to people [NIC].
3. It symbolizes the ineffectiveness of their Christian witness [NIGTC]. Both cold and hot should be taken positively. It is unlikely that Jesus would commend complete disloyalty as some interpret. It rather symbolizes the ineffectiveness of their witness for Christ. Consequently the unbelievers were getting neither spiritual healing nor life from the believers. This is supported by the fact that Jesus introduces himself as the 'faithful and true witness' [NIGTC].
4. It can symbolize either 1 or 2 above [TNTC].

QUESTION—What is symbolized by ζεστός 'hot' here?

It symbolizes: enthusiasm for a cause [BNTC, ICC, TH]; true conversion to a cause [Lns]; fervency of spirit toward a cause (Romans 12:11) [Alf, ICC, Ld, Sw, Wal]; zeal for a cause [Ld]; friendliness and commitment to a cause [WBC]; being zealous, faithful and true witnesses like Christ [NIGTC]; the quality of being able to heal the spiritually sick like the hot springs of nearby Hieropolis [NIC, NTC].

How-I-wish[a] **you-were cold or hot.**

LEXICON—a. ὄφελον (LN 71.28) (BAGD p. 599): 'how I wish' [BNTC; NAB, REB, TEV], 'I wish' [WBC; CEV, NET, NIV, NLT, NRSV, TNT], 'I would' [KJV], 'O that' [BAGD], 'would that' [BAGD, LN, Lns].

3:16 **So**[a] **because you-are lukewarm**[b] **and neither hot nor cold,**

LEXICON—a. οὕτως (BAGD 1.b. p. 597): 'so' [WBC; KJV, NET, NIV, NRSV, TNT], 'thus' [EC], 'but' [BNTC; CEV, NAB, NLT, TEV], 'as it is, since' [BAGD], not explicit [REB]. See this word also at 2:15.

b. χλιαρός (LN **79.74**) (BAGD p. 882): 'lukewarm' [BAGD, BNTC, EC, **LN**; all versions except NLT], 'tepid' [LN, WBC]. This adjective is also translated as a comparative phrase: 'like lukewarm water' [NLT].

QUESTION—What is symbolized by χλιαρός 'lukewarm'?

It symbolizes: spiritual indifference [BNTC, Ld, Lns, TH, Wal]; ineffectiveness in spiritual matters [NIC, NTC, TH]; ineffectiveness in their witness [NIGTC]; powerlessness in spiritual matters [TH]; absence of good works [NIC]; invalid faith [Lns]. The only reason Christ would prefer coldness to lukewarmness is that it symbolizes hypocritical profession of faith [EC]. They could not even be classed with the worldly people around them who had absolutely no concern about the things of Christ [Wal]. They were ineffective to provide either refreshment or healing to others [NIC]. It is worse to have believed and sunk into indifference about one's faith than to have had no faith from the start [Lns].

I-am-about[a] **to-spit-out**[b] **you from my mouth.**[c]
LEXICON—a. pres. act. indic. of μέλλω (See this word also at 1:19 and 3:2): 'to be about to' [EC; NIV, NRSV], 'to be going to' [NET, TEV, TNT], 'to intend to' [BNTC]. This verb is also translated as a future auxiliary verb: 'will' [WBC; CEV, KJV, NAB, NLT, REB]. See this word also at 1:19.
  b. aorist act. infin. of ἐμέω (LN **23.44**) (BAGD p. 254): 'to spit out' [BAGD, BNTC; CEV, NIV, NLT, NRSV, REB, TEV], 'to vomit' [**LN**, WBC; NET, TNT], 'to spew' [EC; KJV, NAB].
  c. στόμα (LN 8.19) (BAGD 1.a. p. 769): 'mouth' [BAGD, BNTC, LN, WBC; all versions].
QUESTION—What is the effect of a lukewarm drink to a person?
  It is: disgusting [EC, Lns, TH]; absolutely abhorrent [ICC]; repulsive [BNTC]; revolting [Ld]; nauseating [Lns, Sw]; intolerable [Wal].
QUESTION—What is indicated by the verb μέλλω 'to be about to'?
  It indicates that the action is only potential and there is a possibility of change [Alf, EC, ICC, Lns, TNTC]. It indicates urgency and divine authority [TH].
QUESTION—What is symbolized by 'spitting something out of one's mouth'?
  It symbolizes: complete rejection [WBC]; strong repudiation [TNTC]; denunciation [ICC]. This indicates final, not immediate judgment, but 3:18–20 show that there is a chance for change [ICC].

3:17 Because you-say that "I-am rich and have-prospered[a] and I-have no need,"[b]
LEXICON—a. perf. act. indic. of πλουτέω (LN 57.25, 57.28) (BAGD 2. p. 674): 'to prosper' [LN (57.28); NRSV], 'to become wealthy' [LN (57.28)], 'to be wealthy, to be well-to-do' [LN (57.25)], 'to acquire wealth' [NIV], 'to acquire great wealth' [NET], 'to be successful' [CEV], 'to be secure' [NAB], 'to be increased with goods' [KJV], 'to have everything one wants' [NLT], 'to make a/one's fortune' [BNTC; REB], 'to be well off' [TEV], 'to have plenty of money' [TNT], 'to become rich' [EC, LN (57.28), Lns, WBC], 'to be rich' [BAGD, LN (57.25)].
  b. χρεία (LN 57.40, 71.23) (BAGD 2. p. 885): 'need' [EC, LN (57.40, 71.23), Lns; KJV], 'lack' [BAGD, LN (57.40)], 'what is needed' [LN (57.40)], 'what should be' [LN (71.23)]. The phrase χρείαν ἔχω 'I have need' is also translated as a verb: 'to need' [WBC; all versions except KJV, NAB, REB], 'to want' [BNTC; NAB, REB].
QUESTION—What relationship is indicated by ὅτι 'because'?
  It indicates the grounds for the conclusion given in 3:18 [Alf, EC, ICC, Lns, NIC, NIGTC, TH; NET, NRSV, TEV]: because you say…, I counsel you…. Together, 3:17–18 are an elaboration of what lukewarmness consists of [EC]. Verse 3:17 explains why God is offended by their works [NIC].
QUESTION—What is the relationship of these three statements?
  They build together into a climax, the first naming the fact, the second describing the process, and the third stating the result, self-sufficiency [Alf].

The three-fold repetition of the same idea functions to emphasize the fact [WBC]. The second statement, 'I have prospered', indicates that they had become rich by their own efforts [Alf, EC, ICC, Ld, NIC, Sw].
QUESTION—Was the wealth being claimed spiritual or material wealth?
  1. It was spiritual wealth [Alf, EC, Ld, Lns, Sw, WBC]. The church members took their material wealth to be indicative of their spiritual condition [Alf, Sw]. They claimed to be rich in that they possessed salvation much like the Corinthians in 1 Corinthians 4:8 [WBC]. The reference to spiritual riches in 3:18 make spiritual riches primary here [EC].
  2. It was material wealth [NTC, TNTC, Wal]. Laodicea was a wealthy city and the church there considered itself, like the city, to be wealthy. However, it was in the spiritual realm that they were lacking [NTC]. Their material wealth blinded them to their true spiritual condition [Wal].
  3. It was both spiritual and material wealth [ICC, NIC, NIGTC]. Laodicea as a city was wealthy and beside this, the believers felt safe in their spiritual achievement [NIC]. They may have been claiming to be in good spiritual condition or that their healthy economic condition indicated a healthy spiritual condition. Their wealth was probably due to considerable cooperation with the idolatrous trade guilds there [NIGTC].

and you-know not that you are the-one (who is) wretched[a] and pitiful[b] and poor[c] and blind[d] and naked,[e]
LEXICON—a. ταλαίπωρος (LN 22.12) (BAGD p. 803): 'wretched' [BAGD, EC, LN, Lns; all versions except CEV, REB, TEV], 'miserable' [BAGD, WBC; TEV], 'pathetic' [LN, TH], 'distressed' [BAGD]. This adjective is also translated as a verb: 'to be bad off' [CEV]; and as a noun: 'wretch' [BNTC; REB]. Ταλαίπωρος also indicates 'unhappy' or 'unfortunate' [TH]. See Romans 7:24 for another instance of this word [ICC, NIC, Sw, TH, Wal].
  b. ἐλεεινός (LN 88.79) (BAGD p. 249): 'pitiful' [BNTC, WBC; CEV, NET, NIV, REB, TEV], 'pitiable' [BAGD, LN, Lns; NAB, NRSV, TNT], 'miserable' [BAGD, EC, LN; KJV, NLT]. Here it describes one who is to be pitied because of his peril of eternal death if he remains in this condition [EC, Lns, Wal].
  c. πτωχός (LN 57.53) (BAGD 1.c. p. 728): 'poor' [BAGD, BNTC, EC, LN, WBC; all versions], 'beggarly' [Lns], 'destitute' [LN], 'begging, dependent on others for support' [BAGD]. Πτωχός means 'extremely poor' to the extent of having to beg [Wal]. The Laodiceans who thought they were rich but in reality were poor, were the exact opposite of the Smyrneans who, in spite of their poverty, were spiritually rich (see 2:9) [NIGTC, TH].
  d. τυφλός (LN 24.38, **32.42**) (BAGD 2.a.β. p. 831): 'blind' [BAGD, BNTC, EC, **LN** (24.38, 32.42), Lns, WBC; all versions], 'unable to see' [LN (24.38)], 'unable to understand' [LN (32.42)], 'incapable of

comprehending' [LN (32.42)]. Here mental and spiritual blindness is indicated [BAGD]. They can not see spiritual values [EC].
   e. γυμνός (LN 49.22) (BAGD 1. p. 167): 'naked' [BAGD, BNTC, EC, LN, Lns, WBC; all versions], 'stripped bare' [BAGD]. Γυμνός can also indicate 'poorly clothed' [Ld, TH]. Salvation is pictured as a garment in 6:11, 7:9, 13, 14 and a number of the church members were without it [EC].
QUESTION—What word is emphasized in this clause?
   The pronoun σύ 'you' is emphatic [Alf, EC, ICC, Lns, NIC, Sw]: You do not know that *it is you who* are wretched.... Coupled with this emphasis the single article with the five adjectives emphasizes that word [Alf, ICC, Lns, Sw, TNTC]: You are *the one* who is wretched.... The repetition of καί 'and' before each adjective after the first is a rhetorical device and serves to emphasize the really appalling condition of the Laodicean church [WBC].

3:18 **I-counsel**[a] **you to-buy**[b] **from me gold refined**[c] **by**[d] **fire so-that you-may-be-rich,**[e]

LEXICON—a. pres. act. indic. of συμβουλεύω (LN 33.294) (BAGD 1. p. 777): 'to counsel' [EC, LN, Lns; KJV, NIV, NRSV], 'to advise' [BAGD, LN, TH, WBC; NLT, REB, TEV, TNT], 'to give advice to' [BAGD], not explicit [CEV]. This verb is also translated as a noun: '(my) advice' [BNTC; NAB, NET]. Συμβουλεύω also means: 'recommend' or 'instruct' and does not carry the sense of force [TH].
   b. aorist act. infin. of ἀγοράζω (LN 57.188) (BAGD 1. p. 12): 'to buy' [BAGD, BNTC, EC, LN, Lns, WBC; all versions], 'to purchase' [BAGD, LN].
   c. perf. pass. participle of πυρόω (See this word at 1:15): 'to be refined' [BNTC, EC, Lns; all versions except KJV, NLT, TEV], 'to be purified' [WBC; NLT], 'to be tried' [KJV]. The phrase πεπυρωμένον ἐκ πυρός 'refined by fire' is translated 'pure (gold)' [TEV]. The figure of refining indicates the removal of dross from gold to attain purity [EC, Sw].
   d. ἐκ with genitive object (LN 89.77, **90.12**) (BAGD 3.e.β. p. 235): 'by' [BAGD, EC, **LN** (90.12), Lns, WBC; NAB, NET, NLT, NRSV, TNT], 'in' [BNTC; CEV, KJV, NIV, REB], 'by means of' [LN (89.77)], not explicit [TEV].
   e. aorist act. subj. of πλουτέω [See this word at 3:17]: 'to be rich' [WBC; KJV, NLT, NRSV, TEV], 'to become rich' [EC; NET, NIV, TNT], 'to be truly rich' [Lns; NAB], 'to make one rich' [BNTC; CEV], 'to make one truly rich' [REB].
QUESTION—What is the significance of the verb συμβουλεύω 'I counsel'?
   It is the soft counterpart of the stern voice of 3:17. It is friendly advice in keeping with the Good News [Lns]. With the following words, it expresses irony and indicates that their attitude of self-sufficiency is groundless [EC].

QUESTION—If the image is buying something from someone, and the topic is 'buying' gold, white clothes, and eye salve, what is the point of similarity?

The point of similarity is the acquiring of goods for a price [Sw]. The person who buys is one who sees he needs the object being offered and who recognizes that the object can be bought from a certain source [Lns]. The cost in this case was nothing (see Isaiah 55:1–3) [Alf, ICC, Ld, Lns, NIC, NIGTC, Sw, Wal, WBC]. Since the advice to buy is spoken to the poor, it is evident that 'buy' in the sense of Isaiah 55 is indicated [Alf]. This counsel is paradoxical since they being poor could afford nothing [WBC]. The cost was the giving up of their own opinion of themselves [Alf, Sw] and their own personal ease [Sw]. The cost to the Laodiceans comes in separating themselves from the idolatrous aspects of their society in which they were involved [NIGTC].

QUESTION—What is indicated by χρυσίον πεπυρωμένον ἐκ πυρός 'gold refined by fire'?

It indicates spiritual riches [Alf, TH]. It indicates spiritual wealth that has been tested and proven reliable (see 1 Peter 1:7) [NIC]. It indicates a spiritual gift that comprises true riches that in effect is Christ in you (see Colossians 1:27). This is the chief gift of which the white clothing and eye salve are by products [ICC]. It indicates true riches which was the glory of God himself [Wal]. It indicates a pure faith accompanied by works (see James 2:5; 1 Timothy 6:18) [EC, Sw]. It indicates salvation in that it takes away poverty [Lns]. Refined gold is a biblical figure for purifying one's life by removing sin (see Job 23:10; Proverbs 27:21; Malachi 3:2–) or a person purified by suffering persecution (see Zechariah 13:9; 1 Peter 1:6–9) [NIGTC].

and white garments so-that you-may-be-clothed[a] and the shame[b] of your nakedness[c] not may-be-revealed,[d]

LEXICON—a. aorist mid. subj. of περιβάλλω (BAGD 1.b.ε. p. 646): 'to be clothed' [EC, WBC; KJV, NAB], 'to be able to be clothed' [NET], 'to be able to cover up' [CEV], 'to dress (oneself)' [BAGD; TEV], 'to clothe yourself' [NRSV, TNT], 'to wear' [NIV], 'to put on' [BNTC; REB], 'to throw around oneself' [Lns], not explicit [NLT]. See this word also at 3:5.

b. αἰσχύνη (LN 25.189) (BAGD 2. p. 25): 'shame' [EC, LN, Lns, WBC; KJV, NAB, NRSV, REB, TNT], 'disgrace' [LN]. This word is also translated as a verb: 'to be shamed' [NLT]. The phrase αἰσχύνη τῆς γυμνότητος 'shame of the nakedness' is translated 'shameful nakedness' [BAGD, BNTC; CEV, NET, NIV, TEV].

c. γυμνότης (LN 49.23) (BAGD 1. p. 168): 'nakedness' [BAGD, BNTC, EC, LN, Lns, WBC; all versions].

d. aorist pass. subj. of φανερόω (LN 24.19, 28.36) (BAGD 1.b. p. 852): 'to be revealed' [BAGD, LN (28.36)], 'to be exposed' [EC; NAB, NET], 'to be seen' [NRSV, TNT], 'to appear' [KJV], 'to be manifest' [WBC], 'to be public' [Lns], 'to be made visible, to be made to appear, to be caused to be seen' [LN (24.19)], 'to become visible, to become known' [BAGD], 'to be made known, to be made plain, to be disclosed, to be brought to the light' [LN (28.36)], not explicit [CEV, NLT]. The negative phrase μὴ φανερωθῇ 'not be revealed' is translated: 'to cover (up)' [NIV, TEV], 'to hide' [BNTC; REB].

QUESTION—What is symbolized by ἱμάτια λευκά 'white garments'?

They symbolize: the righteousness that God gives [Wal]; a life in Christ unstained by the world (see Galatians 3:27; James 1:27) [Sw]; lives similar to the Sardians who did not stain their lives by participating in festivities associated with idol worship [NIGTC]; salvation that covers nakedness [Lns]; an inclination to do righteous deeds [Alf, EC]. White symbolizes: purity [Ld, TH, WBC]; festivity [WBC]; holiness [Lns, WBC]; righteousness [NIC]; sincerity [Ld].

QUESTION—What was connoted by γυμνότης 'nakedness'?

Nakedness symbolized humiliation to people of that day (see Isaiah 20:1–4; 2 Samuel 10:4; Ezekiel 16:37–39) [NIC, TNTC].

and eye-salve[a] to-put-on[b] your eyes so-that you-may-see.[c]

LEXICON—a. κολλούριον (LN **6.203**) (BAGD p. 441): 'eye salve' [BAGD, EC, **LN**, Lns; KJV, NET], 'salve' [NIV, NRSV], 'ointment' [BNTC; NAB, NLT, REB, TEV, TNT], 'medicine' [CEV], 'medication' [WBC].

b. aorist act. infin. of ἐγχρίω (LN **47.15**) (BAGD p. 217): 'to put on' [**LN**; NET, NIV, TEV], 'to apply to' [WBC], 'to smear on' [LN; NAB], 'to anoint' [EC, LN, Lns; KJV, NRSV], 'to rub on' [BAGD, LN]. This verb is also translated as a preposition: 'for' [BNTC; CEV, NLT, REB, TNT].

c. pres. act. subj. of βλέπω (LN 24.7, 24.41) (BAGD 2. p. 143): 'to see' [BNTC, EC, LN (24.7), Lns; KJV, NAB, NRSV, REB, TEV, TNT], 'to be able to see' [BAGD, LN (24.41); CEV, NET, NIV, NLT], 'to regain sight' [WBC].

QUESTION—What is signified by κολλούριον 'eye salve'?

It signifies the conviction of the Holy Spirit in a person's life (see John 16:8) [Alf, Sw]. The Holy Spirit destroys self-deception and gives spiritual insight [EC, Sw]. It signifies the teaching ministry of the Holy Spirit following conversion [EC]. It signifies the Word of God [Lns]. It signifies salvation in that it gives sight and knowledge [Lns].

QUESTION—What is the significance of these particular three objects to the Laodiceans?

The Laodiceans were materially wealthy, they were famous for producing a black cloth from wool, and they were famous for the manufacture of an eye ointment. These correspond to the refined gold, white garments, and eye salve that Christ offered [Sw]. The three objects Christ offered meet the particular needs of the Laodiceans in that they were poor, blind, and naked [TH]. These three objects indicate a renewed relationship to Christ and the only thing that will cure their sickness [NIGTC].

3:19 **As-many-as ever I love[a] I-reprove[b] and discipline;[c]**
LEXICON—a. pres. act. indic. of φιλέω (LN 25.33) (BAGD 1.a. p. 859): 'to love' [BAGD, BNTC, EC, LN, WBC; all versions except NAB], 'to have affection for' [BAGD, LN, Lns], 'to be dear to' [NAB], 'to like' [BAGD]. Φιλέω indicates: 'to love affectionately' [EC, ICC, Lns, NIC, Wal]; 'to love with warm emotion' [TH].
- b. pres. act. indic. of ἐλέγχω (LN 33.417) (BAGD 4. p. 249): 'to reprove' [BNTC, EC, ICC; NAB, NRSV, REB, TNT], 'to rebuke' [LN, Lns; KJV, NET, NIV, TEV], 'to correct' [CEV, NLT], 'to chastise' [WBC], 'to discipline, to punish' [BAGD], 'to reproach' [LN].
- c. pres. act. indic. of παιδεύω (LN 33.226, 36.10, 38.4) (BAGD 2.b.α. p. 604): 'to discipline' [BAGD, BNTC, LN (36.10), Lns, WBC; NET, NIV, NLT, NRSV, REB, TNT], 'to punish' [LN (38.4), TH; CEV, TEV], 'to chastise' [ICC; NAB], 'to chasten' [EC; KJV], 'to instruct, to teach' [LN (33.226)], 'to train' [LN (33.226, 36.10)]. Παιδεύω here involves punishment [BAGD].

QUESTION—What word is emphatic in this clause?
The pronoun ἐγώ 'I' is emphatic [Alf, Lns, NIC, TH, TNTC; NLT]: *I am the one who* reproves and disciplines.

QUESTION—What is the difference between ἐλέγχω 'to reprove', and παιδεύω 'to discipline'?
Ἐλέγχω means to rebuke, reprimand, scold, or censure, while παιδεύω means to train, correct, discipline, punish, or chastise physically [TH]. Ἐλέγχω means to rebuke, expose, convict or punish, while παιδεύω means to train, discipline or educate [Wal]. Ἐλέγχω attempts to accomplish by words what παιδεύω accomplishes by actions [EC, Sw]. Παιδεύω 'instruct, educate' takes the meaning 'chasten' when education concerns correction. If verbal rebuke does not solve the problem, chastening must take place [EC].

be earnest[a] therefore and repent.[b]
LEXICON—a. pres. act. impera. of ζηλεύω (LN 25.76) (BAGD p. 337): 'to be (in) earnest' [BAGD, BNTC, **LN**, WBC; NAB, NET, NIV, NRSV, TEV, TNT], 'to be eager' [BAGD], 'to make up one's mind to' [CEV], 'to be zealous' [EC, Lns; KJV], 'to be diligent' [NLT], 'to be wholehearted' [REB], 'to set one's heart on, to be completely intent upon' [LN]. The present tense imperative indicates a continuous aspect [Alf, ICC, Lns, NIC, TH, TNTC]: continue to be earnest.
- b. aorist act. impera. of μετανοέω (See this word at 2:5): 'to repent' [BNTC, EC, WBC; KJV, NAB, NET, NIV, NRSV, TNT], 'to turn (away) from one's sins' [CEV, TEV], 'to turn from one's indifference' [NLT]. This verb is also translated as a noun: 'repentance' [REB]. The aorist tense indicates a single decisive act [Alf, ICC, Lns, NIC, TH, TNTC].

QUESTION—What relationship is indicated by οὖν 'therefore'?
It indicates a command/urgent advice based on the preceding clause [EC, TH, TNTC]: *because* I reprove and discipline as many as I love, *therefore* be

earnest and repent. They should be earnest and repent so as to avoid punishment [TH].

3:20 **Look,**[a] **I-stand**[b] **at**[c] **the door and knock;**[d] **if anyone hears my voice**[e] **and opens the door,**

LEXICON—a. ἰδού (See this word at 1:7): 'look' [NLT], 'behold' [EC, WBC; KJV], 'listen' [CEV, NET, NRSV, TEV], 'lo' [Lns], 'here I am' [NIV], 'here' [BNTC; NAB, REB, TNT]. 'Here I am' is a vivid rendering for 'behold' [TNTC].
    b. perf. act. indic. of ἵστημι (LN 17.1) (BAGD II.2.b.β. p. 382): 'to stand' [BNTC, EC, LN, Lns, WBC; all versions], 'to be, to exist' [BAGD]. The perfect tense of ἵστημι here is used as a present: 'I stand' [BNTC, Lns; CEV, NET, NRSV, TEV]; 'I am standing' [EC, NIC; KJV, NAB, NLT, REB, TNT].
    c. ἐπί with accusative object (LN **83.23**) (BAGD III.1.a.ζ. p. 288): 'at' [BAGD, BNTC, EC, **LN**, Lns, WBC; all versions], 'by' [LN].
    d. pres. act. indic. of κρούω (LN 19.12) (BAGD p. 454): 'to knock' [BAGD, BNTC, EC, LN, Lns, WBC; all versions]. The present tense indicates a continued knocking [EC, Lns, TNTC; CEV, NET, NRSV, TNT]: I am knocking.
    e. φωνή (LN 33.103) (BAGD 2.a. p. 871): 'voice' [BAGD, BNTC, EC, LN, Lns, WBC; all versions except NAB, NLT], 'call' [BAGD]. This noun is also translated as a participle: 'calling' [NAB, NLT]. See this word also at 1:10.

QUESTION—To whom is this invitation addressed?
    1. It is addressed to believers [Ld, NIC, NIGTC, TH, TNTC]. This plea is to reestablish their fellowship with Christ [NIC]. This invitation is to believers to renew themselves in a relationship they have already begun. It is possible that some members of the church never had known Christ and for them it is a call to make their profession genuine [NIGTC]. The members of this complacent church, like any new converts, must open their lives to Christ's incoming [Ld].
    2. It is addressed to unbelievers [Alf, EC, Lns, Wal]. It is an invitation to the members of a self-satisfied church to obtain spiritual life [Lns]. Saving faith begins fellowship with Christ and assures participation in the supper with Christ, ultimate fellowship with Christ will happen at the Second Coming [EC].

QUESTION—To what does this figure of Christ knocking on a door refer?
    1. It refers to a visit to an individual in the present [Alf, BNTC, ICC, Ld, Lns, NIC, NIGTC, NTC, TH, TNTC, Wal]. The interpretation that this refers to the Second Coming of Christ looks to 3:21 for its support where a final reward is in focus. It is better to see this invitation as a motivation for the repentance called for in 3:19 [NIC, NIGTC]. The choice of this interpretation is also supported by the fact that Christ is currently standing (durative perfect tense) and currently knocking (present active tense)

[NIGTC]. Another reason is the fact that this invitation is addressed to 'anyone' rather than the Church as a whole [ICC, NIGTC]. At the Second Coming, Christ will not knock and seek entrance into men's lives [Wal]. This is similar to John 14:23 in which both the Father and the Son promise to come and live in the person who is obedient to Christ [Lns, TNTC].
2. It refers to the Second Coming of Christ in the future [EC, Sw]. Here the opening of the door is the action of the Church to Christ's final coming [Sw]. A preliminary phase happens with saving faith and the ultimate phase at the time of the Second Coming [EC].

QUESTION—What kind of admission is Christ seeking?

Christ is seeking admission: into the heart of a person [ICC, Ld, TH, Wal]; into a person's soul [Alf].

QUESTION—What is the significance of the clause ἐάν τις ἀκούσῃ φωνῆς μου 'if anyone hear my voice'?

It functions to intensify the knocking [Lns]. It indicates something more than the simple sound of his knocking [Alf]. It was normal to identify oneself when knocking at a person's door and opening the door would be in response to both the knock and the voice [EC].

[and-then][a] **I-will-come-in to him and I-will-eat**[b] **with him and he with me.**

TEXT—Some manuscripts do not include καί 'also/indeed'. GNT includes this word in brackets, indicating uncertainty about its inclusion, but does not mention it in the textual apparatus. Some versions may omit this word for stylistic reasons rather than rejecting it textually.

LEXICON—a. καί (LN 89.87, 91.12): 'and, and then' [LN (89.87)], 'then' [WBC], 'indeed' [LN (91.12)], not explicit [BNTC, Lns; all versions].

b. fut. act. indic. of δειπνέω (LN **23.20**) (BAGD p. 173): 'to eat' [BAGD; CEV, NIV, NRSV, REB, TEV, TNT], 'to share a meal' [WBC; NET, NLT], 'to dine' [BAGD, Lns], 'to have supper' [BNTC; NAB], 'to sup' [KJV], 'to eat a meal' [**LN**], 'to have a meal' [LN].

QUESTION—What relationship is indicated by καί 'and'?

Here it introduces the apodosis of a conditional sentence, so it should be rendered 'then' [NIGTC, WBC]: if anyone hears and opens, *then* I will come in to him. The καί expresses sequence [Alf].

QUESTION—What is meant by ἐισελεύσομαι πρὸς ἀυτόν 'I will come in to him'?

This idiom means to enter his house (see Acts 11:3) [Sw]. It is more natural here to say 'I will come into his house' [TH; TEV]. It means 'to come in to visit him' [WBC].

QUESTION—What is meant by 'eating with a person'?

It indicates: an intimate relationship [Alf, Ld, Sw]; confidence [ICC, Ld]; affection [ICC, Ld, NIC]; companionship [NIC]; fellowship [Lns, NTC, TNTC, Wal]; participation in the marriage supper of the Lamb (19:9) and fellowship in the future kingdom [EC]. Note that Jesus was criticized for not merely associating with sinners but also eating with them (Luke 15:2); and Peter was criticized not for preaching the gospel to Gentiles but for eating with them (Acts 11:3) [Ld].

3:21 The-one conquering I-will-give[a] to-him to-sit[b] with me on my throne,[c] as I-also conquered and sat-down with my Father on his throne.

LEXICON—a. fut. act. indic. of δίδωμι (See this word at 2:7): 'to give' [Lns], 'to give the right' [NAB, NIV, TEV, TNT], 'to grant' [BNTC, EC; KJV, NET], 'to invite' [NLT], 'to allow' [WBC], not explicit [CEV].
- b. aorist act. infin. of καθίζω (LN 17.12) (BAGD 2.a.α. p. 390): 'to sit' [LN, Lns, WBC; all versions except NRSV, REB, TNT], 'to sit down' [BAGD, LN; TNT], 'to be seated' [LN]. This verb is also translated as a noun: 'seat' [BNTC]. The phrase δώσω...καθίσαι 'I will give...to sit' is translated 'I will give a place' [NRSV], 'I will grant a place' [REB].
- c. θρόνος (BAGD 1.c. p. 364): 'throne' [BAGD, BNTC, Lns, WBC; all versions]. See this word also at 2:13.

QUESTION—Who qualifies as one who conquers?
1. All believers who are victorious over evil qualify as conquerors [BNTC, Ld, NIGTC, NTC, Wal]. The victor is the person described in 1 John 5:4, he is the one who believes that Jesus is the Son of God [Wal]. Believers conquer by suffering and death (see 5:5 and 12:11). Also those who suffer with him will reign with him (2 Timothy 2:12) [NTC]. The ones who overcome are those who successfully resist the pressure to participate in idolatry and who are faithful witnesses [NIGTC].
2. All believers who die as martyrs qualify as conquerors [ICC]. Conquerors here refer to those who are victorious to death [ICC].

QUESTION—When will this take place?
It will take place: at the Second Coming of Christ [Alf, EC, ICC, Ld, Lns, NIC]; when the believer dies Jesus will cause him to sit down on his throne [Lns]; either at the Second Coming or at the death of the believer or at both [NIGTC]. The promise of this verse refers to the Millennial Reign of Christ (see Luke 22:30; Matthew 19:28; 2 Tim 2:11, 12). But it is not limited to that only but enters as well into the eternal reign of God [ICC, Ld].

QUESTION—What is indicated by the aorist tenses of νικάω 'to conquer' and καθίζω 'to sit' in the second half of the verse when applied to Christ.
They are both historical aorists and point to Christ's victory at the cross, his resurrection, his ascension into heaven followed by his sitting down at God's right hand [Alf, Lns, Sw].

QUESTION—What is symbolized by 'sitting on a throne'?
It symbolizes: reigning or ruling [Alf, EC, NIGTC, NTC, WBC]; dignity and judicial power [Sw]; royal honor [TNTC, Wal]; glory and power [Sw]. To be seated on the same throne implies equality between those sharing the throne [WBC]. There is no major difference between Christ's being enthroned at the right hand of God and the enthronement of the believer promised in this verse [Ld].

QUESTION—Are there several thrones indicated here or only one?
1. There are several thrones [TH]. It is not appropriate to have two people sitting on the same throne. This concept could be rendered, 'to sit on a throne beside my throne' [TH]. The Father's throne is in heaven and Christ's throne is on earth [EC, Wal].
2. There is only one throne [Alf, Lns, Sw]. The throne of the Father on which Christ sits and the throne of Christ on which the believer sits are the same (see 22:1) [Alf]. 'His throne' and 'the conquering believer's throne' are the same throne, not two [Lns].

3:22 The-one having an-ear let-him-hear what the Spirit says to-the churches.'
QUESTION—Where is this phrase discussed?
It is discussed at 2:7.

DISCOURSE UNIT: 4:1–22:9 [WBC]. The topic is the disclosure of God's eschatological plan.

DISCOURSE UNIT: 4:1–22:5 [EC, TH]. The topic is visions of things to come [TH], future expectation [EC].

DISCOURSE UNIT: 4:1–16:21 [Ld]. The topic is the second vision.

DISCOURSE UNIT: 4:1–8:1 [EC]. The topic is the opening of the seven-sealed scroll.

DISCOURSE UNIT: 4:1–5:14 [EC, NIC, NIGTC, NTC, TH; REB]. The topic is adoration in the court of heaven [NIC], vision of heaven [NTC, TH; REB], the source of the scroll [EC].

DISCOURSE UNIT: 4:1–11 [Alf, BNTC, EC, GNT, Ld, Lns, NIC, NIGTC, NTC, Sw, TNTC, WBC; CEV]. The topic is the worship in heaven [GNT; CEV, KJV, NAB, NLT, TEV], the vision of God's presence in Heaven [Alf], the one sitting on the throne [EC], the vision of the throne in heaven [Sw; NIV], a vision of heaven [TNTC; REB], the creator [BNTC], the throne [Ld, Lns], the throne-room of God [NTC], the worship of God as creator [NIC], wondrous scenes in heaven [NET].

DISCOURSE UNIT: 4:1–2a [NIGTC, WBC]. The topic is introductory vision terminology [NIGTC], John's heavenly ascent [WBC].

4:1 After these-things I-saw, and behold[a] a-door having-been-opened[b] in[c] heaven,[d]
LEXICON—a. ἰδού (See this word at 1:7): 'behold' [EC, WBC; KJV], 'lo' [Lns], 'there was' [NET], 'there before me' [NIV], 'there' [BNTC; NRSV, TNT], 'above me' [NAB], 'I saw' [CEV, NLT]. The phrase εἶδον καὶ ἰδοῦ 'I saw and behold' is translated 'I had a vision' [REB, TEV].
b. perf. pass. participle of ἀνοίγω (LN 79.110): 'to be opened' [EC, LN, Lns, WBC; CEV, KJV], 'to be made open' [LN]. This verb is also

translated as an adjective: 'open (door)' [BNTC; NAB, TEV]. The perfect tense is translated 'stood open' [NRSV, REB], 'standing open' [NET, NIV, NLT, TNT]. The door was already opened when John saw it [Alf, EC].
- c. ἐν with dative object (LN 83.13): 'in' [BNTC, EC, LN, Lns, WBC; all versions except CEV, NAB], 'into' [CEV], 'to' [NAB].
- d. οὐρανός (LN 1.5): 'heaven' [BNTC, EC, Lns, WBC; all versions], 'sky' [LN]. See this word also at 3:12.

QUESTION—What is the function of the phrase μετὰ ταῦτα εἶδον 'after these things I saw'?

It is used to introduce new visions in Revelation (see 7:1, 9; 15:5; 18:1; 19:1) [Alf, EC, ICC, NIGTC, Sw, TNTC, WBC]. The phrase μετὰ ταῦτα 'after these things' is used to close one event and open another [TH].

QUESTION—What is indicated by εἶδον 'I saw'?

It indicates that John was seeing a vision [Alf, EC, TH; probably NAB, REB, TEV]. John saw with spiritual, not physical eyes [BNTC, EC].

QUESTION—To what does οὐρανός 'heaven' refer?

It refers to the dwelling place of God [Alf, NIC, TNTC, Wal]. It refers to the third heaven [Wal]. It refers to part of the physical universe that is seen only by one's spiritual eyes [BNTC]. The door was in the sky and it permitted John to enter heaven [EC].

QUESTION—Who is the implied actor of the passive verb ἠνεῳγμένη 'having been opened'?

The actor is God [WBC]: having been opened by God.

and the first voice[a] that I-heard as of-a-trumpet[b] speaking with me saying,

LEXICON—a. φωνή (See this word at 1:10 and 3:20): 'voice' [BNTC, Lns, WBC; all versions], 'sound' [EC]. This refers to a person speaking and not to some impersonal sound [Sw, TH].
- b. σάλπιγξ (LN 6.93): 'trumpet' [BAGD, BNTC, EC, LN, Lns, WBC; all versions except NAB, NLT], 'mighty trumpet blast' [NLT]. This noun is also translated as an adjective: 'trumpetlike (voice)' [NAB]. See this word also at 1:10.

QUESTION—What is the φωνή 'voice' referred to here?

1. It refers back to the voice that John heard in 1:10 [Alf, EC, ICC, Lns, NIC, NTC, Sw, TH, TNTC]. The definite article with voice marks it as one he had previously heard [Lns].
2. It is simply the first of the voices that he subsequently heard [KJV].

QUESTION—Whose voice was John referring to?

1. It was the voice of Christ [EC, ICC, Lns, NIC, TH, TNTC].
2. It was the voice of an angel [Alf, Sw]. It was a heavenly being or angel [Alf].

"Come-up[a] here,[b] and I-will-show[c] you the-things-which it-is-necessary to-happen after these-things.

LEXICON—a. aorist act. impera. of ἀναβαίνω (LN 15.101) (BAGD 1.a.β. p. 50): 'to come up' [BNTC, EC, LN, Lns, WBC; all versions], 'to ascend' [BAGD], 'to go up' [BAGD].
- b. ὧδε (LN **83.1**); 'here' [BNTC, EC, **LN**, Lns, WBC; all versions except KJV], 'hither' [KJV].
- c. fut. act. indic. of δείκνυμι (See this word at 1:1): 'to show' [BNTC, EC, Lns, WBC; all versions], 'to reveal' [WBC].

QUESTION—To where was John to come?

Rather than watching events through the door, John was taken into heaven through that door [Alf, EC, Lns]. It is not certain whether John only went to the door to look inside at heaven or went through the door into heaven [NIC].

4:2 At-once[a] I-was in-spirit,[b]

LEXICON—a. εὐθέως (LN 67.53) (BAGD p.320): 'at once' [BAGD, BNTC; NAB, NIV, NRSV, REB, TEV, TNT], 'immediately' [BAGD, EC, LN, Lns, WBC; KJV, NET], 'instantly' [NLT], 'right then' [CEV], 'right away, then' [LN].
- b. ἐν πνεύματι (See this phrase at 1:10): 'in spirit' [Lns], 'in the spirit' [EC; NRSV], 'in the Spirit' [KJV, NET, NIV, NLT]. The phrase ἐγενόμην ἐν πνεύματι 'I was in the Spirit' is translated 'the Spirit took control of me' [CEV, TEV], 'the Spirit came upon me' [REB, TNT], 'I fell into a trance' [BNTC, Ld], 'I was in a prophetic trance' [WBC], 'I was caught up in ecstasy' [NAB].

QUESTION—What is the meaning of being ἐν πνεύματι 'in spirit'?

See the question at 1:10 for the explanation of this phrase.

QUESTION—What relationship does this experience of being 'in spirit', have to the one recorded in 1:10?

This experience 'in spirit' was a continuation of the ecstatic state of 1:10, since 4:1 also is part of an ecstatic experience [ICC, NIC]. John is probably combining visions experienced on different occasions [ICC]. This experience was either a separate experience to 1:10, inferring that John had returned to a normal state in the meantime, or this is an even deeper spiritual state than 1:10 [Ld]. After the first vision ended in 3:22 John had returned to his normal senses and immediately afterwards this new ecstatic state happened [EC]. This experience is a recurrence of 1:10 [Alf, Lns, TNTC]. This experience is another spiritual experience, but one with greater force than at 1:10 [Sw].

DISCOURSE UNIT: 4:2b–5:14 [WBC]. The topic is a vision of the heavenly throne room.

DISCOURSE UNIT: 4:2b–11 [WBC]. The topic is the heavenly worship of God.

DISCOURSE UNIT: 4:2b–3 [NIGTC]. The topic is the picture of God sitting on a throne.

and behold[a] **a-throne was-standing**[b] **in heaven, and on the throne one-sitting,**[c]
- a. ἰδού (See this word at 1:7): 'behold' [EC, WBC; KJV], 'lo' [Lns], 'there' [BNTC; NAB, NRSV, REB, TEV, TNT], 'there…I saw' [CEV], 'I saw' [NLT], 'there before me' [NIV], not explicit [NET]. Ἰδού here has the meaning of 'I saw' [TH; NLT].
- b. imperf. mid. (deponent = act.) indic. of κεῖμαι (LN 13.73, 85.3) (BAGD 1.b. p. 426): 'to stand' [BAGD, BNTC, EC, ICC, Lns, Sw; NAB, NET, NRSV, REB], 'to be set' [LN (13.73); KJV, TNT], 'to be situated' [WBC], 'to be' [LN (85.3); NIV, TEV], not explicit [CEV, NLT]. Κεῖμαι has the meaning of 'to be' here [TH, WBC; NIV, TEV] and as such simply indicates the location of the throne [TH].
- c. pres. mid. (deponent = act.) participle of κάθημαι (BAGD 1.a.α. p. 389): 'to sit' [BAGD, BNTC, EC, Lns, WBC; CEV, KJV, NIV, NLT, REB, TEV], 'to be seated' [BNTC, WBC; NAB, NET, NRSV, TNT]. See this word also at 3:21.

QUESTION—Who was sitting on the throne?
Verse 4:8 shows that it was God who was sitting on the throne [NIC, Sw]. Verse 5:7 shows that it was God [Lns]. It was God the Father since he is distinguished from the Lamb in 5:5, 7; 6:16; 7:10 [EC].

4:3 **and the-one sitting (was) like**[a] **in-appearance**[b] **to-(a)-jasper**[c] **and (a)-carnelian**[d] **stone,**[e]
LEXICON—a. ὅμοιος (LN **64.1**): 'like' [BNTC, **LN**, Lns, WBC; KJV, NAB, NET, NRSV, REB], 'similar' [EC], 'his face gleamed like' [TEV], not explicit [NIV, TNT]. See this word also at 1:13 and 2:15. The phrase ὅμοιος ὁράσει 'like in appearance' is translated 'sparkled like' [CEV], 'as brilliant as' [NLT].
- b. ὅρασις (LN **24.31**) (BAGD 2.a. p. 577): 'appearance' [BAGD, BNTC, EC, **LN**, Lns, WBC; NAB, NET, NIV, REB, TNT], 'face' [TEV], not explicit [CEV, NLT]. This noun is also translated as a verb: 'to look (like)' [NRSV], 'to look upon' [KJV].
- c. ἴασπις (LN 2.30) (BAGD p. 368): 'jasper' [BAGD, BNTC, EC, LN, WBC; all versions], 'diamond' [Lns]. It was probably green in color [LN]. It is found in various colors mostly reddish, sometimes green [BAGD].
- d. σάρδιον (LN 2.36) (BAGD p. 742): 'carnelian' [BAGD, LN, WBC; all versions except KJV, REB, TNT], 'cornelian' [BNTC; REB], 'sardine' [KJV], 'sard' [Lns], 'sardius' [BAGD, EC; TNT]. It was usually red in color [Alf, BAGD, EC, ICC, LN, NIC, Sw, TH, TNTC, Wal].
- e. λίθος (LN 2.24, 2.29) (BAGD 1.c. p. 474): 'stone' [BAGD, EC, LN (2.24), Lns; KJV], 'precious stone' [BAGD, LN (2.29); CEV, TEV], 'gemstone' [NLT], 'gem' [LN (2.29)], 'jewel' [BAGD], not explicit

[BNTC, WBC; NET, NIV, NRSV, REB, TNT]. This word is joined with ὅμοιος 'like' and translated: 'gemlike sparkle' [NAB].
QUESTION—What is meant by ἴασπις 'jasper'?
1. It is a clear stone like crystal [EC, Ld, Lns, NIC, Sw, Wal]. In 21.11 it is described as being 'clear as crystal' [EC, Lns, NIC, Sw, Wal]. It is a translucent rock crystal and might be a diamond [EC]. It is a diamond [Lns, NIC, Wal]. It cannot be what we know as jasper which it is opaque and colored [Lns].
2. It is a colored stone of some kind [BAGD, ICC, LN, TH, WBC]. Its color may be: green [BAGD, ICC, LN, TH, WBC]; red [BAGD, TH, WBC]; yellow [TH, WBC]; brown [TH]; or grayish blue [WBC].

and a-rainbow[a] (was) around[b] the throne like-in-appearance[c] to-(an)-emerald.[d]
LEXICON—a. ἶρις (LN **1.38**) (BAGD 2. p. 380): 'rainbow' [BNTC, EC, **LN**, Lns, WBC; all versions], 'halo' [BAGD, LN], 'circle of light' [**LN**], 'colored halo, radiance' [BAGD]. This refers to a circular or semicircular band of light either colored or plain [LN].
b. κυκλόθεν (LN **83.19**) (BAGD 2. p. 456): 'around' [BAGD, EC, **LN**; NAB, NRSV, TNT], 'round about' [Lns; KJV], 'round' [REB], 'in a circle' [LN], 'all around' [BAGD; TEV], 'from all sides' [BAGD]. This preposition is also translated as a verb: 'to encircle' [BNTC, WBC; NET, NIV], 'to circle' [NLT], 'to surround' [CEV]. It formed a complete circle around the throne, possibly like a halo [EC, TH]. It is not known whether it encircled the throne vertically or horizontally [Ld]. Its object was to conceal the one seated on the throne [ICC].
c. ὅμοιος ὅρασις (See these words in this verse above): 'like in appearance' [Lns, WBC], 'similar in appearance' [EC], 'having the appearance of' [TNT], 'looked like' [CEV, NET, NRSV], 'in sight like' [KJV], 'resembling' [NIV], 'like' [NLT], 'as brilliant as' [NAB], 'bright as' [BNTC; REB], 'the color of' [TEV].
d. σμαράγδινος (LN **2.34**) (BAGD p. 758): 'emerald' [BAGD, BNTC, EC, Lns, WBC; all versions except NET, NLT, TEV], 'made of emerald' [NET], 'glow of an emerald' [NLT], 'the color of an emerald' [TEV], 'emerald-like' [**LN**], 'consisting of emerald' [**LN**]. The literal meaning of σμαράγδινος is 'made of emerald' and 'emerald in color' [BAGD]. Σμάραγδος is the actual word for 'emerald' [LN].
QUESTION—What do these three stones symbolize together?
They symbolize the glory and majesty of God [Ld, NIC, NIGTC].
QUESTION—What is the color of σμαράγδινος 'emerald'?
It is: green [Alf, EC, ICC, Lns, NIC, Sw, TH, Wal]; emerald green [ICC, Lns, Sw, Wal]; colorless crystal [NIC]. It is its brilliance, not its color that is in focus here [TH].

QUESTION—In what way was the rainbow like an emerald?
1. The rainbow was all green in color like an emerald [EC, Lns; NET, TEV]: the rainbow was green like an emerald. It looked like it was made of emerald [NET, NRSV], 'the glow of an emerald circled his throne like a rainbow' [NLT]. Probably the rainbow had different shades of green since the symbolism of the emerald lies in its green color [EC]. Green symbolizes grace [Lns].
2. The rainbow was rainbow colored and had a brilliance like an emerald [TH; NAB, REB]: the rainbow gleamed like an emerald. It was as bright as an emerald [REB]

DISCOURSE UNIT: 4:4–8a [NIGTC]. The topic is a picture of the throne and its surroundings.

4:4 **And around**[a] **the throne twenty-four thrones, and on the thrones twenty-four elders**[b]

TEXT—Before the second εἴκοσι 'twenty' some manuscripts possibly include εἶδον τούς 'I saw the', although GNT does not mention this alternative. The words 'I saw the' are included by TR and KJV.

LEXICON—a. κυκλόθεν (LN **83.19**): 'around' [EC; NRSV, TNT], 'round' [BNTC], 'in a circle around' [**LN**; CEV, NET, TEV], 'in a circle about' [REB], 'round about' [Lns; KJV]. This preposition is also translated as a verb: 'surrounding' [NAB, NIV], 'surrounded' [NLT], 'encircled' [WBC]. See this word also at 4:3.

b. πρεσβύτερος (LN 53.77) (BAGD 2.b.γ. p. 700): 'elder' [BAGD, BNTC, EC, LN, Lns, WBC; all versions], 'presbyter' [BAGD]. A πρεσβύτερος is an older person, but one who also bears the qualities of authority and prestige [TH].

QUESTION—Who are these 'elders'?
1. They are angelic beings [BNTC, EC, ICC, Ld, NIC, NIGTC, NTC, TH, TNTC]. They are angels who represent the whole Church [ICC]. They are a group of angels functioning as a kind of heavenly counterpart to the elders of Israel (cf. Exodus 24:11) [Ld]. They are a group of high-ranking angels, the heavenly counterpart of the 24 priestly and the 24 Levitical orders (cf. 1 Chronicles 24:4 and 25:9–13) [NIC]. These angels are identified with the 12 Tribes of Israel and the 12 Apostles who together symbolize all of those whom Christ redeemed [NIGTC].
2. They are representatives of the Church [Alf, Sw, Wal]. The 24 elders symbolize the whole Church. The number 12 is taken from the 12 tribes of Israel, for each one of which there are two members, one for the Jewish side and one for the Gentiles who are joined together in the new Israel [Sw]. The number 24 is made up of the 12 Patriarchs and the 12 Apostles. This view is supported by 21:12, 14, where the 12 gates of the New Jerusalem are inscribed with the names of the 12 tribes of Israel and the 12 foundations stones of it are inscribed with the names of the 12 Apostles [Alf].

3. They are heavenly counterparts of the 24 leaders of the 24 priestly orders as seen in 1 Chronicles 23:6 and 24:7–18 [WBC].
4. They are beings who minister of the Word of God [Lns].

sitting clothed in white clothing and on their heads golden crowns.
TEXT—Some manuscripts possibly include ἔσχον 'they had' before ἐπί 'on', although GNT does not mention this alternative. It is included by TR and KJV.

4:5 And flashes-of-lightning^a and sounds^b and peals-of-thunder,^c come-out^d from the throne
TEXT—Instead of φωναὶ καὶ βρονταί 'sounds and thunders' some manuscripts transpose these words to βρονταὶ καὶ φωναί 'thunders and sounds'. GNT does not mention this alternative. The reading 'thunders and sounds' is taken by KJV.
LEXICON—a. ἀστραπή (LN 14.16) (BAGD p. 118): 'flash of lightning' [BNTC, EC; all versions except KJV], 'lightning' [BAGD, LN, Lns, WBC; KJV].
  b. φωνή (BAGD 1. p. 870): 'sound' [BAGD, LN (14.74), Lns], 'voice' [KJV, TNT], 'roaring' [NET], 'rumbling' [WBC; NIV, NRSV, TEV], 'noise, tone' [BAGD], 'voice' [EC]. The phrase φωναὶ καὶ βρονταί 'sounds and thunder' is translated 'peal of thunder' [BNTC; NAB, REB], 'roar of thunder' [CEV], 'rumble of thunder' [NLT]. Φωνή occurs between 'lightnings' and 'thunders' indicating that it belongs to same phenomena and should translated 'sounds' not 'voices' [Lns]. See this word also at 1:10 and 3:20.
  c. βροντή (LN 14.15) (BAGD p. 147): 'peal of thunder' [EC; NIV, NRSV, TEV, TNT], 'thunder' [BAGD, BNTC, LN, Lns, WBC; CEV, KJV, NAB, NLT, REB], 'crash of thunder' [NET].
  d. pres. mid. (deponent = act.) indic. of ἐκπορεύομαι (LN 15.40) (BAGD 2. p. 244): 'to come out' [BAGD; CEV, NET], 'to come from' [BNTC, WBC; all versions except CEV, KJV, NET], 'to go out' [BAGD, LN, Lns], 'to proceed' [BAGD, EC; KJV], 'to depart out' [LN]. The present tense brings into the foreground these events that occur in heaven continually [WBC].
QUESTION—What does this picture of lightnings and sounds and thunder coming from the throne symbolize?
  It symbolizes: God's awesome power [Alf, Lns, NIC, TNTC]; God's majesty [Ld, NIC]; God's glory [Ld]; God's sovereignty [Alf]; God's displeasure and judgment [EC]. These same three items occur also in 8:5; 11:19 and 16:19 [ICC, NIC, NIGTC].

and seven torches^a of-fire burning^b before the throne, that are the seven spirits of-God,
LEXICON—a. λαμπάς (LN 6.102, 6.104) (BAGD 1. p. 465): 'torch' [BAGD, EC, LN (6.102), Lns, WBC; all versions except KJV, NIV, NLT], 'lamp'

[BNTC, LN (6.104); KJV, NIV], 'lampstands' [NLT]. The λαμπάς is a stick or club having one end wrapped in a pitch-soaked or resinous cloth that burned for a long time [TH]. Torches were used outdoors and are to be distinguished from lampstands [EC].

b. pres. pass. participle of καίω (LN 14.63) (BAGD 1.a. p. 396): 'to burn' [BAGD, BNTC, EC, LN, Lns, WBC; KJV, NAB, NRSV, REB, TEV], 'to be on fire' [LN]. The phrase πυρὸς καιόμεναι 'of fire burning' is translated 'with burning flames' [NLT], 'were burning' [CEV, NET, TNT], 'were blazing' [NIV]. The present tense indicates continual activity [TNTC].

QUESTION—How are the nouns related in the genitive construction τὰ ἑπτὰ πνεύματα τοῦ θεοῦ 'the seven spirits of God'?

The seven spirits belong to God or serve God [TH]. This refers to the Holy Spirit sent by God on a mission to earth [Lns].

QUESTION—What do the seven spirits of God represent?

See 1:4 for a discussion of this question.

4:6 and before the throne something-like[a] (a) sea[b] of-glass[c] like[d] crystal.[e]

LEXICON—a. ὡς (BAGD II.3.a.α. p. 897): 'something like' [BAGD, WBC; NET, NRSV], 'like' [NAB], 'something that looked like' [CEV], 'what looked like' [NIV, REB, TEV], 'what seemed to be' [TNT], 'what appeared to be' [BNTC], 'similar to' [EC], 'as it were' [Lns], not explicit [KJV, NLT]. See this word also at 1:10.

b. θάλασσα (LN 1.69) (BAGD p. 350): 'sea' [BAGD, BNTC, EC, LN, Lns, WBC; all versions].

c. ὑάλινος (LN **6.223**) (BAGD p. 831): 'of glass' [BAGD, BNTC, EC, **LN**; all versions except CEV, NLT], 'shiny (sea) of glass' [NLT], 'glassy' [LN, WBC], 'glass' [CEV], 'transparent' [Lns], 'transparent as glass' [BAGD]. This reminded him of a sea that was made out of glass [EC].

d. ὅμοιος (BAGD 1. p. 566): 'like' [BAGD, BNTC, LN, WBC; NET, NRSV, TNT], 'sparkling like' [NLT], 'like unto' [KJV], 'similar (to)' [BAGD, EC, Lns], 'clear as' [CEV, NIV, TEV], not explicit [NAB, REB]. See this word also at 1:13.

e. κρύσταλλος (LN **2.11, 2.46**) (BAGD p. 454): 'crystal' [BNTC, EC, **LN** (2.46), Lns, WBC; all versions], 'rock-crystal' [BAGD, **LN** (2.11)], 'ice' [LN (2.11)], 'sheet of ice' [REB]. The phrase ὁμοία κρυστάλλῳ 'like crystal' is translated 'crystal clear' [NAB]. Κρύσταλλος is a hard, transparent or translucent kind of quartz [LN].

QUESTION—What is symbolized by the 'sea of glass'?

It symbolizes: God's transcendence [NIC]; his holiness [TNTC]; his providence [Lns]; God's rule being pure, calm, and majestic [Alf]. It is a picture that emphasizes the majesty of God's presence [EC, Ld, NIC, TNTC]. It symbolizes the huge distance separating the throne from others [Sw]. It symbolizes the old order as a sea of evil from which arises the beast of 13:1 [BNTC].

And in (the) middle[a] of-the throne and around[b] the throne four living-creatures[c]

LEXICON—a. μέσος (See this word at 1:13): 'middle' [EC, LN; NET, TNT], 'midst' [LN, Lns, WBC; KJV], 'center' [LN; CEV, NIV, NLT, REB], 'very center' [NAB], 'on each side of' [NRSV, TEV], 'heart' [BNTC].

b. κύκλῳ (LN **83.19**) (BAGD 2. p. 457): 'around' [BAGD, EC, LN, WBC; all versions except KJV, REB, TEV], 'round about' [KJV], 'round' [REB], 'in a circle around' [**LN**], 'in a circle' [BAGD, LN], 'all around' [BAGD, BNTC], 'surrounding' [TEV], 'encircling' [Lns]. Also see a form of this word at 4:4.

c. ζῷον (LN 4.2, **12.32**) (BAGD 1. p. 341): 'living creature' [BNTC, LN (4.2); all versions except KJV, NLT], 'living being' [BAGD, EC, **LN** (12.32); NLT], 'living one' [Lns], 'cherubim' [WBC], 'beast' [KJV], 'living thing' [BAGD]. Ζῷον here refers to supernatural beings [LN (4.2, 12.32)]. It refers to beings that are neither human nor animals [BAGD]. Ζῷα is derived from ζάω 'to be alive' not from κρίζω 'to create', so 'living one' is a more exact translation [EC, Lns] and should not be taken as referring to beasts [EC].

QUESTION—What is the meaning of ἐν μέσῳ τοῦ θρόνου καὶ κύκλῳ θρόνου 'in the middle of the throne and around the throne'?

It indicates that each of the four creatures was located in the middle of each side of the throne and so were around the throne [Alf, ICC]. 'In the middle' should be taken to mean 'near' the throne, while 'around' specifies their relationship to it, that is, in a circle around it [EC, NIC, NIGTC, TH]. The idea is that one creature is in front, two to the sides, and one in back [EC, Sw]. The words have no spatial reference but rather refer to the rule of God that radiates from a center out in a circular pattern [Lns]. It is not indicated whether they were still or in motion around the throne, but a similar description in Ezek. 1:12 suggests a rapid circular movement [EC].

QUESTION—Who are the ζῷα 'living creatures'?

1. They are an order of angels [EC, ICC, NIC, WBC]. They are either one of the higher orders of angels or the highest [ICC]. They are cherubim [WBC] or bear a special relationship to them [EC].
2. They are either angelic beings or they represent the totality of creation [Ld]. They may represent the totality of creation praising God or they are created spirits similar to the seraphim of Isaiah 6:1–3 and the cherubim of Ezekiel 10:14 [Ld].
3. They should not be classified as either angels or cherubim [Lns, TH, TNTC]. In 5:11, 14 the living beings and angels occur together so they must be distinct [Lns]. They are neither animals nor human beings and are like the beings seen in Ezekiel 1:4–14 [TH]. Their closeness to the throne indicates that they are the most important of created beings [TNTC].

being-full[a] of-eyes in-front[b] and in-back.[c]
LEXICON—a. pres. act. participle of γέμω (LN 59.41) (BAGD 1. p. 153): 'to be full (of)' [BAGD, EC, LN; KJV, NET, NRSV, TNT], 'to contain' [LN], 'to be covered with' [WBC; CEV, NAB, NIV, NLT, REB, TEV], 'studded with' [Lns], 'all over' [BNTC].
  b. ἔμπροσθεν (LN **83.36**) (BAGD 1.a. p. 257): 'in front' [BAGD, EC, **LN**, WBC; NET, NIV, NRSV, REB, TEV, TNT], 'on the front' [**LN**], 'front' [BNTC; CEV, NAB, NLT], 'ahead' [BAGD], 'before' [Lns; KJV].
  c. ὄπισθεν (LN **83.41**) (BAGD 1.b. p. 574): 'in back' [EC, **LN**, WBC; NET, NIV], 'on the back of' [LN], 'behind' [BAGD, Lns; KJV, NRSV, REB, TEV, TNT], 'back' [BNTC, LN; CEV, NAB, NLT].
QUESTION—What is symbolized by this clause?
  It symbolizes the awareness and knowledge of the beings so that nothing gets by them [NIC]. It symbolizes vigilance and limitless intelligence [Ld]. It symbolizes alertness and full knowledge so that they are completely aware of what happens pertaining to their judicial responsibilities [EC]. It symbolizes that God knows everything [NTC, Wal].

4:7 **And the first living-creature (was) like (a) lion[a] and the second living-creature (was) like (an) ox[b]**
LEXICON—a. λέων (LN 4.14) (BAGD 1. p. 472): 'lion' [BAGD, BNTC, EC, LN, Lns, WBC; all versions].
  b. μόσχος (LN 4.17) (BAGD p. 528): 'ox' [BAGD, BNTC, EC, WBC; NAB, NET, NIV, NLT, NRSV, REB], 'bull' [CEV, TEV], 'young bull' [BAGD, Lns], 'calf' [BAGD, LN; KJV, TNT].

and the third living-creature had a face[a] like a-man[b]
LEXICON—a. πρόσωπον (LN 8.18) (BAGD 1.a. p. 720): 'face' [BAGD, BNTC, EC, LN, WBC; all versions], 'countenance' [BAGD, Lns].
  b. ἄνθρωπος (LN 9.1, 9.24): 'man' [EC, LN (9.24); KJV, NAB, NET, NIV, TNT], 'human' [WBC; CEV], 'human being' [LN (9.1), Lns], 'person, individual' [LN (9.1)]. This noun is also translated as an adjective: 'human (face)' [BNTC; NLT, NRSV, REB, TEV].

and the fourth living-creature (was) like (a) flying[a] eagle.[b]
LEXICON—a. pres. mid. (deponent = act.) participle of πέτομαι (LN 15.245) (BAGD p. 654): 'to fly' [BAGD, EC, LN, Lns, WBC; CEV, KJV, NET, NIV, NRSV, TNT]. This verb is also translated as a phrase: 'in flight' [BNTC; NAB, REB, TEV], 'with wings spread out as though in flight' [NLT].
  b. ἀετός (LN 4.42) (BAGD p. 19): 'eagle' [BAGD, BNTC, EC, LN, Lns, WBC; all versions], 'vulture' [LN].
QUESTION—What do these four living creatures symbolize?
  They may symbolize four aspects of nature: wild animals (lion), domesticated animals (ox), human beings (man), and birds (eagle) [Ld]. They symbolize the totality of animate creation [EC, NIC, NIGTC, NTC].

What is most noble, strong, wise, and swift in nature is represented by these beings [EC, Sw, TNTC]. The lion symbolizes the wild places of earth; the ox symbolizes the cultivated places, man symbolizes cities and towns, and the eagle symbolizes all the open sky [Lns].

QUESTION—What part of these animals are the living creatures like?

They are like the heads only [EC, TH]. Comparison with Ezek. 1:5 implies that all resemble human beings in form generally [EC].

4:8 **And the four living-creatures, each-one[a] of-them having six wings a-piece,[b]**

LEXICON—a. ἓν καθ' ἕν (BAGD 5.e. p. 232): 'each one' [BAGD, EC, Lns; NET]. The phrase ἓν καθ' ἕν... ἀνά 'each one...apiece' is translated 'each' [BNTC, WBC; all versions except NET].

b. ἀνά (LN 89.91) (BAGD 3. p. 49): 'apiece' [BAGD, EC, LN], 'each' [BAGD, LN], not explicit [BNTC, Lns, WBC; all versions].

QUESTION—What other Scriptural beings were these four living creatures like?

They were like the seraphim of Isaiah 6:2 who also had six wings [EC, Ld, Lns, NIC, Wal, WBC]. The seraphim in Isaiah 6:3 also attribute holiness to the Lord [TH, TNTC, Wal].

on-the-outside[a] and on-the-inside[b] they-are-full of-eyes,

LEXICON—a. κυκλόθεν (LN **83.22**) (BAGD 1. p. 456): 'on the outside' [**LN**, WBC], 'outside' [LN], 'all around' [NET, NIV, NRSV, REB], 'around' [EC, Lns; TNT], 'from all sides' [BAGD], not explicit [CEV, KJV]. The phrase κυκλόθεν καὶ ἔσωθεν 'outside and inside' is translated 'inside and out' [NLT, TEV], 'all over, inside and out' [BNTC; NAB]. See this word also at 4:3.

b. ἔσωθεν (LN 83.16) (BAGD 2. p. 314): 'on the inside' [LN, WBC], 'inside' [BNTC; NAB, NET, NLT, NRSV, REB, TEV], 'within' [BAGD, EC, LN, Lns; KJV, TNT], 'under his wings' [NIV], not explicit [CEV].

QUESTION—What is indicated by their being full of eyes ἔσωθεν 'on the inside'?

The eyes being on the inside indicates that they were on the undersides of their wings [Alf, EC, NIC, TH; NIV]. With eyes all around their bodies [EC, TH; NIV] and on the undersides of their wings, they were able to move their wings without hindering their vision [EC]. It indicates that the beings not only monitored all that was going on outside themselves, but inside as well, where they monitored God's will [Lns].

DISCOURSE UNIT: 4:8b–11 [NIGTC]. The topic is the heavenly beings praise God.

and they-have no pause[a] by-day and by-night saying,[b]

LEXICON—a. ἀνάπαυσις (LN **68.34**) (BAGD 1. p. 58): 'pause' [Lns], 'rest' [EC], 'stopping, ceasing' [BAGD]. The phrase ἀνάπαυσιν οὐκ ἔχουσιν 'they have no rest' is translated 'they never stopped' [**LN**; CEV, NIV,

TEV], 'they do not stop' [NAB], 'they rest not' [KJV], 'they never rest' [NET], 'they keep on' [NLT], 'unceasingly' [REB], 'they do not cease' [WBC], 'they never ceased' [BNTC], 'without ceasing' [BAGD; NRSV], 'without resting' [TNT].
  b. pres. act. participle of λέγω (LN 33.69): 'to say' [EC, LN, Lns; KJV, NET, NIV, NLT], 'to sing' [BNTC; CEV, NRSV, REB, TEV, TNT], 'to chant' [WBC], 'to exclaim' [NAB]. For 'saying', in this context, it is appropriate to translate it 'singing' or 'chanting' [TH].
QUESTION—What is meant by having no pause in what they are saying?
This is not their only activity. In 6:1, 3, 5, and 7 they summon the riders. Having no rest is qualified 'by day and by night'. This expresses the kind of time rather then the extent of time. This is their practice whenever they are not engaged in serving God in some other way [EC].

"Holy,[a] holy, holy, Lord God Almighty,[b] the-one (who) was and the-one being and the-one coming."
LEXICON—a. ἅγιος (BAGD 1.b.δ. p. 10): 'holy' [BAGD, BNTC, EC, Lns, WBC; all versions], 'dedicated to God, sacred' [BAGD]. Here ἅγιος indicates the separateness of God from created beings [EC, Lns, NIC, TH, TNTC], but includes the sense of purity as well [Lns, TH, TNTC]. See this word also at 3:7.
  b. παντοκράτωρ (LN **12.7**): 'Almighty' [EC, **LN**, Lns, WBC; all versions except CEV, NET, REB], 'All-Powerful' [NET], 'all-powerful' [CEV], 'Omnipotent' [BNTC]. This word is also translated as an adjective: 'sovereign (Lord) of all' [REB]. See this word also at 1:8.
QUESTION—To what does the 'coming' refer?
It refers to the time when God will come again to set up his kingdom on earth (see 11:17) [Ld, NIGTC].

4:9 And whenever the living-creatures will-give glory[a] and honor[b] and thanks[c] to-the-one sitting on the throne to-the-one living forever-and-ever,[d]
LEXICON—a. δόξα (See this word at 1:6): 'glory' [BNTC, EC, Lns, WBC; all versions except CEV]. The phrase δώσουσιν...δόξαν 'will give glory' is translated 'kept praising' [CEV]. The meaning of 'give glory' is to declare that God is full of glory, that is, majestic and wonderful [TH].
  b. τιμή (LN 87.4) (BAGD 2.b. p. 817): 'honor' [BAGD, BNTC, EC, LN, Lns, WBC; all versions except CEV], 'respect' [BAGD, LN], 'status' [LN]. The phrase δώσουσιν...τιμήν 'will give honor' is translated 'kept honoring' [CEV]. The meaning of 'give honor' is to declare that God is great, famous, and worthy of praise [TH].
  c. εὐχαριστία (LN 33.349) (BAGD 2. p. 328): 'thanks' [BNTC, EC; all versions except CEV, NAB], 'thanksgiving' [BAGD, LN, Lns, WBC], 'praise' [NAB], 'thankfulness' [LN], 'rendering of thanks' [BAGD]. The phrase δώσουσιν...εὐχαριστίαν 'will give thanks' is translated 'kept thanking' [CEV]. The meaning of 'give thanks' is to state one's gratitude for benefits received [TH].

d. εἰς τοὺς αἰῶνας τῶν αἰώνων (See this phrase at 1:6): 'forever and ever' [BNTC, EC, WBC; all versions], 'for the eons of the eons' [Lns].

QUESTION—Is this act of worship the same as that of 4:8 or different?

1. It is different than the worship of 4:8 [NIGTC, TNTC, Wal, WBC]. Here the fact of the worship is stated, but the content of the worship is not the same as the repetition of 'holy' in 4:8 [WBC]. This is a special worship apart from the activity of 4:8 [Wal]. It probably indicates that a variety of worship songs occur [TNTC].
2. It is the same worship as 4:8 [EC, ICC, TH; CEV]. 'Whenever' indicates that the praise of 4:8 is done repeatedly but not continuously [EC, ICC, TH]. This indicates that the praise of 4:9 and 10 is repeated as often as that of 4:8 [ICC].
3. It is an explanation of the worship 4:8 [Lns]. Saying, "Holy, holy, holy, Lord God Almighty, the one who was, the one being, and the one coming." *That is* they give glory and honor and thanks....

QUESTION—What is the significance of the future tense of 'give'?

'Whenever they shall give' means, 'as often as they give' [Sw]. The future tense should be translated as a present or subjunctive [Lns, Sw, WBC; all versions except CEV]: whenever they give. It should be translated as a past tense [BNTC]: whenever they gave.

4:10 the twenty-four elders will-fall-down[a] before the-(one) sitting on the throne and they-will-worship[b] the-(one) living into the ages of-the ages,

TEXT—Instead of the future tense προσκυνήσουσιν 'they will worship' some manuscripts possibly read the present tense προσκυνοῦσιν 'they worship', although GNT does not mention this alternative. The reading 'they worship' is taken by TR and KJV.

LEXICON—a. fut. mid. (deponent = act.) indic. of πίπτω (LN 17.22) (BAGD 1.b.α. p. 659): 'to fall down' [BAGD, BNTC, Lns; KJV, NAB, NIV, NLT, TEV], 'to kneel down' [CEV], 'to fall' [EC; NRSV, TNT], 'to throw oneself to the ground' [BAGD; NET], 'to prostrate oneself' [LN, WBC; REB]. This is done as a sign of devotion [BAGD]. Πίπτω indicates either to kneel down or to lie prostrate on the ground [TH]. This prone position is assumed in order to worship God [EC]. See this word also at 2:5.

b. fut. act. indic. of προσκυνέω (LN 53.56) (BAGD 2.a. p. 717): 'to worship' [BAGD, BNTC, EC, LN, WBC; all versions], 'to do obeisance to' [Lns], 'to bow down and worship, to prostrate oneself in worship' [LN]. See this word also at 3:9.

QUESTION—What is meant by προσκυνέω 'to worship'?

It means to acknowledge God's unique value and rank [TH]. It means to prostrate oneself in praise [Sw]. It means to convey by one's attitude and possibly by position one's commitment to and respect for God [LN]. It is to express their adoration to God [EC].

and they-will-throw[a] their crowns before the throne saying,

TEXT—Instead of the future tense βαλοῦσιν 'they will throw' some manuscripts read the present tense βάλλουσιν 'they throw'. GNT does not mention this alternative. The reading 'they throw' is taken by KJV.

LEXICON—a. fut. act. indic. of βάλλω (LN 85.34) (BAGD 2.b. p. 131): 'to throw' [Lns], 'to throw down' [NAB, TEV], 'to cast' [EC, WBC; KJV, NRSV], 'to lay down' [BAGD; TNT], 'to place' [CEV], 'to lay' [BNTC; NIV, NLT, REB], 'to put' [LN], 'to offer' [NET]. See this word also at 2.10.

QUESTION—What is symbolized by the crowns of the elders?

The crowns symbolize their: kingly authority [TH]; victory [Lns, Sw]; royalty [Lns]; eternal life [Sw].

QUESTION—What is symbolized by their 'throwing down their crowns before the throne'?

It symbolizes that in reality God is the source of one's: authority [NIC, NTC, TH, TNTC, Wal]; one's honor [Alf, Sw]; or one's victory [Lns, Sw]. It is a symbolic act of reverence [ICC, Sw, WBC]. It symbolizes their subordination to God [EC, Sw, WBC]. It symbolizes an act of honoring God as Creator and benefactor [NIGTC].

4:11 "You-are worthy,[a] our Lord and God, to-receive the glory[b] and the honor[c] and the power,[d]

TEXT—Instead of ὁ κύριος καὶ ὁ θεὸς ἡμῶν 'our Lord and God' some manuscripts read merely κύριε 'Lord'. GNT does not mention this alternative. The reading 'Lord' is taken by KJV.

LEXICON—a. ἄξιος (See this word at 3:4): 'worthy' [BAGD, BNTC, EC, LN, Lns, WBC; all versions]. Ἄξιος has the sense of deserving or having the right to receiving worship [TH]. It indicates that their worship is completely appropriate or fitting [WBC].

b. δόξα (LN 87.4, 33.357): 'glory' [BNTC, EC, Lns, WBC; all versions], 'honor' [LN (87.4)], 'praise' [LN (33.357)].

c. τιμή (LN 87.4) (BAGD 2.b p. 817): 'honor' [BAGD, BNTC, EC, LN, Lns, WBC; all versions], 'respect' [BAGD, LN].

d. δύναμις (LN) (BAGD 1. p. 207): 'power' [BNTC, EC, Lns, WBC; all versions].

QUESTION—What is indicated by the definite articles τὴν δόξαν καὶ τὴν τιμὴν καὶ τὴν δύναμιν '*the* glory and *the* honor and *the* power'?

They refer back to the 'glory' and 'honor' given by the 'living beings' of 4:9, but 'power' is substituted for 'thanks' [Alf, EC, Lns].

QUESTION—How are the nouns related in the genitive construction ὁ κύριος καὶ ὁ θεὸς ἡμῶν 'the Lord and God of us'?

This construction indicates the Lord and God whom we worship or serve [TH].

QUESTION—How does God 'receive power'?

He does not to be given power, he receives praise for his power [TH].

QUESTION—If God is the recipient of glory, honor, and power, who are the givers?

People are the givers of glory, honor, and power to God [TH].

because you created[a] all-things and by[b] your will[c] they-were and they-were-created."

TEXT—Instead of ἦσαν 'they were' some manuscripts read εἰσιν 'they are'. GNT selects the reading 'they were' with an A decision, indicating that the text is certain. 'They are' is apparently taken by CEV, KJV, NIV, NLT, REB.

LEXICON—a. aorist act. indic. of κτίζω (LN 42.35) (BAGD p. 455): 'to create' [BAGD, BNTC, EC, LN, Lns, WBC; all versions]. Κτίζω means to make something that has not existed before [LN, Lns].

    b. διά with accusative object (LN 90.8) (BAGD B.II.1. p. 181): 'by' [BAGD, BNTC, LN (90.8), WBC; CEV, NAB, NIV, NRSV, REB, TEV], 'because of' [EC; NET], 'for' [KJV, NLT], 'due to' [Lns, TNTC], 'in accordance with' [NIC]. This word is also translated: '(they) owe (their existence) to (your will)' [ICC, Sw; TNT]. Διά here indicates the reason why something happens [BAGD]. It indicates that God's will was the cause of creation [Alf, Ld, Lns, NIGTC, Sw].

    c. θέλημα (LN 30.59) (BAGD 2.b. p. 354): 'will' [BAGD, BNTC, EC, LN, Lns, WBC; all versions except CEV, KJV, NLT], 'decision' [CEV], 'pleasure' [KJV, NLT], 'plan, intent, purpose' [LN].

QUESTION—What word is emphasized in this clause?

The pronoun σύ 'you' is emphatic: [Lns, NIC]: you, yourself created all things.

QUESTION—What is the value of repeating κτίζω 'to create' both actively and passively?

It serves to emphasize the actual act of creation by the two historical aorist tenses [Lns].

QUESTION—In the phrase ἦσαν καὶ ἐκτίθησαν 'they were and were created', what is the significance of 'all things' being in existence before they were created?

1. It may be a figure of speech known as *hysteron-proteron* in which the events are simply inverted in time of occurrence [Ld, WBC].
2. The καί 'and' following 'they were' may be explanatory indicating 'that is' [Ld, WBC]: they were, *that is*, they were created.
3. It may mean that they existed in God's mind and/or will before he created them [ICC, Ld, NIC, Sw].
4. In effect it means simply that, 'they exist and were created' [NIGTC; CEV, KJV, NLT, TNT].
5. The two verbs should be reversed [BNTC; NIV, REB, TEV]: they were created and have their being.
6. The two verbs should be kept as they are [Lns; NAB, NET, NRSV]: they existed and were created.

DISCOURSE UNIT: 5:1–8:5 [TNTC]. The topic is the seven seals.

DISCOURSE UNIT: 5:1–8:1 [Ld]. The topic is the seven seals.

DISCOURSE UNIT: 5:1–14 [Alf, BNTC, EC, GNT, Ld, Lns, NIC, NIGTC, NTC, Sw, Wal, WBC; CEV, KJV, NAB, NET, NIV, NLT, TEV]. The topic is the scroll [BNTC], the scroll and the Lamb [EC, GNT, Lns, NIC, Sw, Wal; CEV, NAB, NIV, TEV], the sealed book [Alf, Ld], the Lamb is worthy [NTC], the investiture of the Lamb [WBC], heavenly worship [KJV], the opening of the scroll [NET, NLT].

DISCOURSE UNIT: 5:1–4 [TNTC, Wal]. The topic is the unopened book [TNTC], the book in God's right hand [Wal].

5:1 **And I-saw in[a] the right-hand of-the-one sitting on the throne (a) scroll[b] written on-the-inside[c] and on-the-back[d]**

TEXT—Instead of ὄπισθεν 'on the back', some manuscripts read ἔξωθεν, 'on the outside'. GNT does not mention this alternative, and for most versions it is difficult to determine which text was read.

LEXICON—a. ἐπί with accusative object (LN 83.46) (BAGD III.1.a.ζ. p. 288): 'in' [BNTC, WBC; all versions], 'upon' [LN, Lns], 'on' [EC, LN], 'at' [BAGD].

  b. βιβλίον (See this word at 1:11): 'scroll' [BNTC, EC, WBC; all versions except KJV], 'book' [Lns; KJV].

  c. ἔσωθεν (LN **83.16**): 'on the inside' [EC, **LN**, Lns; CEV, NLT, NRSV], 'inside' [BAGD, BNTC, LN, WBC; TNT], 'within' [BAGD, LN; KJV], 'on the front' [NET]. The phrase ἔσωθεν καὶ ὄπισθεν 'on the inside and on the outside' is translated 'on both sides' [NAB, NIV, REB, TEV]. 'Inside the scroll' refers to the inside before unrolling [EC]. See this word also at 4:8.

  d. ὄπισθεν (LN **83.21**): 'on the back' [BNTC, EC, WBC; NET, NRSV], 'on the back side' [KJV], 'on the outside' [**LN**, Lns; CEV, NLT], 'outside' [TNT], not explicit [NAB, NIV, REB, TEV]. 'On the back' refers to the back side of the scroll after it is unrolled [EC]. See this word also at 4:6.

QUESTION—What is the function of the phrase καὶ εἶδον 'and I saw'?

  It functions to introduce a new scene in the drama (see 5:2, 6, 11; 6:1, 12) [TH, WBC]. It simply marks the division between the contents of chapter 4 and that of 5 [Lns].

QUESTION—Where was the scroll located?

  1. It was located *in* the right hand of the one seated on the throne [NIC, TH, WBC; all versions]. Ἐπί has this meaning in 20:1 where the angel has a chain *in* his hand; and in 1:20 where Jesus speaks of the seven stars *in* his right hand [WBC].

  2. It was located *on* the open palm of the one seated on the throne [Alf, EC, ICC, Sw, TNTC]. The open hand could retain a round object without balancing it if it were cupped [EC].

3. It could be either *in* or *on* his hand so either a flat book or a scroll could be indicated [NIGTC].
4. It was located *at* the right hand of the one seated on the throne [BAGD].

QUESTION—Is the βιβλίον a book or a scroll?
1. It is a scroll [Alf, BNTC, EC, ICC, Ld, Lns, TH, TNTC, Wal, WBC; all versions except KJV]. A scroll consisted of sheets of papyrus joined together at the ends to form a long strip that was then rolled up into a tube-like roll [TH, TNTC]. It is a book-roll [Alf, ICC, Lns].
2. It is a book [KJV].

QUESTION—What are the contents of the scroll?
The contents of the scroll are: the destiny of the world [BNTC, ICC, NIC, Sw, TNTC]; the events described in 7:1–22:21 [Ld]; the events described in 6:1–22:21 [Lns]; the Revelation referred to in 1:1 [NTC]; the events that lead up to the end of the world and introduce us to the next [Ld]; the judgments that will fall upon the earth and the coming of the Messiah [EC].

QUESTION—What is the significance of the scroll's being written 'on the inside and on the back'?
It signifies that the contents were complete and required no addition [Alf, EC]. This fact, coupled with the seven seals, signify that the scroll contains a complete record without any gaps [Lns]. It signifies that the foreknowledge of God was complete and precise [BNTC].

sealed[a] with-seven seals.[b]

LEXICON—a. perf. pass. participle of κατασφραγίζω (LN **6.55**) (BAGD p. 419): 'to be sealed' [BAGD, BNTC, EC, **LN**, Lns, WBC; all versions except TNT], 'to be sealed up' [BAGD; TNT], 'to be made secure' [LN]. use a seal to close or to make something secure [LN].
b. σφραγίς (LN 6.62) (BAGD 1.a. p. 796): 'seal' [BAGD, BNTC, EC, LN, Lns, WBC; all versions except CEV]. The phrase σφραγῖσιν ἑπτά 'with seven seals' is translated 'in seven places' [CEV]. The seal was composed of a quantity of wax attached to the edge of the scroll to keep it closed [TH].

QUESTION—How were the seals placed on the scroll?
1. Each seal sealed a particular part of the scroll [EC, ICC, TNTC, Wal]. Chapter 6 describes what happens as each seal is broken indicating that each seal closed up only a part of the scroll which was then opened one section at a time [TNTC]. The seals would be visible at one end of the roll even though spaced at intervals throughout the inner part of the roll [EC].
2. All seven seals sealed the outside edge of the scroll [Alf, Ld, Lns, TH]. The scroll is inside its case with the seals sealing the case itself. As each seal is opened, the symbolism of the events contained in that section are revealed. [Lns]. The breaking of the seals does not entail the opening of the scroll but is preparatory to it. It is not until the 7th seal is broken that the scroll is opened and its contents are revealed [Ld]. The Apostle John could see all seven seals [Alf].

QUESTION—What is symbolized by the σφραγῖσιν ἑπτά 'seven seals'?
The number seven symbolizes: the fact that the scroll is absolutely inviolable [NIC]; the perfect security of its contents [Sw]; that it was completely sealed [Ld, TH], so it could not be unrolled [TH], and its contents completely hidden [Ld].

5:2 And I-saw (a) mighty^a angel proclaiming^b with (a) loud voice,

LEXICON—a. ἰσχυρός (LN 76.11, 79.63, 87.44) (BAGD 1.a. p. 383): 'mighty' [BAGD, BNTC, WBC; all versions except KJV, NET, NLT], 'strong' [BAGD, EC, LN (76.11, 79.63), Lns; KJV, NLT], 'powerful' [BAGD, LN (76.11, 87.44); NET], 'vigorous' [LN (79.63)], 'great' [LN (87.44)].
  b. pres. act. participle of κηρύσσω (LN **33.206**) (BAGD 1. p. 431): 'to proclaim' [BNTC, EC, **LN**, WBC; all versions except CEV, NLT, TEV], 'to announce' [BAGD, LN; TEV], 'to shout' [NLT], 'to ask' [CEV], 'to herald' [Lns], 'to make known' [BAGD]. Κηρύσσω indicates to announce as a herald [BAGD, LN, TH, Wal].

QUESTION—Why does a *mighty* angel proclaim this with a *loud* voice?
A mighty angel does this with a loud voice because it had to be heard in heaven and earth and under the earth [Alf, EC, Lns, NIC].

QUESTION—Who is this angel?
He may be the angel who ordered the scroll of Daniel 12 to be sealed up [NIGTC, Wal]. Since he is not named here, he was not known by name elsewhere in Scripture [EC].

"Who (is) worthy to-open^a the scroll and to-break^b its seals?"

LEXICON—a. aorist act. infin. of ἀνοίγω (BAGD 1.c. p. 71): 'to open' [BAGD, BNTC, EC, Lns, WBC; all versions]. 'To open' means to unroll the scroll [TH]. See this word also at 3:7.
  b. aorist act. infin. of λύω (LN 18.18) (BAGD 1.a. p. 483): 'to break' [BAGD, BNTC, EC, WBC; all versions except KJV], 'to loose' [Lns; KJV], 'to loosen' [LN]. See this word also at 1:5.

QUESTION—Why are the two actions 'to open' and 'to break' reversed in temporal or logical order?
  1. It is a figure of speech called *hysteron proteron* in which the logical order is reversed [NIC, Sw, TH]. The verb 'to open' is stated first because it is of utmost importance in the context [NIC, Sw].
  2. It is not a figure of speech, the second verb 'to break' explains the first [EC, Lns]: to open *by* breaking its seals.
  3. It is both 1 and 2 [WBC].

QUESTION—What sense of ἄξιος 'worthy' is in focus here?
The sense of being 'morally qualified' is in focus [ICC, NIC, Sw, TNTC]. Being only 'morally qualified' is too weak since it also includes the sense of being worthy in the quality of his being, person, power, and achievements [Lns]. The sense of being able [NIGTC] or having the authority to open the scroll is in focus [NIGTC, TH]. This refers both to Christ's office and to his moral qualifications [EC].

5:3 And no-one in heaven or on the earth or under[a] the earth was-able to-open the scroll or to-look-into[b] it.

TEXT—Some manuscripts include καὶ ἀναγνῶναι 'and to read' following ἀνοῖξαι 'to open'. GNT does not mention this alternative. These words are included by KJV.

LEXICON—a. ὑποκάτω with genitive object (LN 83.51) (BAGD p. 844): 'under' [BAGD, BNTC, EC, LN, WBC; all versions except TEV, TNT], 'beneath' [Lns; TNT], 'below' [BAGD]. The phrase ὑποκάτω τῆς γῆς 'under the earth' is translated 'in the world below' [TEV].

b. pres. act. infin. of βλέπω (BAGD 1.a., 3., p. 143): 'to look into' [BAGD, WBC; NET, NRSV], 'to look inside' [BNTC; NIV, REB TEV], 'to see inside' [CEV], 'to look at' [EC; TNT], 'to look in' [Lns], 'to look on' [KJV], 'to read' [NLT], 'to see' [BAGD]. The phrase βλέπειν αὐτό 'to look into it' is translated 'to examine its contents' [NAB]. See this word also at 3:18.

QUESTION—What is indicated by the phrase 'in heaven or on the earth or under the earth'?

It indicates: the whole universe [EC, Lns, NIC, TH, WBC]; or the whole of creation [ICC, NIC]. These three locales include the realm of heavenly beings, the realm of earthly beings and the realm of the dead [TH]. Another Scriptural reference where this phrase is used is Philippians 2:10 [ICC, NIC, Sw, TH, WBC], and there is an OT pattern in Ex. 20:4, 11; Ps. 146:6 [EC].

QUESTION—What is indicated by the phrase ὑποκάτω τῆς γῆς 'under the earth'?

It indicates: the world of the dead [Alf, EC, Lns, TH]; the underworld [WBC]; Hades (the Greek name) [Alf, ICC, Sw, TH]; or Sheol (the Hebrew name) [TH].

5:4 And I-was-weeping[a] much,[b] because no-one was-found[c] worthy to-open the scroll nor to-look-into it.

TEXT—Some manuscripts include the pronoun ἐγώ 'I' after καί 'and', in addition to its presence in the verb. GNT does not mention this variant. It is included by TR as well as by Alf and Lns.

TEXT—Some manuscripts include καὶ ἀναγνῶναι 'and to read' following ἀνοῖξαι 'to open'. GNT does not mention this alternative. The words 'and to read' is included by KJV.

LEXICON—a. imperf. act. indic. of κλαίω (LN 25.138) (BAGD 1. p. 433): 'to weep' [BAGD, BNTC, EC, LN, WBC; all versions except CEV, TEV], 'to cry' [BAGD; CEV, TEV], 'to sob' [Lns], 'to lament, to wail' [LN]. The imperfect tense indicates an inceptive aspect [BNTC, Lns, TH; NET, NRSV]: I began to weep.

b. πολύς (LN 59.11, 78.3) (BAGD I.2.c.β. p. 689): 'much' [EC, LN (59.11, 78.3), Lns; KJV], 'bitterly' [BNTC; NAB, NET, NRSV, REB, TEV, TNT], 'hard' [CEV], 'profusely' [WBC], 'greatly' [LN (78.3)], 'loudly' [BAGD], 'vehemently' [BAGD (1. p. 433)], 'a great deal' [LN (78.3)],

not explicit [NLT]. The phrase ἔκλαιον πολύ 'I wept much' is translated 'I wept and wept' [NIV].
c. aorist pass. indic. of εὑρίσκω (See this word at 3:2): 'to be found' [BNTC, EC, Lns, WBC; all versions].

QUESTION—Why did John weep?
He wept because he had been promised in 4:1 that he would be shown the future and now this promise was about to be frustrated [Alf, NIC, TNTC]. He wept because God's purposes would not be fulfilled [BNTC, EC, NIC, NIGTC, NTC]. He wept simply because no one was found who could open the scroll [ICC, Lns].

QUESTION—If the pronoun ἐγώ 'I' is included (see TEXT), what is its significance?
It makes the pronoun emphatic [Alf, Lns]: I myself.

DISCOURSE UNIT: 5:5–14 [TNTC]. The topic is the Lion of the Tribe of Judah.

DISCOURSE UNIT: 5:5–7 [Wal]. The topic is the Lamb declared worthy to receive the book.

5:5 And one of the elders says to-me, "Don't weep; look,[a] the Lion of the tribe of-Judah, the Root[b] of-David conquered,

LEXICON—a. ἰδού (See this word at 1:7): 'look' [CEV, NET, NLT, TEV], 'behold' [EC, WBC; KJV], 'see' [NIV, NRSV], 'lo' [Lns], not explicit [BNTC; NAB, REB, TNT].
b. ῥίζα (LN 10.33) (BAGD 2. p. 736): 'Root' [BNTC; KJV, NAB, NIV, NRSV], 'root' [EC; NET], 'Great Descendant' [CEV], 'great descendant' [TEV], 'descendant' [BAGD, LN, WBC; TNT], 'Shoot' [Lns], 'offspring' [LN]. The phrase ἡ ῥίζα Δαυίδ 'the root of David' is translated 'the heir to David's throne' [NLT], 'the shoot growing from David's stock' [REB]. Ῥίζα indicates 'a descendant of' [TH, TNTC].

QUESTION—What is the significance of the present prohibition μὴ κλαῖε 'Don't weep!'?
The present prohibition indicates that the action has already begun [EC, Lns, TH, TNTC, WBC; NET, NLT]: Stop weeping!

QUESTION—What is the purpose of the word ἰδού 'Look!'?
It clearly introduces the scene of the next verse [Alf, ICC]. It indicates that the following announcement is important [Lns].

QUESTION—How are the nouns related in the genitive construction ὁ λέων ὁ ἐκ τῆς πυλῆς Ἰουδά 'the Lion of the tribe of Judah'?
The Lion is from [Lns, TH], or belongs to the tribe of Judah [TH]. This is a Messianic title [Alf, Ld, NIC, TH, WBC]. The Scripture to which this title refers is Genesis 49:9, 10 [BNTC, EC, Ld, NIC, NIGTC, TH, TNTC, Wal, WBC]. The noblest descendant of the tribe is fitly called its lion [EC]

QUESTION—How are the nouns related in the genitive construction ἡ ῥίζα Δαυίδ 'the root of David'?

David is the source of the root [Alf, EC, Ld, Lns, TH, TNTC, WBC; CEV, REB, TEV, TNT]: the root springing out of David. The phrase indicates that Jesus was a descendant of David [Alf, EC, Ld, Lns, TH, TNTC; CEV, TEV]. This is a Messianic title [EC, NIC, NTC, TH]. The Scriptures to which this title refers is Isaiah 11:1, 10 [BNTC, EC, Ld, Lns, NIC, NTC, TH, Wal, WBC]. See a similar reference to this title in Revelation 22:16 [BNTC, LN, NTC, Sw, TH, WBC].

QUESTION—What is the image of the 'root of David' presented here?

It is the picture of a shoot emerging from an old plant [Alf, Ld, Lns]. David's kingdom is like a tree that has fallen, but a new shoot comes out of the stump with the purpose of restoring David's kingdom [Ld]. Since the shoot comes out of the old plant it represents it [Alf]. It is a metaphor meaning 'offspring' [EC].

QUESTION—To what specific event does ἐνίκησεν 'has conquered' refer?

It points to Christ's conquering by his self-sacrifice on the cross [Lns, Wal]. The tense of 'conquered' is aorist pointing to a specific event that occurred in the past [Alf, Lns]. As a lion he defeated the enemies of God [EC].

to-open the scroll and its seven seals."

TEXT—Some manuscripts include λῦσαι 'to loose' following τὸ βιβλίον καί 'the scroll and'. GNT does not mention this alternative. These reading 'to loose' is included by KJV.

QUESTION—What relationship is indicated by the infinitive ἀνοῖξαι 'to open'?

1. It indicates result [Alf, TH, WBC; NET, NRSV, TNT]: He has conquered *with the result that* he may open.
2. It indicates purpose [EC, ICC, Lns]: He has conquered *in order that* he may open. The result of winning the victory was only anticipated and therefore it should be called purpose [EC].

5:6 And I-saw in (the) midst of-the throne and of-the four living-creatures and in (the) midst of-the elders (a) lamb[a] standing as[b] having-been killed,[c]

TEXT—Some manuscripts include καὶ ἰδού 'and behold' following εἶδον 'I saw'. GNT does not mention this alternative. It is included by KJV.

LEXICON—a. ἀρνίον (LN 4.25, 4.26) (BAGD p. 108): 'lamb' [BAGD, LN (4.25), WBC], 'Lamb' [BNTC, EC, LN (4.26), Lns; all versions], 'sheep' [BAGD, LN (4.25)], 'ram' [LN (4.25)]. It is a designation of Christ [BAGD, LN (4.26)].

b. ὡς (See this word at 1:10): 'as' [EC, Lns; KJV], 'as though' [WBC]. The phrase ὡσ ἐσφαγμε'νον 'as having been slain' is translated 'as if it had been slaughtered' [NRSV], 'as if it had once been killed' [CEV], 'that appeared to have been killed' [BAGD; NET, TEV], 'looking as if it had been slain' [NIV, TNT], 'that had been killed' [NAB, NLT], 'with the marks of sacrifice (on him)' [REB], 'bearing the marks of slaughter'

[BNTC]. Ὡς does not indicate that the lamb only appeared to have been slain, but that in fact it had been slain [WBC].
c. perf. pass. participle of σφάζω (LN **20.72**) (BAGD p. 796): 'to be killed' [**LN**; CEV, NET, NLT, TEV], 'to be slain' [EC, Lns; KJV, NAB, NIV], 'to be slaughtered' [BAGD, BNTC, LN, WBC; NRSV, TNT], not explicit [REB]. The perfect tense indicates an action of the past the effects of which continue into the present [Lns, NIC, NIGTC, Sw, TNTC].

QUESTION—What is the significance of the diminutive form of ἀρνός 'sheep'?

It may emphasize the sense of meekness and innocence [Alf]. If the form had validity it stressed the contrast between the powerful Lion and the powerless Lamb [EC, NIGTC]. Although ἀρνίον is the diminutive of ἀρνός, this nuance had been lost by New Testament times [BAGD, NIGTC]. The diminutive distinction should not be insisted on [EC, Sw]. Ἀρνίον designates a sheep of any age [LN (4.25)]. Ἀρνίον indicates a lamb [BNTC, Lns, WBC; all versions].

QUESTION—Who is the Lamb?

The Lamb is Jesus Christ [BAGD, EC, ICC, Ld, LN, Lns, NIC, NIGTC, TH, TNTC, Wal, WBC]. This is the usual word for Christ in Revelation [TNTC].

QUESTION—What is symbolized by the figure of the slain lamb?

The figure symbolizes a sacrificial lamb [EC, NIGTC, NTC, TH, TNTC, Wal]. It was Christ's death to redeem his people as a sacrificial lamb that qualified him to open the scroll [EC].

QUESTION—What is the significance of showing the Lamb as standing?

It indicates: that the Lamb was alive [Alf, EC, Ld, Lns]; that he was ready for action [Lns, NIC]; that he had risen from death [NIGTC, Sw, WBC].

QUESTION—What is the meaning of the phrases: 'in the midst of the throne and the four living creatures' and 'in the midst of the elders'?

1. It has the meaning of 'among' or 'with' and here indicates simply that the Lamb was standing *close to* the throne [NIGTC, Sw, TH, WBC]. The throne is named, but the area around the throne is indicated by the figure of synecdoche [NIGTC].
2. It means that the Lamb was standing in the space between the two concentric circles formed by the four living creatures and the elders respectively [EC, ICC]. The Lamb is standing in the center of both the living beings and the elders who surround the throne. The 'coming' in 5:7 describes his movement from beside the Father to a place where he could receive the scroll [EC].
3. It means between the 24 elders and the combination of the throne and the four living beings [BNTC; REB]. It is probably a Hebrew figure where 'between A and between B' means 'between A and B' [BNTC]. It means he was standing between the throne and the elders but with the four living beings [REB].
4. It means between the four living creatures and the throne [NTC].

5. It means between the four living creatures and the throne but among the 24 elders [NLT, NRSV].
6. It indicates simply that the Lamb is in the center of the scene [Lns, TNTC].

QUESTION—What is the significance of the Lion of Judah of 5:5 being represented here as a Lamb, appearing to have been slain?

The victory of the Lion of Judah was only possible because he had suffered as a Lamb [Ld, NIGTC].

having seven horns[a] and seven eyes, that are the [seven] spirits of-God sent into all the earth.

TEXT—Some manuscripts omit ἑπτά 'seven' before πνεύματα 'spirits'. GNT includes this word in brackets with a C rating, indicating difficulty in deciding whether or not to include it in the text.

TEXT—Instead of the masculine plural without a definite article, ἀπεσταλμένοι 'sent', some manuscripts read the neuter plural with the definite article τὰ ἀπεσταλμένα 'the ones sent'. GNT does not mention this alternative.

LEXICON—a. κέρας (LN **8.17**) (BAGD 1. p. 429): 'horn' [BAGD, BNTC, EC, **LN**, Lns, WBC; all versions].

QUESTION—What do the seven horns symbolize?

The figure of a horn is a symbol of strength or power [BNTC, EC, ICC, Ld, Lns, Sw, TH, WBC]. Seven is the number of perfection [NIGTC, TNTC] or the number of fullness, indicating the fullness of his power [EC]. These coupled together indicate that the Lamb was all-powerful or omnipotent [BNTC, Ld, NIC, NIGTC, NTC, Sw, TNTC]. It indicates with Matthew 28:18 that all power had been given to the Lamb [Alf, Ld]. The figure seven is composed of 3 + 4 (3 for God, 4 for men), so the seven horns symbolize the power of God directed toward the world of men [Lns].

QUESTION—What do the seven eyes symbolize?

They symbolize: vision, intelligence, or wisdom [Ld]; that the Lamb was all-knowing or omniscient [BNTC, EC, ICC, Ld, TH, TNTC]; perfect wisdom [NIC, NTC]; omniscience or omnipresence [WBC]. They symbolize the Lamb as the wisdom of God (1 Corinthians 1:24) [BNTC].

QUESTION—What do the seven spirits of God symbolize?

1. They symbolize the Holy Spirit [Alf, EC, Lns, Wal]. It shows that all the powers of the Holy Spirit belong to Christ [Lns]. It is the Holy Spirit whom Christ sent into the world (John 16:7) [Wal]. The Spirit is Christ's agent for keeping in touch with the world [EC].
2. They may symbolize that the Lamb is omniscient [TNTC].
3. They are archangels, the same as 'the seven angels who stand before God' of 8:2 [WBC].

QUESTION—What is the antecedent of the clause 'that are the seven spirits of God'?

The antecedent is 'seven eyes' and does not include 'seven horns' [Lns, TH]: seven eyes that are the seven spirits of God.

QUESTION—Who is the implied actor of the passive ἀπεσταλμένοι 'sent'?

The implied actor is God [TH]: sent by God. The agent is the Lamb [Ld, Wal]: sent by the Lamb.

5:7 And he-came^a and has-taken (the scroll) from the right-hand of-the-one sitting on the throne.

TEXT—Some manuscripts include τὸ βιβλίον 'the scroll' following εἴληφεν 'took'. GNT does not mention this alternative. These words are included by KJV.

LEXICON—a. ἔρχομαι (BAGD I.1.a.δ. p. 310): 'to come' [BAGD, EC, Lns, WBC; KJV, NAB, NET, NIV, REB, TNT], 'to go' [BNTC; NRSV, TEV], 'to go over' [CEV], 'to step forward' [NLT]. This verb may be rendered 'to come' from the perspective of God, or 'to go' from the perspective of John [TH].

QUESTION—What is the significance of the perfect tense 'has taken'?

It is a historical perfect indicating that the scroll is now in the possession of the Lamb [EC, Lns]. It may be taken as an aoristic perfect indicating a simple past tense (took) or it may be indicating the abiding effects of the action, or it may be used to give the action realism [Sw]. Note: BNTC, WBC and all versions except NAB and REB render this tense as 'took'. NAB and REB render it as 'received'. Lns renders it as 'has taken'.

DISCOURSE UNIT: 5:8–10 [Wal]. The topic is the living creatures and elders worshiping the Lamb.

5:8 And when he-took the scroll, the four living-creatures and the twenty-four elders fell-down before the Lamb, each-one having (a) harp^a and golden bowls^b full of-incense,^c

TEXT—Instead of the singular κιθάραν 'harp' some manuscripts read the plural κιθάρας 'harps'. GNT does not mention this alternative. The reading 'harps' is taken by KJV.

LEXICON—a. κιθάρα (LN **6.83**) (BAGD p. 432): 'harp' [BAGD, BNTC, EC, LN; all versions], 'lyre' [BAGD, **LN**], 'zither' [Lns], 'kithara' [WBC]. A κιθάρα is a small harp [LN], smaller than modern harps [TH].

  b. φιάλη (LN **6.124**) (BAGD p. 858): 'bowl' [BAGD, BNTC, EC, **LN**, Lns; all versions except KJV, NAB], 'bowl used in offerings' [BAGD], 'vessel' [NAB], 'pan' [WBC], 'vial' [KJV]. A φιάλη is a flat bowl, not a vial with a slender neck [EC, Lns].

  c. θυμίαμα (LN **6.211**) (BAGD 1.b. p. 365): 'incense' [BAGD, BNTC, EC, **LN**, WBC; all versions except KJV, NAB], 'incense odors' [Lns], 'aromatic spices' [NAB], 'odor' [KJV].

QUESTION—What is the significance of the Lamb's taking the scroll?

The action of taking and opening the scroll symbolizes the Lamb's authority over God's plan for saving men and judging the world [NIGTC]. It signals the start of converting the contents of the scroll into reality [EC].

QUESTION—Why did the four living beings and 24 elders fall down before the Lamb?

It was an act of worship [Alf, EC, Lns, NIC, Sw, TH, TNTC, Wal, WBC]. The fact that the Lamb is worshiped is proof of his deity for in Revelation God alone is worshiped (see 22:9) [TNTC].

QUESTION—What does a κιθάρα 'harp' symbolize?

A harp is a symbol of the worship of God [EC, Wal]. In Revelation it is always associated with the praise of God [TNTC]. In Psalm 33:2 the harp is associated with praise [Ld, NIC].

QUESTION—Who had the harps and bowls?

1. Only the 24 elders had the harps and bowls [Alf, BNTC, EC, ICC, Lns, NIC, NIGTC, NTC, Sw]. The participle 'having' is masculine, agreeing with the masculine noun 'elders', not with the neuter noun 'living beings' [NIGTC]. The following context shows that the four living beings must not be indicated here [Sw].
2. Both the 24 elders and the four living creatures had the harps and bowls [Ld, TH, TNTC, Wal].

QUESTION—What does this reaction by the living beings and the elders to the Lamb's taking of the scroll indicate?

Their immediate reaction to the Lamb's taking the scroll stresses the significance of that act [WBC].

which are the prayers[a] of-the saints,[b]

LEXICON—a. προσευχή (LN 33.178) (BAGD 1. p. 713): 'prayer' [BAGD, BNTC, EC, LN, Lns, WBC; all versions].

b. οἱ ἅγιοι (LN 11.27): 'saints' [Lns; KJV, NET, NIV, NRSV], 'God's people' [BNTC, Ld, LN, WBC; CEV, NLT, REB, TEV, TNT], 'God's holy people' [NAB]. The ἅγιοι are Christians [ICC, Lns], that is, those who are dedicated to God [ICC]. It is their relationship to God that is in view here, not their purity [WBC].

QUESTION—What is the antecedent of αἵ 'which' in this clause?

1. Only the 'incense' (feminine plural) is the antecedent of 'which' [EC, ICC, Lns, NIGTC, Sw, TNTC]: incense *which is* the prayers of the saints. Although αἵ 'that' is feminine, not agreeing with the neuter 'incense', it is feminine by attraction to the following feminine noun προσευχαί 'prayers' [EC, ICC, NIGTC, Sw]. The prayers are incense and they are offered in golden bowls [TNTC]. The fragrant odor symbolizes the prayers, not the bowls that contained it [Lns]. Prayer is identified with incense in 8:3–4 [NIGTC].
2. The 'bowls' (neuter plural) are the antecedent of 'which' [Alf, TH, Wal; and probably the versions which translate 'which are' in agreement with

the plural 'bowls' and not with the singular 'incense': CEV, NAB, NET, NIV, NRSV, TEV, TNT]: the bowls full of incense *which are* the prayers of the saints. It is the bowls filled with incense that are the prayers of the saints [Alf, TH].

QUESTION—What Scripture shows the relation between incense and prayer?
Psalm 141:2, "May my prayer be set before you like incense; may the lifting up of my hands be like the evening sacrifice," indicates that the psalmist's prayer was like incense [Ld, Lns, NIC, TH, Wal, WBC].

5:9 **and they sing**[a] **(a) new**[b] **song,**[c] **saying, "You-are worthy to-take the scroll and to-open its seals,**

LEXICON—a. pres. act. indic. of ᾄδω (LN 33.109) (BAGD p. 19): 'to sing' [BAGD, BNTC, EC, LN, Lns, WBC; all versions].

b. καινός (LN 28.33, 58.71, 67.115): 'new' [BNTC, EC, LN (28.33, 58.71, 67.115), Lns, WBC; all versions], 'recent' [LN (67.115)], 'previously unknown, previously unheard of' [LN (28.33)]. It means that it is new or recent [LN (58.71, 67.115)] and, because of that, is superior to the old [LN (58.71)], or that it was not known previously [LN (28.33)]. See this word also at 2:17.

c. ᾠδή (LN 33.110) (BAGD p. 895): 'song' [BAGD, BNTC, EC, LN, Lns, WBC; all versions except NAB], 'hymn' [NAB]. In our literature ᾠδή is only a sacred song or song of praise to God [BAGD]. In the New Testament it only indicates a sacred song [TNTC].

QUESTION—Who sang the new song?
1. The elders who held the harps sang the song [ICC, NIC, NIGTC].
2. The elders and the four living beings sang the song [EC, Lns, TH]. Both groups had fallen down before the Lamb (5:8) [EC].

QUESTION—In what sense was the song καίνος 'new'?
Καίνος indicates new in quality and nature, superior to the old [NIC]. It was new in that it depicted the Lamb's new covenant of redeemed people in contrast to the old covenant [Alf, ICC, Ld, NIC, TNTC]. It was new as a song is new that is composed for a special occasion [EC, Ld, WBC]. It was new in the sense of being fresh [Alf, TNTC]. It was new in that it had never been sung before [TH].

QUESTION—What is the function of λέγοντες 'saying'?
It functions to introduce a quote and so is the equivalent of quote marks [BNTC, Lns, TH, WBC; all versions except KJV, NLT].

QUESTION—What does 'opening the seals of the scroll' imply?
It implies the setting up of God's Kingdom on the basis of Christ's having paid the price with his life [Ld].

because you-were-slain and you-purchased[a] **for-God with**[b] **your blood**[c] **some-from every tribe**[d] **and language**[e] **and people**[f] **and nation**[g]

TEXT—Some manuscripts include ἡμᾶς 'us' either before or following τῷ θεῷ 'for God'. It is omitted by GNT with an A rating, indicating that the text is certain. The reading 'us' is included by KJV.

142   REVELATION 5:9

LEXICON—a. aorist act. indic. of ἀγοράζω (LN 37.131) (BAGD 2. p. 13): 'to purchase' [NAB, NET, NIV, TNT], 'to buy' [BAGD, LN, Lns; CEV, REB, TEV], 'to redeem' [EC, LN, WBC; KJV], 'to ransom' [BNTC; NLT, NRSV], 'to set free' [LN], 'to acquire as property' [BAGD]. Ἀγοράζω is used figuratively here to indicate affecting the release of someone by paying a price (see 1 Corinthians 6:20, 7:23) [WBC]. It is based on the idea of a slave obtaining his freedom by paying a sum of money [Ld]. See this word also at 3:18.
  b. ἐν with dative object (LN 90.10) (BAGD III.1.a. p. 260): 'with' [BNTC, EC, LN; CEV, NAB, NIV], 'by' [LN, WBC; KJV, NRSV, REB, TEV, TNT], 'in connection with' [Lns]. The phrase ἐν τῷ αἵματα σου 'with your blood' is translated 'at the cost of your own blood' [NET], 'your blood has ransomed' [NLT]. Ἐν indicates the price of the purchase [ICC, Ld, Lns, NIC, NIGTC, Sw, TH, TNTC, WBC; NET, NLT]. It names the means by which something is accomplished [Alf, TH].
  c. αἷμα (See this word at 1:5): 'blood' [BNTC, EC, Lns, WBC; all versions except TEV, TNT], 'life-blood' [BNTC], 'death' [WBC; TNT], 'sacrificial death' [TEV]. 'Blood' here as in 1:5 indicates Christ's sacrificial death [TH].
  d. φυλή (See this word at 1:7): 'tribe' [BNTC, EC, Lns, WBC; all versions except KJV, NAB], 'race' [NAB], 'kindred' [KJV]. This focuses on those united by family lineage [EC, Lns].
  e. γλῶσσα (LN 33.2) (BAGD 2. p. 162): 'language' [BAGD, LN; all versions except KJV, NAB], 'tongue' [BNTC, EC, Lns, WBC; KJV, NAB], 'dialect, speech' [LN].
  f. λαός (LN 11.55) (BAGD 2. p. 466): 'people' [BAGD, BNTC, EC, LN, Lns, WBC; all versions except CEV, REB, TEV], 'nation' [LN; CEV, REB, TEV].
  g. ἔθνος (See this word also at 2:26): 'nation' [BNTC, EC, Lns, WBC; all versions except CEV, REB, TEV], 'race' [CEV, REB, TEV], 'people' [LN].

QUESTION—What relationship is indicated by ὅτι 'because'?
  It indicates that the following three actions (being slain, purchasing people with his blood, and making them a kingdom and priests) form the *grounds* for the worthiness of the Lamb [EC, Lns, NIC, NIGTC, WBC]. His sacrificial death is the *grounds* of his being worthy [Sw, TNTC]. These three actions are the equivalent of Christ's conquering in 5:5 and therefore being able to open the scroll [NIGTC].

QUESTION—What is the significance of the aorist tense of ἐσφάγης 'were slain'?
  It is a historical aorist and points to Christ's death on Calvary [BNTC, EC, Lns, NIC].

QUESTION—What is the implied object of ἠγόασας 'purchased'?

The implied object is: people [WBC; CEV, NET, NLT, REB, TEV]; us [KJV]; men [BNTC, Ld; NAB, NIV, TNT]; saints [NRSV]; some [Lns]; representatives [Sw].

QUESTION—What is the meaning of τῷ θεῷ 'for God'?

It means: for the purpose of belonging to God [Ld, TH, TNTC]; for God's service [Sw]; for the benefit of God [EC, Lns]. Those who are purchased are destined for serving God [EC].

QUESTION—What is the purpose of the phrase 'from every tribe and language and people and nation'?

It indicates everyone in the whole world [EC, Ld, NIGTC, Wal], in the universe [Alf, NIC, TNTC]. The fourfold repetition functions to emphasize the universality [NIC, WBC]. It functions to include all people who have either a common ancestry, language, nation, or race [TH]. It includes all inhabitants of the earth without distinction but not without exception [NIGTC].

5:10 **and you-made them (a) kingdom and priests for our God, and they-will-reign[a] on the earth."**

TEXT—Instead of αὐτούς 'them', some manuscripts read ἡμᾶς 'us'. GNT selects the reading αὐτούς 'them' with an A rating, indicating that the text is certain. The reading 'us' is taken by KJV.

TEXT—Instead of βασιλείαν 'kingdom', some manuscripts have βασιλεῖς 'kings'. GNT does not mention this alternative. The reading 'kings' is taken by KJV.

TEXT—Instead of βασιλεύσουσιν 'they shall reign' some manuscripts read βασιλεύουσιν 'they reign' while other manuscripts read βασιλεύσομεν 'we shall reign'. GNT reads βασιλεύσουσιν 'they shall reign' with an A rating, indicating that the text is certain. The reading 'they reign' is supported by Alf, ICC, Lns, NIGTC, Sw, TNTC. The reading 'we shall reign' is taken by KJV. All other commentaries and versions support the reading 'they shall reign' with GNT.

LEXICON—a. fut. act. indic. of βασιλεύω (LN 37.64) (BAGD 1.b.δ. p. 136): 'to reign' [BNTC, EC, LN, Lns, WBC; all versions except CEV, TEV], 'to rule' [BAGD, LN; CEV, TEV], 'to be a king' [LN].

QUESTION—Where is a similar clause to this treated?

See an almost identical reference to being made a kingdom and priests for God at 1:6.

QUESTION—What does the phrase τῷ θεῷ ἡμῶν 'for our God' imply?

It implies for the service of God [BNTC, NIC; NAB, NET, NIV, NRSV, TEV]. It implies that they belong to God [TNTC].

QUESTION—Is the pronoun ἡμῶν 'our' inclusive or exclusive?

The pronoun is inclusive since it addresses the Lamb who belongs to God as well [TH].

QUESTION—Does the action βασιλεύσουσιν 'they shall reign' refer to the millennial reign of Christ?
1. It refers to the millennial reign of believers with Christ (see chapter 20) [EC, ICC, Ld, Wal].
2. It does not necessarily refer to the millennial reign [BNTC, Lns, TNTC].

QUESTION—If the present tense βασιλεύουσιν 'they reign' is taken, what does it indicate?
1. It should be taken as a present tense and indicates that the reign of believers on earth has begun [Alf, Lns, NIGTC, Sw]. The reign of believers has begun in life in the Holy Spirit, but a more complete realization of the Kingdom of God is still future [Sw]. Believers began to reign following Christ's death [NIGTC]. As the world and the devil are ruling now, so are believers [Lns]. The present tense adds a sense of certainty to the action [TNTC].
2. It should be taken as a futuristic present [ICC, NIC]: they will reign. The present tense adds a sense of assurance to the fulfillment of the verb [NIC]. The present tense anticipates the Millennial reign of chapter 20 as though it were already occurring [ICC].

DISCOURSE UNIT: 5:11–12 [Wal]. The topic is the worship of the angels.

5:11 **And I-looked, and I-heard (the) voice of-many angels around the throne and the living-creatures and the elders, and the number of-them was ten-thousands[a] of-ten-thousands and thousands[b] of-thousands**

LEXICON—a. μυριάς (LN 60.8, 60.45) (BAGD 2. p. 529): 'ten thousand' [EC, LN (60.45); KJV, NAB, NET], 'myriad' [BNTC, Lns, WBC; NRSV, REB, TNT], 'million' [NLT, TEV], 'innumerable' [LN (60.8)], 'countless' [LN (60.8)], 'many many' [LN (60.8)]. Μυριάς indicates a very large but indefinite number [BAGD]. The phrase μυριάδες μυριάδων 'ten thousands of ten thousands' is translated 'countless thousands' [BAGD], 'ten thousand times ten thousand' [KJV, NET, NIV], 'myriad(s) on myriad(s)' [BNTC; REB], 'myriads and myriads' [WBC]. The phrase μυριάδες μυριάδων καὶ χιλιάδες χιλιάδων 'ten thousands of ten thousands and thousands of thousands' is translated 'millions and millions' [CEV], 'thousands and millions' [NLT, TEV], 'countless (in number) thousands and tens of thousands' [NAB].

b. χιλιάς (LN **60.80**) (BAGD p. 882): 'thousand' [BAGD, EC, LN, Lns; KJV, NAB, NIV, NLT, NRSV, REB, TEV, TNT]. The phrase χιλιάδες χιλιάδων 'thousands of thousands' is translated 'thousands upon thousands' [BAGD, BNTC, **LN**; NIV, REB], 'thousands and thousands' [WBC]. The phrase χιλιάδες χιλιάδων 'thousands of thousands' is a way of expressing an enormous number [LN].

QUESTION—What is the function of the phrase καὶ εἶδον 'and I saw'?
It introduces a new part of the vision [ICC, Sw].

QUESTION—What is the meaning of μυριάδες μυριάδων καὶ χιλιάδες χιλιάδων 'ten thousands of ten thousands and thousands of thousands'?

It is an expression that indicates an innumerable number [Alf, EC, ICC, Ld, NIC, TNTC]. A similar expression in a similar scene occurs in Daniel 7:10 [ICC]. The genitives 'ten thousands *of ten thousands* and thousands *of thousands*' indicate 'times' or 'multiplied by' [Lns]: ten thousand *times* ten thousand and thousands *times* thousands.

5:12 saying with-(a) loud voice, "Worthy is the Lamb who was-slain to-receive the power[a] and riches[b] and wisdom[c] and strength[d] and honor[e] and glory[f] and praise."[g]

LEXICON—a. δύναμις (See this word at 4:11): 'power' [BNTC, EC, Lns, WBC; all versions].

b. πλοῦτος (LN 57.30) (BAGD 2. p. 674): 'riches' [EC, LN, Lns; CEV, KJV, NAB, NLT, REB, TNT], 'wealth' [BAGD, BNTC, LN, WBC; NET, NIV, NRSV, TEV], 'abundance' [BAGD, LN].

c. σοφία (LN 32.32, 32.37) (BAGD 3.a. p. 760): 'wisdom' [BAGD, BNTC, EC, LN (32.32, 32.37), Lns, WBC; all versions], 'insight, understanding' [LN (32.37)].

d. ἰσχύς (LN 79.62) (BAGD p. 383): 'strength' [BAGD, EC, LN, Lns;, all versions except NET, NRSV, REB], 'might' [BAGD, BNTC, WBC; NET, NRSV, REB], 'power' [BAGD].

e. τιμή (See this word at 4:11): 'honor' [BAGD, BNTC, EC, LN, Lns, WBC; all versions], 'respect' [BAGD, LN].

f. δόξα (See this word at 4:11): 'glory' [BNTC, EC, Lns, WBC; all versions].

g. εὐλογία (LN 33.356, 33.470) (BAGD 1. p. 322): 'praise' [BAGD, LN (33.356), WBC; all versions except KJV, NLT, NRSV], 'blessing' [BNTC, EC, LN (33.470), Lns; KJV, NLT, NRSV].

QUESTION—What is the function of the single article with all seven attributes?

The single article functions to unite the seven attributes as though they were a single unit [Alf, EC, ICC, NIC, WBC]. It may indicate that these all as a unit describe God and that the Lamb shares in these attributes [Alf]. Even though viewed as a group, the repetition of 'and' between each attribute stresses the dignity of each one [EC].

QUESTION—What does it mean 'to receive power, riches, wisdom....'?

It means to receive praise for these qualities [Alf, EC, TH]: worthy to receive praise for his power, riches, wisdom....

QUESTION—How are the seven attributes divided?

The first four nouns, power, riches, wisdom, and strength, are qualities that the Lamb possesses [ICC, NIC, TNTC], the last three nouns, honor, glory, and praise, are the response toward him of others [ICC, Lns, NIC, TNTC]. The first six are attributes or qualities of the Lamb, the last is praise that is offered to him [TH]. The first four are either qualities the Lamb possesses or qualities that he will soon assume [ICC]. The seven form a complete ascription of praise indicating that all that belongs to God also belongs to the Lamb [Ld]. This praise to the Lamb is similar to the praise of God in 4:11 [TH].

DISCOURSE UNIT: 5:13–14 [Wal]. The topic is the worship all creation.

5:13 **And I-heard every creature[a] that (is) in heaven and on the earth and under the earth and on the sea and all-things in them saying,**

TEXT—Some manuscripts include ἅ ἐστιν 'that are' after θαλάσσης 'sea'. It is omitted by GNT with a B rating, indicating that the text is almost certain. The words 'that are' are included by KJV.

LEXICON—a. κτίσμα (LN 42.38) (BAGD p. 456): 'creature' [BAGD, EC, LN, Lns; all versions except CEV, REB, TNT], 'created thing' [REB, TNT], 'created being' [WBC], 'being' [CEV], '(the whole) creation' [BNTC].

QUESTION—What is the function of the phrase τὰ ἐν αὐτοῖς πάντα 'all things in them'?

It functions to emphasize the fact that *all* creatures are included [Lns, NIC, TH, TNTC].

QUESTION—Who is included in this group?
1. Absolutely every creature is included [BNTC, NIGTC]. It even includes hostile beings (see Colossians 1:20) [BNTC].
2. All creatures except the demons are included [Alf, Ld, Lns]. It includes angels, believers who have died, inhabitants of Hades and sea life [Alf].

QUESTION—To what place does the phrase ὑποκάτω τῆς γῆς 'under the earth'?

It refers to Hades [ICC].

"To-the-one sitting on the throne and to-the Lamb (be) the praise[a] and the honor and the glory and the might[b] into-the-ages-of-the-ages."[c]

LEXICON—a. εὐλογία (LN **33.356**): 'praise' [BAGD, **LN**, WBC; all versions except KJV, NLT, NRSV], 'blessing' [BNTC, EC, Lns; KJV, NLT, NRSV]. See this word also at 5:12.

b. κράτος (See this word at 1:6): 'might' [BNTC, EC, LN, Lns; NAB, NRSV, REB, TEV], 'power' [WBC; KJV, NIV, NLT], 'ruling power' [NET], 'strength' [CEV], 'sovereignty' [TNT].

c. εἰς τοὺς αἰῶνας τῶν αἰῶνον (See this phrase at 1:6 and 1:18): 'forever and ever' [BNTC, EC, Lns, WBC; all versions except REB], 'for ever' [WBC; REB], 'for the eons of the eons' [Lns].

QUESTION—What is the significance of this praise being given to both the One Sitting on the throne and to the Lamb?

It shows that the Lamb also receives the worship reserved for God alone [ICC, Ld, NIGTC, TNTC]. They share the throne, and worship that is offered to one is offered to the other [EC, ICC].

QUESTION—What is the significance of the article being repeated before each attribute in the phrase ἡ εὐλογία καὶ ἡ τιμή καὶ ἡ δόξα καὶ τὸ κράτος 'the praise and the honor and the glory and the might'?

The presence of the article before each noun serves to emphasize that particular noun [EC, Lns, Sw, TNTC].

5:14 And the four living-creatures were-saying, "Amen." And the elders fell-down and worshiped.

TEXT—Some manuscripts possibly include εἰκοσιτέσσαρες 'twenty-four' before πρεσβύτεροι 'elders', although GNT does not mention this alternative. It is included by TR and KJV.

TEXT—Some manuscripts include ζῶντι εἰς τοὺς αἰῶνας τῶν αἰῶνον '(the one) living into the ages of the ages' after προσεκύνησαν 'worshiped'. GNT does not mention this alternative. It is included by TR and KJV.

LEXICON—a. ἀμήν (See this word at 1:6): 'amen' [BNTC, Lns, WBC; all versions]. This word means 'so be it' or 'it is so' [TH], showing that the four living creatures agree with the praise of all creation [Alf, ICC, NIGTC, TH].

QUESTION—What is the significance of the imperfect tense ἔλεγον 'were saying'?

It signifies a repetitive aspect [EC, Lns]: they kept saying. If the imperfect does signify a repetitive aspect, then it indicates that the living creatures say "Amen" after the naming of each of the seven in 5:12, followed by the four attributes in 5:13 [Lns, NIC].

DISCOURSE UNIT: 6:1–8:5 [NIGTC, NTC]. The topic is the seven seals.

DISCOURSE UNIT: 6:1–8:1 [Alf, NIC, TH; REB]. The topic is the seven seals.

DISCOURSE UNIT: 6:1–17 [GNT, ICC, Ld, Lns, Sw, WBC; CEV NET]. The topic is the seals [GNT; KJV, NIV, TEV], the six seals [ICC, Ld, Lns, Sw, WBC; NAB, NLT], the seven seals [NET].

DISCOURSE UNIT: 6:1–8 [Alf, BNTC, NIC, NIGTC, WBC]. The topic is the first four seals [Alf, NIC, NIGTC], the four horsemen [BNTC, WBC].

DISCOURSE UNIT: 6:1–2 [EC, Ld, NTC, TNTC, Wal, WBC]. The topic is the first seal.

6:1 And I-saw when the Lamb opened[a] one of the seven seals, and I-heard one of the four living-creatures saying as (with a) voice[b] of-thunder,[c] "Come."[d]

TEXT—Some manuscripts include καὶ ἴδε 'and see' after ἔρχου 'Come!'. The words are omitted by GNT with a B rating, indicating that the text is almost certain. The words 'and see' are included by KJV.

LEXICON—a. aorist act. indic. of ἀνοίγω (BAGD 1.d. p. 71): 'to open' [BAGD, EC, Lns, WBC; CEV, KJV, NET, NIV, NRSV, TNT], 'to break' [BNTC; NLT, REB], 'to break open' [NAB, TEV].
- b. φωνή (BAGD 1. p. 870): 'voice' [BNTC, EC, Lns, WBC; all versions except KJV], 'noise' [KJV], 'sound' [BAGD]. See this word also at 1:10 and 3:20.
- c. βροντή (See this word at 4:5): 'thunder' [BNTC, EC, Lns, WBC; all versions except NET]. This noun is also translated as an adjective: 'thunderous' [NET].
- d. pres. mid. (deponent = act.) impera. of ἔρχομαι (See this word at 1:4): 'to come' [BNTC, EC, WBC; all versions except CEV, NAB], 'to come out' [CEV], 'to come forward' [NAB], 'to go' [Lns]. Ἔρχομαι may indicate either 'to come' or 'to go' [Lns, WBC]. Here it has the sense of 'Be on your way!' [Lns].

QUESTION—To whom is the command Ἔρχου, 'Come!' addressed?
1. It is addressed to a horseman [EC, ICC, Ld, Lns, NIC, NIGTC, NTC, TH, TNTC, WBC]. The horsemen are summoned, this is the most natural interpretation. If it were addressed to John, the verb δεῦρο 'come' would have been used as in 17:1 and 21:9 [ICC]. The response to this command is the appearance of the first horseman in 6:2 [EC].
2. It is addressed to John [Wal; KJV]: Come and see!
3. It is addressed to Christ [Alf, Sw]. This reflects the groaning of all creation to see the revealing of the sons of God, and it is expressed as a prayer to Christ [Alf]. In Revelation the verb ἔρχομαι 'to come' is used of God or of Christ [Sw].

QUESTION—In the figure of 'thunder', what particular feature is being symbolized?

The aspect of loudness is being symbolized [TH, WBC]: loud like thunder. Elsewhere in Revelation thunder is used to depict a very loud voice (see 14:2 and 19:6) [WBC].

QUESTION—From where was the one addressed expected to come?

Since he was a messenger of God he probably came from heaven [TH].

6:2 **And I-looked, and behold[a] (a) white horse, and the-one sitting on it having (a) bow[b] and (a) crown was-given to-him**

TEXT—The words καὶ εἶδον 'and I saw' do not occur in some manuscripts. They are included by GNT with a B rating, indicating that the text is almost certain.

LEXICON—a. ἰδού (See this word at 1:7): 'behold' [EC; KJV], 'behold, there was' [WBC], 'here came' [NET], 'there was' [BNTC; NRSV, REB, TEV, TNT], 'there before me was' [NIV], 'to my surprise' [NAB], 'lo' [Lns], not explicit [CEV, NLT]. Ἰδού indicates the startling nature of what John saw [EC, Wal].
- b. τόξον (LN **6.37**) (BAGD p. 822): 'bow' [BAGD, BNTC, EC, **LN**, Lns, WBC; all versions].

QUESTION—What is the function of the phrase καὶ εἶδον 'and I looked'?
Instead of reading from the scroll, John saw the prophetic event enacted in a vision [EC]. See this phrase treated at 5:1.

QUESTION—What other Scriptural reference is similar to these four horses?
The description of different colored horses in Zechariah 6:1ff. is similar to these [Alf, EC, ICC, NIGTC, NTC, Sw, TNTC, WBC].

QUESTION—What does the figure of the rider of the white horse symbolize?
1. It has a negative interpretation [BNTC, EC, ICC, NIC, NIGTC, Sw, TNTC, Wal, WBC]. The interpretation of this horseman should be consistent with the three following ones that are negative [BNTC, Sw]. The figure symbolizes military conquest [NIC, Sw]. This figure symbolizes primarily war [ICC, TNTC, WBC], but then symbolizes the Parthians [ICC, NTC, Sw] who were excellent archers and may have ridden white horses [ICC]. The verb ἐδόθη 'was given' is frequently used to indicate God's permission to evil forces to carry out their work (see 9:1, 3, 5; 13:5, 7, 14, 15) [BNTC, NIC]. It symbolizes the ruler of Daniel 9:26 who comes to lead the revived Roman empire. He will appear in the 70th week of Daniel and will be the world ruler during the tribulation and is the same as the beast coming out of the sea in 13:7 [Wal]. The rider is an agent of judgment of the last days [NIC]. The rider is a satanic force whose purpose is to persecute and defeat believers (see 11:7 and 13:7) [NIGTC].
2. It has a positive interpretation [Alf, Ld, Lns]. The rider of the white horse symbolizes the gospel in the sense of the whole Word of God and its victory over all the world's opposition (see Matthew 24:14) [Lns]. The color white throughout Revelation is always associated with Christ or spiritual victory and this gives us a clue to its interpretation here. Here the figure symbolizes the announcing of the Gospel of Christ as it is proclaimed around the world winning victories as it goes (see Matthew 24.14) [Ld]. The figure symbolizes the victory of God's people. The rider is not Christ himself, but one who symbolizes Christ's victorious power [Alf].

QUESTION—What is symbolized by a white horse?
The white horse symbolizes victory [Lns, TH, TNTC, Wal, WBC]. White refers to the persevering righteousness of believers and may indicate that the evil forces attempt to deceive by appearing to be righteous [NIGTC]. In Revelation the color white always symbolizes Christ [Ld]. It refers to a feigned righteousness of an imposter of Christ [EC].

and he-went-out[a] conquering and that[b] he-might-conquer.
LEXICON—a. aorist act. indic. of ἐξέρχομαι (BAGD 1.a.ζ. p. 274): 'to go out' [BAGD, Lns, WBC; CEV, TNT], 'to come out' [BAGD; NRSV], 'to ride out' [BNTC; NET, NIV, NLT, TEV], 'to ride forth' [NAB, REB], 'to go forth' [EC; KJV]. See this word also at 3:12.

b. ἵνα (See this word at 2:10): 'that' [EC, WBC], 'to' [BNTC, Lns; all versions except NIV, TNT], 'for (victory)' [NIV, TNT].

QUESTION—How is the phrase νικῶν καὶ ἵνα νικήσῃ 'conquering and that he might conquer' translated in the versions?

'Conquering, and to conquer' [Lns; KJV, NRSV, REB], 'as a conqueror to conquer' [TEV], 'as a conqueror to win his victory' [BNTC], 'as a conqueror (he rode out) to conquer his enemies' [NET], 'as a conqueror bent on conquest' [NIV], 'he had already won some victories, and he went out to win more' [CEV], 'to win many battles and gain the victory' [NLT], 'a victor seeking for victory' [TNT], 'victorious, to conquer yet again' [NAB], 'the conqueror (went out) that he might conquer even more' [WBC]. The participle 'conquering' plus the purpose phrase 'and to conquer' means to completely conquer [Lns]. The purpose clause, 'in order to conquer', indicates a victory that lasts forever [Alf].

QUESTION—What is symbolized by a bow?

The bow symbolizes victory [EC, Ld, Wal, WBC], or warfare [TH]. The fact that arrows are not mentioned supports the view that the victories will come through peaceful means [EC].

QUESTION—What is symbolized by a crown?

The crown symbolizes: victory [EC, ICC, Ld, Lns, NTC, TNTC, Wal]; or the authority and power of a king [TH].

QUESTION—Who is the implied actor of ἐδόθη 'was given'?

The implied actor is God [BNTC, EC, Lns, NIC, NIGTC, TH, WBC]. God is the ultimate source though there may have been an intermediate agent [TNTC]. An angel may have been the actor [TH]. This verb is used in Revelation to indicate God's permission to evil forces to carry out their work EC, [BNTC, NIC]. Rather than indicating permission by God, it is his authorization to carry out this act [NIGTC].

DISCOURSE UNIT: 6:3–4 [Ld, NTC, TNTC, Wal, WBC]. The topic is the second seal.

6:3 And when he-opened the second seal, I-heard the second living-creature saying, "Come."

TEXT—Some manuscripts include καὶ ἴδε or καὶ βλέπε 'and see' after ἔρχου 'come'. GNT does not mention this variant. One of these two forms is included by KJV.

QUESTION—Who is the antecedent of the pronoun 'he'?

The antecedent is the Lamb [EC, NIC, NIGTC, Sw, TH, TNTC, Wal; CEV, NAB, NIV, NLT, REB, TEV, TNT]: when the Lamb opened the second seal.

6:4 And another horse, fiery-red,[a] went-out, and (it) was-given[b] to-the-one sitting on it to-take[c] peace from the earth and so-that they-should-kill[d] each-other,

TEXT—Some manuscripts include εἶδον καὶ ἰδού 'I saw and behold' after καί 'and'. It is omitted by GNT with a B rating, indicating that the text is almost certain.

LEXICON—a. πυρρός (LN **79.31**) (BAGD p. 731): 'fiery red' [BNTC, EC, LN, WBC; CEV, NET, NIV], 'red (as fire)' [BAGD], 'bright red' [NRSV], 'fiery' [Lns], 'red' [KJV, NAB, NLT, REB, TEV, TNT], 'blood red' [Alf, NTC, Sw].
- b. aorist pass. indic. of δίδωμι (LN 37.98) (BAGD 1.b.β. p. 193): 'to be given' [BAGD, EC, Lns; KJV], 'to be given (the) power' [BNTC, WBC; CEV, NAB, NIV, REB, TEV], 'to be given the authority' [NLT], 'to be given permission' [TNT], 'to be granted permission' [NET], 'to be permitted' [NRSV], 'to be granted' [BAGD], 'to be appointed, to be assigned' [LN]. See this word also at 2:7.
- c. aorist act. infin. of λαμβάνω (See this word at 3:11): 'to take' [BNTC, EC, Lns; CEV, NET, NIV, NRSV], 'to take away' [CEV, REB, TNT], 'to remove' [WBC; NLT], 'to rob' [NAB]. The phrase λαβεῖν τὴν εἰρήνην 'to take peace' is translated 'to bring war' [TEV].
- d. aorist act. subj. of σφάζω (See this word at 5:6): 'to kill' [CEV, TEV, TNT], 'to slaughter' [BNTC, WBC; CEV, NAB, NRSV, REB], 'to butcher' [NET], 'to slay' [EC, Lns; NIV]. This verb is also translated as a noun: 'slaughter' [NLT].

QUESTION—What is 'fiery red' symbolic of?
It is symbolic of: warfare [EC, Lns, TH]; bloodshed [Lns]; killing [NTC, TH]; burning [Lns]; or strife [NTC]. The rider is not a particular person; he represents the forces of war with its consequent horrors [EC].

QUESTION—Who is the implied actor of ἐδόθη '(it) was given'?
The implied actor is God [BNTC, EC, TH, TNTC, WBC], or an angel [TH].

and (a) large[a] sword[b] was-given to-him.

LEXICON—a. μέγας (LN 79.123) (BAGD 1.a. p. 497): 'large' [LN, WBC; NIV, TEV], 'great' [BNTC, EC, LN, Lns; KJV, NRSV, REB, TNT], 'big' [LN; CEV], 'huge' [NAB, NET], 'mighty' [NLT], 'long' [BAGD].
- b. μάχαιρα (LN 6.33) (BAGD 1. p. 496): 'sword' [BAGD, EC, LN; all versions], 'short sword' [Lns], 'dagger' [LN], 'saber' [BAGD]. In John 18:10 this word refers to a short knife carried in a sheath, but here it refers to a long sword carried in battle [EC].

QUESTION—What is the 'sword' symbolic of?
It is symbolic of: killing [Lns]; civil and international conflict [Sw]; a specific period of bloodshed [EC]; or the absence of peace (See Matthew 10:34) [Alf]. Its large size indicates how constant and terrible it is [Lns].

QUESTION—What is the figure of the whole verse symbolic of?
It is symbolic of: civil war [NIC, NTC, TNTC]; rebellion [NIC]; international war [Alf, Lns, NIGTC, Sw]; warfare [Ld, Wal]; or bloodshed [Ld]. It primarily symbolizes the persecution of believers and secondarily international conflict [NIGTC].

DISCOURSE UNIT: 6:5–6 [EC, Ld, NTC, TNTC, Wal, WBC]. The topic is the third seal.

6:5 **And when he-opened the third seal, I-heard the third living-creature saying, "Come."**
TEXT—Some manuscripts include καὶ ἴδε 'and see' after ἔρχου 'come'. It is omitted by GNT with a B rating, indicating that the text is almost certain. The words 'and see' are included by KJV.

And I-looked, and behold[a] **a black**[b] **horse, and the-one sitting on it having (a) pair-of-scales**[c] **in his hand.**
TEXT—Some manuscripts omit καὶ εἶδον 'and I looked'. GNT includes these words with a B decision, indicating that the text is almost certain.
LEXICON—a. ἰδού (See this word at 1:7): 'behold' [EC; KJV], 'behold, there was' [WBC], 'here came' [NET], 'there' [BNTC], 'there was' [NRSV, REB, TEV, TNT], 'there before me was' [NIV], 'this time' [NAB], 'lo' [Lns], not explicit [CEV, NLT]. Ἰδού indicates the startling nature of what John saw [EC, Wal]. It highlights the figure of the rider on a black horse with the pair of scales [Lns].
  b. μέλας (LN **79.26**) (BAGD p. 500): 'black' [BAGD, BNTC, EC, **LN**, Lns, WBC; all versions].
  c. ζυγός (LN **6.214**) (BAGD 2. p. 340): 'pair of scales' [BAGD, BNTC; all versions except CEV, KJV, NET], 'balance scale' [BNTC, **LN** (6.214); CEV, NET], 'pair of balances' [KJV], 'balance' [BAGD, EC, Lns], 'lever of a balance' [BAGD]. The scales consisted of a rod suspended from a cord or hook with pans suspended from each end. Weights in one side determined the weight of the commodity in the other [LN, WBC]. It could be two pans on either side, or a pan on one side and weights on the other [EC, Lns]. The ζυγός referred to the rod itself [ICC].
QUESTION—What does the black horse symbolize?
  It symbolizes: famine [TH, TNTC, WBC]; death from famine [TH, WBC]; lamentation and mourning resulting from famine and the anxiety resulting from it [EC]; or the somber nature of the rider's task [Alf]. Black symbolizes suffering (Lamentations 5:10 KJV) [Wal]. The color is insignificant [NTC].
QUESTION—What do the pair of scales symbolize?
  They symbolize: scarcity [Alf, ICC, Ld, NIC, NTC, Sw]; or famine [EC, ICC, NIC, NIGTC]. In the ancient world when essential commodities are sold by weight it indicates scarcity (see Leviticus 26:26 and Ezekiel 4:16) [Alf, EC, ICC, NIC, NIGTC, TNTC, WBC]. Famine is the normal result of conquest by an invading army when the army lives off the land [NIC].

6:6 And I-heard as-it-were[a] (a) voice in (the) midst of-the four living-creatures saying,

TEXT—Some manuscripts do not include ὡς 'as it were'. GNT does not mention this alternative. This word is omitted by WBC; KJV, NLT.

LEXICON—a. ὡς (See this word at 1:10 and 4:6): 'as it were' [Lns], 'what sounded like' [BNTC; CEV, NIV, REB, TEV], 'what seemed to be' [NAB, NRSV, TNT], 'something like' [EC; NET], not explicit [WBC; KJV, NLT].

QUESTION—Whose voice did John hear?

It may have been the voice of Christ, the Lamb [ICC, NIGTC]. It is probably Christ's voice since it comes from the middle of the throne and the four living beings [NIGTC]. It was God's voice [EC, Wal]. It was a divine person [TNTC]. It was not one of the four living beings [TH]. It was the voice of Nature objecting to the miseries of famine [Sw].

"(A) quart[a] of-wheat[b] for-(a)-denarius[c] and three quarts of-barley[d] for-(a)-denarius,

LEXICON—a. χοῖνιξ (LN **81.24**) (BAGD p. 883): 'quart' [BNTC, **LN**; CEV, NET, NIV, NRSV, REB, TEV], 'liter' [WBC], 'choinix' [BAGD, Lns; TNT], 'measure' [EC; KJV], 'ration' [NAB], 'loaf' [NLT]. A χοῖνιξ was a dry measure almost equivalent to a quart [BAGD]. It was equal to a quart or a liter [LN]. It amounted to the daily ration of grain for one man [Alf, BAGD, ICC, Ld, NIGTC, Sw, TNTC, WBC]. It was barely one slave's daily ration of food [Lns]. It was the amount a working man would eat in one meal [Wal]. This was equal to about a quart in the English system but a little over a liter in the metric system. By weight it was about 2 pounds or 1 kilogram—precisely 570 grams [TH].

b. σῖτος (LN 3.41) (BAGD p. 752): 'wheat' [BAGD, BNTC, EC, LN, Lns, WBC; all versions except NLT, REB], 'wheat bread' [NLT], 'flour' [REB], 'grain' [BAGD, LN]. Wheat flour rather than grain is indicated by this word [TH].

c. δηνάριον (LN 6.75) (BAGD p. 179): 'denarius' [BAGD, EC, LN, Lns, WBC; TNT], 'a day's pay' [NAB, NET, NLT, NRSV], 'a day's wage(s)' [BNTC; NIV, REB, TEV], 'a whole day's wages' [CEV], 'penny' [KJV]. It was the laborer's average daily wage [Alf, BAGD, BNTC, ICC, Ld, LN, Lns, NIC, NIGTC, NTC, Sw, TH TNTC, Wal, WBC; all versions except KJV, TNT].

d. κριθή (LN **3.44**) (BAGD p. 450): 'barley' [BAGD, BNTC, EC, **LN**, Lns, WBC; all versions except REB], 'barley-meal' [REB]. Barley flour rather than grain is indicated by this word [TH]. Barley was considered the food of the poor [Ld, Sw].

QUESTION—Does this price for wheat and barley reflect a fair price?

It is an exorbitant price [NIC, TH, WBC]. It was about 8 times the normal price for wheat and 5 times the normal price for barley [WBC]. The price was about 10 times what was normally given [NTC]. The price was about 10 to 12 times what was normally given [NIC]. The price was between 8 and 16 times the normal price [ICC, NIGTC]. The price was 12 to 15 times the normal price [Ld]. The prices are high but do not reflect famine prices [Lns, TNTC].

and (do) not damage^a the olive-oil^b and the wine."^c

LEXICON—a. aorist act. subj. of ἀδικέω (See this word at 2:11): 'to damage' [Lns; NET, NIV, NRSV, REB, TEV, TNT], 'to harm' [BNTC, WBC], 'to ruin' [CEV], 'to hurt' [EC; KJV], 'to waste' [NLT]. The phrase μὴ ἀδικήσῃς 'do not harm' is translated 'to spare' [NAB]. The aorist tense indicates that no damage has yet been done [WBC].
  b. ἔλαιον (LN 6.202) (BAGD 3. p. 248): 'olive oil' [EC, LN; CEV, NAB, NET, NLT, NRSV], 'oil' [BNTC, Lns, WBC; KJV, NIV, TNT], 'olive' [REB], 'olive trees' [TEV], 'olive orchard' [BAGD]. Here effect is given for the cause [BAGD].
  c. οἶνος (LN 6.197) (BAGD 3. p. 562): 'wine' [BNTC, EC, LN, Lns, WBC; all versions except REB, TEV], 'vine' [REB], 'vineyard' [BAGD; TEV]. Οἶνος is a fermented beverage made from grape juice [LN].

QUESTION—To whom is the command addressed?
  It is second person singular and is therefore addressed to the horseman [Alf, NTC, Sw, TH, WBC].

QUESTION—What is indicated by olive oil and wine?
  They is a figure of metonymy in which the product is named but the source is indicated [BAGD, Sw, TH, WBC; TEV]: olive orchards and vineyards. Damage to the orchard would affect the supply for a long period [WBC]. Olive and wine were considered basic necessities [Alf, Ld, NIGTC, Sw]. Olive oil and wine were luxury items [BNTC, ICC, TNTC]. The oil and wine were not luxury items but they were a step up in comfort from wheat and barley [Lns]. Scarcity of wheat, barley, oil, and wine indicates famine in Joel 1:10, 11 [NIGTC]. Psalms 104:14, 15 indicate that all four are staples of life [Alf].

QUESTION—What is the purpose of this command?
  It functions to limit the severity of the famine [Alf, Ld, NIC, TH]. It further describes the severity of the famine; although severe, it is limited [NIGTC]. The horseman is to keep sufficient available for sustenance [Alf].

QUESTION—What is generally indicated by this verse?
  It indicates that conditions will be bad but not unbearable [BNTC, ICC, TNTC]. It indicates that though there will be scarcity, food will still be available [Alf, BNTC]. It indicates a time of great shortage but not actual famine [Ld]. It indicates a time of great scarcity when life is reduced to barest essentials [Wal]. It indicates hardship but forbids severe losses in these four crops [Sw]. It indicates a time when only the basic necessities will be attainable by man with nothing left over for other necessities such as oil and wine [NIGTC]. It indicates a time when the essentials of life are scarce for the poor but luxury items for the wealthy are abundant [EC, ICC]. It

indicates an unjust distribution of the products of the earth where the rich have but the poor suffer [Lns].

DISCOURSE UNIT: 6:7–8 [EC, Ld, NTC, TNTC, Wal, WBC]. The topic is the fourth seal.

6:7 **And when he-opened the fourth seal, I-heard (the) voice of-the fourth living-creature saying, "Come."**
TEXT—Some manuscripts include καὶ ἴδε or καὶ βλέπε 'and see' after ἔρχου 'come'. GNT omits them with a B decision, indicating that the text is almost certain. The words 'and see' are included by KJV.

6:8 **And I-looked, and behold[a] (a) pale[b] horse, and the-one sitting on it (the) name to-him (was) Death,[c] and Hades[d] was-following with him**
TEXT—Some manuscripts do not include καὶ εἶδον 'and I saw'. GNT includes these words with a B decision, indicating that the text is almost certain.
LEXICON—a. ἰδού (See this word at 1:7): 'behold' [EC, WBC; KJV], 'lo' [Lns], 'here came' [NET], 'there was' [BNTC; NRSV, REB, TEV, TNT], 'there before me was' [NIV], not explicit [CEV, NAB, NLT]. 'Behold' indicates that what he saw startled him [Wal].
  b. χλωρός (LN **79.35**) (BAGD 2. p. 882): 'pale' [BAGD, BNTC; KJV, NIV], 'pale-colored' [**LN**, WBC; TEV, TNT], 'pale green' [EC, Wal, WBC; CEV, NET, NRSV], 'pale green like a corpse' [NLT], 'sickly pale' [REB], 'sickly green' [NAB], 'pale greenish-gray' [LN], 'livid' [Alf, Lns, NTC]. This word is regarded as typical of a corpse, since this color is used as a symbol of death [**LN**]; it is the color of a sick person [BAGD]. Χλωρός indicates: 'green' [TH, WBC]; 'yellowish green' [TH, TNTC]; the color of a corpse [Alf, Ld, LN, NIC, NTC, TNTC; NLT]; the color of a person pale from fear [NIC, Sw, WBC]; or someone pale as though from sickness [Alf, WBC].
  c. θάνατος (See this word at 1:18): 'Death' [BNTC, EC, Lns, WBC; all versions], 'death' [BAGD, LN]. Death here is treated as a person [Alf, BAGD, EC, ICC, NTC, Sw, WBC].
  d. ᾅδης (LN 23.108): 'Hades' [BNTC, EC, WBC; NET, NIV, NRSV, REB, TEV, TNT], 'hades' [Lns], 'Death's Kingdom' [CEV], 'Hell' [KJV], 'Grave' [NLT] 'the nether world' [NAB], 'death' [LN (23.108)]. Hades is personified here [Alf, EC, ICC, Lns, NTC]. It is the place of the departed dead [Alf, Lns, NIGTC, Wal] and it follows death in order to accommodate those who die [Alf, Ld, Lns]. It is the underworld or the grave [Ld]. Since the believing dead go under the altar (see 6:9), the inhabitants here must be the souls of unbelievers [Lns]. Hades is the domain of death [WBC]. See this word also at 1:18.
QUESTION—What is symbolized by the pale horse?
  It symbolizes: terror [Sw]; death from famine, pestilence, and wild beasts [Ld]; tragic death as judgment [Lns].

QUESTION—What is the function of the imperfect tense ἠκολούθει 'was following' and what does it mean?
It indicates a continuous aspect [Lns]: kept following. It is not clear if Hades is riding a second horse or is mounted on the same horse behind Death since it is unlikely to be on foot [Ld]. There is no fifth horse, so apparently he is on foot and able to keep up with the horse [Alf, EC]. He follows Death in order to gather in the victims of Death [EC, Lns]. Hades swallows up those killed by famine, pestilence, and wild beasts [Ld].

and authority[a] was-given to-them over[b] the fourth-part[c] of-the earth
LEXICON—a. ἐξουσία (LN 76.12): 'authority' [EC, Lns, WBC; NAB, NET, NLT, NRSV, TEV, TNT], 'power' [BNTC, LN; CEV, KJV, NIV, REB]. See this word also at 2.26.
  b. ἐπί with accusative object (LN 37.9) (BAGD III.1.b.α. p. 288): 'over' [BAGD, BNTC, EC, LN, Lns, WBC; all versions], 'with responsibility for' [LN].
  c. τέταρτον (LN **60.64**) (BAGD p. 813): 'fourth part' [BAGD, **LN**, Lns; KJV], 'fourth' [LN], 'quarter' [BAGD]. The phrase τὸ τέταρτον 'the fourth part' is translated 'a/one fourth' [EC, WBC; CEV, NET, NIV, NLT, NRSV, TEV], 'a/one quarter' [BNTC; NAB, REB, TNT]. 'The fourth part' here indicates a quarter of the population rather than of the land [NIC, NTC, TH, Wal].
QUESTION—Who is the implied actor of ἐδόθη 'was given'?
The implied actor is God [BNTC, TH, TNTC]: God gave. The implied actor is the Lamb [Lns]: the Lamb gave.

to-kill with[a] sword[b] and with famine[c] and pestilence[d] and by[e] the wild-animals[f] of-the earth.
LEXICON—a. ἐν with dative object (LN 90.10) (BAGD III.1.a. p. 260): 'with' [BAGD, EC, LN, WBC; CEV, KJV, NAB, NLT, NRSV], 'by' [BNTC, LN; NET, NIV, REB, TNT], 'by means of' [TEV], 'in connection with' [Lns]. Here ἐν indicates instrumentality [Alf, EC, TH].
  b. ῥομφαία (LN **55.6**): 'sword' [BNTC, EC, WBC; all versions except TEV], 'a great sword' [Lns], 'war' [**LN**; TEV], 'battle' [TH]. It is possible that the literal meaning of 'broad sword' should be taken here [LN]. Here 'sword' is not limited to war since other violent deaths such as murder are also included [Ld]. See this word also at 1:16.
  c. λιμός (LN 23.33) (BAGD 2. p. 475): 'famine' [BAGD, BNTC, EC, LN, Lns, WBC; all versions except KJV], 'hunger' [LN; KJV].
  d. θάνατος (LN **23.158**) (BAGD 1.e. p. 351): 'pestilence' [Alf, BAGD, BNTC, EC, **LN**, Lns, NIGTC, NTC, Sw; NET, NRSV, REB, TNT], 'plague' [LN, NIC, WBC; NAB, NIV], 'disease' [NIGTC, TH; CEV, NLT, TEV], 'epidemic' [TH], 'fatal illness' [BAGD], 'death' [BAGD, Lns; KJV]. In the LXX θάνατος translates the Hebrew word meaning pestilence and here it refers to disease or epidemic [TH].

e. ὑπό with genitive object (LN 90.1) (BAGD 1.d. p.843): 'by' [BAGD, BNTC, EC, LN, Lns, WBC; NET, NIV, NRSV, REB, TNT], 'by means of' [TEV], 'with' [CEV, KJV, NAB, NLT]. Ὑπό here indicates agency [Alf, TH].

f. θηρίον (LN 4.3, 4.4) (BAGD 1.a.β. π.361): 'wild animal' [BAGD, LN (4.4), WBC; CEV, NET, NIV, NLT, NRSV, TEV], 'wild beast' [BNTC, Lns; NAB, REB, TNT], 'animal' [LN (4.3, 4.4)], 'beast' [BAGD, EC; KJV], 'quadruped' [LN (4.4)]. Θηρίον refers to dangerous animals [BAGD].

DISCOURSE UNIT: 6:9–11 [Alf, BNTC, Ld, NIC, NIGTC, NTC, TNTC, Wal, WBC]. The topic is the fifth seal [Alf, BNTC, Ld, NIGTC, NTC, TNTC, WBC], the fifth seal: cry of the martyrs [NIC, Wal].

6:9 **And when he-opened the fifth seal, I-saw underneath the altar[a] the souls[b] of-the-ones killed because-of[c] the word of-God and because-of the testimony[d] that they had.[e]**

LEXICON—a. θυσιαστήριον (LN 6.114) (BAGD p. 366, 1.b.β.): 'altar' [BAGD, BNTC, EC, LN, Lns, WBC; all versions]. A θυσιαστήριον was a thing where gifts to a deity were placed and a ceremony performed in honor of that deity [LN]. An altar is a place where sacrifices are made [WBC].

b. ψυχή (LN 9.20) (BAGD 1.a.α. p. 893): 'soul' [BAGD, BNTC, EC, Lns, WBC; all versions except NAB], 'spirit' [NAB], 'person' [LN], 'breath of life, life-principle' [BAGD]. The ψυχή is the immaterial part of a person that continues to live after the body dies [TH, WBC]. There is no difference between 'souls' and 'spirits' [Alf, TH]. See this word at 20:4 and compare similar references to 'spirits' at Acts 7:59 and Hebrews 12:23 [Lns].

c. διά with accusative object (See this word at 1:9 and 2:3): 'because of' [EC, Lns, WBC; NAB, NET, NIV], 'because' [TEV], 'for' [BNTC, WBC; CEV, KJV, NLT, NRSV, REB], 'for the sake of' [TNT], 'for speaking…and telling about' [CEV].

d. μαρτυρία (BAGD 2.d.γ. p. 493): 'testimony' [BAGD, BNTC, EC, Lns; KJV, NET, NIV, NRSV, REB, TNT], 'witness' [WBC; NAB]. The phrase τὴν μαρτυρίαν ἣν εἶχον 'the testimony that they had' is translated 'telling about their faith' [CEV], 'being faithful in their witness' [NLT], 'had been faithful in their witnessing' [TEV]. The phrase 'because of the word of God and because of the testimony that they had' is translated 'because of the witness they bore to the word of God' [NAB]. This refers to testimony concerning Jesus [BAGD]. See this word also at 1:2.

e. imperf. act. indic. of ἔχω (LN 57.1) (BAGD I.1.c.β. p. 332): 'to have' [EC, LN, Lns], 'to bear' [WBC; NAB, REB], 'to maintain' [NIV, TNT], 'to give' [NET, NRSV], 'to hold to' [BNTC], 'to hold' [KJV], 'to possess' [LN], 'to keep, to preserve' [BAGD], not explicit [CEV, NLT, TEV].

QUESTION—Who is the antecedent of 'he'?
   He is the Lamb [Sw, TH].
QUESTION—What altar is represented here?
   The vision reverts from the horsemen on earth to heaven and what was a throne room in chapters 4–5 is now God's temple [EC].
   1. It is the altar of burnt offerings [Alf, BNTC, Ld, Sw, TH, Wal, WBC]. This altar is the heavenly counterpart of the altar on which sacrifices were made [TH].
   2. It is the altar of incense [BAGD, EC, ICC, NIGTC, NTC, TNTC]. It is the altar of incense because the altar of burnt offering was already finished at the Cross [TNTC]. It had the characteristics of both, but mainly of the altar of incense [ICC]. On this the prayers of the saints were offered up to God (see 8:3) [NTC].
   3. It makes little difference whether one or the other. The idea of sacrifice recalls the burnt offering while the prayers of the souls recalls the altar of incense [NIC].
QUESTION—Why were the souls *underneath* the altar?
   Since these souls were martyred and their blood, in which their lives resided, was poured out, they are represented as being beneath the altar in heaven [Alf, BNTC, Ld, NIC]. This does not indicate their state or location in the intermediate state. It is just a vivid way of picturing their martyrdom [Ld]. It may be in keeping with the fact that when sacrifices were made in the OT, the blood was poured around the base of the altar (Leviticus 4:7; Exodus 29:12). The blood cries out for vengeance from there [Alf]. Martyrs are thought of as sacrifices offered to God (2 Timothy 4:6; Philippians 2:17). Though the sacrifice is made on earth, the soul is offered to God on the altar in heaven [ICC]. The souls are under the altar because they have been sacrificed on it [BNTC, ICC]. This is a way of saying that from God's perspective, their martyrdom is viewed as a sacrifice on the altar of heaven [NIC]. Being under the altar symbolizes: a place of safety [NIGTC, TH, TNTC]; nearness to God [WBC].
QUESTION—Were they killed for testifying about Jesus, or for possessing the testimony that Jesus gave?
   1. They were killed for testifying about Jesus [Alf, BNTC, NIGTC, Sw TH; CEV, NAB, NET, NLT, NRSV, REB, TEV]. By proclaiming the Word of God the believers were testifying the same testimony that caused Jesus' death [BNTC]. The word καί 'and' is explanatory, 'because of the word of God, *that is*, the testimony that they had', indicating it was because of the witness that they bore to the Word of God that they were killed [TH; NAB].
   2. They were killed for possessing the testimony that Jesus gave [BAGD, EC, ICC, Ld, Lns, NIC, TNTC, WBC; KJV]. The word καί 'and' is explanatory, 'because of the word of God, *that is*, the testimony that they had' [EC]. The word εἶχον 'they had' indicates that this is the testimony that Christ gave them and that they had preserved [ICC, WBC]. It was for

REVELATION 6:9 159

accepting the witness that Jesus gave that they were put to death [Ld]. They refused to renounce the testimony of Jesus [Lns]. It was because of the testimony that they had received from Jesus (see 12:17 and 20:4) [NIC]. This testimony received from Jesus would also involve their own testimony of it [NIC].

QUESTION—What does this seal symbolize?

It symbolizes a time of persecution and its relation to God's plan for history [Sw]. This seal explains the reason for the martyrdom of believers [NIC].

6:10 And they-cried with-a-loud voice saying, "How-long,ᵃ Masterᵇ holyᶜ and true,ᵈ

LEXICON—a. ἕως πότε (BAGD II.1.c. p. 335): 'how long' [BAGD, EC, Lns; KJV]. The phrase ἕως πότε...οὐ κρίνεις 'until when...do you not judge' is translated 'how long before/until you judge' [BNTC, WBC; all versions except KJV].

b. δεσπότης (LN 37.63, 57.13) (BAGD p. 176): 'Master' [EC, WBC; CEV, NAB, TNT], 'Sovereign Master' [NET], 'master' [BAGD, LN (37.63, 57.13)], 'lord' [BAGD, LN (37.63, 57.13)], 'Lord' [LN; KJV], 'Sovereign Lord' [BNTC; NIV, NLT, NRSV, REB], 'Almighty Lord' [TEV], 'Lord Absolute' [Lns], 'owner' [BAGD, LN (57.13)], 'ruler' [LN (37.63)]. Δεσπότης indicates someone who has absolute power over another [LN (37.63)], or an owner of slaves [LN (57.13)].

c. ἅγιος (BAGD 1.b.δ. p. 9): 'holy' [BAGD, BNTC, EC, LN, Lns, WBC; all versions]. The characteristics, 'holy' and 'true', are also ascribed to Christ in 3:7 [TH]. See this word also at 3:7.

d. ἀληθινός (See this word at 3:7): 'true' [BAGD, BNTC, EC, LN, WBC; all versions except CEV], 'faithful' [CEV], 'Genuine One' [Lns]. God is true in faithfulness to his word [EC, Ld]. He is genuine in that he is the only real God [Lns].

QUESTION—Who is being addressed here as δεσπότης 'Master'?

God is being addressed [Alf, EC, ICC, Ld, Lns, NIC, NIGTC, NTC, Sw, TH, TNTC, Wal, WBC].

do-you-judgeᵃ and avengeᵇ not our bloodᶜ from the-ones living on the earth?"

LEXICON—a. pres. act. indic. of κρίνω (LN 56.20, 56.30) (BAGD 4.b.α. p. 452): 'to judge' [BAGD, EC, **LN** (56.20), Lns, WBC; all versions except NAB, REB, TNT], 'to pass judgment' [TNT], 'to pass sentence' [BNTC], 'to judge someone's cause' [NAB], 'to vindicate' [REB], 'to condemn, to judge as guilty' [LN (56.30)], 'to decide a legal question, to act as a judge making a legal decision, to arrive at a verdict, to try a case' [LN (56.20)], 'to administer justice' [BAGD].

b. pres. act. indic. of ἐκδικέω (LN 56.35, 38.8) (BAGD 2. p. 238): 'to avenge' [BNTC, EC, Lns, WBC; all versions except CEV, TEV], 'to punish' [BAGD, LN (38.8); CEV, TEV], 'to cause someone to suffer' [LN (38.8)], 'to take vengeance for something' [BAGD], 'to give someone justice' [LN (56.35)], 'to pay back, to revenge, to seek retribution' [LN (39.33)].

c. αἷμα (LN 8.64, 23.107) (BAGD 2.a. p. 22; 2.a. p. 23): 'blood' [BAGD, BNTC, EC, LN (8.64), Lns; KJV, NAB, NET, NIV, NLT, NRSV], 'death' [LN (23.107), WBC; REB, TNT], 'violent death' [LN (23.107)]. It refers figuratively to the seat of life [BAGD]. The phrase τὸ αἷμα ἡμῶν 'our blood' is translated '(who) killed us' [CEV], '(for) killing us' [TEV].

QUESTION—Is this a real or rhetorical question?

It is rhetorical in that it is a request that God act at once in their behalf [TH]. It is a prayer either of vengeance or a prayer of vindication [Ld]. [Note that all versions render it as a question, however.] It is the perplexing question asked by the righteous almost since the start of the human race [EC].

QUESTION—Who or what is the object of κρίνω 'to judge'?

The object is 'the ones living on the earth' [EC, NIGTC; CEV, NET, NIV, NLT, TEV]: to judge the people who live on the earth. The object is 'our cause' [NAB]: to judge our cause. The verb means 'to vindicate' and the object is 'us' [REB]: to vindicate us.

QUESTION—What is the object of ἐκδικέω 'to avenge'?

The object is: 'our blood' or 'our death' [NET, NIV, NLT, REB]: to avenge our blood/death. The verb means 'to punish' and the object is 'the ones living on the earth' [CEV, TEV]: to punish those living on the earth.

QUESTION—Is this a cry for vengeance or for justice?

1. It is a cry for justice or vindication of wrong [BNTC, Ld, Lns, NIC, NIGTC, NTC, TNTC, WBC]. It is an appeal to God to reverse the judgment of the world against them [TNTC]. They are not asking for personal revenge but that the reputation of God and his people be vindicated [NIC, NIGTC]. Luke 18:7 is a parable told by Jesus about good people suffering under evil people and concluding, "Will not God vindicate his elect, who cry to him day and night? Will he delay long over them? I tell you, he will vindicate them speedily." The cry of the martyrs was not for revenge, but for vindication [Ld].

2. It is a cry for vengeance [Alf, ICC, Sw, TH, WBC; all versions]. This verb only occurs here and in 19:2 where the vengeance is carried out [WBC]. 'Avenge' has the sense of 'get even' and here indicates some form of punishment [TH]. The martyrs are asking God to execute vengeance and in so doing are refraining from personal revenge [Sw].

QUESTION—Who are 'the ones living on the earth'?

They are: those who are hostile to God [Ld, Lns, NIC, NTC, WBC]; unbelievers [ICC, NIGTC, TNTC]; those who killed them [TH]. This term is used to refer to the enemies of Christianity nine times in Revelation (3:10; 6:10; 8.13; 11:10; 13:8, 14; 17:8) [WBC]. See this question also at 3:10.

6:11 And (a) white robe[a] was-given to-them each and it-was-told them that they-should-rest[b] yet (a) short time,

LEXICON—a. στολή (LN 6.174) (BAGD p. 769): 'robe' [BAGD, BNTC, EC, WBC; all versions except NAB, NET], 'long robe' [LN; NAB, NET], 'flowing robe' [Lns], 'long, flowing robe' [BAGD]. It was a robe of state, that flowed to the feet [EC].

b. fut. mid./mid. (deponent = act.) indic. of ἀναπαύω (LN 23.80, **85.58**) (BAGD 2. p. 59): 'to rest' [EC, LN (23.80), WBC; all versions except NAB, NIV], 'to wait' [BAGD, Lns; NIV], 'to wait patiently' [BNTC], 'to be patient' [NIGTC; NAB], 'to abide' [**LN** (85.58)], 'to remain' [LN (85.58)], 'to remain quiet' [BAGD]. The verb indicates that they must wait but meanwhile they should rest [Ld, Sw]. They are to refrain from their cry for vengeance and to rest in blessedness [EC].

QUESTION—Who is the implied actor of ἐδόθη 'given', and ἐρρέθη 'told'?

The implied actor is God [TH, WBC]: God gave them robes and told them. The actor is an angel [TH]: an angel gave them robes and told them.

QUESTION—What does the στολὴ λευκή 'white robe' symbolize?

It symbolizes: victory [BNTC, Sw, TH, TNTC]; purity [BNTC, NIC, NIGTC, TH, WBC]; bliss [BNTC, EC, Ld, NIC, NTC]; righteousness [Alf, NIGTC, Wal]; immortality or salvation [WBC]; rest [Ld]; the beauty of holiness [Lns]; a new resurrection body [ICC]. This robe was their heavenly body, a special reward given to martyrs [ICC]. It is implied that they received a temporary body but not the final resurrection body [Wal]. It is pressing the symbolism too far to conclude that the saints must have physical bodies to have white robes because this vision does not teach the condition of the saints between death and the Lord's coming. The giving of the robes symbolizes the honor bestowed on them [EC]. It indicates that the honors of victory are already awarded to them [Sw]. The white robes assure the souls of their purity and rescinds the guilty verdict against them by the world [NIGTC]. It assures them of individual vindication [BNTC].

until (the number) also (of) their fellow-servants[a] and their brothers[b] the-ones being-about[c] to-be-killed[d] as they-themselves also would-be-completed.[e]

LEXICON—a. σύνδουλος (LN 87.81) (BAGD 3. p. 785): 'fellow servant' [WBC; all versions except CEV, NLT, TEV], 'fellow slave' [BAGD, EC, LN, Lns], 'other servant' [TEV], 'the Lord's other servant' [CEV], 'servant of Jesus' [NLT]. Here σύνδουλος indicates 'fellow Christian' [BAGD]. This is noun is also translated as a phrase: '(killed) in Christ's service' [BNTC].

b. ἀδελφός (See this word at 1:9): 'brother' [BNTC, EC, Lns, WBC; KJV, NAB, NET, NIV, TNT], 'brother and sister' [NRSV], 'Christian brother' [LN], 'believer' [TEV], 'the Lord's other followers' [CEV], 'fellow believer' [LN], not explicit [NLT]. The phrase 'their fellow servants and their brothers' is translated 'their brothers in Christ's service' [REB].

c. pres. act. participle of μέλλω (See this word at 1:19): 'to be about to' [EC, LN, Lns], 'were to be' [BNTC, WBC; REB, TNT], 'to be going to be' [NET], 'soon to be' [NRSV], 'to be' [CEV, KJV, NAB, NIV, NLT, TEV].

d. pres. pass. infin. of ἀποκτείνω (See this word at 2:13): 'to be killed' [BNTC, EC, LN, WBC; all versions except NAB, NLT, REB], 'to be killed off' [Lns], 'to be martyred' [NLT], 'to be put to death' [REB], 'to be slain' [NAB].

e. aorist pass. subj. of πληρόω (LN **59.33**) (BAGD 5., 6. p. 672): 'to be completed' [BAGD; NIV, TNT], 'to be complete' [BNTC, **LN**, WBC; NRSV, REB], 'to be reached' [NET], 'to be filled' [NAB], 'to be filled full' [Lns], 'to be fulfilled' [KJV], 'to be made complete' [EC, LN]. This verb is also translated as an adjective: 'complete (number)' [CEV, TEV], 'full (number)' [NLT]. See this word also at 3:2.

QUESTION—Does the phrase 'and their fellow servants and their brothers' refer to two groups or to one?

It refers to a single group [Alf, EC, ICC, NIC, Sw, TH, WBC; NLT, REB], and the second καί 'and' functions to explain the first [NIC, WBC]: and their fellow servants, *that is*, their brothers. It should be translated '*both* their fellow servants *and* their brothers' but it still refers to a single group viewed from two perspectives [Alf, Sw]. It refers both to saints in general and to martyrs in particular [Sw].

QUESTION—What word should be supplied as subject of 'to be completed'?

The word 'number' should be supplied [Alf, Ld, Lns, NIC, NIGTC, Sw, TH, TNTC, WBC; all versions except KJV, NAB]: number to be completed. The word 'quota' should be supplied [NAB]: quota to be filled. The word 'roll' should be supplied [BNTC]: roll to be completed.

QUESTION—What is implied by the completion of the number of martyrs?

It implies that God will accomplish his final victory over the forces of evil only by the death of the full number of martyrs [BNTC]. It implies that suffering is necessary in God's plan [WBC]. It implies that there will be more persecution [Sw, TH], by God's decision [TH]. It indicates that a certain number of believers must die before God will answer their prayer for justice [WBC]. It implies that God will answer their request [NIGTC].

DISCOURSE UNIT: 6:12–7:17 [Alf]. The topic is opening the sixth seal and its attendant visions.

DISCOURSE UNIT: 6:12–17 [Alf, EC, Ld, NIC, NIGTC, NTC, TNTC, Wal, WBC]. The topic is the sixth seal [EC, Ld, NIGTC, NTC, TNTC, Wal, WBC], the coming of the day of the Lord [Alf]. This section comprises the Lord's reply to the prayer of the saints in 6:10 [NIC, NIGTC], the answer is that their deaths will be vindicated [NIC]. Similar Scriptures that prophesy similar event are: Isaiah 2:12–17; 13:10–13; 24:1–6; 18–23; 34:2–4; Jeremiah 4:23–28; Haggai 2:6, 7; Zechariah 14:4–5; Joel 2:28–3:3; 3:15–16; Malachi 3:2; Matthew 24:7,

29; Mark 13:8, 24–25; Luke 21:11, 25–26; 23:30; Hebrews 12:26–27; 2 Peter 3:10, 12.

DISCOURSE UNIT: 6:12–14 [Ld, Lns, NIGTC, WBC]. The topic is cosmic upheavals [WBC].

6:12 And I-saw when he-opened the sixth seal,
TEXT—Some manuscripts include ἰδού 'behold' after καί 'and'. GNT does not mention this alternative. 'Behold' is included by KJV.
QUESTION—What is symbolized by the opening of the sixth seal?
It symbolizes: the end of the world [Ld, Lns, Wal]; the coming of the Lord [Alf]; the events that announce the last days [NIC, Sw]; the inauguration of God's final judgment [NIGTC, TH]; the Day of the Lord (2 Peter 3:10) [WBC]. The events do not proclaim the very end since that cannot happen until there is first a great persecution of believers [ICC]. This does not symbolize a temporal judgment [NIGTC]. Though not the very end, as it described later in Revelation, the sixth seal seems to indicate that God is intervening directly into human affairs to punish an evil world [Wal].
QUESTION—Is this section to be taken literally or figuratively?
  1. It should be taken literally [Lns, Wal]. This is the end of the first cycle of visions and it pictures the end of the world and what happens is literal. In the following visions each cycle ends with another aspect of the end [Lns].
  2. It should be taken figuratively [BNTC, NIGTC, NTC, Sw]. This is figurative language portraying God's judgment against an unbelieving world [NIGTC].
  3. It is mid-way between literal and figurative [EC, ICC, Ld, NIC, TNTC]. It denotes a real catastrophe but it is not completely literal. Stars can not literally fall to the earth [Ld]. If it denoted only social upheaval, this would not cause men to run in terror to the mountains and plead for death [NIC]. This is not the absolute end of the earth. Upheavals of even greater scale will come at the very end [EC].

and (a) great earthquake^a occurred
LEXICON—a. σεισμός (LN 14.87) (BAGD p. 746): 'earthquake' [BNTC, EC, LN, WBC; all versions], 'great shaking' [Lns].
QUESTION—What is indicated by σεισμός 'earthquake' here?
Σεισμός indicates 'shaking' and here refers to a shaking of more than the earth, a shaking of heaven, sea, and land [Alf]. It indicates the dislocation of the whole universe [Lns]. It probably indicates earthquake but in the context it could include the heavens [EC, WBC]. Earthquakes are one of the signs that frequently indicate the end of the world [TH] or the coming of the Lord [WBC]. It is a symbol of the defeat of the worldly political order hostile to God. In Hebrews 12:27 it symbolizes the removal of all that can be shaken [BNTC]. Here it symbolizes social and racial revolution [Sw]. It is a precursor to the end of the world [ICC].

and the sun became black[a] as sackcloth[b] made-of-hair[c] and the whole[d] moon became as blood[e]

TEXT—The word ὅλη 'whole' does not occur in some manuscripts. GNT does not mention this alternative. It is omitted by BNTC; CEV, KJV, NAB, NLT.

LEXICON—a. μέλας (LN **79.26**): 'black' [BNTC, EC, **LN**, Lns; all versions except CEV, NLT], 'dark' [WBC; CEV, NLT]. See this word also at 6:5.

b. σάκκος (LN 6.164) (BAGD p. 740): 'sackcloth' [BAGD, BNTC, EC, LN, Lns; all versions except NAB, NLT, REB], 'black cloth' [NLT], 'coarse black cloth' [TEV], 'tent cloth' [NAB], 'funeral pall' [REB], 'sack' [BAGD]. The phrase σάκκος τρίχινος 'sackcloth made of hair', is translated 'haircloth' [WBC]. Σάκκος is a rough cloth [Lns, NIC, TH]. Made from black goat hair [NIC, Sw] and worn in times of mourning [LN, Lns, NIC, TH]. It is worn as a sign of repentance [LN].

c. τρίχινος (LN **8.13**) (BAGD p. 827): 'made of hair' [BAGD; NET], 'made of goat hair' [NIV], 'goat's hair' [NAB], 'of hair' [EC, LN, Lns; KJV], 'hairy' [**LN**], not explicit [BNTC, WBC; CEV, NLT, NRSV, REB, TEV, TNT].

d. ὅλη (LN 63.1) (BAGD p. 564): 'whole' [BAGD, EC, LN, Lns; NIV, TNT], 'entire' [BAGD, LN, WBC], 'full' [NET, NRSV], 'all', [LN] 'complete' [BAGD], not explicit [BNTC; CEV, KJV, NAB, NLT]. This word is also translated as modifying 'red': 'all (red)' [REB], 'completely (red)' [TEV]. The whole moon indicates a 'full' moon [Alf, Lns; NET, NRSV].

e. αἷμα (BAGD 3. p. 23): 'blood' [EC, Lns; KJV, NRSV], 'blood red' [NET, NIV, TNT], 'red like blood' [TEV], 'red as blood' [BNTC, WBC; CEV, NAB, NLT, REB]. The point of similarity here is the color red, not the liquid characteristic of blood [TH]. See this word also at 1:5

QUESTION—What is the significance of the sun becoming black?

It means that the sun stopped shining [TH]. The darkening of the sun and moon seem to symbolize the decay and collapse of society [Sw]. The sun and moon failing to fulfill their usual function along with the stars falling from the sky indicated the nearness of the end of the world [ICC].

QUESTION—What is the significance of the moon becoming blood?

The moon's darkening symbolizes the cataclysm at the world's end [Lns]. It symbolizes disaster [BAGD]. The color of deep copper is how the moon appears in a total eclipse [EC, Sw].

6:13 and the stars of-the sky fell to the earth, as (a) fig-tree[a] being-shaken[b] by (a) great wind drops[c] its unripe-figs[d]

LEXICON—a. συκῆ (LN 3.5) (BAGD p. 776): 'fig tree' [BAGD, BNTC, EC, LN, Lns, WBC; KJV, NET, NIV, NRSV, TNT], 'tree' [NLT, REB, TEV], not explicit [CEV, NAB]. A fig tree typically produces two crops a year, one ripening in June and another in August or September [LN].

b. pres. pass. participle of σείω (LN **16.7**) (BAGD 1. p. 746): 'to be shaken' [BAGD, EC, **LN**, Lns, WBC; KJV, NET, NIV, NLT, NRSV, TNT], 'to

be battered' [BNTC]. This verb is also translated as though 'figs' were its subject: 'to be shaken loose' [CEV, NAB], 'to be blown off' [REB]. It is also translated actively: 'to shake' [TEV].
- c. pres. act. indic. of βάλλω (LN **15.122**) (BAGD 1.c. p. 131): 'to drop' [**LN**, WBC; NET, NRSV], 'to cast' [EC, Lns; KJV], 'to let fall' [BAGD, LN], not explicit [CEV, NAB, REB]. This verb is also translated as though 'figs' were its subject: 'to drop' [BNTC; NIV], 'to fall' [NLT, TEV, TNT].
- d. ὄλυνθος (LN **3.37**) (BAGD p. 565): 'unripe fig' [BNTC, WBC; NET, TEV, TNT], 'late fig' [BAGD, **LN**; NIV], 'untimely fig' [KJV], 'green fig' [NLT], 'summer fig' [BAGD], 'winter fig' [Alf, Lns], 'winter fruit' [NRSV], 'fig' [EC; CEV, NAB, REB]. An ὄλυνθος is a fig that grows in the winter [Alf, Lns, NIC, Sw] and easily drops in a wind [Alf, Lns, NIC]. It is produced in late summer and often falls off before ripening [LN, WBC]. For translation purposes, the important component of meaning is that this is unripe fruit, not that it is a particular kind of fruit [TH].

QUESTION—What other Scripture describes similar scenes?

Isaiah 34:4, Matthew 24:29, Mark 13:25 and Luke 21:26 describe similar scenes.

QUESTION—What is symbolized by the stars falling from the sky?

It symbolizes the collapse of established authority [NTC]. Since the world depends on the orderly functioning of the sun, moon, and stars, when they are shaken like this, it indicates the nearness of the end of the world [ICC]. To the ancient world this indicated the end of the world [NIC]. It marks the end of the world [TH]. In the ancient world, stars were thought of as living beings with divine authority. The falling of the stars therefore symbolized God's punishment of the powerful beings who stood behind the authority of earthly kings [BNTC]. While οἱ ἀστέρες 'the stars' can refer to the larger heavenly bodies, it can refer to smaller objects such as meteors and comets. Here stars are not referred to since they are still in place at the fourth trumpet, so this is a literal meteor shower intended to cause terror among the people of the earth (Luke 21:11) [EC].

6:14 and the sky[a] split-open[b] like (a) scroll being-rolled-up[c]

LEXICON—a. οὐρανός (LN 1.5, 1.11): 'sky' [BNTC, LN (1.5); all versions except KJV], 'heaven' [EC, LN (1.11), Lns, WBC; KJV]. See this word also at 3:12.
- b. aorist pass. (deponent = act.) indic. of ἀποχωρίζομαι (LN **15.14, 63.30**) (BAGD p. 102): 'to split open' [BNTC, **LN** (63.30)] 'to be split apart' [NET], 'to be split' [BAGD], 'to be separated' [Lns], 'to be separated into parts' [EC], 'to be separated definitely, to be split up' [LN (63.30)], 'to disappear' [**LN** (15.14); NAB, TEV, TNT], 'to disappear from sight' [WBC], 'to vanish' [NRSV, REB], 'to be taken away' [NLT], 'to depart' [KJV], 'to recede' [NIV], 'to move away' [LN (15.14)], not explicit [CEV].

c. pres. pass. participle of ἑλίσσω (LN **79.120**) (BAGD p. 251): 'to be rolled up' [BAGD, EC, **LN**, Lns, WBC; all versions except KJV, NIV, NRSV], 'to be rolled together' [KJV], 'to be made into a roll' [LN]. This verb is also translated actively with 'sky' as its subject: 'to roll up' [BNTC; NIV], 'rolling itself up' [NRSV].

QUESTION—What figure is being described here to symbolize the action of the sky?

It is the figure of a rolled-out scroll that is split in the middle with each side rolling back in two directions [EC, ICC, NIC, Sw]. It is the figure of something separated from its place and then shriveled up like paper [Lns]. It is the figure of a scroll being rolled up [Alf, TH], and placed off by itself [Alf]. It is the figure of a scroll rolling into itself [TH].

QUESTION—What other Scriptures portray a similar event?

Isaiah 34:4; Matthew 24:35; 2 Peter 3:10; and Hebrews 1:12 portray a similar event.

and every mountain and island was-moved^a from its place.

LEXICON—a. aorist pass. indic. of κινέω (LN 15.1): 'to be moved' [EC, LN (15.1, 15.3), Lns; CEV, KJV, NET, TEV, TNT], 'to be removed' [NIV, NRSV], 'to be dislodged' [BNTC; REB], 'to be uprooted' [NAB], 'to be shaken' [WBC]. The phrase ἐκ τῶν τόπων αὐτῶν ἐκινήθησαν 'were moved from their places' is translated 'disappeared' [NLT]. See this word also at 2:5.

QUESTION—What is the significance of the mountains and islands being moved?

It symbolizes political upheaval [NTC]. Mountains and islands are the most stable features of the world. Their being shaken implies God's judgment [WBC]. It should not be taken literally [ICC, TNTC], otherwise men would not be able to hide themselves as in the following context [TNTC]. It is a literal upheaval, probably tied to a shifting of the earth's crust during the earthquake (6:12); mountains and islands rise and disappear [EC].

QUESTION—What other Scriptures portray a similar event?

Isaiah 13:6–13 and Revelation 16:20 portray a similar event.

QUESTION—Who is the implied actor of ἐκινήθησαν 'were moved'?

This verb indicates divine activity [TH]: God moved/caused to be moved.

DISCOURSE UNIT: 6:15–17 [Ld, Lns, NIC, WBC]. The topic is human reactions [WBC].

6:15 **And the kings of-the earth and the great-men^a and the military-leaders^b and the rich^c (persons) and the powerful^d (persons) and every slave and free^e (person)**

LEXICON—a. μεγιστάν (LN 87.41) (BAGD p. 498): 'great man' [BAGD; KJV], 'great person' [LN], 'important person' [LN, WBC], 'chief one' [EC], 'very important person' [LN; NET], 'famous person' [CEV], 'magnate' [BAGD, Lns; NRSV], 'ruler' [NLT, TEV], 'prince' [NIV],

'noble' [NAB, REB], 'leading man' [TNT], 'courtier' [BAGD, BNTC]. These were high-ranking officials in the kings' courts [EC, Lns].
b. χιλίαρχος (LN 55.15) (BAGD p. 882): 'military leader' [BAGD, EC; CEV], 'military chief' [TEV], 'general' [LN, Lns, WBC; NET, NIV, NLT, NRSV], 'commander' [REB, TNT], 'commanding officer' [LN], 'officer' [BNTC], 'chief captains' [KJV], 'military tribune' [BAGD], 'chiliarch' [LN, Lns]. This noun is also translated as a phrase: 'those in command' [NAB]. A χιλίαρχος was the commander of 1000 soldiers [BAGD, LN], or the commander of a Roman cohort of 600 soldiers [BAGD, NIC].
c. πλούσιος (BAGD 1. p. 673): 'rich' [BAGD, BNTC, EC, Lns; all versions except KJV, NAB, NLT], 'rich man' [KJV], 'wealthy' [BAGD, WBC; NAB], 'wealthy person' [NLT]. See this word also at 2:9.
d. ἰσχυρός (LN **87.44**) (BAGD 1.b. p. 383): 'powerful' [BAGD, BNTC, LN, WBC; all versions except KJV, NIV, NLT], 'strong' [BAGD, EC, Lns], 'mighty' [BAGD; NIV], 'mighty man' [KJV], 'great' [**LN**]. This adjective is also translated as a phrase: 'person with great power' [NLT]. This probably refers to those who are either physically [Alf, Lns], or intellectually strong [Alf]. They had great influence over large groups of people [EC]. See this word also at 5:2.
e. ἐλεύθερος (LN 87.84) (BAGD 1. p. 250): 'free' [BAGD, BNTC; NAB, NET, NRSV, REB, TEV], 'free person' [EC, LN, WBC; CEV, NLT], 'free man' [LN, Lns; KJV, NIV, TNT].

QUESTION—What does this list of classes of people indicate?
It indicates that people from all classes of society, from highest to lowest, are included [EC, ICC, Ld, NTC, Sw, Wal]. It is a collective way to refer to God's enemies [NIC, TNTC, WBC]. It refers to all unbelievers on earth [NIGTC]. There are only six classes since the last two indicate a single class, united by the word 'every'. Six is the number of the ungodly [Lns]. Prominence is given to the first four, the great and powerful [TH, TNTC]. The first five classes comprise all those who might have been able to put their trust in a permanent world [Alf]. Stress is given to those who might have reason to feel secure in their own position in life [NIC]. The number seven indicates completeness [NIC, TNTC].

QUESTION—What is indicated by the final two classes 'slave' and 'free'?
These two classes comprised the most significant class division of the ancient world [Sw]. It is way of expressing 'everyone' [BNTC; NRSV, REB]: everyone, slave or free. It is a way of expressing 'all other people' [TEV]: all other people, slave or free. It indicates the whole lower class of society, those who are slaves and those slaves who have been set free [EC, Lns].

hid themselves in the caves[a] **and among the rocks of-the mountains**

LEXICON—a. σπήλαιον (LN **1.57**) (BAGD p. 762): 'cave' [BAGD, BNTC, EC, **LN**, Lns, WBC; all versions except KJV], 'den' [BAGD, LN; KJV], 'hideout' [LN].

QUESTION—What does this action indicate?

It indicates that the people recognize this as the end of the world [Ld]. It is a picture terror and hopelessness [Lns]. They did not dread death as much as standing before God [EC]. In the OT it indicated that such people were running away from God's judgment [WBC].

QUESTION—What other Scriptures portray a similar event or similar groupings?

Isaiah 2:10, 18, 19, 21; Luke 21:26; Revelation 13:16; and 19:18 portray a similar event or similar groupings.

6:16 **And they-say to-the mountains and rocks,**[a] **"Fall on us and hide us from (the) face**[b] **of-the-one sitting on the throne and from the anger**[c] **of-the Lamb,**

LEXICON—a. πέτρα (LN **2.21**) (BAGD 1.a. p. 654): 'rock' [BAGD, EC, Lns; all versions except REB], 'rock cliff' [**LN**], 'cliff' [Lns, WBC], 'crag' [BNTC; REB], 'bedrock' [LN]. Πέτρα indicates a rocky crag or mountain ledge rather than the rock pieces referred to by λίθος [LN].

b. πρόσωπον (LN 85.26) (BAGD 1.c.α. p. 721): 'face' [EC; all versions except CEV, REB, TEV], 'presence' [BAGD, LN], 'countenance' [Lns], 'the One' [WBC; REB], 'the one' [CEV], 'sight' [BNTC], 'eyes' [TEV]. Here πρόσωπον 'face' is either a reference to God's presence [TH, WBC; REB], or to his eyes [BNTC, TH; TEV]. See this word also at 4:7.

c. ὀργή (LN 88.173) (BAGD 2.b. p. 579): 'anger' [LN; CEV, TEV], 'wrath' [BAGD, BNTC, EC, Lns, WBC; all versions except CEV, TEV], 'fury' [LN]. The ὀργή here is not the strong emotion but the punishment that the anger expresses [TH].

QUESTION—What other Scriptures speak of a similar concept?

Genesis 3:8, 9; Isaiah 2:19; Hosea 10:8; and Luke 23:30 all speak of a similar concept.

QUESTION—Who is the one sitting on the throne?

This refers to God [Lns, TH, WBC; REB]. This is a lengthy way to refer to God that is frequently used in Revelation [WBC].

QUESTION—Why do the people want to be hidden?

They want to be hidden because they prefer death to having to face the Lamb's wrath [Alf, EC, NIC], or God's presence [Sw]. The people did not seek death, but only protection from God's wrath [TH]. The impending threat is so great than anything is better than having to face it [TNTC].

6:17 because the great[a] day of-their wrath came, and who is-able to-stand?"[b]

TEXT—Some manuscripts have αυτοῦ 'his', before 'wrath' instead of αὐτῶν 'their'. GNT selects the reading 'their' with an A rating, indicating that the text is certain. The reading 'his' is taken by WBC and KJV.

LEXICON—a. μέγας (LN 87.22) (BAGD 2.b.β. p. 498): 'great' [BAGD, BNTC, EC, LN, Lns, WBC; KJV, NAB, NIV, NLT, NRSV, REB, TNT], 'terrible' [TH; CEV, TEV], 'important' [BAGD, LN].

b. aorist. pass. (deponent = act.) infin. of ἵστημι (BAGD II.1.d. p. 382): 'to stand' [BNTC, EC, Lns; KJV, NIV, NRSV, REB, TNT], 'withstand (it)' [WBC; NAB, NET], 'to stand up against (it)' [TEV], 'to stand firm' [BAGD], 'to face (it)' [CEV], 'to survive' [NLT], 'to hold one's ground' [BAGD, Sw]. The aorist refers to what has come and people connect the arrival of this day at least with the cosmic upheavals that came with the sixth seal [EC, Sw]. See this word also at 3:20.

QUESTION—What is the significance to the definite article in the phrase ἡ ἡμέρα ἡ μεγάλη 'the day, the great'?

It signifies a special day, one that is well known to the readers, the Day of the Lord (see 16:14) [WBC].

QUESTION—What other Scriptures refer to the Day of the Lord or to his wrath?

Nahum 1:6; Joel 2:11, 31; Zephaniah 1:14, 18 2:2; Malachi 4:5; Jude 6; and Revelation 16:14 refer to the Day of the Lord or to his wrath.

QUESTION—Who is the antecedent of αὐτῶν 'their' wrath?

The antecedent of 'their' is God's and the Lamb's wrath [NIGTC, NTC, Sw, TH].

QUESTION—How long is the 'day'?

Day does not refer to a 24-hour period, but to an indefinite period of time including the great tribulation and the Second Coming of Christ [Ld, Wal].

QUESTION—What is the nature of the day?

It will be a day: of judgment [TH, WBC]; of punishment [TH]; a day of accounting for evildoers [TNTC]. It will be a day of accounting that has to occur in a moral universe, a day when God gives his response to the world's evil [NTC].

QUESTION—What reply is expected to the question, 'Who is able to stand' and what does it mean 'to stand'?

The expected reply to the question is: 'no one is able to stand' [EC, NIGTC, TNTC], at least none of those who utter this cry [Lns]. 'To stand' means to survive what the future holds as the hardships worsen as God's wrath is revealed [EC]. It means to endure God's fierce anger [NIC]. This is the viewpoint of the terrified inhabitants of the earth, not that of the author [ICC].

DISCOURSE UNIT: 7:1–17 [EC, Lns, NIC, NTC, TNTC, Wal, WBC; CEV, KJV, NET, NIV, NLT]. The topic is the 144,000 [Lns, WBC; CEV, KJV, NET], an interlude [NTC, TNTC], interlude: the two multitudes [Ld], interlude: security and salvation [NIC], the saints of the great tribulation [Wal], the slaves of God [EC], the seals [NIV], God's people preserved [NLT]. This chapter gives the answer to the question, "Who can stand?" It is those who are sealed [BNTC, Ld].

DISCOURSE UNIT: 7:1–8 [Alf, GNT, Ld, NIC, NIGTC, NTC, TNTC, WBC; NAB, NIV, NRSV, TEV]. The topic is the sealing of the elect [Alf], the sealing of the martyrs [BNTC], the sealing of God's servants [NIC, NTC, TNTC], the sealing of the 144,000 of Israel [GNT, Sw, WBC; NAB, NIV, NRSV], the 144,000 [Ld; TEV], the 144,000 on earth [EC].

DISCOURSE UNIT: 7:1–3 [Wal]. The topic is the vision of the four angels.

7:1 After^a this I-saw four angels standing on the four corners^b of-the earth, holding-back^c the four winds^d of-the earth

TEXT—Some manuscripts include καί 'and' before μετά 'after'. GNT does not mention this alternative. It is included by KJV.

TEXT—Instead of the singular τοῦτο 'this', some manuscripts have the plural ταῦτα 'these'. GNT does not mention this alternative. The reading 'these' is taken by KJV.

LEXICON—a. μετά with accusative object (LN 67.48) (BAGD B.II.3. p. 510): 'after' [BAGD, BNTC, EC, LN, Lns, WBC; all versions except NLT], not explicit [NLT]. The phrase μετὰ τοῦτο is translated 'after this' [BAGD, BNTC, Lns, WBC; CEV, NAB, NET, NIV, NRSV, TEV, TNT], 'after that' [REB], 'then' [NLT], 'after these things' [KJV], 'afterward' [BAGD].

    b. γωνία (LN **79.107**) (BAGD p.168): 'corner' [BAGD, BNTC, EC, **LN**, Lns; all versions], 'quarter' [WBC].

    c. pres. act. participle of κρατέω (BAGD 2.d. p. 448): 'to hold back' [BAGD, EC, Lns; all versions except KJV, NAB], 'to hold' [LN; KJV], 'to hold in check' [BNTC, ICC; NAB], 'to restrain' [BAGD, WBC], 'to hold fast, to detain' [Sw], 'to hinder' [BAGD]. See this word also at 2:1.

    d. ἄνεμος (LN **14.4**) (BAGD 1.a. p. 64): 'wind' [BAGD, BNTC, EC, **LN**, Lns, WBC; all versions], 'blowing' [LN].

QUESTION—What is the function of the phrase μετὰ τοῦτο 'after this'?

It introduces a new section or vision [Alf, EC, ICC, Sw, TH, WBC]. It simply states that what John saw in chapter seven is subsequent to what he saw in chapter 6 [Lns, NIGTC]. It introduces an interlude between the sixth and seventh seals. The singular 'this' takes the events of the sixth seal as a single unit [EC].

QUESTION—Who are the angels?

They are God's angels and do not represent anything further [Alf, Lns].

QUESTION—What is the significance of the angels' standing on the four corners of the earth?

It symbolizes their complete control over the earth [NIGTC, TNTC].

QUESTION—What do the four corners of the earth symbolize?
They symbolize the four cardinal directions of the earth from which the wind blows, North, South, East, and West [Alf, EC]. They symbolize the complete known world [NIGTC] and the world-wide responsibilities of the angels [EC].
QUESTION—What is symbolized by wind?
Wind symbolizes harmful or destructive activity [BNTC, EC, NIC, NIGTC, TNTC]. We assume that the winds will cause damage [Ld, WBC]. It symbolizes judgment as 7:2 and 3 show that they are kept from harming the earth [NTC].
QUESTION—What do the four winds symbolize?
1. They symbolize the plagues that are shortly to happen [EC, Ld]. Instead of referring to the release of these winds later, the picture changes to the plagues associated with the seven angels with trumpets.
2. They symbolize the four horsemen of 6:1–8 [BNTC, NIGTC, TNTC]. The four winds symbolize the destructive power of the four horsemen. See Zechariah 6:1–8 (ASV) where the four horsemen are identified with the four winds of heaven. This interpretation places this chapter in chronological order before chapter six [BNTC, NIGTC]. Taken this way, we can see what happened to believers during the destruction portrayed in chapter 6 [TNTC].
3. They do not symbolize the four horsemen [NIC, WBC]. The passage in Zechariah (RSV) does not identify the horsemen with the winds, but simply states that they go forth *to* the winds [NIC]. They symbolize the four cardinal directions, North, South, East, and West, and include all winds [WBC].

so-that no wind should-blow[a] **on the earth nor on the sea nor on any tree.**
LEXICON—a. pres. act. subj. of πνέω (LN 14.4) (BAGD 1.a. p. 679): 'to blow' [BAGD, BNTC, LN, Lns, WBC; all versions]. The present subjunctive indicates that the winds had already begun to blow [EC, Lns, NIC]: should not keep on blowing.

7:2 And I-saw another angel coming-up[a] **from (the) rising**[b] **of-(the) sun having (the) seal**[c] **of-(the) living God,**
LEXICON—a. pres. act. participle of ἀναβαίνω (LN 15.101): 'to come up' [LN, Lns; CEV, NAB, NIV, TEV, TNT], 'to come' [NLT], 'to ascend' [EC, LN, WBC; KJV, NET, NRSV], 'to rise' [BNTC; REB], 'to go up' [LN]. The angel comes up to Heaven [Alf, TH], as indicated by the following context [TH].
b. ἀνατολή (LN 15.104, 82.1) (BAGD 2.a. p. 62): 'rising' [BAGD, EC; NRSV], 'east' [LN (82.1)]. The phrase ἀνατολῆς ἡλίου 'rising of the sun' is translated 'the east' [BAGD, BNTC, WBC; all versions except CEV, NRSV], 'where the sun rises in the east' [CEV], 'sunrise' [Lns].
c. σφραγίς (LN **6.54**) (BAGD 1.b. p. 796): 'seal' [BNTC, EC, LN, Lns; all versions except CEV], 'signet' [BAGD, **LN**, WBC], 'signet ring' [NIC,

Sw, TH, WBC], 'mark' [CEV]. It is the instrument with which one seals or stamps [BAGD, EC, Lns, TH]. See this word also at 5:1 where it refers to a seal of wax that has been impressed with a signet ring.

QUESTION—How are the nouns related in the genitive construction σφραγῖδα θεοῦ ζῶντος 'seal of the living God' related?

God uses the seal, or people use the seal to put God's mark on people [TH]. God possesses the seal or the seal puts God's mark of the people [Alf, TH].

QUESTION—What is the function of a seal as well as its nature here?

The purpose of a seal was to mark an object or person as being owned by someone [BAGD, Lns, NIC, Sw, TH, TNTC, WBC], or to validate official documents [NIC, Sw]. Here the mark was a symbol of God's protection (see 9.4) [BAGD, NIC, TNTC, WBC]. The seal put the name of the Lamb and His Father on a person (see 14:1 and 22:4) [NIC, NTC, TH, WBC]. Here the seal protects believers in the coming judgments [EC, NIC], and from attacks by demonic powers [ICC, NIC].

QUESTION—Why is God called 'the living God'?

It is used to show the contrast between the true God and false idols [EC, ICC, NIC].

and he-called-out^a with-(a) loud voice to-the four angels to-whom it-was-given to-damage^b the earth and the sea

LEXICON—a. aorist act. indic. of κράζω (LN 33.83) (BAGD 2.a. p. 447): 'to call out' [BAGD; NIV, TEV], 'to call' [NRSV], 'to shout' [LN; CEV], 'to shout out' [NET, NLT], 'to cry out' [EC, WBC; NAB, REB, TNT], 'to cry' [BNTC, Lns; KJV].

b. aorist act. infin. of ἀδικέω (See this word at 2:11): 'to damage' [NET, NRSV, TEV], 'to do damage' [TNT], 'to hurt' [EC, Lns, WBC; KJV], 'to harm' [WBC; CEV, NIV], 'to injure' [NLT], 'to ravage' [NAB, REB], 'to make havoc of' [BNTC]. The damage is done by loosing the winds [Alf, Sw].

QUESTION—Who is the implied actor of the passive verb ἐδόθη 'it was given' and what was given?

The implied actor is God [NIGTC, TH, WBC]: God gave. They were given power [BNTC, NIGTC, TH, WBC; CEV, NIV, NLT, NRSV, REB, TEV]. They were given the assignment [WBC]. They were given the permission [NET, TNT].

7:3 saying, "(Do) not damage the earth nor the sea nor the trees, until we-mark-with-a-seal^a the servants of-our God on their foreheads."^b

LEXICON—a. aorist act. subj. of σφραγίζω (LN **33.484**) (BAGD 2.b. p. 796): 'to mark with a seal' [BAGD, **LN**, TH; NRSV, TEV, TNT], 'to mark' [LN; CEV], 'to seal' [EC, LN, Lns, WBC; KJV], 'to put a seal' [NET, NIV], 'to place a seal' [NLT], 'to set a seal' [BNTC; REB], 'to imprint a seal' [NAB].

b. μέτωπον (LN 8.16) (BAGD p. 515): 'forehead' [BAGD, BNTC, EC, LN, Lns, WBC; all versions].

QUESTION—Is the plural subject of the verb σφραγίσωμεν 'we mark with a seal' inclusive or exclusive?

The plural subject 'we' is exclusive in that it does not include the four angels being spoken to [TH]. Those included in the 'we' are: other angels [TH] or the angel's helpers [NIC, NIGTC]. The plural is an editorial 'we' [CEV]: I have marked with a seal.

QUESTION—Who are the 'servants of our God'?

They are the same as the 144,000 of the 7:3 and 14:1, and their number includes all the martyrs alive at that time, but not the whole church [BNTC]. They are the complete number of believers who are alive when this event occurs [Alf, NIC]. They are the same as those spoken about in Matthew 24:31 who are alive when Christ returns. Although not identical with the group referred to in 7:9, they are included in that group [Alf]. They are the same as those servants addressed in 1:1 and include all those who become believers throughout the NT era [Lns]. It refers to all of God's people without limit [TNTC].

QUESTION—What is indicated by the phrase τοῦ θεοῦ ἡμῶν 'our God'?

It indicates that angels and believers are linked together as servants of God (see 19:10 and 22:9) [EC, ICC, NIC, Sw]. It also includes the four angels who are being addressed [TH].

QUESTION—What is the purpose of 'marking with a seal'?

It protects those sealed from God's wrath [NIC]. It protects believers from the disasters that the winds that are being held in check will inflict [EC, NIGTC]. It protects martyrs from the disasters that the winds that are being held in check will inflict [BNTC]. It protects the 144,000 from the harm of the fifth trumpet spoken of in 9:4 [WBC].

DISCOURSE UNIT: 7:4–8 [Wal, WBC]. The topic is the sealing of the twelve tribes.

7:4 And I-heard the number of-the-ones marked-with-a-seal, (a) hundred forty four thousand, marked-with-a-seal from every tribe of-(the)-sons of-Israel:

QUESTION—Should the number be taken literally or figuratively?

1. It should be taken figuratively [Alf, BNTC, ICC, Ld, Lns, NIC, NIGTC, NTC, Sw, TH]. It refers to the church as spiritual Israel (see Romans 2:28–29, 4:11; Galatians 3:29, 6:16; Philippians 3:3; Revelation 2:9, 3:9) [Alf, ICC, Ld, NIC, NIGTC, NTC, Sw, TNTC]. It refers to all of God's people [Lns, NIGTC, TH]. The number 144,000 represents completeness [Alf, Ld, Lns, NIC, NIGTC]. The number means: that all of God's people will be brought safely through the tribulation [Ld]; that these are the believers who are about to enter the final period of testing [NIC]. It is the same group as the 'servants of God' of 7:2 and the 'great throng' of 7:9, but is limited to martyrs [BNTC].
2. It should be taken literally [EC, Wal, WBC]. This refers literally to the 12 Tribes of Israel. Although only 12,000 from each tribe are sealed, others

from Israel will be saved but may be martyred. However, only these 144,000 will be protected from persecution and brought safely through the time of tribulation [Wal].

7:5 **from (the) tribe of-Judah twelve thousand sealed, from (the) tribe of-Reuben twelve thousand, from (the) tribe of-Gad twelve thousand,**

TEXT—Some manuscripts possibly include ἐσφραγισμένοι 'sealed' after χιλιάδες 'thousands' beginning with the tribe of Reuben and after each of the following phrases through the second phrase in 7:8. GNT does not mention these. The reading 'sealed' is included by the TR and KJV.

QUESTION—Why is the tribe of Judah mentioned first?

The tribe of Judah is mentioned first probably because the Messiah comes from this tribe [BNTC, ICC, Lns, NIC, NIGTC, NTC, TNTC, WBC].

7:6 **from (the) tribe of-Asher twelve thousand, from (the) tribe of-Naphtali twelve thousand, from (the) tribe of-Manasseh twelve thousand, 7:7 from (the) tribe of-Simeon twelve thousand, from (the) tribe of-Levi twelve thousand, from (the) tribe of-Issachar twelve thousand, 7:8 from (the) tribe of-Zebulun twelve thousand, from (the) tribe of-Joseph twelve thousand, from (the) tribe of-Benjamin twelve thousand sealed.**

DISCOURSE UNIT: 7:9–17 [Alf, BNTC, EC, GNT, ICC, Ld, NIC, NIGTC, NTC; CEV, KJV, NAB, NIV, NRSV, TEV]. The topic is the multitude from every nation [Alf, GNT; CEV, NRSV], the innumerable multitude [Ld, Sw, TNTC, WBC; KJV, NIV, NLT, TEV], the innumerable multitude in heaven [EC], the triumph of the martyrs [ICC, NTC], the triumph of the elect [NAB], the song of victory [BNTC], the bliss of the redeemed in Heaven [NIC].

7:9 **After these-things I-looked, and behold**[a] **(a) great crowd,**[b] **that no-one was-able to count,**[c] **from every nation and tribe and people and tongue**

LEXICON—a. ἰδού (See this word at 1:7): 'behold' [EC, WBC], 'lo' [Lns; KJV], 'here' [NET], 'there' [BNTC; NRSV, TEV, TNT], 'there before me' [NIV], not explicit [CEV, NAB, NLT, REB].

b. ὄχλος (LN 11.1): 'crowd' [LN, WBC; CEV, NAB, NET, NLT, TEV, TNT], 'multitude' [EC, LN, Lns; KJV, NIV, NRSV], 'throng' [BNTC; REB].

c. aorist act. infin. of ἀριθμέω (LN **60.3**) (BAGD p. 106): 'to count' [BAGD, EC, **LN**; all versions except KJV], 'to number' [LN, Lns, WBC; KJV].

QUESTION—What is the significance of the phrase μετὰ ταῦτα 'after these things'?

It introduces a new vision [Alf, EC]. It only indicates that this is the next thing that John sees [Lns]. It does not indicate that the next event is subsequent in time to what has gone before but only that John saw this vision after the preceding one [NIGTC].

QUESTION—At what time will this vision here portrayed come to pass?
This occurs during the tribulation period between the sixth and seventh seals [EC]. This innumerable crowd appears after the final judgment takes place when the righteous enter at last into eternal life (see Matthew 25.46) [Alf]. It is definite future and is a picture of what will occur after 22:3 when God's throne comes down to be with men [Ld, Sw]. This is a glimpse of the final state of bliss of believers given to encourage those who are about to suffer greatly [NIC]. This vision portrays a time before the great tribulation and is given to encourage those who will suffer [ICC].

QUESTION—Where are the words 'nation, tribe, people, and tongue' treated previously?
All these words occur in 5:9 only in a different order. Together they indicate the whole human race [TH]. All these together indicate the universality of the crowd [NIC, TNTC]. The four-fold reference highlights the size of the crowd [Lns].

standing before the throne and before the Lamb, clothed in-white robes and (holding) palm-branches[a] in their hands,

LEXICON—a. φοῖνιξ (LN **3.53**) (BAGD I.2. p. 864): 'palm-branch' [BAGD, EC, LN; all versions except KJV], 'palm frond' [WBC], 'palm' [BNTC, Lns; KJV], 'palm-leaf' [BAGD].

QUESTION—To what does τοῦ θρόνου 'the throne' refer?
It is a reference to God who sits on the throne (see 4:10 and 8:3) [WBC]. It is a symbol of God's power, rule and dominion [Lns].

QUESTION—Who is this great crowd?
1. It is the same as the one just described as being sealed [ICC, Lns, NIGTC, TNTC]. The symbolic number of 144,000 is now shown to be beyond counting [Lns].
2. It is different from the one just described as being sealed [Alf, EC, NIC, NTC, Wal, WBC]. The group in 7:4–8 was a specific number, this one is innumerable. That group was taken from one nation, this is taken from every nation. That group may be included in this one [WBC]. This group is far larger than the 144,000 and includes believers of all time [NIC].

QUESTION—Are these people martyrs?
It is probable that they are martyrs [ICC, Ld, NTC, Wal]. The group is the martyrs spoken of in 6:11 [ICC]. Like those in chapter 6 they are martyrs but now their number is complete [NTC]. Some of them may be martyrs [NIC]. There is no indication here that they are martyrs [NIC]. This refers to the entire church [Lns].

QUESTION—What is symbolized by the white color of their robes?
White symbolizes: holiness [Lns]; justification [TNTC]; bliss [NTC]; victory [Ld, NIC]; the righteousness of Christ [NIC]; purity through testing [NIGTC]. White robes are the dress of martyrs (see 6:11) [Wal].

QUESTION—What is symbolized by palm branches?

Palm branches symbolize: joy (see John 12:13) [Alf, ICC, NIC, Sw, TH]; victory [BNTC, EC, ICC, Ld, NIC, NIGTC, NTC, Sw, TNTC, Wal, WBC]; purity [BNTC, NIC]; life and salvation [Lns].

7:10 and they-call-out with-(a)-loud voice saying, "Salvation[a] to-our God the-one sitting on the throne and to-the Lamb."

LEXICON—a. σωτηρία (LN 21.25, 21.26) (BAGD 2. p. 801): 'salvation' [BAGD, EC, LN (21.25, 21.26), Lns; all versions except CEV, REB], 'victory' [BNTC, NTC, WBC; REB]. The phrase σωτηρία τῷ θεῷ ἡμῶν 'salvation to our God' is translated 'our God has the power to save his people' [CEV].

QUESTION—Does 'salvation' here refer to general deliverance from sin or to deliverance from the recent persecution?

1. It refers to deliverance from recent persecution [BNTC, EC, ICC, NIGTC, Sw, TH, WBC]. It refers to deliverance from the great tribulation they have come out of (see 7:14) [Sw]. It has the connotation of 'victory' [EC].
2. It refers to general deliverance from sin [Ld, Lns, NIC]. It refers to deliverance from sin, death and condemnation [Lns]. It refers both to deliverance from persecution and to sin and its consequences (see 7:15–17) [NIC].

QUESTION—What is the meaning of the phrase σωτηρία τῷ θεῷ ἡμῶν 'salvation to our God'?

The sense is: salvation *belongs* to our God [WBC; NET, NIV, NRSV]; salvation *comes from* our God [NLT, TEV]; salvation *is from* our God [NIGTC; NAB, TNT]. It is an acknowledgment that God is the source of their salvation [Alf, Ld, Lns, NIC, NIGTC, Sw, TNTC, Wal, WBC; CEV, NAB, NET, NIV, NLT, NRSV, TEV, TNT].

QUESTION—Is the pronoun ἡμῶν 'our (God)' inclusive or exclusive?

If the crowd is speaking to each other, the pronoun is inclusive, that is, all of ours. But if the crowd is speaking to God, of course the pronoun is exclusive [TH].

7:11 And all the angels stood around the throne and the elders and the four living-beings and they-fell-down on their faces before the throne and they worshiped God

QUESTION—Who is the antecedent of the pronoun in ἔπεσαν 'they fell down'?

The antecedent is 'the angels' [Alf, BNTC, ICC, NIC, NIGTC, Sw, TNTC; all versions except CEV]. The antecedent is the angels and all those in heaven [Wal]. The antecedent is the angels, the twenty-four elders, and the four living beings [EC, Lns, WBC; CEV], the same ones as in 5:11–12 [EC].

QUESTION—What is the meaning of εσαν ἐνώπιον 'they fell down before'?

It means that they prostrated themselves before [Sw, TH].

7:12 saying, "Amen, the praise[a] and the glory and the wisdom and the thanks and the honor and the power and the strength to-our God forever-and-ever;[b] amen."

LEXICON—a. εὐλογία (See this word at 5:12): 'praise' [BNTC, WBC; CEV, NAB, NET, NIV, REB, TEV], 'blessing' [EC, Lns; KJV, NLT, NRSV, TNT].

b. εἰς τοὺς αἰῶνας τῶν αἰώνων (See this phrase at 1:6 and 1:18): 'forever and ever' [BNTC, EC, WBC; all versions except NLT, REB], 'for ever' [REB], 'forever and forever' [NLT], 'for the eons of the eons' [Lns].

QUESTION—What is the meaning of the first ἀμήν 'amen'?

It means that the angels take the praise of 7:10 and make it their own [ICC] while solemnly confirming it [EC, ICC, Lns, TH, TNTC]. It emphatically confirms the praise of 7:10 [NIGTC].

QUESTION—Where are the nouns of this verse also treated?

Six of the seven are treated at 5:12, while the word εὐχαριστία 'thanks' is treated at 4:9 [TH].

QUESTION—What is the function of the definite article's being repeated before each noun?

It emphasizes each word [NIC, Sw]. The article means in each case 'the …above all others' [TNTC].

QUESTION—What is the function of the final ἀμήν 'amen'?

It asserts the reliability of the whole verse [TNTC].

7:13 And one of the elders answered[a] saying to-me, "These ones clothed with-the white robes who are-they and from-where did-they-come?"

LEXICON—a. aorist pass. (deponent = act.) indic. of ἀποκρίνομαι (LN 33.28, 33.184) (BAGD 1. p. 93): 'to answer' [BAGD, EC, LN (33.184), Lns; KJV], 'to address' [NRSV], 'to reply' [BAGD, LN (33.184)], 'to speak' [BNTC, LN (33.28)], 'to declare, to say' [LN (33.28)]. The phrase ἀπεκρίθη…λέγων 'answered…saying' is translated 'asked' [CEV, NAB, NET, NIV, NLT, TEV], 'turned and asked' [REB], 'said' [WBC; TNT]. Ἀποκρίνομαι indicates a response to a particular situation rather than to a question [EC, ICC, Lns, TH, WBC]. 'Spoke up' is a good translation of the phrase 'answered saying' [TH].

QUESTION—Did the elder know the answers to these question?

The elder did know the answers, he was asking rhetorically [NIC]. The elder was anticipating John's question [NIC, Sw]. The purpose of these questions was to focus interest in the scene portrayed in verses 9 and 10 [WBC]. The elder intends to interpret the scene for John [TH, WBC].

7:14 And I-said to-him, "My lord,[b] you know."

TEXT—The word μου 'my' does not occur in some manuscripts. GNT does not mention this alternative.

LEXICON—a. κύριος (LN 87.53) (BAGD 1.b. p. 459): 'lord', [BNTC, EC, Lns; NET, REB], 'sir' [BAGD, LN], 'mister' [LN]. The phrase κύριε μου 'my lord' is translated 'Sir' [WBC; all versions except NET, REB]. This form of address indicates an attitude of subordination, courtesy, respect [NIGTC] or reverence [Alf, EC, Lns, NIC].

QUESTION—What is the significance of the explicit pronoun σύ 'you'?

The explicit pronoun is emphatic [BNTC, EC, NIC; NAB, NLT, NRSV, REB, TEV]: You yourself know. Or, it is you who knows.

QUESTION—What is implied in John's reply σύ οὖδας 'you know'?

It implies that John does not know [Alf, EC, ICC, NIC, Sw, Wal], but wants to [ICC]. It is a request to the elder to give the answer [Lns, Sw].

And he-said to-me, "These are the-ones coming out-of the great tribulation and they-washed their robes and made-white[a] them in the blood of-the Lamb.

LEXICON—a. aorist act. indic. of λευκαίνω (LN **79.28**) (BAGD 2. p. 472): 'to make white' [BAGD, BNTC, EC, **LN**, Lns, WBC; all versions], 'to whiten' [LN]. The aorist tense of this verb and ἔπλυναν 'they washed' indicates an action completed some time in the past [ICC, Lns, NIC, Sw, TNTC] on earth [ICC, Sw]. the two aorists 'washed' and 'made white' indicate one action, not two [Lns].

QUESTION—What is the significance of the present tense participle ἐρχόμενοι 'coming'?

1. It is descriptive and has no reference to time [Alf, Lns, NIC, NTC, Sw, WBC]. It means 'they who have just come out'. The aorist 'did come' of 7:3 indicates that it should not be taken as though they were just arriving [NIC]. It simply describes these people as being those that come out of the great tribulation [Alf]. If it refers to time, it should be taken as a past [NTC]. The participle indicates action that is simultaneous with the two aorist verbs 'washed' and 'made white' and so should be translated as a past [WBC].
2. It should be translated as an imperfect indicating that they were at that very time coming out of the great tribulation [BNTC, EC, ICC].

QUESTION—To what does τῆς θλίψεως τῆς μεγάλης 'the tribulation the great' refer?

1. It refers to the great tribulation spoken of in Daniel 12:1, Matthew 24:21, Mark 13:19, 1 Thessalonians and Revelation 3:10 that occurs before the end [EC, ICC, NIC, NIGTC, Sw, TH, Wal, WBC]. The definite article indicates that the readers already know the tribulation referred to, that it is the one that will introduce the final days [WBC]. The definite article indicates the final series of troubles that will precede the end [NIC]. The tribulation referred to is future and not the same thing that all believers experience in the world [ICC].
2. It refers to all the tribulation that believers have gone through from the beginning [Alf, Lns, NTC, TNTC]. It indicates the great tribulation, but also includes all the trials that believers have endured (see John 16:33 and Acts 14:22) [Alf, TNTC]. The reference is to the persecution that began in John's day and continues until Christ's final victory [NTC].

QUESTION—How can these people make their robes white in red blood?
This is figurative language in which whiteness symbolizes forgiveness of sins by means of Christ's sacrificial death [TH]. The figure indicates that their ability to stand in God's presence has been earned through the sacrifice of Christ [NTC]. Whiteness refers to spiritual purity and the washing away of sins [Wal]. This figure stresses the effectiveness of Christ's atoning death [TNTC]. Blood can make sins clean (see Hebrews 9:24 and 1 John 1:7). Here blood refers to the sacrifice of the Lamb on the cross [NIC]. Here washing robes symbolizes believing in and receiving Christ's sacrificial death for oneself (Acts 15:9) [Alf, Lns]. The blood of Christ symbolizes by metonymy the atoning death of Christ [WBC].

QUESTION—Are these people all martyrs?
They are all martyrs [BNTC, ICC, Ld, Wal]. They are not all martyrs [NIC, NIGTC, TNTC, WBC]. See this same question about this group at verse 9.

7:15 Therefore[a] they-are before the throne of God and they-serve[b] him day and night in his temple,[c]

LEXICON—a. διά τοῦτο: 'therefore' [KJV, NIV, NRSV], 'that is why' [BNTC; NLT, REB, TEV, TNT], 'for this reason' [WBC; NET], 'because of this' [EC, Lns], 'it was this that' [NAB], 'and so' [CEV].
   b. pres. act. indic. of λατρεύω (LN 53.14) (BAGD p. 467): 'to serve' [BAGD, EC, Lns, WBC; KJV, NET, NIV, NLT, TEV], 'to serve as one's minister' [BNTC], 'to minister to' [NAB], 'to worship' [LN; CEV, NRSV, REB, TNT] 'to perform religious rites' [BAGD, LN], 'to venerate' [LN].
   c. ναός (See this word also at 3:12): 'temple' [BAGD, BNTC, EC, LN, WBC; all versions except NLT], 'Temple' [NLT] 'sanctuary' [LN, Lns].

QUESTION—What relationship is indicated by the phrase διά τοῦτο 'therefore'?
It indicates that the preceding verse is the *reason* for their ability to be before the throne of God [Alf, BAGD, BNTC, EC, Lns, NIC, NIGTC, Sw, TH, WBC; KJV, NAB, NET, NIV, NLT, NRSV, TEV, TNT]: They washed their robes and made them white in the blood of the Lamb, *therefore* they are before the throne of God. It indicates that the preceding verse explains why they are able to serve God [ICC].

QUESTION—What is the significance of their being before the throne of God?
It signifies that: they are in fellowship with God [Ld]; they have direct access to God [TNTC]; they are in a place of honor and distinction [Wal].

QUESTION—What is implied by λατρεύω 'to serve'?
It implies that: they worship God (see Romans 12:1) [EC, ICC, NIC, TH; CEV, NRSV, REB, TNT]; they praise God (see 22:3–5) [Alf, EC, NIC]; they serve God as a priests (see 20:6 and 22:3) [EC, NTC].

QUESTION—What does ναός 'temple' refer to?
It does not refer to a literal building but to the presence of God and the Lamb (see 21:22) [NIGTC, Sw]. Heaven is God's temple (see 21:22) [EC, NIC,

TH, TNTC]. The temple refers to God's very presence [Wal]. The temple is where God lives (see 4:2ff) [NTC].

QUESTION—What is indicated by the phrase ἡμέρας καὶ νυκτός 'day and night'?

The phrase indicates 'unceasingly' [EC, ICC, NIC, Sw, TH, Wal, WBC]. The fact that a literal day and night are not in focus here is seen in 20:10 where the Devil is tormented day and night forever and ever [NIC]. See a similar phrase at 4:8 [ICC].

and the-(one) sitting on the throne will-dwell[a] over[b] them.

LEXICON—a. fut. act. indic. of σκηνόω (LN 85.75) (BAGD p. 755): 'to dwell' [BAGD, BNTC, LN; KJV], 'to come to dwell' [LN], 'to spread one's tent/tabernacle' [Lns; CEV, NIV, TNT], 'to be a tabernacle' [EC], 'to come to reside, to take up residence' [LN], 'to live' [BAGD]. The phrase σκηνόω ἐπί 'to dwell over' is translated 'to give shelter' [NAB], 'to spread one's tent/tabernacle over' [Lns; CEV, NIV, TNT], 'to dwell among' [BNTC; KJV], 'to live among and shelter' [NLT], 'to protect with one's presence' [REB, TEV].

b. ἐπί with the gen. (LN) (BAGD 3.1.a.ζ. p. 288): 'over' [BAGD, EC, Lns; CEV, NIV, TNT], 'among' [BNTC; KJV]. The phrase σκηνόω ἐπί 'to dwell over' is translated 'to shelter' [WBC; NET, NRSV], 'to give shelter to' [NAB], 'to live among and shelter' [NLT], 'to dwell among' [BNTC; KJV], 'to protect' [Alf], 'to protect with one's presence' [REB, TEV].

QUESTION—What is indicated by σκηνόω ἐπί 'to dwell over'?

It indicates that God will be in fellowship with them [Wal]. It indicates that he will spread his tent over them, that is, that God's presence will be with them as though living in the same tent with them [Lns]. It corresponds to the OT promise to dwell in their midst [EC]. It indicates the actual presence of God with them [ICC, NIC, NTC, Sw, TNTC]. It indicates: 'to shelter' [BAGD, NIC, NTC, TH]; 'to protect' [NIC, Sw, TH].

7:16 They-will-be-hungry[a] not again[b] nor will-they-be-thirsty[c] again

LEXICON—a. fut. act. indic. of πεινάω (LN 23.29) (BAGD 1. p. 640): 'to be hungry' [BAGD, BNTC, LN; NLT, TNT], 'to hunger' [BAGD, EC, Lns, WBC; CEV, KJV, NIV, NRSV, TEV], 'to go hungry' [NET], 'to feel hunger' [REB], 'to know hunger' [NAB], 'to have hunger' [LN].

b. ἔτι (See this word at 3:12): 'again' [BNTC; all versions except KJV, NRSV], 'anymore' [EC, Lns], 'any longer' [WBC], 'no more' [KJV, NRSV].

c. fut. act. indic. of διψάω (LN 23.39) (BAGD 1. p. 200): 'to be thirsty' [BAGD, BNTC, LN; NET, NLT, TNT], 'to thirst' [EC, Lns, WBC; CEV, KJV, NIV, NRSV, TEV], 'to feel thirst' [REB], 'to know thirst' [NAB], 'to suffer from thirst' [BAGD].

QUESTION—What other Scripture is similar to this?

Isaiah 49:10 is similar to these two verses, 7:16–17 [EC, TH].

QUESTION—What is implied by not being hungry or thirsty again?
It implies that they will have no unsatisfied desire [TNTC]. It implies that their souls' deep desires for spiritual wholeness will be satisfied [NIC]. Hunger and thirst symbolize whatever they endured in the tribulation [Wal]. Thirst implies the pain of unfulfilled desire (see John 4:14) [ICC].

nor the sun nor any[a] scorching-heat,[b] will-fall-on[c] them
LEXICON—a. πᾶς (LN 59.24) (BAGD 1.a.α. p. 631): 'any' [BAGD, BNTC, LN, Lns, WBC; all versions except NAB, NLT, TNT], not explicit [EC; NAB, NLT, TNT].
  b. καῦμα (LN **14.67**) (BAGD p. 425): 'scorching heat' [BNTC, **LN**, WBC; CEV, NIV, NRSV, REB, TEV], 'heat' [BAGD, EC, LN, Lns; KJV], 'heat of the sun' [NAB], 'burning heat' [NET, TNT], 'burning' [BAGD]. The phrase ὁ ἥλιος οὐδὲ πᾶν καῦμα 'the sun nor any scorching heat' is translated 'the scorching noontime heat' [NLT], 'burning heat of the sun' [TNT].
  c. aorist act. subj. of πίπτω 'επι' (LN **24.93**) (BAGD 2.b.α. p. 660): 'to fall on' [EC, Lns, WBC; TNT], 'to cause to suffer, to cause pain to' [LN]. The idiom πίπτω ἐπί 'to fall on' is translated 'to beat down on' [NAB, NET, NIV], 'to beat on' [REB], 'to strike' [BNTC; NRSV], 'to be troubled by' [CEV], 'to light on' [KJV], 'to burn' [TEV], 'to make someone suffer' [**LN**]. This idiom is also translated positively: 'to be fully protected from' [NLT].

7:17 **Because the Lamb in-the-middle[a] of-the throne will-shepherd[b] them**
LEXICON—a. ἀνὰ μέσον (LN **83.10**) (BAGD 1.b. p. 49): 'in the middle' [NET, TNT], 'in the midst' [LN (83.10), Lns, WBC; KJV], 'in the center' [BAGD; CEV, TEV], 'at the center' [NIV, NRSV, REB], 'at the midpoint' [EC], 'in the heart' [BNTC], 'in front of' [NLT]. The phrase ἀνὰ μέσον τοῦ θρόνου 'in the middle of the throne' is translated 'on the throne' [NAB].
  b. fut. act. indic. of ποιμαίνω (LN 36.2, 44.3) (BAGD 2.b. p. 684): 'to shepherd' [EC, Lns, WBC; NET], 'to be one's shepherd' [BNTC; all versions except KJV, NET], 'to feed' [KJV], 'to guide and take care of, to guide and help' [LN (36.2)], 'to take care of' [LN (44.3)], 'to care for, to nurture, to protect' [BAGD]. See this word also at 2:27.
QUESTION—What relationship is indicated by ὅτι 'because'?
It indicates that this verse is the reason for 7:16 [EC, Lns, NIGTC]: they will not hunger or thirst...*because* the Lamb will shepherd them. It is because the Lamb is in the middle of the throne, a divine position, that he is able to provide these benefits [NIGTC].
QUESTION—If the image is a shepherd tending his sheep and the topic is what Jesus does for his followers, what is the point of similarity?
The point of similarity is: care [BAGD, EC, LN, NIC, TH]; provision for needs [NIC, TNTC, Wal; KJV]; leadership [LN, Lns, NTC, Wal, WBC]; protection [BAGD].

QUESTION—What is the significance of the paradoxical image of a lamb being a shepherd?

It brings out the fact that the Lamb identifies with his people [NIGTC, Sw].

and will-lead^a them to springs^b of waters of-life,

LEXICON—a. fut. act. indic. of ὁδηγέω (LN **15.182**) (BAGD 1. p. 553): 'to lead' [BAGD, EC, **LN**, Lns; all versions except NRSV, REB, TEV], 'to guide' [BAGD, BNTC, LN, WBC; NRSV, REB, TEV].

b. πηγή (LN 1.78) (BAGD 2. p. 656): 'spring' [BAGD, BNTC, EC, LN, Lns, WBC; all versions except CEV, KJV], 'stream' [CEV], 'fountain' [KJV].

QUESTION—What is the significance of the forward position of the word 'life' in the phrase ζωῆς πηγὰς ὑδάτων 'of life springs of waters'?

It signifies that the words 'of life' are emphatic [Alf, EC, NIC, Sw]: *life's water springs*. This figure indicates the final satisfaction of the longing of people's spirits [NIC].

and God will-wipe-away^a every tear^b from their eyes."

LEXICON—a. fut. act. indic. of ἐξαλείφω (LN **47.18**) (BAGD 1.a. p. 272): 'to wipe away' [BAGD, EC, **LN**, Lns, WBC; all versions except CEV, NAB, REB, TNT], 'to wipe' [BNTC; CEV, NAB, REB, TNT]. See this word also at 3:5.

b. δάκρυον (LN **8.73**) (BAGD p. 170): 'tear' [BAGD, BNTC, EC, LN, Lns, WBC; all versions].

QUESTION—What is signified by God wiping every tear from their eyes?

It signifies that he will remove the source of all pain and sadness (see Isaiah 25:8 and Revelation 21:4) [TH]. It signifies that he rescues them from all evil and they enjoy his fellowship [TNTC]. It signifies that when they get to heaven, all that caused tears in the tribulation will be over [Wal].

DISCOURSE UNIT: 8:1–14:20 [Ld]. The topic is the seventh seal and the six trumpets.

DISCOURSE UNIT: 8:1–11:19 [TH]. The topic is the seven trumpets.

DISCOURSE UNIT: 8:1–11:14 [WBC]. The topic is the seventh seal and the first six trumpets.

DISCOURSE UNIT: 8:1–9:21 [Lns; NET]. The topic is the seventh seal and the first six trumpets [Lns].

DISCOURSE UNIT: 8:1–13 [Lns, Sw]. The topic is the seventh seal and four trumpets.

DISCOURSE UNIT: 8:1–5 [BNTC, GNT, NIGTC, NTC, TNTC; CEV, KJV, NIV, NLT, NRSV, TEV]. The topic is the seventh seal and the golden censer [GNT; NIV, NRSV], the seventh seal [BNTC, NIGTC, NTC, TNTC; CEV, KJV, NLT, TEV].

DISCOURSE UNIT: 8:1–2 [NAB]. The topic is the seven trumpets.

DISCOURSE UNIT: 8:1 [EC, Ld, Lns, NIC, Wal, WBC]. The topic is the seventh seal [EC, Ld, Wal, WBC], a dramatic pause [NIC].

8:1 **And when he-opened the seventh seal, there-was silence[a] in heaven (for) about[b] half-an-hour.[c]**

LEXICON—a. σιγή (LN **33.120**) (BAGD p. 749): 'silence' [BAGD, BNTC, EC, **LN**, Lns; all versions], 'quiet' [BAGD].
  b. ὡς (LN 78.42) (BAGD IV.5. p. 899): 'about' [BAGD, EC, LN, Lns; all versions], 'approximately' [BAGD, LN], 'nearly' [BAGD], 'what seemed' [BNTC], not explicit [WBC].
  c. ἡμίωρον (LN **67.200**) (BAGD p. 348): 'half an hour' [BNTC, **LN**, Lns; all versions except KJV], 'the space of half an hour' [KJV], 'a half hour' [BAGD, EC]. Half an hour signifies a short period of time in case time in minutes and hours is foreign to a culture [TH].

QUESTION—How does this chapter relate to what has gone before?
  It resumes the opening of the seals from the end of chapter 6 [EC, NIGTC, Sw, Wal]. It continues the description of the final judgment [NIGTC].

QUESTION—What is the significance of this seventh seal?
  Since this is the final seal, it signifies that the scroll is now fully opened [Alf, BNTC, Ld, Sw, WBC]. All the events before this in 6:1–7:17 have corresponded to the breaking of the seals. Starting with the breaking of the seventh seal, we now see the actual contents of the scroll, which constitute the remainder of Rev. 8:2–22:5 [WBC].

QUESTION—What is the purpose of the half hour of silence?
  1. It may function as a dramatic silence before the final judgments are enacted [BNTC, EC, Ld, Lns, NIC, Sw, TH]. The silence increases the tension remarkably [Lns, NIC].
  2. It may function to emphasize the importance of what is to follow [NIGTC, TH, Wal]. It shows that the contents of the seventh seal are significant [NIGTC].
  3. It may be to allow the prayers of the believers to be heard [BNTC, ICC, TNTC]. The praising of the angels stops so that the prayers of God's people may be heard (see 4:8f) [BNTC, TNTC].
  4. Silence is appropriate in the presence of God (see Psalm 62:1 and Habakkukk 2:20) [TNTC, WBC].

DISCOURSE UNIT: 8:2–14:20 [Ld]. The topic is the six trumpets.

DISCOURSE UNIT: 8:2–11:19 [EC, NIC; REB]. The topic is the seventh trumpets.

DISCOURSE UNIT: 8:2–9:21 [WBC]. The topic is the first six trumpets.

DISCOURSE UNIT: 8:2–6 [EC, Ld, Wal, WBC]. The topic is preparation [Ld], introduction of the seven angels [Wal], the third throne room scene [WBC], the setting of the trumpets: the prayers of the saint's [EC].

DISCOURSE UNIT: 8:2–5 [NIC]. The topic is preparation.

8:2 **And I-saw the seven angels who stand before God, and seven trumpets**[a] **were-given to-them.**

LEXICON—a. σάλπιγξ (See this word at 1:10): 'trumpet' [BAGD, BNTC, EC, LN, Lns, WBC; all versions]. This could either indicate a ram's horn or a metal musical instrument [TH].

QUESTION—Who are these angels?

The definite article in τοὺς ἑπτὰ ἀγγέλους 'the seven angels' indicates that they are a well-known group of angels [Ld, NIGTC, Sw, WBC]. The definite article indicates that they are a special group of angels [EC, NIC, TNTC]. They may be the seven angels of Jewish apocalyptic tradition named in 1 Enoch 20:1–8: Uriel, Raphael, Raguel, Michael, Sariel, Gabriel and Remiel (see Tobit 12:15) [ICC, Ld, NIC, NIGTC, NTC, Sw, TNTC, WBC]. That each name ends with *el* ('God') indicates that they had a close relationship to God [TNTC]. The angels spoken of in Enoch are described as archangels [ICC, NTC, Sw]. In Luke 1:19 the angel Gabriel describes himself as one who stands in God's presence possibly indicating that there were a class of angels so designated. They are probably archangels who fill a very special role among the angels [WBC]. They are special simply because they are to sound the trumpets [EC]. These are not archangels [Alf, Lns].

QUESTION—What is the significance of 'standing before God'?

It indicates a place of prominence as in Luke 1:19 [Wal]. They are stand before God in readiness to serve him [EC].

QUESTION—Who is the implied actor of ἐδόθησαν 'were given'?

The implied actor is either God or an angel [TH].

QUESTION—What is the significance of trumpets?

They are a signal for the Second Coming of Christ or the end times (see Matthew 24:31; 1 Corinthians 15:52; 1 Thessalonians 4:16) [BNTC, TNTC, WBC]. They announce the day of God's anger (see Zephaniah 1:14–16) [NIC].

DISCOURSE UNIT: 8:3–5 [NAB]. The topic is the golden censer.

8:3 **And another angel came and stood at the altar having (a) golden censer,**[a] **and much incense was-given to-him,**

LEXICON—a. λιβανωτός (LN **6.138**) (BAGD 2. p. 473): 'censer' [BAGD, BNTC, EC, **LN**, Lns, WBC; all versions except CEV, NLT, TEV], 'incense container' [CEV, TEV], 'incense burner' [NLT]. It is a bowl in which incense is burned [BAGD, LN].

QUESTION—Who is the implied actor of ἐδόθη 'was given'?

The implied actor is God [EC], or an angel [TH]. The incense was given by God's command [Alf].

in-order-that he-will-offer[a] **(it) with-the prayers of-all the-saints**[b] **on the golden altar before the throne.**

TEXT—Instead of the δώσει 'he will offer', some manuscripts have the aorist subjunctive δώσῃ 'he might offer'. GNT does not mention this alternative. Most versions translated the phrase ἵνα δώσει/δώσῃ 'in order that he will/might offer' with the infinitive 'to offer'.

LEXICON—a. fut. act. indic. of δίδωμι (LN 57.71, 85.33): 'to offer' [BNTC, TH, TNTC, WBC; all versions except NAB, NET, NLT], 'to offer up' [NET], 'to mix' [NLT], 'to dispense' [EC], 'to deposit' [NAB], 'to put' [LN (85.33)], 'to give' [LN (57.71), Lns].

    b. οἱ ἅγιοι (See this word at 5:8): 'the saints' [EC, Lns; KJV, NET, NIV, NRSV], 'God's people' [BNTC, WBC; CEV, NLT, REB, TEV, TNT], 'God's holy ones' [NAB]. All the saints are indicated here, not just the martyrs under the altar of 6:9 [Alf, ICC, Ld, NIC, Sw].

QUESTION—Are the prayers of the saints and the incense the same thing?

    1. The incense is the prayers of the saints [BNTC, NIC, NTC]: he with offer the incense consisting of the prayers of the saints. The dative case translated 'with (the prayers)' is best taken as the same as the Hebrew *le* (defining incense) in both 8:3 and 4 (see 5:8) [NIC, NTC]: to offer the incense, *consisting of* the prayers of all the saints. It should be translated: 'to offer...*in token of* the prayers of all of God's people' [BNTC].

    2. The incense is different than the prayers of the saints [EC, ICC, Lns, Sw, TH, TNTC, Wal, WBC; all versions]: he will offer the incense along with the prayers of the saints. The angel adds much more incense to increase the volume of smoke so that the prayers and the incense arise together [EC]. The incense is put on the live coals that are the prayers of the saints [Sw]. See also the following question.

QUESTION—What is the purpose of the incense?

    1. It is to make the prayers acceptable to God [EC, ICC, TH, WBC]. The incense makes the prayers either more acceptable or more pleasing to God [WBC]. This does not mean that the angel is a mediator, but that the prayers are enforced by the accompanying incense [EC].

    2. It is not to make the prayers acceptable to God [Ld, Lns, NIC, TNTC]. The prayers are already rising like incense, the purpose is simply to significantly increase the amount of aromatic smoke [Lns]. The idea that an angel makes the prayers of the saints acceptable to God is not Scriptural [TNTC]. If the incense enabled the prayers, this would go against the fact that believers are priests themselves. The incense adds a sweet smell to the prayers [Ld].

QUESTION—What is the significance of τοῦ θρόνου 'the throne'?

    It is the throne of God [EC, TH]. This expression is another way of indicating God himself without saying his name directly (see 8:4) [WBC].

QUESTION—What may have been the content of the prayers?

They were prayers for vengeance on their enemies as seen in the catastrophe that they, with the incense, effect in 8:5 [WBC]. They were prayers for God's judgments against evil opposition forces [Alf, Ld, NIC].

8:4 **And the smoke[a] of-the incense went-up with-the prayers of-the saints from (the) hand of-the angel before God.**

LEXICON—a. καπνός (LN 1.37) (BAGD p. 403): 'smoke' [BAGD, BNTC, EC, LN, Lns, WBC; all versions].

QUESTION—Should the phrase ἐνώπιον τοῦ θεοῦ 'before God' be construed with the verb ἀνέβη 'went up', or with τοῦ ἀγγέλου 'the angel'?

1. It should be construed with the verb 'went up' [Alf, BNTC, EC, TH, WBC; CEV, KJV, NAB, NET, NIV, NLT, NRSV, REB, TNT]: the smoke of the incense *went up before God.*
2. It should be construed with 'the angel' [TEV]: the angel who was before God.

QUESTION—Did the smoke go from the angel's actual hand?

It went up from the censer that was in the angel's hand [Sw, TH].

QUESTION—What is symbolized by the prayers going up before God?

It symbolizes that God accepts the prayers (see Psalms 141:2) [WBC].

QUESTION—What made the smoke?

When the incense is put on hot coals, sweet smelling smoke from the incense is produced [NIC].

8:5 **And the angel took the censer and filled it from the fire of-the altar and threw (it) to the earth, and there-were thunders and sounds and lightnings and (an) earthquake.**

QUESTION—What is signified by this verse?

It signifies that the judgments of God that follow are in answer to the prayers of the saints (see 6:9–10 and 8:3, 4) [Alf, EC, ICC, Ld, Lns, NIC, NIGTC, NTC, Sw, TNTC, Wal, WBC]. It signifies God's final judgment of the world [NIGTC].

QUESTION—What is the function of the perfect tense εἴληφεν 'has taken'?

The perfect must be translated as an aorist 'took' since it is coupled with the aorist 'filled' [Alf]. It is used to increase the drama being played out [NIC]. It is as though John is reporting what he has just seen [Lns]. He took the censer because he had put it down [ICC, Sw].

QUESTION—What is signified by the throwing of fire to the earth?

It indicates that God's judgment is about to happen there (see Ezekiel 10:2) [EC, ICC, Ld, Lns, WBC]. It indicates God's final judgment on the earth [NIGTC].

QUESTION—What did the angel throw to the earth?

He threw: fire [Alf, ICC, Lns, NIGTC, Sw, WBC]; live coals and incense [TH]. He may have thrown the fire, or the incense and possibly the censer [NIC]. The fire indicates live coals or glowing embers [TH, WBC].

QUESTION—What is signified by the thunders, sounds, lightnings, and earthquake
They signal that something great is about to happen [Sw]. They indicate that God's judgment is about to happen [Ld]. They indicate that God is about to answer the prayers of 6:10 [Ld, NIC]. They indicate the close of the seventh seal as they also indicate the close of the seventh trumpet (11:19) and seventh bowl (16:18) [ICC]. They indicate God's final judgment on the earth (see Isaiah 29:6; Revelation 11:19; 16:18) [NIGTC].

DISCOURSE UNIT: 8:6–11:19 [NIGTC, NTC, TNTC]. The topic is the seven trumpets.

DISCOURSE UNIT: 8:6–9:21 [GNT, NIGTC; CEV, KJV, NIV, NRSV, TEV]. The topic is the trumpets [GNT; CEV, KJV, NIV, NRSV, TEV], the first six trumpets [NIGTC].

DISCOURSE UNIT: 8:6–13 [NAB, NLT]. The topic is the first four trumpets.

DISCOURSE UNIT: 8:6–12 [BNTC, NIC, NIGTC, NTC]. The topic is the natural plagues [BNTC], the first four trumpets [NIC, NIGTC].

8:6 **And the seven angels having the seven trumpets prepared[a] them so-that they-might-blow-(the)-trumpets.[b]**
TEXT—Instead of αὐτούς 'them', some manuscripts have ἑαυτούς 'themselves'. GNT does not mention this alternative. The reading 'themselves' is taken by Lns; KJV.
LEXICON—a. aorist act. indic. of ἑτοιμάζω (LN 77.3) (BAGD 2. p. 316): 'to prepare' [BAGD, BNTC, EC, LN, Lns; all versions except CEV, NRSV], 'to get ready' [WBC; CEV], 'to make ready' [LN; NRSV].
  b. aorist act. subj. of σαλπίζω (LN 6.90, 6.92) (BAGD p. 741): 'to blow a trumpet' [BNTC; CEV, NRSV, REB, TEV, TNT], 'to sound a trumpet' [BAGD, LN (6.92), WBC; NET, NIV], 'to sound' [EC; KJV], 'to blow a mighty blast' [NLT], 'to trumpet' [BAGD, Lns], 'to play (the) trumpet' [LN (6.90)].
QUESTION—How did the angels prepare to sound their trumpets?
They took their positions [EC, Sw]. They picked up their trumpets [Lns]. They raised them to their mouths [Alf, EC, NIC, Sw].

DISCOURSE UNIT: 8:7–12 [Alf, EC, ICC, Lns, WBC]. The topic is the first four trumpets.

DISCOURSE UNIT: 8:7 [EC, Ld]. The topic is the first trumpet.

8:7 **And the first blew-(his)-trumpet; and there-occurred hail[a] and fire mixed[b] with blood and it-was-thrown on the earth,**
LEXICON—a. χάλαζα (LN **2.13**) (BAGD p. 874): 'hail' [BAGD, BNTC, EC, **LN**, Lns, WBC; all versions], 'hailstorm' [LN].

b. perf. pass. participle of μίγνυμι (LN 63.10) (BAGD 1. p. 499): 'to be mixed' [BAGD, BNTC, EC, LN, Lns, WBC; all versions except KJV, REB], 'to be mingled' [BAGD, LN; KJV, REB].

QUESTION—Who is the implied actor of ἐβλήθη 'it was thrown'?

The implied actor may be God [EC, TH], or an angel [TH]. The implied actor is some heavenly being [TNTC].

and the third-part^a of-the earth was-burned-up^b and the third-part of-the trees^c was-burned-up and all green grass^d was-burned-up.

TEXT—Some manuscripts do not include καὶ τὸ τρίτον τῶν δένδρων κατεκάη 'and the third part of the trees was burned up'. GNT does not mention this alternative.

LEXICON—a. τρίτον (LN **60.63**) (BAGD 2. p. 826): 'third part' [BAGD, EC, LN, WBC; KJV], 'third' [BAGD, BNTC, **LN**, Lns, WBC; all versions except KJV, NLT], 'one-third' [BAGD; NLT]. One third here indicates a sizeable proportion but less than the majority [TNTC]. It indicates that God shows kindness to more than he judges [Alf].

b. aorist pass. indic. of κατακαίω (LN 14.66) (BAGD p. 411): 'to be burned up' [BAGD, BNTC, EC, LN, Lns; KJV, NET, NIV, NRSV, TEV, TNT], 'to be burned' [BNTC; CEV], 'to be reduced to ashes' [LN], 'to be set on fire' [NLT], 'to be scorched' [NAB], 'to be burned down' [BAGD, LN], 'to be consumed' [BAGD].

c. δένδρον (LN 3.2) (BAGD p. 174): 'tree' [BAGD, BNTC, EC, LN, Lns, WBC; all versions], 'bush' [LN].

d. χόρτος (LN 3.15) (BAGD p. 884): 'grass' [BAGD, BNTC, EC, LN, Lns, WBC; all versions except CEV, NAB], 'plant' [CEV, NAB], 'small plant' [LN], 'herbage' [Lns].

QUESTION—Does this indicate that only one-third of the earth was affected or all the earth?

1. It indicates that only one-third of the earth was affected [Ld, NIC, TH, TNTC]. It means that all grass in that area was burned up [TNTC] or all the trees and all the grass in that part were burned up [NIC, TH].
2. It indicates all the earth but only one third of the trees and all of the grass were burned up [Alf].

QUESTION—What is the significance the three-fold repetition of κατεκάη 'was burned up'?

The repetition functions to emphasize the verb [Lns].

QUESTION—What is the purpose of this action?

This judgment of God is not final. He is sending punishment, but he means to give them a chance to turn to him from their sinful ways [NIC].

DISCOURSE UNIT: 8:8–9 [EC, Ld]. The topic is the second trumpet.

8:8 And the second angel blew-(his)-trumpet; and something-like[a] (a) great mountain burning with-fire was-thrown into the sea, and the third-part of-the sea became blood[b]

LEXICON—a. ὡς (BAGD II.3.a.α. p. 897): 'something like' [BAGD, EC, WBC; CEV, NAB, NET, NIV, NRSV], 'something that looked like' [TEV], 'what looked like' [REB], 'what seemed like' [TNT], 'what seemed' [BNTC], 'as it were' [Lns; KJV], not explicit [NLT]. This might be a flaming meteoric chunk as large as a mountain [Alf, EC, Wal]. See this word also at 6:6.

b. αἷμα (LN **8.64**) (BAGD 3. p. 23): 'blood' [BAGD, BNTC, EC, **LN**, Lns, WBC; all versions]. The reference may be not to literal blood but to a blood-like color [LN]. Blood here refers to the color red [BAGD]. See this word also at 1:5.

QUESTION—Who is the implied actor of ἐβλήθη 'it was thrown'?

The implied actor may be either an angel or God [TH].

8:9 and the third-part of-the creatures[a] in the sea having lives[b] died and the third-part of-the ships were-destroyed.[c]

LEXICON—a. κτίσμα (LN **42.38**): 'creature' [BAGD, BNTC, EC, **LN**, Lns; all versions except NLT], 'thing' [NLT]. Κτίσμα refers to marine life here [TH, TNTC].

b. ψυχή (LN 23.88): 'life' [BAGD, EC, LN, Lns; KJV]. This noun is also translated as an adjective: 'living' [BNTC, WBC; all versions except KJV, NAB, NET], 'alive' [NET]. It is also translated as a verb: '(creatures) living (in)' [NAB]. See this word also at 6:9.

c. aorist pass. indic. of διαφθείρω (LN **20.40**) (BAGD 1. p. 190): 'to be destroyed' [BAGD, EC, Lns, WBC; all versions except NAB, NET], 'to be completely destroyed' [**LN**; NET], 'to be utterly destroyed' [LN], 'to be wrecked' [NAB], 'to be sunk' [BNTC].

QUESTION—Does this indicate that the destruction occurred on the whole sea or only on the third part that was turned to blood?

1. It indicates that the destruction of the creatures and ships occurred only on the one-third of the sea that was turned to blood [TH]. It indicates that the destruction of the ships occurred only on the one-third of the sea that was turned to blood [NIC, Wal]. It probably occurred closest to the impact of the fiery mass [Wal].
2. It indicates that one third of the ships on the whole sea was destroyed [Alf].

DISCOURSE UNIT: 8:10–11 [EC, Ld]. The topic is the third trumpet.

8:10 And the third angel blew-(his)-trumpet; and (a) great star burning like (a) torch[a] fell out-of heaven and it-fell on the third-part of-the rivers and on the springs[b] of-the waters,

LEXICON—a. λαμπάς (See this word at 4:5): 'torch' [BNTC, EC, Lns, WBC; all versions except KJV], 'lamp' [KJV].

b. πηγή (LN **1.78**) (BAGD 1. p. 655): 'spring' [BAGD, LN, Lns, WBC; all versions except KJV, NAB, REB], 'fountain' [EC; KJV]. The phrase πηγὰς τῶν ὑδάτων 'springs of the waters' is translated 'springs' [**LN**; NAB, REB], 'fresh-water springs' [BNTC]. Rivers and springs indicate fresh water [ICC, Lns, NIC, Sw, TH]. See this word also at 7:17.

QUESTION—Was this a literal star?

It could have been a meteor [Ld, NIC, WBC] or a comet [TH, WBC]. It was some kind of object that was burning as it entered the earth's atmosphere from outer space [Wal].

QUESTION—Did the star fall on all the rivers and springs or only on one-third of them?

1. It fell on one-third of the rivers and springs of the earth [EC, NIC, TH]. Verse 8:11 indicates that only one-third of the waters became bitter [NIC].
2. It fell on all the rivers and springs of the earth [Alf].

8:11 **and the name of-the star is-called Wormwood,**[a] **and the third-part of-the waters became wormwood**[b]

LEXICON—a. Ἄψινθος (LN **3.21**) (BAGD p. 129): 'Wormwood' [BAGD, BNTC, EC, **LN**; all versions except CEV, NLT, TEV], 'Bitterness' [**LN**; NLT, TEV], 'Bitter' [**LN**; CEV], 'Absinthe' [Lns], 'Apsinth' [WBC], 'wormwood' [LN].

b. ἄψινθος (LN **79.43**) (BAGD p. 129): 'wormwood' [BAGD, BNTC, EC; KJV, NAB, NET, NRSV, REB, TNT], 'bitter' [LN; CEV, NIV, NLT, TEV], 'bitter like wormwood' [LN, WBC], 'absinthe' [Lns]. Ἄψινθος belongs to the plant genus *Artemesia*. One ingredient in this herb is the agent hujone that can cause, among other symptoms, permanent damage to the nervous system [WBC]. The phrase ἐγένετο...εἰς ἄψινθον 'became into wormwood' is translated 'became like wormwood' [**LN**], 'turned bitter' [**LN**].

QUESTION—Does the phrase ἐγένετο...εἰς ἄψινθον 'became...into wormwood' mean, 'became wormwood' or 'became like wormwood'?

1. It means that it became wormwood [BAGD, Ld, Sw; KJV, NAB, NET, NRSV, REB, TNT]. Wormwood was mixed with the water [Ld].
2. It means that they became bitter like wormwood [ICC, LN, NIC, WBC; CEV, NIV, NLT, TEV]. It does not mean that the waters became the herb by this name, but that they became as bitter as that herb [LN, WBC].

and many of-the men[a] **died from**[b] **the waters because they-were-made-bitter.**[c]

LEXICON—a. ἄνθρωπος (BAGD 1.b. p. 68): 'man' [BAGD, EC; KJV], 'person' [BNTC, Lns, WBC; all versions except KJV, NRSV], 'many' [NRSV], 'human being' [BAGD]. See this word also at 4:7.

b. ἐκ ((LN **90.12**) (BAGD 3.e.b. p. 235): 'from' [EC, Lns; NAB, NET, NIV, NRSV], 'from drinking' [REB, TEV], 'of' [BNTC; KJV, TNT], 'as a result of' [**LN**, WBC], 'by' [BAGD, LN], 'because of' [BAGD, NIGTC], not explicit [CEV, NLT].

c. aorist pass. indic. of πικραίνω (LN **79.42**) (BAGD 1. p. 657): 'to be made bitter' [BAGD, EC, LN, Lns; KJV, NRSV, REB, TNT], 'to be poisoned' [BNTC]. This passive is also translated actively: 'to turn bitter' [**LN**, WBC; NET, TEV], 'to be/become bitter' [CEV, NIV, NLT]. The phrase ὑδάτων…ἐπικράνθησαν 'waters…they were made bitter' is translated 'this polluted water' [NAB].

DISCOURSE UNIT: 8:12–13 [EC, Ld]. The topic is the fourth trumpet.

DISCOURSE UNIT: 8:12 [WBC]. The topic is the fourth trumpet.

8:12 And the fourth angel blew-(his)-trumpet; and was-struck[a] the third-part of-the sun and the third-part of-the moon and the third-part of-the stars, so-that[b] the third-part of-them might-be-darkened[c] and the third-part of the day not might-shine[d] and the night likewise.

LEXICON—a. aorist pass. indic. of πλήσσω (LN **19.1**) (BAGD 2. p. 673): 'to be struck' [BAGD, **LN**, WBC; all versions except KJV, NAB], 'to be stricken' [EC], 'to be hit hard' [NAB], 'to be smitten' [Lns; KJV], 'to fall (of a plague)' [BNTC].
   b. ἵνα (LN 89.49): 'so that' [BNTC, EC, LN, Lns; NET, NIV, NRSV, REB, TEV, TNT], 'with the result that' [WBC], 'so' [KJV], 'and' [NLT], 'to' [NAB], 'so as a result, that' [LN], not explicit [CEV].
   c. aorist pass. (deponent = act.) subj. of σκοτίζω (LN 14.55) (BAGD 1. p. 757): 'to be darkened' [BAGD, EC, LN, WBC; KJV, NET, NRSV, TNT], 'to be plunged into darkness' [NAB], 'to be made dark' [Lns], 'to lose light' [CEV], 'to lose brightness' [TEV]. This passive verb is also translated actively: 'to turn dark' [BNTC; NIV, REB], 'to become dark' [NLT].
   d. aorist act. subj. of φαίνω (BAGD 2.a. p. 851): 'to shine' [BAGD, Lns; KJV, NRSV], 'to brighten' [EC], 'to appear' [WBC]. The phrase μὴ φάνῃ 'might not shine' is translated: '(light) failed to appear' [REB], '(there) was no light' [BNTC; CEV, NET, TEV], 'was without light' [NIV], 'was dark' [NLT], 'had no light' [TNT], 'lost (its) light' [NAB]. See this word also at 1:16.

QUESTION—Does the one-third refer to intensity of light or to duration of time?
   1. It refers to the duration that they shone [Alf, EC, ICC, NIC, TH]. It means that the sun, moon, and stars only shined two-thirds of the time. This is made clear by the latter part of the verse [TH]. The one-third refers to the amount of time they were darkened, and there is no way to reconcile the second part of the verse to the first [ICC]. This indicates that for one-third of the day and night there was complete darkness [NIC].
   2. It refers to intensity [Ld, NIC, NIGTC, Sw, TNTC, Wal, WBC]. If one-third of the heavenly bodies are darkened, the result would be a decrease in the intensity of the light, not the length of time they shone [WBC]. Each heavenly body only gave two-thirds of its light after being struck.

The second part of the verse must be figurative language to indicate a corresponding lack of intensity of light day and night [NIGTC]. John is not so concerned with logic but strongly states that one-third of all light was gone [TNTC].

DISCOURSE UNIT: 8:13–9:21 [WBC]. The topic is the last three trumpets [NIC].

DISCOURSE UNIT: 8:13–9:12 [BNTC]. The topic is the first woe.

DISCOURSE UNIT: 8:13 [Alf, NIC, NIGTC, NTC]. The topic is the eagle's warning [NIC], introduction to the last three trumpets [Alf, NIGTC], the three woes [NTC].

8:13 And I-looked, and I-heard one[a] eagle[b] flying in midheaven,[c] saying with-(a) loud voice, "Woe,[d] woe, woe, to-the-ones living on the earth

TEXT—Instead of ἀετοῦ 'eagle', some manuscripts have ἀγγέλου 'angel'. GNT does not mention this variant. 'Angel' is followed by KJV.

LEXICON—a. εἷς (LN 60.10, 92.22) (BAGD 3.b. p. 231): 'one' [LN (60.10, 92.22)], 'an' [Alf, BAGD, BNTC, EC, ICC, LN (92.22), Lns, WBC; all versions except CEV, NLT], 'a lone' [CEV], 'a single' [Alf; NLT], 'one solitary' [TNTC].

b. ἀετός (LN 4.42) (BAGD p. 19): 'eagle' [BAGD, BNTC, EC, LN, Lns, WBC; all versions], 'vulture' [BNTC, LN, NIC, TNTC]. An eagle is a symbol of swiftness [BAGD].

c. μεσουράνημα (LN **1.10**) (BAGD p. 508): 'midheaven' [BAGD, BNTC, EC, Lns, WBC; NAB, NRSV, REB, TNT], 'high in the sky, midpoint in the sky, straight above in the sky' [LN]. The phrase ἐν μεσουρανήματι 'in midheaven' is translated 'overhead in the sky' [**LN**], 'across the sky' [CEV], 'through the midst of heaven' [KJV], 'through the air' [NLT], 'directly overhead' [LN; NET], 'in midair' [TNTC; NIV], 'in the air' [TEV].

d. οὐαί (LN 22.9) (BAGD 1.c. p. 591): 'woe' [BAGD, BNTC, EC, Lns, WBC; KJV, NAB, NET, NIV, NRSV, REB], 'trouble' [CEV], 'terror' [NLT], 'calamity' [TNT], 'horror' [LN; TEV], 'alas' [BAGD], 'disaster' [LN].

QUESTION—What is the function of the phrase καὶ εἶδον 'and I looked'?
It introduces a new scene [EC, NIGTC, WBC], within a vision [WBC]. It is a transition to the last two trumpets [EC].

QUESTION—What does the phrase ἐν μεσουρανήματι 'in mid-heaven' signify?
It signifies that the eagle was flying directly overhead where the sun is at noon [Alf, EC, ICC, Ld, NIC, Sw]. This central place allows the eagle to be seen by everyone [Alf, EC, Ld, NIC, Sw], and to be heard by everyone [Alf, NIC].

QUESTION—What is the significance of the loud voice of the eagle?
It strongly highlights the final three trumpet soundings [BNTC]. It assures that everyone will hear him [EC].

QUESTION—To whom does the phrase τοὺς κατοικοῦντασ ἐπὶ τῆς γῆς 'those living on the earth' refer?
It refers to those who are hostile to God, but not to believers [Alf, EC, ICC, Ld, Lns, NIC, NIGTC, NTC]. It refers to all people even though believers will not be killed [TH]. Implied is the idea that believers will not be affected by these woes (see 9:4) [ICC, Ld, TH]. See this question also at 3:10.

QUESTION—What is the significance of announcing woe to those on earth?
It signifies that the last three trumpets will be worse than the last four [BNTC, Ld, Lns, Sw, Wal]. It emphasizes the severity of the last three trumpets [NIGTC]. It introduces the last three trumpets [TH].

because-of[a] the remaining sounds of-the trumpet of-the three angels being-about to-trumpet."

LEXICON—a. ἐκ with genitive object (LN 89.25, 90.16, 67.33) (BAGD 3.f. p. 235): 'because of' [BAGD, BNTC, EC, LN (89.25), WBC; NET, NIV, NLT, TNT], 'by reason of' [BAGD, Sw; KJV], 'due to' [Lns], 'from' [LN (90.16); NAB], 'at' [NRSV, REB], 'when' [LN (67.33); TEV], 'by' [LN (90.16)], 'as a result of' [BAGD], 'at the time of' [LN (67.33)], not explicit [CEV].

DISCOURSE UNIT: 9:1–11:19 [Alf]. The topic is the last three trumpets.

DISCOURSE UNIT: 9:1–12 [Alf, EC, ICC, Ld, NIC, NIGTC, NTC, Sw, TNTC, WBC; NLT]. The topic is the fifth trumpet.

DISCOURSE UNIT: 9:1–11 [Lns; NAB]. The topic is the fifth trumpet and the firs woe.

DISCOURSE UNIT: 9:1–2 [Wal]. The topic is the fifth trumpet: the fallen star and the abyss.

9:1 And the fifth angel trumpeted; and I-saw a-star fallen from heaven to the earth, and there-was-given to-it the key of-the shaft[a] of-the abyss[b]

LEXICON—a. φρέαρ (LN 1.58) (BAGD p. 865): 'shaft' [BAGD, BNTC, Lns, WBC; all versions except CEV, KJV, TEV], 'tunnel' [CEV], 'pit' [BAGD, EC, LN], 'deep pit' [LN], not explicit [KJV, TEV].

b. ἄβυσσος (LN 1.20) (BAGD 2. p. 2): 'abyss' [BAGD, BNTC, EC, LN, Lns, WBC; NAB, NET, NIV, REB], 'bottomless pit' [NLT, NRSV, TNT], 'deep pit' [CEV], 'very deep place, abode of evil spirits' [LN]. The phrase τοῦ φρέατος τῆς ἀβύσσου 'the pit of the abyss' is translated 'the abyss' [LN; TEV], 'bottomless pit' [KJV], 'the tunnel that leads down to the deep pit' [CEV].

QUESTION—Is the star literal or figurative?
The star is a figure representing a personal being of some kind (see 1:20) [Alf, BNTC, EC, ICC, Ld, NIC, NIGTC, NTC, Sw, TH, TNTC, Wal, WBC].

QUESTION—Is the being represented by the star good or evil?
1. The being is good [EC, ICC, Ld, Lns, NIC, TH, TNTC, WBC]. This being is one of the many agents of God seen in Revelation. He is probably the same as the angel pictured in 20:1 [NIC]. He is an angelic being or messenger [EC, ICC, Ld, TH, TNTC, WBC] like the angel of 20:1 [TNTC]. He may be a minor deity [TH]. The verb 'fallen' simply indicates 'descended' [EC, ICC, Ld].
2. The being is evil [Alf, BNTC, NIGTC, NTC, Sw, Wal]. The being represented is probably Satan (see Isaiah 14:12; Luke 10:18; Revelation 12:9) [Alf, NIGTC, Sw, Wal], or one of his subordinates [NIGTC]. It was probably a fallen angel and may have been Apollyon-Abaddon (see 11:9) [NTC]. The being is an evil agent acting by God's permission [BNTC].

QUESTION—What is indicated by the perfect tense of πεπτωκότα 'fallen'?
It indicates that John did not see the star fall but just saw it in its fallen state [Alf, NIGTC, Sw, TH, WBC]. It indicates that he saw an angel just as he was landing [ICC].

QUESTION—What is indicated by the passive ἐδόθη 'was given'?
God had given him the key [EC]. It indicates that the action of the angel is limited by the sovereignty of God [NIGTC, Sw, TNTC].

QUESTION—What is symbolized by the κλείς 'key'?
It symbolizes the authority given to the angel to open the abyss [Sw, Wal].

QUESTION—How are the nouns related in the genitive construction τοῦ φρέατος τῆς ἀβύσσου 'the shaft of the abyss'?
The shaft leads to the abyss [Alf, EC, NIGTC; CEV].

QUESTION—What is indicated by ἄβυσσος 'abyss'?
The abyss is: the place where the dead are (see Romans 10:7) [BAGD, Ld, NIC, TH, TNTC]; the place where the demons live or are imprisoned (see Luke 8:31) [Alf, BAGD, BNTC, EC, ICC, Ld, NTC, TH, TNTC, Wal]; the place where Satan is imprisoned (see 20:1–3) [BAGD, ICC, Ld, LN, NIC, TNTC, Wal, WBC]; the place where the angel Abaddon or Apollyon lived (see 11:9) [BAGD, NIC, WBC]; the place from which the beast comes up (see 11:7; 17:8) [BAGD, Ld, NIC, WBC]; the beginning place of punishment of the fallen angels, demons, the Beast and the false Prophet [ICC]; Hell [Alf, Lns]; Sheol [Sw, TH]. It is located in the depths of the earth [TH]. Ἄβυσσος is composed of ἀ- 'without' and βυθός 'depth'. It is a huge region beneath the earth [WBC], a subterranean cavern connected [EC]. The underground region of the abyss is connected with the surface by means of a shaft [EC, Ld, NTC] The opening of the shaft has a lid of some sort [EC].

9:2 And he-opened the shaft of-the abyss, and smoke rose out-of the shaft like smoke[a] of-(a) great furnace,

LEXICON—a. καπνός (LN **1.37**) (BAGD p. 403): 'smoke' [BAGD, BNTC, EC, **LN**, Lns, WBC; all versions]. This does not mean the smoke of a small controlled fire, but the billowing smoke of a forest fire or volcano [EC, LN, Sw].

QUESTION—What did the star-being open?

He opened the cover or door to the abyss [EC, NTC, WBC].

and was-darkened[a] the sun and the air[b] by[c] the smoke of-the shaft.[d]

LEXICON—a. aorist pass. (deponent = act.) indic. of σκοτόω (LN **14.55**) (BAGD 1. p. 758): 'to be darkened' [BAGD, BNTC, EC, Lns, WBC; all versions except CEV, REB, TNT]. This verb is also translated actively: 'to become dark' [**LN**; TNT], 'to become darkened' [BAGD, LN], 'to turn dark' [CEV], '(the smoke) darkened' [REB]. There was so much smoke that the light from sun was darkened as it passed through it [EC].

b. ἀήρ (LN **1.6**) (BAGD p. 20): 'air' [BAGD, BNTC, EC, **LN**, Lns, WBC; all versions except NIV], 'sky' [NIV]. For translation purposes it may be more logical to render this 'sky' to correlate with 'become dark' [**LN**].

c. ἐκ with genitive object (LN 85.25, 89.77) (BAGD 3.e.β. p. 235): 'by' [BAGD, BNTC, WBC; NAB, NIV, NLT, TEV], 'by reason of' [KJV], 'because of' [BAGD, EC, LN (85.25); CEV, TNT], 'due to' [Lns], 'with' [NET, NRSV], 'from' [LN (89.77)], 'by means of' [LN (89.77)], not explicit [REB]. See this word also at 8:13.

d. φρέαρ (LN **1.58**): 'shaft' [BNTC, Lns, WBC; NAB, NET, NRSV, TNT], 'pit' [BAGD, **LN**; KJV], 'Abyss' [NIV], 'abyss' [TEV], not explicit [CEV, NLT, REB]. See this word also at 9:1.

QUESTION—What other Scripture describes a similar event?

Joel 2:10 describes a plague of locusts that darkened the sun and moon [Ld, NIC].

DISCOURSE UNIT: 9:3–6 [Wal]. The topic is the fifth trumpet: demonic torment loosed on the earth.

9:3 **And from the smoke locusts[a] came-out on the earth,**

LEXICON—a. ἀκρίς (LN **4.47**) (BAGD p. 33): 'locust' [BAGD, BNTC, EC, LN, WBC; all versions], 'grasshopper' [BAGD, **LN**, Lns]. The ἀκρίς is an insect of the Acrididae family [LN].

QUESTION—What were these locusts?

They were demon-like beings [NIGTC]. They were demonic locusts [BNTC, NTC]. They were demons or fallen angels [EC]. They are creatures that symbolize evil powers (see Luke 10:19) [Ld, NIGTC]. They were unlike ordinary locusts since they had the stinging tails like scorpions [ICC].

and power[a] was-given to-them like the scorpions[b] of-the earth have power.

LEXICON—a. ἐξουσία (LN 76.12) (BAGD 2. p. 278): 'power' [BAGD, LN; all versions except NAB, NRSV], 'authority' [EC, WBC; NRSV], 'ability, capability, might' [BAGD]. This noun is also translated as an adjective: '(as) powerful (as scorpions in their sting)' [NAB]. Here ἐξουσία indicates 'capacity' or 'capability' [TEV]. See this word also at 2:26.

b. σκορπίος (LN 4.56) (BAGD 1. p. 757): 'scorpion' [BAGD, BNTC, EC, LN, Lns, WBC; all versions].

QUESTION—What was the power that was given to them?

The power was the ability to sting like a scorpion (see 9:10) [Alf, BNTC, EC, TH]. People fear the sting of the scorpion so the power that the locusts had was the ability to terrorize people [WBC].

QUESTION—Who is the implied actor of ἐδόθη 'was given'?

The implied actor is God [EC, NIGTC] or Christ [NIGTC]. The passive indicates the activity of God [WBC]. An indefinite phrase like 'someone gave' could be used [TH].

9:4 **And it-was-told them that they-should-harm[a] not the grass of-the earth nor any plant[b] nor any tree,**

LEXICON—a. aorist act. indic. of ἀδικέω (See this word at 2:11): 'to harm' [BNTC; NAB, NIV, TEV, TNT], 'to hurt' [EC, Lns; KJV], 'to damage' [WBC; NET, NRSV, REB], 'to attack' [NLT], 'to punish' [CEV].

b. χλωρός (LN **3.13**, **3.13 fn 3**) (BAGD 1. p. 882): 'plant' [BNTC, LN, WBC; CEV, NAB, NIV, NLT, REB, TEV], 'green plant' [LN (**3.13**); NET], 'green growth' [NRSV], 'green thing' [EC, Lns; KJV, TNT]. In contrast with grass and trees, this word refers to larger annuals and smaller perennial plants [LN (**3.13 fn 3**)].

QUESTION—Who is the implied actor of the passive ἐρρέθη 'it was told'?

The implied actor is God [EC, TH, Wal, WBC] or his angelic agent [TH, WBC]. In the ultimate sense God was in back of the command [TNTC]. It may have been Satan [Wal].

QUESTION—What is the significance of the three-fold prohibition 'not the grass of the earth nor any plant nor any tree'?

It emphasizes that all vegetable life should be excluded from harm [TH].

except[a] the men[b] who have not the seal[c] of-God on the foreheads.[d]

LEXICON—a. εἰ μή (LN 89.131): 'except' [EC, LN, WBC], 'but only' [BNTC, LN; all versions except CEV, NLT, TEV], 'only' [Lns; CEV, TEV], 'but all' [NLT].

b. ἄνθρωπος (BAGD 1.a.β. p. 68): 'man' [BNTC, EC; KJV, NAB, TNT], 'person' [WBC; all versions except KJV, NAB, TNT], 'human being' [BAGD, Ld]. Here it is used in contrast with animals and plants [BAGD]. See this word also at 8:11.

c. σφραγίς (LN **33.483**) (BAGD 1.c. p. 796): 'seal' [BNTC, EC, LN, Lns, WBC; all versions except CEV, TEV], 'mark' [**LN**; CEV], 'mark of a seal' [BAGD; TEV], 'impression of a seal' [BAGD]. This word may also be translated 'mark that shows that they belong to God' [LN]. See this word also at 5:1.

d. μέτωπον (LN **8.16**) (BAGD p. 515): 'forehead' [BAGD, BNTC, EC, **LN**, Lns, WBC; all versions].

QUESTION—Who are the ones who have not the seal?
They are: the unbelieving inhabitants of the world [Alf, NIGTC]; evil people [NIC]; godless people [TNTC].

QUESTION—Who are those who have the seal of God?
They are: believers, God's people [ICC, Ld, Lns, NIC, NIGTC, TH]; the new Israel [Sw]; the 144,000 of chapter 7 and it may include all believers of that time [Wal].

QUESTION—From what harm are those who are sealed protected?
They are protected from the demonic activity of the locusts but not from other physical evils [ICC, Ld]. This shows that believers are protected from the tribulation in the sense of its being God's wrath [Ld].

9:5 And it-was-given to-them that not they-should-kill them, but that they-shall-be-tormented[a] five months,

TEXT—Instead of the future pass. indic. βασανισθήσονται 'they shall be tormented', some manuscripts have the aorist act. subj. βασανισθῶσιν 'they may torment'. GNT does not mention this alternative.

LEXICON—a. fut. pass. indic. of βασανίζω (LN 38.13) (BAGD 2.a. p. 134): 'to be tormented' [BAGD, EC, LN, Lns; KJV], 'to be made to suffer' [CEV], 'to be tortured' [BAGD, LN]. This passive verb is also translated actively: 'to torture' [all versions except CEV, KJV, REB], 'to torment' [BNTC, WBC; REB].

QUESTION—Who is the implied actor of the passive verb ἐδόθη 'it was given'?
The implied actor is God who commissions the task [NIGTC, TH].

QUESTION—Who is the implied object of ἐδόθη 'it was given'?
The implied object is 'permission' [BNTC, TH; CEV, NAB, NET, NRSV, REB, TEV, TNT]: permission was given. The implied object is: 'power' [TNTC; NIV]: power was given. The object is 'command' [WBC]: command was given.

QUESTION—Who is the antecedent of the three pronouns 'they...them... they'?
The first pronoun refers to the locusts, the second and third to the people who are being tortured [Alf]: the locusts should not kill the people, but the people shall be tormented.

QUESTION—What is the significance of the period of five months?
It signifies a limited period of time [NIC, NIGTC, Sw, TNTC, WBC]. It signifies a rather long period of suffering [TH]. It may refer to the normal life span of a locust [ICC, NIC, NIGTC, NTC, TH, TNTC]. It may refer to the five months of the year when locusts are active [Alf, EC, NIC, NIGTC, Wal].

and their torment[a] (is) as (the) torment of-(a)-scorpion when it-stings[b] (a) man.[c]

LEXICON—a. βασανισμός (LN 24.90) (BAGD 2. p. 134): 'torment' [BAGD, BNTC, EC, LN, Lns, WBC; KJV, REB], 'torture' [BAGD, LN; NET,

NRSV, TNT], 'suffering' [CEV], 'agony' [NIV, NLT], 'pain' [NAB, TEV], 'severe pain, severe suffering' [LN]. The sting of a scorpion is excruciating [Ld, Sw].
  b. aorist act. subj. of παίω (LN **19.16**) (BAGD 1. p. 605): 'to sting' [BAGD, EC, **LN**; NET, NRSV, TNT], 'to strike' [Lns; KJV, NIV]. This verb is also translated as a noun: 'sting' [BNTC, WBC; CEV, NAB, NLT, REB, TEV]. It possibly has the more generic sense of 'to strike' [LN (**19.16 fn 3**)].
  c. ἄνθρωπος (See this word at 9:4): 'man' [EC; KJV, NIV, TNT], 'person' [WBC; NET], 'someone' [NRSV], 'human being' [Lns], not explicit [BNTC; CEV, NAB, NLT, REB, TEV].

9:6 And in those days men[a] will-seek[b] death and in-no-way[c] they-will-find[d] it,
LEXICON—a. ἄνθρωπος (See this word at 9:4): 'man' [BNTC, EC; KJV, NAB, NIV, TNT], 'person' [WBC; CEV, NET, NLT, NRSV, REB], 'they' [TEV], 'human being' [Lns].
  b. fut. act. indic. of ζητέω (LN **25.9**, 13.19) (BAGD 2.b.α. p. 339): 'to seek' [BNTC, EC, Lns, WBC; all versions except CEV], 'to attempt to find' [LN (13.19)], 'to desire' [BAGD, LN (25.9)], 'to strive for, to aim at, to wish' [BAGD]. The phrase ζητήσουσιν...τὸν θάνατον 'will seek death' is translated 'will want to die' [**LN** (25.9); CEV].
  c. οὐ μή (See this phrase at 2:11 and 3:3): 'in no way' [EC, Lns], 'not' [BNTC, WBC; all versions]. Ὀυ μή expresses definiteness and certainty [Alf].
  d. fut. act. indic. of εὑρίσκω (BAGD 1.a. p. 324): 'to find' [BAGD, BNTC, EC, Lns, WBC; all versions except CEV]. The phrase οὐ μὴ εὑρήσουσιν αὐτὸν 'will not find it' is translated 'will not be able to' [CEV]. See this word also at 3:2.

and they-will-desire[a] to-die and death flees[b] from them.
TEXT—Instead of the pres. indic. φεύγει 'flees' some manuscripts read the fut. indic. φεύξεται 'will flee'. GNT does not mention this alternative. BNTC, WBC and all versions render this as a present. Only Lns preserves the future tense.
LEXICON—a. fut. act. indic. of ἐπιθυμέω (LN 25.12) (BAGD p. 293): 'to desire' [BAGD, EC, Lns, WBC; KJV], 'to long' [BAGD, BNTC, LN; NET, NIV, NLT, NRSV, REB, TNT], 'to want' [TEV], 'to hope for' [CEV], 'to yearn' [NAB], 'to desire very much' [LN], 'vehemently desire' [Alf].
  b. pres. act. indic. of φεύγω (LN 15.61, 21.14) (BAGD 1. p. 855): 'to flee' [BAGD, EC, LN (15.61), Lns; KJV, NET, NLT, NRSV, TEV], 'to escape' [LN (21.14); CEV, NAB, TNT], 'to elude' [BNTC, WBC; NIV, REB], 'to avoid' [LN (21.14)], 'to run away' [LN (15.61)], 'to seek safety in flight' [BAGD]. The present tense is a vivid way of expressing continual avoidance [Alf, ICC, NIC, TNTC]: keeps running from them. It

is a vivid way of stressing that death will evade those who desire it [NIGTC].

QUESTION—What is the significance of repeating the same idea: (1) 'men will-seek death and in-no-way will they find it'; and (2) 'they will desire to die and death flees from them'?

The repetition serves to emphasize the idea that although people will want to die, they will continue to live [NIGTC, TH, TNTC].

9:7 And the appearances^a of-the locusts^b (were) like horses prepared for battle,^c

LEXICON—a. ὁμοίωμα (LN 64.3) (BAGD 3. p. 567): 'appearance' [BAGD, WBC], 'likeness' [EC, LN, Lns], 'shape' [Alf; KJV]. This noun is also translated as a verb phrase: '(the locusts) looked like' [CEV, NET, NIV, NLT, TEV], or as a prepositional phrase: 'in appearance' [BAGD, BNTC; NAB, NRSV, REB, TNT]. The phrase τὰ ὁμοιώματα τῶν ἀκρίδων ὅμοια ἵπποις 'the appearances of the locusts were similar to horses' is translated 'the locusts resembled horses in appearance' [BAGD].

b. ἀκρίς (See this word at 9:3): 'locust' [BAGD, BNTC, EC, LN, WBC; all versions], 'grasshopper' [Lns]. The reference is to locusts as being very destructive [LN].

c. πόλεμος (LN 55.5) (BAGD 1.b. p. 685): 'battle' [BAGD, BNTC, EC, Lns, WBC; all versions], 'war, fighting' [LN], 'fight' [BAGD].

QUESTION—What is the similarity between these locusts and horses prepared for battle?

The locusts being arrayed in ranks like cavalry lines was similar to horses prepared for battle [TNTC]. Their physical features resembled war horses outfitted with armor [EC, Ld, Lns].

and on their heads as crowns like gold, and their faces like faces of-men,^a

LEXICON—a. ἄνθρωπος (See this word also at 9:4): 'man' [EC; KJV, NAB, NET], 'human being' [Lns]. This noun is also translated as an adjective: 'human (faces)' [BNTC, WBC; all versions except KJV, NAB, NET].

QUESTION—What did the crowns indicate?

The crowns probably symbolized victory or success [EC, Ld, Lns, NIC, Sw]. They could carry out their missions to a successful end [Ld, NIC].

QUESTION—What did the comparison with men's faces indicate?

It probably indicated that they were intelligent beings [EC, Ld, Lns, Sw]. The reference to a man's face may have included the whole head including the ears [TH].

9:8 And they-had hair^a like hair of-women, and their teeth were like lions' (teeth),

LEXICON—a. θρίξ (LN 8.12) (BAGD 1. p. 364): 'hair' [BAGD, BNTC, EC, LN, Lns, WBC; all versions].

QUESTION—What feature of women's hair was like the locusts' hair?
The features of being long and flowing were like women's hair [Alf, NIC]. It was long and wavy [TH]. It was long and possibly disheveled [WBC]. It was long [TNTC]. It may have indicated their speed as they carried out their work [NIC].

QUESTION—What did the lion's teeth symbolize?
The lion's teeth symbolized fierceness [Ld, NIC, TNTC].

9:9 and they-had chests^a like iron^b breastplates,^c

LEXICON—a. θώραξ (LN **8.38**) (BAGD 2. p. 367): 'chest' [BAGD, BNTC, **LN**, Lns; CEV, NAB, REB, TEV], 'thorax' [WBC], 'breastplate' [EC; KJV, NET, NIV, TNT], 'scale' [NRSV], 'armor' [NLT]. From this word for 'chest' developed the meaning of breastplate armor that covered the chest and back [EC].
  b. σιδηροῦς (LN 2.59) (BAGD p. 750): 'iron' [BAGD, BNTC, EC, LN, Lns, WBC; all versions except CEV, NLT], 'made of iron' [BAGD, LN; CEV, NLT].
  c. θώραξ (LN **6.39**) (BAGD 1. p. 367): 'breastplate' [BAGD, BNTC, EC, **LN**, Lns, WBC; all versions except CEV, NLT], 'armor' [CEV, NLT].

QUESTION—What is implied by the iron breastplate-like chests of the locusts?
The iron breastplate-like chests imply that they were well-protected [TNTC], or invincible [EC, Ld, Lns, NIC, Sw, Wal].

and the sound of-their wings^a (was) like (the) sound of chariots^b of-many horses rushing^c into battle,

LEXICON—a. πτέρυξ (LN **8.29**) (BAGD p. 727): 'wing' [BAGD, BNTC, EC, LN, Lns, WBC; all versions]. The reference is to wings of insects [**LN**].
  b. ἅρμα (LN **6.52**) (BAGD p. 107): 'chariot' [BNTC, EC, LN, Lns, WBC; all versions except CEV, NET, TEV], 'war chariot' [BAGD]. The phrase ἁρμάτων ἵππων 'chariots of horses' is translated 'horse-drawn chariots' [CEV, NET, TEV]. A ἅρμα is a two-wheeled cart drawn by one or more horses [TH].
  c. pres. act. participle of τρέχω (LN **15.230, 6.52**) (BAGD 1. p. 825): 'to rush' [BAGD, **LN** (6.52), WBC; CEV, NIV, NLT, NRSV, TEV], 'to charge' [BNTC; NAB, NET, REB], 'to run' [EC, **LN** (15.230), Lns; KJV], 'to gallop' [TNT].

QUESTION—How is the phrase ἁρμάτων ἵππων πολλῶν 'chariots of many horses' translated?
It is translated 'many horse-drawn chariots' [NET, TEV], 'an army of horse-drawn chariots' [CEV], 'an army of chariots' [NLT], 'chariots of many horses' [Lns; KJV], 'many horses and chariots' [NAB, NIV, REB], 'many chariots with horses' [NRSV], 'many chariots with teams of warhorses' [WBC], 'chariots drawn by many horses' [TNT], 'many chariots...horses' [BNTC].

9:10 And they-have tails like scorpions and stingers,[a] and in their tails (is) their power[b] to-hurt men[c] five months,

TEXT—Some manuscripts have ἦν 'was' after κέντρα 'stingers', instead of καί 'and'. Then καί 'and' is included before ἡ ἐξουσία 'the power' reading, '...scorpions, and stingers were in their tails, and their power (is) to hurt...' Neither GNT nor Nestle-Aland mention this alternative. It is taken by TR and KJV.

LEXICON—a. κέντρον (LN **8.45**) (BAGD 1. p. 428): 'stinger' [**LN**, WBC; CEV, NAB, NET, NRSV], 'sting' [BAGD, BNTC, EC, LN, Lns; KJV, NIV, REB, TEV, TNT]. This noun is also translated as a verb: 'to sting' [NLT].

b. ἐξουσία (LN 76.12) (BAGD 2. p. 278): 'power' [BAGD, BNTC, LN, Lns, WBC; all versions except NAB, NET], 'enough venom' [NAB], 'ability' [NET], 'capability' [BAGD, TH], 'authority' [EC, TH].

c. ἄνθρωπος (See this word also at 9:4): 'man' [EC; KJV, NAB, TNT], 'person' [LN (9.1), WBC; NET, NIV, NLT, NRSV, REB, TEV], 'human being' [Lns], 'someone' [CEV], 'mankind' [BNTC].

QUESTION—What is the significance of the present tense ἔχουσιν 'they have'?

It contributes to the vividness of John's description [NIC, TNTC].

QUESTION—Are the tails of these beings like scorpions or like the tails of scorpions?

They are like the tails of scorpions [Alf, ICC, Ld, Sw, TH, WBC; CEV, TEV].

QUESTION—Of what previous verse is this a further description?

Verse 9:9 speaks of these beings as having the power to torment people and the torment they inflicted as being like the sting of a scorpion [Ld].

9:11 they have over them (a) king the angel[a] of-the abyss,[b]

TEXT—Some manuscripts include καί 'and' before ἔχουσιν 'having'. GNT does not mention this alternative. 'And' is included by KJV.

LEXICON—a. ἄγγελος (BAGD 2.c. p. 8): 'angel' [BNTC, EC, Lns, WBC; all versions]. This refers to an evil spirit [BAGD]. See this word also at 1:1.

b. ἄβυσσος (LN **1.20**): 'abyss' [BNTC, EC, Lns; NAB, NET, REB, TEV], 'Abyss' [NIV], 'deep pit' [CEV], 'bottomless pit' [KJV, NLT, NRSV, TNT], 'underworld' [**LN**]. See this word also at 9:1.

QUESTION—How are the nouns related in the genitive construction τὸν ἄγγελον τῆς ἀβύσσου 'the angel of the abyss'?

The angel is in charge of the abyss [NIGTC, Sw, TH; CEV, NAB, TEV]. The angel is from the abyss [NLT]. The abyss defines who the angel is [Alf]: the abyss angel.

QUESTION—Who is this angel?

He may be the same angel as opened the abyss in 9:1 [ICC, Ld, NIGTC, NTC]. He is not the angel of 9:1 [EC, Lns, NIC, WBC]. He is an evil angel

[Alf, BAGD, EC, NIGTC, TNTC, WBC]. He may be Satan [NIGTC, WBC] or his representative [NIGTC]. He is not Satan [Alf, EC, Lns].

(the) name to-him in-Hebrew (is) Abaddon,[a] **and in the Greek he-has (the) name Apollyon.**[b]

LEXICON—a. Ἀβαδδών (LN **93.2**) (BAGD p. 1): 'Abaddon' [BAGD, BNTC, EC, **LN**, Lns, WBC; all versions]. Ἀβαδδών means 'Destroyer' [EC, **LN**]. Ἀβαδδών in Hebrew means 'destruction' [ICC, NIC, NIGTC, TH, TNTC].

b. Ἀπολλύων (LN **93.32**) (BAGD p. 95): 'Apollyon' [BAGD, BNTC, EC, **LN**, Lns, WBC; CEV, KJV, NAB, NET, NIV, NRSV], 'the Destroyer' [BAGD], 'Apollyon, the Destroyer' [NLT, REB], 'Apollyon (meaning "The Destroyer")' [TEV, TNT]. Ἀπολλύων means 'Destroyer' [BNTC, **LN**, NIC, NIGTC, TH, TNTC, Wal].

DISCOURSE UNIT: 9:12–21 [Lns; NAB]. The topic is the sixth trumpet.

9:12 **The first**[a] **woe**[b] **passed;**[c] **behold,**[d] **comes yet two woes after these-things.**

LEXICON—a. εἷς (LN 60.10) (BAGD 4. p. 232): 'first' [BAGD, BNTC, EC, Lns, WBC; all versions except KJV], 'one' [**LN**; KJV].

b. οὐαί (LN **22.9**) (BAGD 2. p. 591): 'woe' [BAGD, BNTC, EC, Lns; KJV, NAB, NET, NIV, NRSV, REB], 'horrible thing' [CEV], 'horror' [TEV], 'terror' [NLT], 'calamity' [BAGD; TNT], 'disaster' [**LN**, WBC]. See this word also at 8:13.

c. aorist act. indic. of ἀπέρχομαι (LN **13.93**) (BAGD 1.b. p. 84): 'to pass' [NET, NRSV, REB], 'to pass away' [BAGD, EC, LN], 'to happen' [CEV], 'to occur' [WBC], 'to go' [Lns], 'to cease' [**LN**], 'to cease to exist' [**LN**]. This verb is also translated as an adjective: '(is) past' [KJV, NAB, NIV, NLT, TNT], '(is) over' [BNTC; TEV]. The aorist describes the vision of the first woe as having gone from John's sight [Lns]. It refers to the time of fulfillment, not that it had passed away at the time of writing [EC].

d. ἰδού (See this word at 1:7): 'behold' [EC, WBC; KJV], 'lo' [Lns], 'but look' [NLT], 'but wait' [CEV], 'but' [BNTC; NET, REB], not explicit [NAB, NIV, NRSV, TEV, TNT].

QUESTION—What is the significance of ἰδοῦ 'behold', plus the present tense ἔρχεται 'comes'?

They increase the vividness of the scene [TNTC].

DISCOURSE UNIT: 9:13–21 [Alf, EC, ICC, Ld, NIC, NIGTC, NTC, Sw, TNTC, WBC]. The topic is the sixth trumpet.

DISCOURSE UNIT: 9:13–15 [Wal]. The topic is the sixth trumpet.

9:13 And the sixth angel trumpeted; and I-heard a voice from the [four] horns[a] of-the golden altar the-one before God,

TEXT—Some manuscripts omit τεσσάρων 'four' before κεράτων 'horns'. GNT includes this word in brackets with a C decision, indicating difficulty in deciding whether or not to include it in the text. It is also omitted by BNTC, EC, Lns, NIGTC, WBC; NIV, REB.

LEXICON—a. κέρας (LN **8.17, 79.105**) (BAGD 2. p. 429): 'horn' [BNTC, EC, LN (8.17), Lns; KJV, NAB, NET NIV, NLT, NRSV, REB], 'corner' [BAGD, **LN** (79.105), WBC; CEV, TEV, TNT], 'projection' [LN (79.105)], 'extension, end' [BAGD]. Κέρας here refers to the four horn-shaped corners of the altar [EC, **LN** (8.17), TH].

QUESTION—What altar is referred to here?

It is the golden altar of incense, the one referred to in 8:3 [Alf, BNTC, EC, GNT, ICC, Ld, Lns, NTC, Sw, TH, WBC].

QUESTION—Whose voice was speaking?

It was the horn itself that was given the ability to speak by God [WBC]. It was the voice of the altar itself (see 16:7) [Alf]. The altar speaks, but this is symbolical of the prayers of the martyrs from under it [Ld]. It may have been the voice of the souls from under the altar (see 6:9) [NIC]. It may have been the voice of the angel referred to as standing at the altar in 8:3 [EC, NIC, NTC]. It may have been the voice of Christ or of an angel [NIGTC].

QUESTION—What is the significance of this verse?

It signifies that the judgments that are occurring are in answer to the prayers of God's people [BNTC, NIC, NIGTC, Sw, Wal].

9:14 saying to-the sixth angel, the-one having the trumpet, "Release[a] the four angels bound[b] at[c] the great river Euphrates."

LEXICON—a. aorist act. impera. of λύω (LN 18.18) (BAGD 2.a. p. 483): 'to release' [BNTC, WBC; all versions except KJV, NET], 'to set free' [BAGD; NET], 'to loose' [BAGD, EC, Lns; KJV], 'to untie' [BAGD, LN].

b. perf. pass. participle of δέω (LN 18.13) (BAGD 2. p. 178): 'to be bound' [EC, Lns, WBC; all versions except CEV, NAB], 'to be tied up' [LN; CEV, NAB], 'to be held in bonds' [BNTC], 'to be tied' [BAGD, LN], 'to be tied together' [LN].

c. ἐπί with dative object (LN 83.23) (BAGD II.1.a.δ. p. 287): 'at' [BNTC, EC, LN, Lns, WBC; all versions except CEV, KJV, NAB], 'beside' [CEV], 'on the banks of' [NAB], 'on' [Alf], 'in' [KJV], 'by' [LN], 'near' [BAGD].

QUESTION—Who are these four angels?

These four angels are not the same as those angels mentioned in 7:1 [Alf, ICC, Ld, Lns, NIC, NIGTC, TNTC, Wal], because those angels were at the four corners of the earth not at the Euphrates [Alf, ICC, Ld, NIC, TNTC], and because they were holding back the four winds but these angels are themselves bound [Alf, ICC, NIGTC]. They may rather be the four winds mentioned in 7:1 [NIGTC]. They are good angels who perform God's bidding [Lns]. The fact that they are bound indicates that they were evil angels [EC, Ld, TNTC, Wal], there is no occasion in Scripture where good angels are bound [Wal]. It indicates that God is the one in control of their being bound and released [TH].

9:15 And the four angels the-ones prepared for the hour and day and month and year were-released, in-order-that they should-kill the third-part of-the men.[a]

LEXICON—a. ἄνθρωπος (See this word at 9:4): 'man' [EC; KJV], 'person' [CEV, NLT], 'mankind' [BNTC, NTC, TNTC; NAB, NIV, REB, TNT], 'humankind' [NRSV], 'human race' [TEV], 'human being' [Lns], 'humanity' [WBC; NET].

QUESTION—Is the purpose clause, ἵνα ἀποκτείνωσιν 'in order that they should kill', construed with 'were released' or with 'prepared'?
1. It should be construed with 'were released' [BNTC, EC, Ld, NIC, NIGTC, TH, WBC; CEV, NET, NIV, NLT, REB, TNT]: the angels, who were prepared for the hour, day, and month, were released in order that they should kill.
2. It should be construed with 'prepared' [Alf, Lns, NIGTC, Wal; NAB, NRSV, TEV]: the angels, who were prepared for this hour, day and month to kill, were released.

QUESTION—What is the significance of the four-fold reference to the time of their release?

The four-fold reference to the time specifies the exact hour that it occurred [Ld]. The single article governing all four time words centers attention on the precise time that God had decided [EC, NIC]. The single article indicates that they all point to a single time, the hour of the day of the month of the year [Alf, Sw]. If a particular language does not have words for all of these time references, a generic translation like, 'at this exact time' could be used [TH].

QUESTION—Who was the implied actor in the passive ἐλύθησαν 'were released'?

The implied actor is the angel [TH, TNTC WBC].

QUESTION—Who were to be killed?

The unbelievers of the world were to be killed since believers were exempt from this judgment (see 9:4, 20) [Alf, ICC, Ld, NIC].

9:16 And the number of-the troops[a] of-the cavalry[b] (was) twice-ten-thousands[c] of-ten-thousands, I-heard their number.

LEXICON—a. στράτευμα (LN 55.7, 55.10) (BAGD p. 770): 'troop' [BAGD; NAB, NRSV], 'army' [BAGD, EC, LN (55.7), Lns; KJV, NLT], 'squadron' [BNTC; REB], 'soldier' [WBC], 'some soldiers, a few soldiers, a small group of soldiers' [LN (55.10)]. The phrase τῶν στρατευμάτων τοῦ ἱππικοῦ 'the troops of cavalry' is translated 'soldiers

on horseback' [NET], 'war horses' [CEV], 'mounted troops' [NIV, TEV], 'cavalry' [TNT].
    b. ἱππικός (LN **55.21**) (BAGD p. 380): 'cavalry' [BAGD, BNTC, EC, **LN**, Lns, WBC; NAB, NRSV, REB], 'horseman' [LN; KJV], 'mounted troops' [NLT], 'cavalryman' [LN], not explicit [CEV, NET, NIV, TEV, TNT].
    c. δισμυριάς (LN **60.9**) (BAGD p. 199): 'twice ten thousand' [BNTC, WBC; REB], 'twenty thousands' [EC], 'two myriad' [Lns], 'double myriad' [BAGD], 'countless, incalculable, great number of' [LN]. A δισμυριάς amounts to 20,000 [BAGD]. The phrase δισμυριάδες μυριάδων 'twice ten thousand of ten thousand' is translated 'two hundred million' [NAB, NET, NIV, NLT, NRSV, TEV, TNT], 'two hundred thousand' [KJV], 'twice ten thousand times ten thousand' [BNTC, WBC; REB], 'more than two hundred million' [CEV], 'countless' [**LN**], 'enormous number' [**LN**]. The phrase indicates an indefinite number of incalculable immensity [BAGD].

QUESTION—What happened to the four angels?

They are the commanders of this vast cavalry [NIGTC, Sw]. The four angels obey the command to kill by means of this huge army [NIGTC].

QUESTION—Is this number literal or figurative?
1. It is literal [Alf, EC, Lns, TH, TNTC; all versions]. The fact that John states that he heard the number indicates that it is intended literally [TNTC]. If a language does not have specific numbers to express this, a generic translation like 'a very large number' or 'too many to count' can be used [TH].
2. It is figurative indicating a very large number [BAGD, Ld, LN, NIC, NIGTC, NTC, Sw, Wal]. The number indicates the concept of innumerability [BAGD, Ld, LN, NIC, NIGTC]. The plural of both numbers (twice ten thousands of ten thousands) yields a too indefinite sum to be taken literally [NIGTC]. A literal number sacrifices the evocative connotations that are intended [NTC].

QUESTION—What is the nature of this army?

It is a large number of evil spiritual beings [Ld, NIGTC, WBC]. They are demons [EC].

9:17 And this-was-how[a] I-saw the horses in the vision[b] and the-ones sitting on them,

LEXICON—a. οὕτως (See this word also at 2:15): 'this was how (I saw/looked)' [BNTC; NAB, NRSV, REB, TNT], 'like this' [WBC; NIV], 'this is what…(looked like)' [NET], 'thus' [EC, Lns; KJV], not explicit [CEV, NLT, TEV].
    b. ὅρασις (LN **33.488**) (BAGD 3. p. 577): 'vision' [BAGD, BNTC, EC, **LN**, Lns, WBC; all versions]. Ὅρασις here refers to supernatural vision [BAGD]. See this word also at 4:3. A ὅρασις is an experience in which a person sees a scene clearly and believably in his/her mind's eye. Such an

experience is given by the agency of God or some other supernatural power [LN].

QUESTION—What is implied by the mention of the word ὅρασις 'vision'?

It implies that what he was seeing were demonic creatures and not natural horses and riders [Ld]. It implies that he was seeing symbolic things [NIC].

having fiery-red[a] and dark-blue[b] and sulfur-yellow[c] breastplates, and the heads of-the horses (were) like (the) heads of-lions,

LEXICON—a. πύρινος (LN **79.33**) (BAGD p. 731): 'fiery red' [BNTC, **LN**, WBC; CEV, NAB, NET, NIV, NLT, REB], 'fiery' [BAGD, Lns], 'the color of fire' [BAGD; NRSV], 'red as fire' [TEV, TNT], 'of fire' [EC; KJV].

b. ὑακίνθινος (LN **79.37**) (BAGD p. 831): 'dark blue' [BAGD, BNTC; CEV, NET, NIV], 'deep blue' [NAB], 'sky blue' [NLT], 'blue' [LN; TNT], 'blue as sapphire' [TEV], 'color of sapphire' [NRSV], 'blue like hyacinth' [EC, WBC], 'turquoise' [REB], 'hyacinth-colored' [BAGD], 'blue as hyacinth' [**LN**], 'jacinth' [KJV], 'hyacinthine' [Lns]. Ὑακίνθινος indicates a dusky blue [NIC, TNTC] or smoky blue color [ICC].

c. θειώδης (LN **79.36**) (BAGD p. 354): 'sulfur yellow' [BNTC; REB], 'sulfureous yellow' [LN], 'yellow as sulfur' [**LN**; NIV, TEV], 'yellow like sulfur' [WBC; NET, TNT], 'yellow' [CEV, NLT], 'pale yellow' [Alf; NAB], 'sulfurous' [BAGD], 'color of sulfur' [NRSV], 'brimstony' [Lns], 'brimstone' [EC; KJV].

QUESTION—Who are described as having breastplates?
1. The riders have the breastplates [BNTC, ICC, Ld, Lns, NIC, NTC, Sw; CEV, NET, NLT, NRSV]. The Greek grammar allows for both interpretations, but it is simpler to assign this to the riders alone [Ld].
2. Both the riders and the horses have breastplates [Alf, EC, NIGTC, WBC; KJV, NAB, NIV, REB, TEV, TNT]. It applies to the horses also since they are the main subject of the rest of the description [EC].

and fire and smoke and sulfur[b] goes-out from their mouths.

LEXICON—a. θεῖον (LN 2.26) (BAGD p. 353): 'sulfur' [BAGD, BNTC, LN, Lns, WBC; all versions except KJV, NLT], 'burning sulfur' [NLT], 'brimstone' [EC, LN, Lns; KJV].

9:18 By[a] **these three plagues[b] the third-part of-the men[c] were-killed, by[c] the fire and the smoke and the sulfur coming-out of their mouths.**

TEXT—Some manuscripts do not include πληγῶν 'plagues'. GNT does not mention this variant. It is omitted by KJV.

LEXICON—a. ἀπό with genitive object (LN 90.11, 90.15): 'by' [BNTC, LN (90.11, 90.15), WBC; all versions], 'from' [EC, LN (90.11, 90.15), Lns], 'arising from, springing out of' [Sw].

b. πληγή (LN **22.13**, 23.158) (BAGD 3. p. 668): 'plague' [BAGD, BNTC, EC, LN (**22.13**, 23.158), WBC; all versions except CEV, KJV],

'infliction' [Lns], 'pestilence' [LN (23.158)], 'misfortune' [BAGD], 'terrible troubles' [CEV], 'great suffering distress' [LN (22.13)], not explicit [KJV].
  c. ἄνθρωπος (See this word at 9.4): 'man' [EC; KJV] 'mankind' [BNTC; NAB, NIV, REB, TNT], 'person' [CEV, NLT], 'humanity' [WBC; NET], 'humankind' [NRSV], 'human race' [TEV], 'human being' [Lns].
  d. ἐκ with genitive object (LN 90.16, 89.77): 'by' [BNTC, LN (90.16), WBC; all versions except CEV], 'as a result of' [Lns], 'caused by' [CEV], 'by means of' [LN (89.77)], 'from' [EC, LN (89.77, 90.16)].

QUESTION—What specific three plagues are being referred to?
The fire and the smoke and the sulfur are the three plagues [EC, ICC, Ld, Lns, NIC, NIGTC, Sw, TNTC].

QUESTION—What is the significance of the repeated article before each of the nouns in the phrase 'by *the* fire and *the* smoke and *the* sulfur'?
It indicates that each of these entities is thought of as a distinct agent causing death [EC, Sw].

QUESTION—Does the verb 'to kill' refer to literal death?
It should be taken literally to refer to physical death, but spiritual death is also implied [NIGTC]. (Note that although no other commentary spoke about this, their silence probably argues for physical death.)

9:19 For the power[a] of-the horses is in their mouth and in their tails,

TEXT—Some manuscripts read αἱ γὰρ ἐξουσίαι αὐτῶν 'for their power' instead of ἡ γὰρ ἐξουσία τῶν ἵππων 'for the power of the horses'. GNT does not mention this alternative. 'For their power' is followed by the TR and KJV.

TEXT—Some manuscripts do not include the phrase καὶ ἐν ταῖς οὐραῖς 'and in their tails'. GNT does not mention this alternative.

LEXICON—a. ἐξουσία (LN **76.12**): 'power' [BNTC, **LN**, Lns, WBC; all versions except CEV, NAB], 'deadly power' [NAB], 'authority' [EC]. This noun is also translated as an adjective: 'powerful (mouths)' [CEV]. See this word also at 9:10.

QUESTION—What relationship is indicated by γάρ 'for'?
It indicates the explanation of how the horses were able to kill [EC, Lns]: *You see*, the power of the horses is in their mouth and in their tails.

QUESTION—Does the power to kill lie in both their mouth and their tail?
  1. They have power to kill with both their mouth and their tail [EC, TH, WBC; NAB]. This indicates lethal power and should be understood as their having power in their tails *as well as* in their mouths [WBC].
  2. They have power to kill with the mouth only, the tail is used to cause suffering [Ld, Lns, NIC].

for their tails (are) like snakes,[a] having heads and with[b] them they-inflict-injury.[c]

LEXICON—a. ὄφις (LN 4.52) (BAGD 1. p. 600): 'snake' [BAGD, BNTC, LN, Lns, WBC; NAB, NET, NIV, NLT, TEV], 'serpent' [BAGD, EC; KJV, NRSV, REB, TNT], 'poisonous snake' [CEV], 'reptile' [LN].

b. ἐν with dative object (LN 90.10): 'with' [EC, LN, WBC; KJV, NET, NIV, NRSV, REB, TNT], 'in connection with' [Lns], 'by' [LN], not explicit [BNTC; CEV, NAB, NLT]. This preposition is also translated by a verb: '(they) use (them)' [TEV].

c. pres. act. indic. of ἀδικέω (See this word at 2:11): 'to inflict injury' [BNTC, WBC; NIV, REB], 'to injure' [NET, NLT], 'to hurt' [Lns; TEV], 'to do hurt' [KJV], 'to inflict harm' [NRSV], 'to do harm' [EC; TNT], 'to bite and hurt' [CEV], 'to strike' [NAB].

9:20 **And the rest[a] of-the men,[b] the-ones not were-killed by[b] these plagues, not-even repented from the works of-their hands,**

LEXICON—a. λοιπός (LN **63.21**) (BAGD 1.b. p. 479): 'rest' [BNTC, EC, **LN**, Lns, WBC; all versions except CEV, NAB, NLT], 'part' [NAB], not explicit [CEV, NLT]. The phrase οἱ λοιποί 'the rest' is translated 'those who were left' [BAGD]. See this word also at 2:24.

b. ἄνθρωπος (See this word at 9:4): 'man' [EC; KJV], 'mankind' [BNTC; NAB, NIV, REB, TNT], 'person' [CEV, NLT], 'humanity' [WBC; NET], 'human being' [Lns], 'human race' [TEV], 'humankind' [NRSV].

c. ἐν with dative object (LN 83.13, 90.10): 'by' [EC, LN (90.10), WBC; KJV, NET, NIV, TEV, TNT], 'in' [LN (83.13), Lns; NLT], 'with' [LN (90.10)], 'inside, within' [LN (83.13)], not explicit [BNTC; CEV, NAB, REB].

QUESTION—What category of men does this refer to?

It refers to unbelieving mankind [Alf, NIC, Sw, TNTC].

that[a] they-will-worship not demons[b] and idols[c] made-of-gold, and of-silver and of-bronze[d] and of-stone and of-wood, that are-able neither to-see nor to-hear nor to-walk,

LEXICON—a. ἵνα (LN 89.49) (BAGD I.2. p. 377; II.2. p. 378): 'that' [BAGD, EC, LN; KJV], 'so that' [LN], 'so as to' [Lns; NET], 'that is' [WBC], 'so as a result' [LN], not explicit [BNTC; all versions except KJV, NET]. See this word also at 2:10 and 2:21.

b. δαιμόνιον (LN 12.37) (BAGD 2. p. 169): 'demon' [BAGD, BNTC, EC, LN, Lns, WBC; all versions except KJV], 'devil' [KJV], 'evil spirit' [BAGD, LN]. A δαιμόνιον is an evil spiritual being who does physical or psychological harm to people [TH].

c. εἴδωλον (LN 6.97) (BAGD 1. p. 221): 'idol' [BAGD, BNTC, EC, LN, Lns, WBC; all versions except NAB], 'image' [BAGD, LN], 'god' [NAB]. An εἴδωλον is an object that resembles a person, animal, or god, and is an object of worship [LN].

d. χαλκοῦς (LN **2.56**) (BAGD p. 875): 'made of bronze' [BAGD, BNTC, **LN**, Lns, WBC; CEV, NET, NLT], 'fashioned from bronze' [REB], 'of/from bronze' [NAB, NIV, NRSV, TEV, TNT], 'bronze' [Lns], 'made of brass' [BAGD, LN], 'of brass' [KJV], 'made of copper' [BAGD, LN]. While χαλκοῦς means 'made of bronze', the word χαλκός means 'bronze' (an alloy of copper and tin), 'brass' (an alloy of copper and zinc), and 'copper' [LN (2.54)]. See a related word meaning 'bronze' at 1:15.

QUESTION—What relationship is indicated by ἵνα 'that'?

1. It expresses the result of repenting [ICC, Lns, WBC]: they did not repent so as to stop worshipping demons and idols.
2. It expresses the purpose of repenting [Alf, EC]: they did not repent, *in order that* they will not worship demons and idols.
3. It expresses the content of repenting [TH, TNTC, WBC]: they did not repent of worshiping demons and idols.

QUESTION—What is indicated by the phrase τῶν ἔργων τῶν χειρῶν αὐτῶν 'the works of their hands'?

It indicates 'idols' [Alf, BNTC, TH, WBC; CEV, NAB, REB] or 'idolatry' [NIC, NIGTC]. It indicates evil works [Lns; NLT].

9:21 And they-repented not of their murders^a nor of their sorceries^b

LEXICON—a. φόνος (LN 20.82) (BAGD p. 864): 'murder' [BAGD, BNTC, LN, Lns, WBC; all versions except CEV], 'killing' [BAGD]. This noun is also translated as a verb: 'to murder' [CEV].

b. φάρμακον (LN **53.100**) (BAGD 2. p. 854): 'sorcery' [BNTC, EC, LN, Lns, TNTC, WBC; KJV, NAB, NRSV, REB, TNT], 'magic' [**LN**; TEV], 'magic spell' [NET], 'magic art' [NIV], 'magic potion, charm' [BAGD], 'witchcraft' [NLT]. This noun is also translated as a verb: 'to practice witchcraft' [CEV].

QUESTION—What is meant by φάρμακον 'sorcery'?

It indicates the use of mysterious words and acts involving evil spiritual forces. Their purpose is to injure, kill or curse people (see Galatians 5:20; Revelation 18:23; 21:8; and 22:15). It could be translated 'black magic', 'evil spells' or 'witchcraft' [TH]. It either indicates magic spells or poison [WBC]. It indicates witchcraft [NIC] and the use of magic potions or drinks [Ld, NIC]. It indicates the putting of evil spells on people [Lns]. It includes the use of evil charms [Ld].

nor of their fornication^a nor of their thefts.^b

LEXICON—a. πορνεία (See this word at 2:21): 'fornication' [BNTC, EC, Lns; KJV, NAB, NRSV, REB], 'sexual immorality' [NET, NIV, TEV], 'immorality' [WBC; NLT], 'sexual vice' [TNT]. This noun is also translated as a verb: 'to be immoral' [CEV]. Πορνεία refers in general to sexual sin and not specifically to the sin of fornication [Ld, Lns, TNTC, WBC].

b. κλέμμα (LN **57.232**) (BAGD p. 434): 'theft' [BAGD, EC, LN, Lns, WBC; KJV, NAB, NIV, NLT, NRSV, TNT], 'stealing' [BAGD, **LN**; CEV, NET, TEV], 'robbery' [BNTC; REB].

DISCOURSE UNIT: 10:1–11:14 [Alf, NIC, NTC, TNTC]. The topic is interlude [NIC, NTC]. The interlude functions to emphasize the events associated with the seventh trumpet [TH, TNTC]. It is parenthetical and prepares for the final trumpet by reviewing developments leading up to it [EC]. It instructs the church about its role during the final period of world history [NIC].

DISCOURSE UNIT: 10:1–11:13 [ICC, Ld, Lns]. The topic is interlude [Ld], the rainbow angel and the two witnesses [Lns].

DISCOURSE UNIT: 10:1–11 [Alf, BNTC, EC, GNT, Ld, Lns, NIC, NIGTC, NTC, Sw, Wal, WBC; CEV, KJV, NAB, NET, NIV, NLT, NRSV, TEV]. The topic is the angel and the little scroll [GNT, Ld, NIC, NTC, Sw, Wal, WBC; CEV, KJV, NAB, NET, NIV, NLT, NRSV, TEV], the little book [Alf, BNTC], the rainbow angel [Lns], announcement of the end of delay [EC].

DISCOURSE UNIT: 10:1–4 [Alf, TNTC, Wal]. The topic is the little book and the seven thunders.

10:1 And I-saw another strong angel coming-down from heaven wrapped[a] **(with a) cloud,**

LEXICON—a. perf. pass. participle of περιβάλλω (BAGD 1.b.α. p. 646): 'to be wrapped' [WBC; NAB, NET, NRSV, REB, TEV], 'to be clothed' [EC; KJV, TNT], 'to be robed' [BNTC; NIV], 'to be covered' [CEV], 'to be surrounded' [NLT], 'to throw around' [Lns], 'to have put on, wear' [BAGD]. See this word also at 3:5.

QUESTION—Who is this angel?

1. He may be the same as the strong angel spoken of in 5:2 [Alf, NIC, Sw, TH, Wal, WBC]. The strong angel of 5:2 also spoke with a loud voice and was associated with opening the seven-sealed scroll [NIC].
2. The angel of 5:2 is the only strong angel mentioned previously and this present angel is described as 'another strong angel', so he is similar to, but distinct from, the angel in 5:2 [EC, Lns]. His strength refers to his appearance and actions [EC, Lns].
3. He is Christ himself [NIGTC]. The rainbow on the angel's head is similar to the description of a divine being described in Ezekiel 1:26–28. His face shining like the sun is very similar to the description of Christ in 1:16, while his legs being like pillars of fire correspond to Christ's feet being like bronze refined in a furnace of 1:15 [NIGTC].

and the rainbow^a (was) on his head and his face (was) like the sun and his legs^b (were) like pillars^c of-fire,

LEXICON—a. ἶρις (LN **1.38**) (BAGD 1. p. 380): 'rainbow' [BAGD, BNTC, EC, LN, Lns; all versions], 'halo' [LN, WBC]. The reference may be either to a rainbow or to a halo [**LN**]. See this word also at 4:3.

b. πούς (LN **8.49**) (BAGD 1.a. p. 696): 'leg' [BAGD, BNTC, ICC, WBC; all versions except KJV, NLT], 'foot' [EC, LN, Lns; KJV, NLT]. In view of the context, the reference here may be to the 'leg', but this is not certain since this is a supernatural vision [**LN**]. It clearly means 'leg' [BAGD]. The reference to his 'feet' being like 'pillars of fire' requires the translation of 'legs' here [EC, TH].

c. στῦλος (See this word at 3:12): 'pillar' [BNTC, EC, Lns; all versions except CEV, TEV], 'column' [WBC; CEV, TEV].

10:2 and having in his hand (an) opened little-scroll.^a And he-placed his right foot on the sea, and the left (one) on the land,

LEXICON—a. βιβλαρίδιον (LN 6.65) (BAGD p. 141): 'little scroll' [BNTC, EC, LN; all versions except KJV, NLT, TEV], 'small scroll' [WBC; NLT, TEV], 'little book' [BAGD, Lns; KJV].

QUESTION—Which hand held the little scroll?

It is likely that the left hand held the scroll in view of 10:5 which says that he raised his right hand to heaven [Alf, EC, Ld, WBC]. If it is necessary to specify the hand, it is better to say the scroll was in his right hand [TH].

QUESTION—What does the verb 'opened' imply in connection with the scroll?

It signifies that the scroll was unrolled [TH; CEV, NLT]. It signifies that the scroll was unsealed, not that it was unrolled [WBC]. It implies that the contents of the scroll were in plain view for all to see [TH]. It was disclosed to those for whom it was intended [Ld].

QUESTION—What is the significance of the angel's feet being on the land and the sea?

It signifies that the contents of the message he brings is for the whole world [BNTC, EC, ICC, Ld, Lns, Sw, TH, TNTC]. It also indicates the gigantic size of the angel [Ld, Sw, TH, TNTC].

10:3 and he-shouted^a with-(a)-loud voice like (a) lion roars.^b

LEXICON—a. aorist act. indic. of κράζω (BAGD 1. p. 447): 'to shout' [CEV, NET, NRSV], 'to give a shout' [BNTC, Lns; NIV, NLT, REB], 'to call out' [TEV], 'to cry out' [BAGD; TNT], 'to cry' [EC, WBC; KJV], 'to give a cry' [NAB]. See this word also at 7:2.

b. pres. mid. (deponent = act.) of μυκάομαι (LN **14.77**) (BAGD p. 529): 'to roar' [BAGD, EC, LN, Lns; KJV, NET, NRSV], 'to growl' [CEV], 'to bellow' [LN]. This verb is also translated as a noun: '(the) roar' [BNTC; NAB, NIV, NLT, REB, TEV, TNT]; and as an adjective: 'roaring (lion)' [WBC]. The phrase ὥσπερ λέων μυκᾶται 'just as a lion roars' is translated 'which sounded like the roar of lions' [**LN**].

QUESTION—What is the significance of the angel's loud voice?
   A loud voice is a literary device that stresses the importance of the message and the supernatural quality of the speaker [WBC].
QUESTION—What is the point of similarity between the angel's shout and the lion's roar?
   The point of similarity is: the loudness of the sound [EC, Ld, NIGTC, TH]; its frightening quality [TH]; or its deep resonance that commands attention [TNTC]. It does not imply that the words were unintelligible [EC].

And when he-shouted, the seven thunders[a] uttered[b] their own sounds.[c]
LEXICON—a. βροντή (See this word at 4:5): 'thunder' [BAGD, BNTC, LN, Lns, WBC; all versions], 'peal of thunder' [EC].
   b. aorist act. indic. of λαλέω (LN 33.70) (BAGD 1. p. 463): 'to utter' [EC, Lns, WBC; KJV], 'to sound' [BAGD; NRSV], 'to speak' [LN; NIV], 'to roar' [CEV], 'to talk, to say, to tell' [LN], 'to give forth sounds/tones' [BAGD]. The phrase ἐλάλησαν...τὰς ἑαυτῶν φωνάς 'uttered... their own sounds' is translated 'answered' [NLT], 'answered with a roar' [TEV], 'spoke' [BNTC; NIV, REB, TNT], 'raised their voices' [NAB].
   c. φωνή (LN 14.74, 33.103) (BAGD 2.c. p. 871): 'sound' [LN (14.74), WBC], 'voice' [EC, LN (33.103), Lns; KJV, NAB, NET, NIV], 'crashing peal' [BAGD], not explicit [BNTC; CEV, NLT, NRSV, REB, TEV, TNT]. The thunders uttered words that John was going to record until told not to (10:4) [EC]. See this word also at 1:10.
QUESTION—What is the significance of the definite article in αἱ ἑπτὰ βρονταί '*the* seven thunders'?
   It indicates a definite group [TNTC], or that the group was known to the readers [EC, ICC, NIC, WBC]. It merely points to a particular group of seven [Lns].

10:4 **And when the seven thunders sounded, I-was-about[a] to-write, and I-heard (a) voice out-of heaven saying, "Seal-up[b] the-things-that the seven thunders uttered, and write them not."**
TEXT—Instead of ὅτε 'when', some manuscripts have ὅσα 'as many things as', and other manuscripts have ἤκουσα ὅσα 'I heard as many things as'. GNT selects the reading 'when' with a B rating, indicating that the text is almost certain.
TEXT—Some manuscripts include αὐτά 'them' either before or after ἤμελλον γράφειν 'I was about to write'. It is omitted by GNT with a B rating, indicating that the text is almost certain.
LEXICON—a. imperf. act. indic. of μέλλω (BAGD 1.c.α. p. 501): 'to be about to' [BAGD, BNTC, EC, Lns, WBC; all versions except NAB, NET], 'to be about to start' [NAB], 'to be preparing to' [NET], 'to be on the point of' [BAGD]. Here μέλλω has nearly the meaning of 'to begin' [BAGD]. See this word also at 1:19.
   b. aorist act. impera. of σφραγίζω (LN 6.55) (BAGD 2.a. p. 796): 'to seal up' [BAGD, BNTC; KJV, NAB, NET, NIV, NRSV], 'to seal' [EC, LN,

Lns], 'to put under seal' [REB], 'to put a seal on, to make secure' [LN]. The phrase σφράγισον ἃ ἐλάλησαν αἱ ἑπτὰ βρονταί 'seal the things that the seven thunders spoke' is translated 'keep secret what the seven thunders said' [NLT, TEV, TNT], 'conceal the message of the seven thunders' [WBC], 'keep it secret' [CEV]. The purpose of sealing is to keep the material secret [BAGD].

QUESTION—Whose voice did John hear?

It was either the voice of God or Christ [EC, Ld]. It was probably the voice of God [TH], of Christ [ICC]. God was the ultimate source of the voice [TNTC].

QUESTION—What is the action implied in the command σφράγισον 'Seal up!'?

It implies that these words should be concealed or kept secret [BAGD, Ld, TH, TNTC; CEV, NLT, TEV, TNT]. It is nearly synonymous with the following command, 'Write them not!' [EC, ICC].

DISCOURSE UNIT: 10:5–7 [Alf, NIGTC, TNTC, Wal, WBC]. The topic is the angel's oath [NIGTC, TNTC, WBC], the announcement of the end of the age [Wal].

10:5 **And the angel, whom I-saw standing on the sea and on the land, raised[a] his right hand to heaven**

TEXT—Some manuscripts do not include τὴν δεξιάν 'the right'. GNT does not mention this alternative. The reading 'the right' is not included by KJV.

LEXICON—a. aorist act. indic. of αἴρω (BAGD 1.a. p. 24): 'to raise' [BNTC, WBC; all versions except CEV, KJV, NLT], 'to lift' [EC, Lns; NLT], 'to lift up' [BAGD; KJV], 'to take up, to pick up' [BAGD], 'to hold up' [CEV].

QUESTION—What is the significance of the angel raising his right hand to heaven?

It was a sign that indicated that he was taking an oath (see Genesis 14:22; Exodus 6:8; Numbers 14.30; Deuteronomy 32:40; Daniel 12:7) [Alf, EC, Ld, NIC, Sw, TH, TNTC, WBC]. This gesture symbolically appeals to God to bear witness to the oath [WBC].

10:6 **and he-swore[a] by[b] the-one living forever-and-ever,[c] who created the heaven and the-things in it and the earth and the-things in it and the sea and the-things in it,**

TEXT—Some manuscripts do not include the phrase καὶ τὴν θάλασσαν καὶ τὰ ἐν αὐτῇ 'and the sea and the things in it'. GNT includes it with an A decision, indicating that the text is certain.

LEXICON—a. aorist act. indic. of ὀμνύω (LN 33.463) (BAGD p. 566): 'to swear' [BAGD, BNTC, EC, LN, Lns; KJV, NET, NIV, NRSV, REB, TNT], 'to swear an oath' [WBC; NLT], 'to take a vow' [TEV], 'to take an oath'. [BAGD; NAB], 'to make an oath' [LN]. The phrase ὤμοσεν ἐν 'he swore by', is translated 'he made a promise in the name of' [CEV].

ὈΜνύω indicates to verify the truth of a statement by calling on deity to penalize the person if the statement is not true [LN].
b. ἐν with dative object (LN 90.30) (BAGD IV.5. p. 261): 'by' [BAGD, BNTC, EC, LN, Lns, WBC; all versions except CEV, NLT, TEV], 'in the name of' [CEV, NLT, TEV].
c. εἰς τῶν αἰῶνας τῶν αἰώνων (See this word at 1:18): 'forever and ever' [BNTC, EC, LN (84.22); all versions except CEV, REB], 'forever' [WBC; CEV, REB], 'for the eons of the eons' [Lns].

that (there)-will-be delay/time[a] no-longer,
LEXICON—a. χρόνος (BAGD p. 888): 'delay' [BAGD, BNTC, EC; all versions except CEV, KJV, NLT], 'time' [Lns; KJV], 'interval of time' [WBC]. This clause is also translated: 'you won't have to wait any longer' [CEV], 'God will wait no longer' [NLT]. See this word also at 2:21.
QUESTION—What sense of χρόνος 'delay/time' is indicated here?
1. The sense of 'delay' is indicated [BNTC, EC, ICC, Ld, NIC, NIGTC, NTC, Sw, TH, TNTC, Wal, WBC; all versions except KJV].
2. The sense of 'time' is indicated [Lns; KJV]. 'Time' as we know it, to record the passage of months, days, and years, will cease to be [Lns].
QUESTION—If 'delay' is the sense taken for χρόνος, what event(s) are being referred to as happening without delay?
There will be no delay before the fulfillment of the mystery of God (10:7) [EC]. It is the blowing of the seventh trumpet that will occur without delay [NTC, TH, TNTC, WBC]. The reign of the Antichrist will occur without delay (see Daniel 12:6, 7 and 2 Thessalonians 2:3ff) [ICC, NIC]. It is the end of the age that will occur without delay [Ld, NIC, NIGTC, TNTC]. It is in contrast with the statement made to the martyrs in 6:9–12 who are told to rest a little longer [Ld, NIC].

10:7 **But in the days of-the voice of-the seventh angel, when he-is-about to-trumpet, and the mystery[a] of-God has-been-fulfilled[b], as he-announced[c] (to) his-own servants the prophets.**
TEXT—Instead of the aorist pass. indic. ἐτελέσθη 'has been fulfilled', some manuscripts read the aorist pass. subj. τελεσθῇ 'should be fulfilled'. GNT does not mention this alternative. The reading 'should be fulfilled' is taken by KJV.
LEXICON—a. μυστήριον (See this word at 1:20): 'mystery' [EC, Lns; KJV, NET, NIV, NRSV], 'secret plan' [WBC; CEV, TEV], 'mysterious plan' [NAB, NLT], 'secret purpose' [BNTC; TNT], 'hidden purpose' [REB]. The phrase τὸ μυστήριον τοῦ θεοῦ 'the mystery of God' refers to the whole content of the book [BAGD].
b. aorist pass. indic. of τελέω (LN 13.126, 68.22) (BAGD 1., 2. p. 811): 'to be fulfilled' [LN (13.126), WBC; NLT, NRSV, REB], 'to be completed' [BAGD, EC, LN (68.22); NET], 'to be accomplished' [BNTC, LN (13.126, 68.22); NIV, TNT], 'to be accomplished in full' [NAB], 'to be finished' [BAGD, LN (68.22); KJV], 'to be brought to an end' [BAGD,

Lns], 'to be brought to fruition' [LN (13.126)], 'to be made to happen' [LN (13.126)], 'to be ended' [LN (68.22)]. This passive voice is also translated actively: 'to happen' [CEV], 'to accomplish' [TEV]. Τελέω indicates to bring something to a proposed final form [TH]. This aorist tense is translated as a future by CEV, NAB, NIV, NLT, NRSV, TEV, and TNT: will be fulfilled. It is translated as a future perfect by BNTC, WBC and REB: will have been fulfilled. It is the prophecy of Daniel 11:29–12:13 that will be fulfilled [NIGTC].

c. aorist act. indic. of εὐαγγελίζω (LN 33.215) (BAGD p. 317; 1): 'to announce' [WBC; NAB, NIV, NLT, NRSV, TEV, TNT], 'to proclaim' [NET], 'to tell' [CEV], 'to preach' [EC], 'to declare' [KJV], 'to promise' [REB], 'to assure' [BNTC], 'to give the good news' [Lns], 'to bring good news' [BAGD], 'to announce the gospel' [LN], 'to announce good news' [BAGD], 'to tell the good news' [LN]. Amos 3:7 speaks of God revealing his plan to his servants the prophets [NTC]. What God told them was the time when he would fulfill his plans [TH].

QUESTION—What relationship is indicated by ἀλλά 'but'?

Ἀλλά indicates a strong contrast [Alf, EC, Ld, NIC, TNTC]. It indicates: 'on the contrary' [Lns]. The contrast is with the final statement in 10:6 [EC, NIC]: there will be delay no longer *but*.... The strong contrast stresses the interpretation that 'delay' rather than 'time' is indicated in 10:6 [TNTC].

QUESTION—Who is the implied actor of ἐτελέσθη 'has been fulfilled'?

The implied actor is God [Lns; CEV, TEV]: God fulfilled the mystery.

QUESTION—Does this verse indicate that the mystery of God will be fulfilled before the seventh angel sounds?

Yes, it means this [CEV, REB]. No, it does not mean this [ICC, Ld, NIC, NIGTC]. The verb μέλλειν can mean 'to be about to', which could then indicate that the mystery would be fulfilled before the angel sounded [ICC, Ld, NIC, NIGTC], but it can also be taken as a simple future and that is its meaning here [EC, ICC, Ld, NIC, NIGTC, WBC; KJV]: when he will blow his trumpet. What the verse indicates is that God's mystery will be fulfilled within the period of time that will be brought about by the blowing of the seventh trumpet [EC, NIC]. The blowing of the seventh trumpet is not a singular act, but indicates a series of events occurring over a period of time [Ld].

QUESTION—What is meant by τὸ μυστήριον τοῦ θεοῦ 'the mystery of God'?

Mystery refers to the truth about God that has not been completely revealed. It has to do with how evil is allowed to have its way over good [Wal]. The mystery is God's purpose revealed to man (see Romans 16:25, 26) [Ld]. It refers to God's purpose(s) for man [BNTC, ICC, Ld, NIC, NIGTC, NTC, Sw, TH, TNTC; REB, TNT]. It refers to God's plan to accomplish his purpose through Christ [TH]. It has to do with God's plan to save man and judge evil [Ld, TNTC]. The mystery concerns the details revealed in the rest of the chapters [EC]. John is saying that what God purposed for man in creation and brought about by Jesus' sacrificial death, will be brought to completion at the sounding of the seventh trumpet [NIC].

QUESTION—What is the correct translation for καί 'and' here?

It should be translated 'then' [Alf, EC, ICC, Sw, WBC; NET, TEV, TNT]: *then* the mystery of God has been fulfilled. It should be translated 'also' [Lns]: the mystery of God has *also* been fulfilled.

QUESTION—What particular prophets are being referred to?

It refers to: OT prophets [WBC]; NT prophets [ICC, TH]; both OT and NT prophets [EC, Ld, Lns, NIC, Sw, TNTC].

DISCOURSE UNIT: 10:8–11 [Alf, NIGTC, TNTC, Wal, WBC]. The topic is the little book [TNTC], the eating of the scroll [Wal, WBC], renewal of John's commission to prophesy [Alf, NIGTC].

10:8 **And the voice that I-heard from heaven (was) again speaking with me and saying, "Go take the opened scroll in the hand of-the angel standing on the sea and on the land."**

TEXT—Instead of βιβλίον 'scroll', some manuscripts have βιβλαρίδιον 'little scroll'. GNT does not mention this alternative. The reading 'little scroll' is taken by KJV.

QUESTION—What voice spoke to John here?

It is the same voice that spoke to him in 10:4 [EC, ICC, Ld, Lns, NIC, NIGTC, Sw, TH, TNTC, Wal, WBC].

QUESTION—What is the significance of the repetition the angel's stance on land and sea?

The repetition indicates that it is important [Ld, TNTC]. It functions to emphasize the angel's sovereignty over the earth [NIGTC]. The stance symbolizes the fact that the angel is sovereign over all the earth [NIGTC, Wal] or that his message is meant for the whole world [Ld]. It is probably only rhetorical (see 10:2, 5, 8) [NIC].

QUESTION—What is the significance of the interchange of the words βιβλαρίδιον 'little scroll', and βιβλίον 'scroll' in 10:2, 8, and 9?

It appears that there is no difference in meaning [EC, NIC, TNTC].

QUESTION—What is the significance of repeating that the book was open and what does it signify?

The repetition indicates that the fact of its being open is important [TNTC], or is being emphasized [NIGTC]. It symbolizes that the Revelation of the scroll is available to everyone [TNTC]. It symbolizes the angel's (Christ's) sovereignty [NIGTC].

10:9 **And I-went to the angel telling him to-give me the little-scroll.**

TEXT—Instead of δοῦναι 'to give', some manuscripts have the imperative δός 'Give!' GNT does not mention this alternative. The reading 'Give!' is taken by KJV.

QUESTION—Did John *tell* the angel to give him scroll?

It is better to translate 'tell' as 'ask' [NIC, TH, WBC; CEV, NET, NIV, NLT, REB, TEV], 'request' [EC].

And he-says to-me, "Take and eat[a] it, and it-will-make-bitter[b] your stomach,[c]

LEXICON—a. aorist act. impera. of κατεσθίω (LN 23.11) (BAGD 1. p. 422): 'to eat' [BNTC, EC, WBC; all versions except KJV, TNT], 'to eat up' [BAGD, LN, Lns; KJV, TNT], 'to eat down' [Lns, TNTC], 'to swallow, to consume' [BAGD], 'to devour' [BAGD, NIC, TNTC].

    b. fut. act. indic. of πικραίνω (LN **79.42**): 'to make bitter' [EC, **LN**, Lns; KJV, NET], 'to become bitter in' [**LN**], 'to be sour in' [NAB], 'to be bitter to' [NRSV], 'to turn sour' [NIV, REB], 'to turn sour in' [TEV], 'to make sour' [NLT], 'to sour' [TNT]. The phrase πικρανεῖ σου τήν κοιλίαν 'it will make your stomach bitter' is translated 'it will be bitter to swallow' [BNTC], 'your stomach will turn sour' [CEV], 'it will irritate your stomach' [WBC]. The stomach is the digestive organ and this is where John will feel the bitter sensation [EC]. See this word also at 8:11.

    c. κοιλία (LN 8.67) (BAGD 1. p. 437): 'stomach' [BAGD, EC, WBC; all versions except KJV], 'belly' [LN, Lns; KJV], 'internal organ' [LN], not explicit [BNTC].

QUESTION—What are the contents of the scroll?

The contents of the scroll is probably 11:1–13 [NIC, NTC], a message for believers about to suffer persecution [NIC]. The contents are not only 11:1–3, but comprise the 'mystery of God' referred to in 10:7 [Alf]. The scroll is the gospel [Lns]. The scroll is probably the Word of God [Wal]. The contents are the word of God containing words of salvation and judgment [Ld]. It is the message that John must proclaim (see 10:11) [TNTC].

QUESTION—What is symbolized by eating the scroll?

'Eating' signifies: 'to make its contents completely your own' or 'take them into your innermost being' [TNTC]. It symbolizes: John's assimilation of the message [BNTC, EC, Ld, NIC, NTC, Wal]; intake and mental digestion of the contents [Sw]; complete compliance with God's will [NIGTC]; John's taking the gospel into his heart [Lns].

QUESTION—What is symbolized by the 'bitterness'?

1. The bitterness symbolizes God's judgment on unbelievers [Ld, NIGTC, NTC, Sw, TNTC]. Knowing the judgment that would come would cause John deep sorrow [Sw]. John must proclaim judgment with a broken heart and bitter spirit [Ld].
2. The bitterness symbolizes the persecution of believers [BNTC, NIC]. The scroll is a message for believers about suffering before the end [NIC]. The prophets who spoke God's word with their mouths, were also called on to suffer in their bodies [BNTC].

3. The bitterness symbolizes both 1 and 2 [Alf, Wal]. It is bitter especially because of the God's judgments against the evil world but also because of the persecution that John experiences [Wal].
4. The bitterness symbolizes a negative reception to the gospel that results in being lost [Lns].

but in your mouth it-will-be sweet[a] like honey."[b]
LEXICON—a. γλυκύς (LN **79.39**) (BAGD p. 162): 'sweet' [BAGD, BNTC, EC, **LN**, Lns, WBC; all versions], 'fresh, not bitter' [LN]. The meaning is that it will be pleasant to read [BAGD].
  b. μέλι (LN **5.20**) (BAGD p. 500): 'honey' [BAGD, BNTC, EC, **LN**, Lns, WBC; all versions].
QUESTION—What is symbolized by the 'sweetness'?
The scroll is sweet because it is the Word of God (see Psalms 19:10 and 119:103) [Alf, Ld, NIC, Sw]. It is sweet because to proclaim the good news is sweet to the proclaimer [Lns]. It is sweet because John's strict personality matched the severity of the scroll's contents [BNTC]. It refers to John's present satisfaction in learning God's will for the future [EC].

10:10 **And I-took the little-scroll from the hand of-the angel and ate it, and it-was like sweet honey in my mouth and when I-ate it, my stomach was-made-bitter. 10:11 And they-say to-me, "It-is-necessary (for) you to-prophesy[a] again about/against[b] peoples[c] and nations[d] and languages[e] and many kings."**
TEXT—Instead of the plural λέγουσιν 'they say', some manuscripts have the singular λέγει 'he says'. GNT does not mention this alternative. The reading 'he says' is taken by KJV, NAB, NLT.
LEXICON—a. aorist act. infin. of προφητεύω (LN 33.459) (BAGD 3. p. 723): 'to prophesy' [BAGD, BNTC, EC, LN, Lns, WBC; all versions except CEV, REB, TEV], 'to utter prophesies' [REB], 'to tell what will happen (to)' [CEV], 'to proclaim God's message' [TEV], 'to make inspired utterances' [LN], 'to foretell the future' [BAGD]. Προφητεύω means to speak a message under the influence of divine inspiration either about the future or about matters in general [LN]. It indicates that John will reveal to others the contents of the scroll [NIGTC, NTC]. To prophesy is to proclaim God's messages [TH]. The prophesy can be either about the present or the future [NIGTC].
  b. ἐπί with dative object (LN 83.35, 90.23, 90.57) (BAGD II.1.b.δ. p. 287): 'about' [LN (90.23), NIC, TH, TNTC; NET, NIV, NLT, NRSV, TEV, TNT], 'concerning' [EC, LN (90.23)], 'with reference to, with respect to' [LN (90.23)], 'to' [BAGD, LN (90.57), Lns; CEV], 'against' [NIGTC, WBC], 'before' [LN (83.35); KJV], 'over' [BNTC; REB], 'for' [NAB].
  c. λαός (See this word at 5:9): 'people' [BAGD, BNTC, EC, LN, Lns, WBC; all versions except TEV], 'nation' [TEV]. Λαός refers to people as a nation [BAGD]. The phrase λαοῖς καὶ ἔθνεσιν 'peoples and nations' is translated 'people of...nations' [CEV].

d. ἔθνος (See this word at 2:26): 'nation' [BNTC, EC, Lns, WBC; all versions except TEV], 'race' [TEV].
e. γλῶσσα (LN 9.18): 'language' [WBC; all versions except KJV], 'tongue' [BNTC, EC, Lns; KJV], 'person, 'individual' [LN]. See this word also at 5:9.

QUESTION—Who is referred to by the pronoun 'they' in λέγουσιν 'they say'?

It probably is the equivalent of the indefinite 'it was said/I was told' (see 13:16 and 16:15) [Alf, BNTC, EC, ICC, NIC, Sw, TH, TNTC, WBC; NIV, REB, TEV, TNT]. It indicates a divine impulse felt by John [EC]. It may refer to an angel or to God [TH]. (This verb is translated as 'they say/said' or its equivalent by Lns, WBC; CEV, NET, and NRSV.)

QUESTION—What is the specific meaning of ἐπί 'about' here?

1. It means 'about', 'concerning', or 'in regard to' [Alf, EC, ICC, Ld, NIC, Sw, TH, TNTC; NET, NIV, NLT, NRSV, TEV, TNT]: to prophesy about peoples, etc. The sense of 'prophesy about' is frequently is used in the Greek Bible to translate a Hebrew idiom and this is probably its meaning here (see 22:16) [Ld]. Although it is against opponents of the Lamb, it is also favorable toward the redeemed [EC]. See a similar use in John 12:16 after the verb 'to write' [ICC].
2. It means 'against' [NIGTC, WBC]: to prophesy against peoples.... Since the context is one of judgment, the sense of 'against' is more fitting here. Most of the occurrences in the LXX in Jeremiah, Amos, and Ezekiel the preposition is used with the sense of 'against'. Also from here on in Revelation, the compound 'peoples, nations, tongues and kings' is used to refer to unbelievers which would further warrant the sense of 'against' here (see 11:9; 13:7–8; 14:6ff.; 17:15) [NIGTC].
3. It has other meanings [BNTC]. It indicates; 'over' [BNTC; REB]; 'to' [BAGD, Lns; CEV]; 'before' [KJV]; 'for' [NAB].

QUESTION—To what does the word πάλιν 'again' refer?

It merely refers to a continuation of the prophesying that John had already been doing [NIGTC]. It means after the seventh trumpet in 11:15 [ICC, NIC, Sw], when John will reveal more fully the destinies of the nations [NIC]. It means in addition to the previous part of Revelation [Alf]. John has called his writing a prophecy in 1:3. He is now going to prophesy further [TNTC].

DISCOURSE UNIT: 11:1–14 [Alf, EC, GNT, NTC, Sw, TNTC, WBC; CEV, KJV, NAB, NET, NIV, NLT, NRSV, TEV]. The topic is the two witnesses. This unit is difficult to interpret [Alf, NIC, TNTC, Wal]. It is one of the most difficult in the book of Revelation [Alf].

DISCOURSE UNIT: 11:1–13 [Ld, Lns, NIGTC]. The topic is measuring the temple and the two witnesses [Ld], the witnesses [Lns].

DISCOURSE UNIT: 11:1–3 [BNTC]. The topic is measuring the temple.

DISCOURSE UNIT: 11:1–2 [Alf, ICC, NIC, Wal, WBC]. The topic is the measuring of the temple [Alf, ICC, NIC, WBC], the measuring rod of God [Wal].

11:1 And there-was-given to-me (a) reed[a] like (a) rod,[b]

LEXICON—a. κάλαμος (LN 6.213) (BAGD 3. p. 398): 'reed' [EC, Lns, WBC; KJV, NIV], 'stick' [TEV], 'cane' [BNTC; TNT], 'long cane' [REB], 'measuring rod' [BAGD, LN; NAB, NET, NRSV], 'measuring stick' [LN; CEV, NLT]. The κάλαμος is a cane known as *Arundo donax* that grows to as much as 15 or 20 feet tall [Sw]. It is straight and strong like a ῥάβδος 'rod' [Lns, Sw]. It was like a bamboo cane, sufficiently long and rigid for this kind of work [NIC].

b. ῥάβδος (LN 6.218) (BAGD p. 733): 'rod' [BAGD, EC, LN, Lns; KJV], 'measuring rod' [BNTC; NIV, REB, TEV, TNT], 'staff' [BAGD, WBC; NET, NRSV], 'stick' [BAGD, LN]. A rod was used for walking or leaning [EC]. The phrase κάλαμος ὅμοιος ῥάβδῳ 'a reed like a rod' is translated 'a measuring stick' [CEV, NLT], 'a measuring rod' [NAB].

QUESTION—Should this chapter be taken literally or figuratively?
  1. It is largely figurative [Alf, BNTC, ICC, Ld, Lns, NIC, NIGTC, Sw, TH, TNTC].
  2. It is largely literal [Wal, WBC].

QUESTION—Who is the implied actor in ἐδόθη 'it was given'?
  Either God or an angel gave John the reed [TH, WBC]. It was probably the strong angel of 10:9–11 who was already present [EC]. God's authority was behind the giving [TNTC]. The passive mood indicates that the question of who is speaking should be considered irrelevant [Lns]

saying, "Get-up[a] and measure[b] the temple[c] of-God and the altar and the-(ones) worshiping in[d] it.

TEXT—Some manuscripts include καὶ εἰστήκει ὁ ἄγγελος 'and the angel stood' before λέγων 'saying'. It is omitted by GNT with an A rating, indicating that the text is certain. It is included by KJV.

LEXICON—a. pres. act. impera. of ἐγείρω (LN 17.9) (BAGD 1.b. p. 215): 'to get up' [BAGD, LN; NET, TNT], 'to rise' [EC; KJV], 'to stand up' [LN], 'to go' [BNTC, WBC; NIV, NLT, REB, TEV], 'to come' [BAGD; NAB, NRSV], not explicit [CEV]. This verb is also translated as an adverb: 'Up!' [Lns]. This verb acts as an auxiliary verb to the main action verb 'measure' [TH]. It functions to call a person to action without necessarily assuming that they were either sitting or lying down [WBC].

b. aorist. act. impera. of μετρέω (LN 81.2) (BAGD 1.a. p. 514): 'to measure' [BAGD, BNTC, EC, LN, Lns, WBC; all versions except CEV, NAB], 'to measure around' [CEV], 'to take measurement' [NAB]. To measure people means to count them [EC, NIC, Sw, TH, TNTC, WBC; NAB, NIV, NLT, REB, TEV, TNT].

c. ναός (BAGD 1.a. p. 533): 'temple' [BAGD, BNTC, EC, **LN**, Lns, WBC; all versions except TNT], 'sanctuary' [Lns; TNT]. Ναός refers to the complex of the Holy Place, the Holy of Holies, the court of the priests, the court of Israel and the court of women [Ld]. See this word also at 3:12.

d. ἐν with dative object (LN 83.13, 83.23): 'in' [EC, LN (83.13); TEV], 'within' [WBC], 'in connection with' [Lns], 'at' [LN (83.23)], not explicit [NLT, REB]. The phrase ἐν αὐτῷ 'in it' is translated 'there' [BNTC; CEV, NAB, NET, NIV, NRSV, TNT], 'therein' [KJV].

QUESTION—Who is the speaker in the verb λέγων 'saying'?

The speaker is: God [TH]; God or Christ [Lns, WBC]; God or an angel [Wal]. The speaker is the strong angel of 10:9–11 who has given him the reed and now gives added instructions [EC].

QUESTION—What is the significance of measuring the temple, altar, and worshipers?

It signifies that these entities will be protected [BNTC, ICC, Ld, NIC, NIGTC, Sw, TH, TNTC, WBC]. The protection is not physical, but spiritual since there will still be physical persecution and suffering [BNTC, ICC, NIC]. The protection is from the Antichrist and his demonic forces [ICC, NIC]. The thing that is measured at God's command is under his care and control [TNTC]. Measuring indicates a kind of special ownership of God over the thing measured [Wal]. Measuring indicates God's presence [NIGTC] or favor [EC]. This measuring is similar to, or synonymous with, the sealing of the servants of God in 7:3 [ICC, NIC, NIGTC, NTC]. It signifies God's ownership of the Temple and altar [Wal]. It signifies getting a grasp of the temple's dimensions and setting [Alf]. It serves to make a dividing line between what is inside the temple and belongs to it, and what is outside and is evil [Lns].

QUESTION—How are the nouns related in the genitive construction τὸν ναὸν τοῦ θεοῦ 'the temple of God'?

The temple either belongs to God or is the place where He is worshiped [TH].

QUESTION—What does the temple symbolize?

1. The temple symbolizes the Church, the body of believers [Alf, BNTC, ICC, Lns, NIC, NIGTC, NTC, Sw, TNTC], (see 1 Corinthians 3:16; 2 Corinthians 6:16; Ephesians 2:20, 21; 1 Peter 2:5) [BNTC, TNTC]. Both the temple and the altar symbolize the Church [Alf]. The temple, the altar, and the worshipers symbolize the Church (see 3:12 and Ephesians 2:19ff.) [ICC, Lns]. The temple, the outer court, and the Holy City all refer to the Christian community [NIGTC].

2. The temple symbolizes the Jewish people [Ld]. This chapter indicates the salvation of Israel, that is, spiritual Israel, that will be grafted into the church (see Romans 11:26; Matthew 23:29 and Luke 21:24). So the temple symbolizes the remnant of true worshipers of the Lord among Israel [Ld].

2. The temple is the literal temple rebuilt in Jerusalem [EC, Wal].

QUESTION—Which altar is being referred to?
1. The reference is to the altar of incense [Alf, Lns, NIC]. It must be the golden altar of incense since worshipers are connected with it (see 8:3) [Lns, NIC].
2. The reference is to the altar of burnt offering [EC, NIGTC, Sw, TH, TNTC, Wal, WBC]. The definite article in the phrase τὸ θυσιαστήριον 'the altar' suggests 'the altar of burnt offering'. Since the altar of incense was located in the temple, to measure it would be unnecessary as it would be included in the temple measurement [WBC]. This is the brazen altar where people could gather [EC].

QUESTION—What does the altar symbolize?
It symbolizes the worship of God's people as seen in their sacrificial witness to the Good News [NIGTC].

QUESTION—To what does ἐν αὐτῷ 'in it' refer?
It refers to the altar, taking 'altar' to be a metonymy for the altar room [WBC]: in the altar room. It refers to the altar and means 'in connection with the altar' [Lns]. It refers to the temple [EC, TH]: in the temple.

11:2 And the outside[a] court[b] of-the temple leave-out[c] and measure it not,

TEXT—Instead of the first ἔξωθεν 'outside', some manuscripts have ἔσωθεν 'inside' GNT selects the reading 'outside' with an A rating, indicating that the text is certain.

LEXICON—a. ἔξωθεν (LN 83.20) (BAGD 2.b. p. 280; 3. p.121): 'outside' [BAGD, EC, LN, Lns, WBC; CEV, NRSV, TNT], 'without' [KJV], 'apart from' [LN]. This adverb is also translated as an adjective: 'outer' [BAGD (p. 121), BNTC; NAB, NET, NIV, NLT, REB, TEV]

b. αὐλή (LN **7.56**) (BAGD 3. p. 121): 'court' [BAGD, BNTC, EC, Lns; all versions except CEV, NET, NLT], 'courtyard' [**LN**, WBC; CEV, NET, NLT].

c. aorist act. impera. of ἐκβάλλω ἔξωθεν (LN 7.56) (BAGD 3. p. 237): 'to leave out' [BAGD; CEV, KJV, NET, NRSV, REB, TNT], 'exclude' [WBC; NAB, NIV], 'to reject' [Lns], 'cast out' [EC], 'omit' [LN], 'to leave exposed' [BNTC], not explicit [NLT, TEV].

QUESTION—To what does the outer court refer?
It refers to the Court of the Gentiles [EC, ICC, Ld, Lns, NIC, TH, WBC]. It refers to everything that is outside of the ναός 'temple' itself, not only to the Court of the Gentiles [Alf].

QUESTION—What is symbolized by the 'outer court'?
1. The outer court symbolizes the Church [BNTC, NIC, NIGTC]. It refers to some part of the Church [BNTC], or the Church seen from a different point of view [NIC]. It is that part of the Church that the Gentiles have power over, the Church as represented by the outer court, may be physically persecuted [NIC, NIGTC], but it cannot be harmed in an eternal sense [NIC].

REVELATION 11:2 223

2. The outer court symbolizes Israel [Ld, Sw]. The outer court and Jerusalem symbolize Israel as a whole in contrast to a believing remnant represented by the temple and its worshipers [Ld]. While the temple symbolizes the Church, the outer court may symbolize Israel which is given over to the heathen [Sw].
3. The outer court symbolizes the unbelieving heathen [EC, ICC, Lns, TH, TNTC]. It symbolizes those who are consigned to the domination of the Antichrist for 42 months [ICC]. It symbolizes everything that is not holy and that belongs to the world [Lns].

QUESTION—What does the command 'not to measure the outer court' signify?
It signifies that God does not give physical protection from suffering and death to his church. It is only in regard to their faith that they are protected [BNTC]. It signifies the lack of protection and being given over to persecution [NIC]. It signifies that this part is rejected by God [EC, ICC]. It signifies that this part is to be considered evil [Alf].

because it-was-given to-the-nations,ᵃ and they-will-trampleᵇ the holyᶜ city forty [and] two months.

TEXT—Some manuscripts do not include the second καί 'and' following τεσσεράκοντα 'forty'. GNT does not deal with this alternative, but includes it in brackets, indicating that the Committee had doubts about including it. This καί 'and' is written in italics in KJV, indicating that this word was not in its Greek text.

LEXICON—a. τὰ ἔθνη (LN 11.37): 'the nations' [NLT, NRSV], 'the Gentiles' [EC, WBC; KJV, NAB, NET, NIV, REB, TNT], 'the heathen' [BNTC, LN, Lns; TEV], 'those people who don't know God' [CEV], 'pagans' [LN]. See this word also at 2:26.
  b. fut. act. indic. of πατέω (LN **20.22**, 19.51) (BAGD 1.a.γ. p. 635): 'to trample' [BAGD, LN (19.51); NLT], 'to trample on' [EC, LN (20.22); NET, NIV, TEV], 'to trample upon' [**LN** (20.22)], 'to trample over' [NRSV], 'to trample all over' [CEV], 'to trample underfoot' [BNTC; REB, TNT], 'to tread on' [BAGD], 'to tread under foot' [KJV], 'to tread down' [Lns], 'to crush' [NAB], 'to keep under subjection' [WBC], 'to subdue by force' [LN (20.22)], 'to plunder' [BAGD]. Πατέω here indicates 'to dominate, to rule' [TH].
  c. ἅγιος (BAGD 1.a.α. p. 9): 'holy' [BAGD, BNTC, EC, LN, Lns, WBC; all versions except TEV], 'Holy' [TEV], 'sacred, dedicated to God' [BAGD]. See this word also at 3:7.

QUESTION—Who is the implied actor in ἐδόθη 'it was given'?
The implied actor is God [ICC, TH]: God gave it to the nations.

QUESTION—Who are 'the Gentiles'?
They are non-Christians [TH]. They are the heathen who cannot worship God or Christ [Lns]. They are the people in rebellion against God and who will oppress the Jewish remnant in Jerusalem [EC].

QUESTION—What is implied by the word πατήσουσιν 'they will trample'?
It implies the great martyrdom of the church [BNTC]. It implies a period of tribulation for the church [NIGTC]. It implies that the holy city will be profaned but not destroyed [ICC]. It implies that Israel will be judged by God because of its apostasy [Ld]. It implies a time of trouble for Israel [EC, Wal].

QUESTION—To what does τὴν πόλιν τὴν ἁγίαν 'the holy city' refer?
It refers to Jerusalem [Alf, EC, Lns, TH, WBC], God's city [TH]. It refers to the new or heavenly Jerusalem (see 21:2, 10; 22:19) [ICC, NIGTC]. It refers to Jerusalem as rejected by God, under Muslim domination [Lns].

QUESTION—What does the forty-two month period signify?
It signifies the three and a half year reign of the Antichrist as prophesied by Daniel (Daniel 7:25 and 12:7) [ICC, Ld]. It signifies the three and a half year period of Gentile domination over Israel [EC, Sw, Wal]. The domination of the Holy City by the Gentiles, the testimony of the two witnesses (11:3), the woman's wilderness stay (12:6, 14) and the beast's reign (13:5) all refer to the same three and a half year period [TNTC]. It signifies the temporary period before the end of the age when evil triumphs over good (see 12:14; Daniel 7:25; 12:7) [Ld, NIC, TH]. It signifies the period that Jesus predicted in Luke 21:24 when, "the times of the Gentiles are fulfilled" [Lns, NIC, TH, TNTC, Wal]. It signifies the period prophesied by Daniel, but it is figurative and indicates a period of tribulation of the witnessing church beginning from Christ's Resurrection [NIGTC].

DISCOURSE UNIT: 11:3–14 [NIC]. The topic is the two witnesses.

DISCOURSE UNIT: 11:3–13 [Alf, ICC, Wal, WBC]. The topic is the two witnesses.

DISCOURSE UNIT: 11:3–6 [Wal, WBC]. The topic is the prophecy of two witnesses [Wal], their mission and authority [WBC].

11:3 And I-will-give[a] to-my two witnesses[b] and they-will-prophesy[c] (a) thousand two-hundred sixty days clothed with-sackcloth.

LEXICON—a. fut. act. indic. of δίδωμι (LN 37.98): 'to give' [BNTC, Lns; KJV, NIV, NLT, REB, TNT], 'to grant' [NET, NRSV], 'to commission' [ICC; NAB], 'to send' [TEV], 'to appoint, to assign' [LN]. This verb is also used to express permission: 'to let…(preach)' [CEV], 'to permit…(to prophesy)' [ICC, WBC]. It is also translated supplying the implied object of 'give': 'to give power' [KJV, NIV, NLT], 'to give/grant authority' [EC; NET, NRSV, REB, TNT], 'to give free scope' [BNTC]. The verb δίδωμι 'to give' is used here in the sense of 'to supply' [Lns]. See this word also at 2:7.

b. μάρτυς (BAGD 2.c. p. 494): 'witness' [BAGD, BNTC, EC, Lns, WBC; all versions]. Here μάρτυς means a person who bears a message from God, but here it approaches the sense of 'martyr' [BAGD]. See this word also at 1:5.

c. fut. act. indic. of προφητεύω (BAGD 1. p. 723): 'to prophesy' [BAGD, BNTC, EC, LN, Lns, WBC; all versions except CEV, TEV], 'to proclaim God's message' [TEV], 'to proclaim a divine revelation' [BAGD], 'to preach' [CEV]. See this word also at 10:11.

QUESTION—Who is the speaker?

The speaker is God [NIC, TH]. Since 11:8 talks about Christ in the third person, Christ cannot be the speaker [EC, NIC]. The speaker is God or Christ [ICC, WBC], in light of the pronouns 'I' and 'my' [WBC]. The speaker is Christ or an angel [Sw]. It is a heavenly voice that speaks in Christ's name [Alf]. The speaker is still unidentified. Here the speaker quotes the Lord's words [Lns]. The angel speaks as God's mouthpiece and God's voice enters the narrative in an inconspicuous manner [EC]. See this question also at verse 11:1.

QUESTION—What is the significance of the definite article in the phrase τοῖς δυσὶν μάρτυσίν μου '*the* two witnesses of me'?

It indicates that these were two well-known persons [Alf, ICC, WBC].

QUESTION—Who are these two witnesses?

1. They are literal people, but their identity cannot be definitely decided [Ld, Wal]. The fact that their work is described in such detail argues that they were historical people [Ld]. These two are prophets whom God will raise up after the rapture from among those who turn to Christ then [Wal].
2. They are literal people: Moses and Elijah [EC, ICC]. According to 2 Kings 2:11, Elijah was taken up without dying and there was a similar tradition about Moses. The return of these two men at the end of the age was expected by Christians while the Jews expected Elijah to return. In the account of the Transfiguration, it is Moses and Elijah who appear with Jesus. These factors justify the position that the two witnesses are Moses and Elijah. Also the similarity of the work of these two to the work of Moses and Elijah, as seen in 11:5–6, tends to support this view.
3. They are literal people: Enoch and Elijah, who had been translated to heaven without having died [WBC].
4. They are symbolic of the Church [BNTC, NIC, NIGTC, NTC, Sw, TNTC]. They symbolize the Church as being royal and priestly in keeping with the symbolism in 11:4 [NTC]. Although modeled after Moses and Elijah [NIC], they symbolize the Church as a witnessing church [NIC, NIGTC, Sw]. They symbolize part of the church since in chapter one there were seven lampstands, here there are only two [TNTC]. They are the Christian martyrs [BNTC, NIC] who will supply sufficient evidence (two witnesses) against the Church's opposition [BNTC].
5. They are symbolic of an adequate witness to the Word of God [Lns]. Deuteronomy 17:6, 15, and 19 establish the principle that for a charge to be considered valid it must have at least two witnesses. These two witnesses at the end of Revelation confirm the validity of its contents [Lns].

QUESTION—What was the nature of their prophesying?
Their prophesying will include preaching of repentance, but will also foretell the future [EC]. They proclaimed: the need for repentance [Alf, ICC, Lns]; the coming judgment [Alf]; God's message to a persecuted people to bring about their conversion [Ld]. They prophesied: doom [TNTC, Wal]; judgment against their oppressors [WBC].

QUESTION—What is the purpose of their wearing σακκός 'sackcloth'?
It is the typical clothing for prophets (see 2 Kings 1:8, Isaiah 20:2, Zechariah 13:4) [Ld]. It was symbolic of mourning [EC, NIC, NIGTC, TH, TNTC] over the trampling of the holy city [EC], in keeping with the message of judgment that they had to proclaim [NIGTC, TH]. It symbolized the doom they proclaimed [Wal]. It indicated that the attitude of the Church during this period of persecution should be contrite, not triumphant [Sw]. It was symbolic of being repentant (see Matthew 11:21) [Alf, Lns, NIC]. It symbolized the seriousness of their message [ICC].

QUESTION—What is the relationship between the forty-two months of 11:2 and the 1260 days of this verse?
The period of forty-two months of 11:2, the length of time that the Gentiles will trample the holy city, is the same length of time that the two witnesses will prophesy [Lns, NIC, TH, TNTC, Wal, WBC], and these two periods refer to the same period of time in history [NIC, TH, TNTC, Wal, WBC]. It is expressed in two ways for literary variation. A solar month is 30 days [NIC].

DISCOURSE UNIT: 11:4–14 [BNTC]. The topic is the two witnesses.

11:4 **These are the two olive-trees[a] and the two lampstands[b] standing before the Lord of-the earth.**

TEXT—Instead of κυρίου 'Lord', some manuscripts have θεοῦ 'God'. GNT does not mention this alternative. The reading 'God' is taken by KJV.

LEXICON—a. ἐλαία (LN 3.9) (BAGD 1. p. 247): 'olive tree' [BAGD, BNTC, LN, Lns, WBC; all versions], 'olive branch' [EC].
b. λυχνία (See this word at 1:12): 'lampstand' [EC; CEV, NAB, NET, NIV, NLT, NRSV], 'lamp pedestal' [Lns], 'lamp' [BNTC; REB, TEV, TNT], 'candlestick' [KJV], 'menorah' [WBC].

QUESTION—What Scripture is similar to this description?
Zechariah 4:1–14 is similar to these two metaphors [Alf, BNTC,EC, ICC, Ld, Lns, NIC, NIGTC, NTC, Sw, TH, TNTC, Wal, WBC]. The definite article in the phrase αἱ δύο ἐλαῖαι 'the two olive trees' refers back to the Zechariah passage [Alf, WBC]. The definite article in the phrase αἱ δύο λυχνίαι 'the two lampstands' may refer back to the Zechariah passage [WBC].

QUESTION—To what function of the olive trees are the two witnesses being compared?
They are compared with the product of the olive tree, that is, olive oil, and this figure indicates a plentiful supply. In Zechariah the oil is associated with

the Holy Spirit and the promise, "'Not by might nor by power, but by my Spirit', says the Lord Almighty" Zechariah 4:6. Here their dependence on the Spirit of God is indicated [TNTC]. In the Zechariah passage the olive trees supplied oil to the lampstands [EC, Lns, NIC, NIGTC, Wal]. This indicates that the two witnessed by the strength supplied by the Spirit of God [Wal]. This figure and the following show that the Spirit of God is the power to make witnessing effective [NIC]. As olive trees, the two are full of God's Spirit who empowers their witness [Lns]. This verse shows that God's authority is behind these two witnesses and is enabling them [Ld].

QUESTION—To what function of the lampstands are the two witnesses being compared?

A lampstand carries God's light (Matthew 5:15, 16) [NIC]. A lampstand is a figure symbolizing witness [WBC]. As two lampstands, the two bear the light of God's Word [Lns].

QUESTION—Why is the verb ἑστῶτες 'standing' in the masculine gender?

It is masculine to agree with οὗτοι 'these' (the two witnesses), and not with either 'olive trees' or 'lampstands', both of which are feminine [TH].

QUESTION—Who is τοῦ κυρίου τῆς γῆς 'the Lord of the earth'?

It refers to God [WBC].

11:5 **And if anyone wants^a to-harm them fire comes-out of their mouth and consumes^b their enemies;^c**

LEXICON—a. pres. act. indic. of θέλω (LN 30.58) (BAGD 2. p. 355): 'to want' [BAGD, Lns, WBC; NET, NRSV, TNT], 'to try' [BNTC; CEV, NAB, NIV, NLT, REB, TEV], 'to will' [BAGD; KJV], 'to be minded' [BAGD], 'to wish' [BAGD], 'to desire' [EC], 'to purpose' [LN]. See this word also at 2:21.
  b. pres. act. indic. of κατεσθίω (LN **20.45**) (BAGD 2. p. 422): 'to consume' [BAGD, BNTC; NET, NLT, NRSV, REB, TNT], 'to consume completely' [LN], 'to destroy' [CEV, TEV], 'to utterly destroy' [**LN**, WBC], 'to devour' [EC, Lns; KJV, NAB, NIV].
  c. ἐχθρός (LN 39.11): 'enemy' [BAGD, BNTC, EC, LN, Lns, WBC; all versions except NRSV], 'foe' [NRSV].

QUESTION—What is the thrust of this verse?

It indicates that no one can harm these witnesses until their mission is complete [Ld, TNTC].

and if anyone wants to-harm them, thus it-is-necessary (for) him to-be-killed.

QUESTION—What is the purpose of this clause?

It repeats the content of the first clause in order to emphasize it [Lns]. It emphasizes the horrible death by which they will die [WBC].

QUESTION—To what specifically does οὕτως 'thus' refer?

It refers to being consumed by fire [BNTC, Lns, TH; NAB, NIV, NLT, NRSV, TEV, TNT].

11:6 These have the power[a] to-shut-up[b] the sky,[c] so-that no rain[d] may-rain[e] (during) the days of-their prophecy,

LEXICON—a. ἐξουσία (See this word at 2:26 and 9:3): 'power' [BNTC, Lns, WBC; all versions except NRSV, TEV TNT], 'authority' [EC; NRSV, TEV, TNT].
  b. aorist act. infin. of κλείω (LN 79.112) (BAGD 2. p. 434): 'to shut up' [BNTC, WBC; NIV, REB, TEV, TNT], 'to shut' [BAGD, EC, LN; KJV, NLT, NRSV] 'to close' [LN], 'to close up' [NAB, NET], 'to lock up' [Lns; CEV]. See this word also at 3:7.
  c. οὐρανός (LN 1.5) (BAGD 1.b. p. 594): 'sky' [BAGD, BNTC, LN; all versions except KJV], 'heaven' [BAGD, EC, Lns, WBC; KJV].
  d. ὑετός (LN **2.10**) (BAGD p. 833): 'rain' [BAGD, BNTC, **LN**, Lns, WBC; all versions except KJV, NET, NIV], 'rain water' [LN], not explicit [EC; KJV, NET, NIV]. The phrase ἵνα μὴ ὑετὸς βρέχῃ 'in order that rain may not rain' is translated 'that no rain may fall' [BAGD], 'that it rain not' [KJV], 'so that it does not rain' [NET, NIV], 'so that there will be no rain' [TEV].
  e. pres. act. subj. of βρέχω (LN 14.10) (BAGD 1. p. 147): 'to rain' [LN; KJV, NET, NIV], 'to give forth rain' [EC], 'to fall' [BAGD, BNTC, WBC; CEV, NAB, NLT, NRSV, REB, TNT], 'to wet' [Lns], not explicit [TEV].

and they-have power over the waters to-turn[a] them into blood and to-strike[b] the earth with every plague[c] as-often-as[d] they-want.

LEXICON—a. pres. act. infin. of στρέφω (LN **13.63**) (BAGD 1.a.β. p. 771): 'to turn' [BAGD, BNTC, EC, **LN**, Lns, WBC; all versions], 'to change' [BAGD, LN].
  b. aorist act. infin. of πατάσσω (LN 19.3) (BAGD 2. p. 634): 'to strike' [BAGD, WBC; NET, NIV, NRSV, TEV, TNT], 'to smite' [BNTC, EC, Lns; KJV], 'to afflict' [NAB, REB], 'to cause' [CEV], 'to send' [NLT], 'to strike a blow' [LN], 'to hit' [BAGD].
  c. πληγή (LN **23.158**): 'plague' [BNTC, EC, **LN**, WBC; all versions except CEV], 'terrible trouble' [CEV], 'smiting' [Lns]. See this word also at 9:18. It is also possible to interpret plague in Revelation 11:6 as being somewhat more generic in meaning, that is to say, trouble or distress causing widespread suffering (see 22.13) [LN].
  d. ὁσάκις ἐάν (LN 67.36) (BAGD p. 585): 'as often as' [BAGD, EC, LN, Lns; KJV, NIV, NLT, NRSV, TEV], 'whenever' [LN, WBC; CEV, NET, REB, TNT], 'at will' [BNTC; NAB].

11:7 And when they-complete[a] their testimony, the beast[b] the-one coming-up from the abyss[c] will-make war[d] with them and will-conquer them and will-kill them.

LEXICON—a. aorist act. subj. of τελέω (LN **68.22**) (BAGD 1. p. 810): 'to complete' [BAGD, BNTC, LN; NET, NLT, REB, TNT], 'to finish' [BAGD, EC, **LN**, Lns, WBC; CEV, KJV, NAB, NIV, NRSV, TEV], 'to

bring to an end' [BAGD]. See this word also at 10:7. Τελέω includes the sense of achieving a goal [LN, TNTC].
b. θηρίον (LN 4.4) (BAGD 1.b. p. 361): 'beast' [BAGD, EC, WBC; all versions except NAB], 'wild beast' [Lns; NAB], 'monster' [BNTC], 'animal' [BAGD, LN]. This is a beast of prey like a lion or panther, and connotes unreasoning violence arising from a cruel nature [EC]. Probably this is the beast described in 13:1 [TH]. See this word also at 6.8.
c. ἄβυσσος (LN 1.20): 'abyss' [BNTC, EC, LN, Lns, WBC; NAB, NET, REB, TEV], 'Abyss' [NIV], 'bottomless pit' [KJV, NLT, NRSV, TNT], 'deep pit' [CEV], 'abode of evil spirits' [LN]. It is the abode of the beast as the antichrist [BAGD, LN]. His association with the abyss indicates his connection with the powers of evil [EC, NIC, TNTC]. He owes his authority to the demonic empire [Ld]. See this word also at 9:1.
d. πόλεμος (BAGD 1.a. p. 685): 'war' [BAGD, BNTC, EC, LN, WBC; all versions except CEV, NIV, TEV], 'battle' [Lns; CEV]. The phrase ποιήσει πόλεμον 'he will make war' is translated '(he) will attack' [NIV], '(he) will fight' [TEV]. This verb 'to make war' indicates that the two witnesses may be symbolic of a larger group [NIC, TNTC, WBC]. It is best not to see much more in this verb than a general reference to conquering by whatever means, not necessarily military [Ld]. See this word also at 9:7.

QUESTION—To what specific μαρτυρία 'testimony' does this refer?

It refers back to 11:3 and the work given to the two witnesses to prophesy for 1260 days [WBC]. It refers to the message that God gave them to proclaim [TH].

QUESTION—Who might this θηρίον 'beast' be?
1. It may be the Antichrist and/or the beast referred to in Daniel 7:22ff. [Alf, ICC, Ld, LN, NIC, NIGTC, NTC, Sw, TNTC]. It is the same as the little horn of Daniel 7:8, 21, who will wear out the saints of God; the 'desolating sacrilege' referred to by Jesus in Matthew 24:15 and Mark 13:15; and the man of lawlessness referred to by Paul in 2 Thessalonians 2:3–4. He is the one who will come at the end of the age [Ld]. It refers to the antichrist and is the same as the beast of 13:1ff. and 17:3ff. [ICC, NTC]. It may be a reference to the four beasts of Daniel 7:3 conceived of as one, or a reference to the fourth [Sw].
2. It is Satan himself [Wal].
3. It is a not a person, but a spirit of antagonism to God and his kingdom [BNTC, Lns]. It symbolizes all the antichristian force in the world [Lns]. Wherever men of power refuse to be responsible to God, there this beast is seen coming up from the abyss [BNTC].

QUESTION—What is the signified by the definite article in the phrase τὸ θηρίον 'the beast'?

It signifies that he is a well-known figure [NIC, WBC]. It signifies that this beast is the one that Daniel prophesied about [NIGTC].

QUESTION—What is the significance of the present tense participle τὸ ἀναβαῖνον 'the one coming up'?
It describes where the beast comes from, and does not indicate that he came up at that particular time [WBC]. The participle describes the character of the beast [Alf, BNTC, EC, Lns].

11:8 **And their corpse[a] (will lie) on the street[b] of-the great city,**
TEXT—Instead of the singular τὸ πτῶμα αὐτῶν 'their corpse' some manuscripts have the plural τὰ πτώματα αὐτῶν 'their corpses'. GNT does not mention this alternative. BNTC, EC, WBC and all versions render this phrase as 'their corpses' whether they read it as singular or plural.
LEXICON—a. πτῶμα (LN 8.7) (BAGD p. 728): 'corpse' [BAGD, EC, LN; NAB, NET, TNT], 'fallen corpse' [Lns], 'dead body' [BAGD, LN; KJV, NRSV], 'body' [BNTC, WBC; CEV, NIV, NLT, REB, TEV]. Πτῶμα refers to whatever had been killed, one or many [Alf]. The singular may be used to indicate the close unity between the two witnesses [TNTC]. It refers especially to a corpse that was killed by violence [BAGD].
b. πλατεῖα (LN 1.103) (BAGD p. 666): 'street' [BAGD, BNTC, EC; all versions except NLT], 'main street' [NLT], 'public square' [WBC], 'avenue' [LN, Lns], 'wide street' [LN], 'wide road' [BAGD]. The word πλατεία indicates a broad street, the Broadway of the city [Lns].
QUESTION—To what city does the phrase τῆς πόλεως τῆς μεγάλης 'of the great city' refer?
  1. It refers to Jerusalem [EC, ICC, Ld, NTC, TH, Wal, WBC]. The following clause, 'where their Lord was also crucified' argues that we interpret this city as Jerusalem [EC, Ld, NTC, TH, WBC]. Although Jerusalem is the city, here it symbolizes the command center of all that is anti-Christian [Lns]. The pronoun ὅπου 'where' refers back to 'the great city', not to the words 'Sodom and Egypt' [TH].
  2. It refers to Rome [BNTC]. The phrase 'the great city' elsewhere in Revelation always refers to Rome (see 16:19; 17:18; 18:10, 16, 18, 19, 21). Even then, however, Rome indicates more than just the literal city, it symbolizes the imperial power of Rome. It is the tower of Babel, the home of this world's inhabitants [BNTC].
  3. It refers to something else [Alf, NIC, NIGTC, TNTC]. No single city is indicated. Rather it refers to sophisticated man in organized society [TNTC]. It is the world under the rule of the Antichrist [NIC]. The pronoun ὅπου 'where' does not refer back to 'the great city' but to the nearer words 'Sodom and Egypt'. The phrase is a general reference to the ungodly world, Babylon [NIGTC]. It has a wider reference than to Jerusalem itself for Jesus was crucified outside of the city by the authority of Rome [Alf].
QUESTION—What is the significance of the article in the phrase ἐπὶ τῆς πλατείας 'on the street'?
It indicates that the street was well-known [WBC].

QUESTION—What is implied by the corpses lying unburied?
It was shameful not to be buried to the people of the ancient world (see 1 Kings 21:24; Jeremiah 8:1, 2; 14:16) [EC, Ld, NIC, NIGTC, Sw, TH].

that is-called spiritually[a] Sodom and Egypt, where also their Lord was-crucified.

TEXT—Some manuscripts do not include καί 'also' before ὁ κύριος αὐτῶν 'their Lord'. GNT does not mention this alternative. It is omitted or not translated by CEV, NLT, TEV and TNT.

TEXT—Instead of ὁ κύριος αὐτῶν 'their Lord', some manuscripts have ὁ κύριος ἡμῶν 'our Lord'. GNT does not mention this alternative. The reading 'our Lord' is taken by KJV.

LEXICON—a. πνευματικῶς (LN **33.17**) (BAGD 2. p. 679): 'spiritually' [BAGD, EC, Lns; KJV], 'spiritually like' [CEV], 'figuratively' [BNTC, **LN**; NIV], 'symbolically' [LN; NET, TNT], 'prophetically' [WBC; NRSV], 'in prophetic language' [REB], 'allegorically' [Alf, LN], 'so to speak' [LN], not explicit [NLT]. This is word signifies the language of allegory or metaphor [EC]. This adverb is also translated by a noun phrase: 'the symbolic name' [NAB, TEV]. Πνευματικῶς here indicates that Jerusalem is implied by the name Sodom [BAGD].

QUESTION—What is symbolized by the name 'Sodom'?
Sodom symbolized: evil [ICC, NIGTC, NTC, TNTC, WBC]; moral degradation [BNTC, EC, NIC, Sw]; oppression [TNTC]; complete ruin [Sw]; hostility to God [Ld]; abomination [Lns].

QUESTION—What is symbolized by the name 'Egypt'?
Egypt symbolized: slavery [EC, NIC, Sw, TNTC, WBC]; oppression [BNTC, EC, NIC, NTC, Sw]; persecution [NIGTC, TNTC]; evil [ICC]; abomination [Lns]; hostility to God [Ld]. Sodom and Egypt have in common an unmitigated enmity towards God and his people [EC].

QUESTION—Who is ὁ κύριος 'the Lord'?
The Lord refers to Jesus [EC, TH, WBC].

QUESTION—Who is the antecedent of 'their' in the phrase ὁ κύριος αὐτῶν 'their Lord'?
1. The antecedent is the two witnesses [Alf, BNTC, EC, TH]: the Lord of the two witnesses. The word 'also' indicates their Lord '*as well as*' they were killed [Alf].
2. The antecedent is the people around the world in 11:9 [NIGTC]: the Lord of the peoples and tribes and nations.

11:9 **And some-of[a] the peoples and tribes and languages and nations see[b] their corpse (for) three days and (a) half**

TEXT—Instead of the present tense βλέπουσιν 'they see', some manuscripts possibly have the future tense βλέψουσιν 'they will see', although GNT does not mention this alternative. The reading 'they will see' is taken by TR and KJV.

TEXT—Instead of the singular τὸ πτῶμα αὐτῶν 'their corpse', some manuscripts have the plural τὰ πτώματα αὐτῶν 'their corpses'. GNT does not mention this alternative. The reading 'their corpses' is taken by KJV.
LEXICON—a. ἐκ with genitive object (BAGD 4.a.γ. p. 235): 'some of' [BAGD, ICC, WBC], 'those from' [EC; NET], 'men from' [BNTC; NAB, NIV, TNT], '(people) from' [REB, TEV], 'members of' [NRSV], '(people) of' [CEV] 'they of' [KJV], 'of' [Lns], not explicit [NLT]. Ἐκ here indicates part or representatives of each of the following groups that are named [TNTC]. See this word also at 2:10 and 3:9.
   b. pres. act. indic. of βλέπω (LN 24.7): 'to see' [EC, LN, WBC; KJV], 'to stare at' [BNTC; CEV, NAB, NLT], 'to look at' [NET, TEV], 'to look upon' [Lns], 'to gaze on' [NIV, REB, TNT], 'to gaze at' [NRSV].
QUESTION—What is the significance of the single article with the four nouns peoples, tribes, languages and nations?
   The single article joins all four into one group [Lns].

and do-not allow[a] their corpses to-be-placed into (a) tomb.[b]
TEXT—Instead of the present tense ἀφίουσιν 'they allow', some manuscripts have the future tense ἀφήσουσιν 'they will allow'. GNT does not mention this alternative. The reading 'they will allow' is taken by KJV.
TEXT—Instead of the singular μνῆμα 'tomb', some manuscripts have the plural μνήματα 'tombs'. GNT does not mention this alternative. The reading 'tombs' is taken by KJV.
LEXICON—a. pres. act. indic. of ἀφίημι (See this word at 2:20): 'to allow' [Lns; TEV, TNT], 'to be allowed' [NLT], 'to permit' [EC, WBC; NET], 'to let' [CEV], 'to suffer' [KJV]. The phrase οὐκ ἀφίουσιν 'they do not allow', is translated 'they refuse' [BNTC; NAB, NIV, NRSV, REB].
   b. μνῆμα (LN 7.75) (BAGD p. 524): 'tomb' [BAGD, EC, LN, Lns; NET, NRSV, TNT], 'grave' [BAGD, LN; KJV]. The phrase τεθῆναι εἰς μνῆμα 'to be placed into a tomb', is translated 'to be buried' [WBC; CEV, TEV], 'to bury' [NAB, NLT], 'burial' [BNTC; NIV, REB].
QUESTION—What is implied by the corpses lying unburied?
   It implies disgrace [Ld, NIC] or harsh persecution [NIGTC]. The purpose was to cause them greater shame [EC, ICC, TNTC]. This action also expressed triumph over them [TNTC]. It was an expression of anger against the two witnesses [WBC]. The normal custom was to bury a corpse either the same day, or at most within a twenty-four hour period [TH].
QUESTION—What is the significance of the use of the plural of πτῶμα 'corpse' here?
   It may be because each body needed individual treatment in burial [Sw, WBC]. The plural brings out the fact that although the body of Christ is singular, it is composed of many witnesses scattered over the world [NIGTC].

REVELATION 11:9 233

QUESTION—What should be done about the change in tense between 11:9–11. In verse 9 the present tense is used; in verse 10 the future tense is used; in verse 11 the past tense is used?
As it is difficult to account for these tense changes, it is best to use the appropriate tense that will best fit the context of the narrative [TH].

11:10 And the-ones dwelling on the earth rejoice[a] over them and celebrate[b] and will-send gifts[c] to-each-other,

TEXT—Instead of the present tense χαίρουσιν 'they rejoice', some manuscripts have the future tense χαρήσονται 'they will rejoice'. GNT does not mention this alternative. The reading 'they will rejoice' is taken by KJV.

TEXT—Instead of the present tense εὐφραίνονται 'they celebrate', some manuscripts have the future tense εὐφρονθήσονται 'they will celebrate'. GNT does not mention this alternative. The reading 'they will celebrate' is taken by KJV.

LEXICON—a. pres. act. indic. of χαίρω (LN 25.125) (BAGD 1. p. 873): 'to rejoice' [BAGD, EC, LN, Lns, WBC; KJV, NET], 'to gloat' [BNTC; NAB, NIV, NRSV, REB, TNT], 'to be happy' [TEV], 'to be glad' [BAGD, LN], 'to celebrate' [CEV]. The phrase χαίρουσιν...καὶ εὐφραίνονται 'rejoice...and celebrate' is translated 'to celebrate' [NLT]. To 'rejoice over them' means 'to rejoice because they have been killed' [TH].

b. pres. pass. indic. of εὐφραίνω (LN 25.131) (BAGD 2. p. 327): 'to celebrate' [BNTC; NET, NIV, NRSV, REB, TEV], 'to make merry' [EC, Lns; KJV], 'to be joyful' [WBC], 'to rejoice' [BAGD; TNT], 'to be happy' [CEV], 'to be gladdened' [BAGD], 'to be made glad, to be cheered up, to be caused to be happy' [LN], not explicit [NLT]. This verb is also translated as a noun: 'merriment' [NAB]. The passive voice should be taken as a middle indicating 'to make merry', as seen in the celebration of the prodigal son's return home (see Luke 15:23) [Lns].

c. δῶρον (LN **57.84**) (BAGD 1. p. 210): 'gift' [BAGD, BNTC, EC, LN, WBC; CEV, KJV, NAB, NET, NIV, TNT], 'present' [BAGD, **LN**, Lns; NLT, NRSV, REB, TEV]. The gifts are an expression of the happiness of the celebrants [Ld].

QUESTION—Who were 'those who dwell on the earth'?
It refers to the unbelieving people of the world [EC, Ld, Lns, NIC, NIGTC, NTC, Sw, TH, TNTC, Wal, WBC]. It refers to the inhabitants of Palestine including some Jews [ICC]. See this question also at 3:10; 6:10; and 8:13.

because these two prophets tormented[a] the-ones dwelling on the earth.

LEXICON—a. aorist act. indic. of βασανίζω (LN 38.13) (BAGD 2.a. p. 134): 'to torment' [BAGD, EC, LN, Lns, WBC; KJV, NET, NIV, NLT, TNT], 'to be a torment to' [BNTC; NRSV, REB], 'to harass' [NAB], 'to torture' [BAGD, LN], 'to cause much trouble' [CEV], 'to bring much suffering to' [TEV].

QUESTION—How did the two prophets torment the ones dwelling on the earth?

They tormented them by: inflicting the suffering described in 11:5–6 [Alf, EC, NIC, NIGTC, TH, WBC]; exposing the sins of the people of the world through their preaching and pricking their consciences [EC, NIC, Sw]; announcing judgments against the people [Lns, NIC, NIGTC, NTC].

11:11 **And after the three days and a-half (the) breath/spirit[a] of-life from God entered in them, and they-stood-up on their feet,**

TEXT—Some manuscripts do not include τάς 'the' before τρεῖς 'three'. GNT does not mention this alternative. It is omitted by KJV.

TEXT—Instead of ἐν αὐτοῖς 'in them', some manuscripts have εἰς αὐτούς 'into them', and other manuscripts have ἐπ' αὐτούς 'on them'. GNT does not mention these alternatives. The reading 'into them' is probably taken by KJV.

LEXICON—a. πνεῦμα (LN 12.18, 23.186) (BAGD 2. p. 674): 'breath' [BAGD, BNTC, EC, LN (23.186), Lns, WBC; all versions except CEV, KJV, NLT], 'spirit' [NLT], 'Spirit' [Alf, LN (12.18); KJV], 'life-spirit' [BAGD], 'Spirit of God, Holy Spirit' [LN (12.18)]. The phrase πνεῦμα ζωῆς ἐκ τοῦ θεοῦ 'breath of life from God' is translated 'God will breathe life' [CEV]. See this word also at 1:4.

QUESTION—What is meant by πνεῦμα ζωῆς ἐκ τοῦ θεοῦ 'a breath/spirit from God'?

1. It means a breath from God that gives life [TH; CEV, TEV; and probably those who translate this 'a breath of life from God': BNTC, EC, Ld, Lns, WBC; all versions except KJV, NLT]: God breathed life into them.
2. It means the Holy Spirit from God who gives life [Alf; KJV]: God's Spirit gave them life.
3. It means God gave them a spirit of life [NLT]: God gave them a living spirit.

QUESTION—What is the significance of the clause, 'they stood on their feet'?

It functions to emphasize the fact that they had come back to life [WBC].

and great fear fell on the-ones seeing[a] them.

LEXICON—a. pres. act. participle of θεωρέω (LN 24.14) (BAGD 1. p. 360): 'to see' [BAGD, LN, WBC; all versions except NET, NLT], 'to watch' [BNTC; NET], 'to stare at' [NLT], 'to behold' [EC, Lns], 'to observe, to look at' [BAGD, LN], 'to be a spectator' [LN].

11:12 **And they-heard (a) loud voice from heaven saying to-them, "Come-up here."**

TEXT—Instead of ἤκουσαν 'they heard', some manuscripts have ἤκουσα 'I heard'. GNT does not mention this alternative.

QUESTION—Who is the antecedent of ἤκουσαν 'they heard'?

The two witnesses/prophets heard [ICC, Lns, NIC, TH, TNTC].

QUESTION—Whose voice was heard?
It was the voice of God or an angel. [TH]. It was Christ, the one who had summoned John in 4:1 [EC].

And they-went-up to[a] heaven in the cloud, and their enemies saw them.
LEXICON—a. εἰς with accusative object (LN 84.16, 84.22): 'to' [BNTC, LN (84.16), WBC; all versions except TEV, TNT], 'into' [EC, LN (84.22), Lns, NIC; TEV, TNT], 'toward, in the direction of' [LN (84.16)].
QUESTION—What is the significance of the definite article in the phrase ἐν τῇ νεφέλῃ 'in *the* cloud'?
There is no reference to a particular cloud in the context. This usage is similar to the English phrase 'in the clouds' [Alf]. Note: BNTC, WBC and all versions translate the definite article as an indefinite article: '*a* cloud'. Only Lns preserves the definite article: '*the* cloud'.
QUESTION—What is the function of the cloud?
It is the means of transportation to Heaven (see Acts 1:9 and 1 Thessalonians 4:17) [TH, WBC].

11:13 **And in that hour[a] (a) great earthquake occurred and the tenth[b] of-the city fell[c]**
LEXICON—a. ὥρα (LN 67.199): 'hour' [EC, LN, Lns, WBC; KJV, NLT]. The phrase ἐν ἐκείνῃ ὥρᾳ 'in that hour' is translated 'in the same/very hour' [KJV, NLT], 'at that moment' [NAB, NRSV, REB], 'at that same/very moment' [BNTC, TH; CEV, TEV, TNT], 'just then' [NET],
b. δέκατον (LN **60.65**) (BAGD 2.a. p. 174): 'tenth' [BAGD, BNTC, **LN**, Lns, WBC; all versions except KJV, TNT], 'tenth part' [BAGD, EC, LN; KJV, TNT]. Δέκατον here indicates a 'tenth' of the buildings of the city [TH].
c. aorist act. indic. of πίπτω (LN **20.60**) (BAGD 1.b.β. p. 659): 'to fall' [BAGD, BNTC, EC, Lns; KJV, NRSV], 'to fall in ruins' [NAB, TNT], 'to collapse' [BAGD, TNTC; NET, NIV, REB], 'to fall to pieces' [BAGD], 'to experience destruction' [LN]. It is also translated using the passive voice: 'to be destroyed' [**LN**, WBC; TEV]; and active voice with 'earthquake' as agent: 'to destroy' [CEV, NLT].

and seven thousand names[a] of-men[b] were-killed in the earthquake
LEXICON—a. ὄνομα (LN **9.19**, 33.126) (BAGD III. p. 573): 'name' [BAGD, LN (33.126)]. The phrase ὀνόματα ἀνθρώπων 'names of persons' is translated 'people' [BAGD, BNTC, EC, **LN** (9.19), WBC; all versions except KJV, NAB], 'persons' [ICC, Lns, Sw; NAB], 'men' [Alf; KJV]. See this word also at 3:4.
b. ἄνθρωπος (See this word at 4:7 and 8:11): 'man' [KJV], not explicit [BNTC, EC, Lns, WBC; all versions except KJV].

and the rest became terrified[a] and gave glory[b] to-the God of-heaven.
LEXICON—a. ἔμφοβος (LN 25.256) (BAGD p. 257): 'terrified' [BAGD, LN, Lns, WBC; NAB, NET, NIV, NLT, NRSV, TEV], 'frightened' [CEV],

'affrighted' [KJV], 'filled with fear' [REB], 'very frightened' [LN], 'very much afraid' [LN], 'afraid' [BAGD, EC], 'startled' [BAGD]. This adverb is also translated as a noun phrase: 'in their terror' [TNT], 'in terror' [BNTC].

b. δόξα (BAGD 3. p. 204): 'glory' [EC, Lns, WBC; KJV, NET, NIV, NLT, NRSV], 'homage' [REB], 'praise' [TNT], 'fame, renown' [BAGD], 'honor' [BAGD]. The phrase ἔδοκαν δόξαν 'gave glory' is translated 'praised' [CEV], 'praised the greatness' [TEV], 'worshiped' [NAB], 'did homage' [BNTC]. See this word also at 1:6.

QUESTION—Does the statement, ἔδοκαν δόξαν τῷ θεῷ τοῦ οὐρανοῦ 'they gave glory to the God of Heaven', indicate that they repented and turned to Christ?

1. It indicates that they were converted [Alf, BNTC, EC, ICC, Ld, NTC, Sw, WBC]. Elsewhere in Revelation this action seems to indicate conversion (see 14:7; 15:4; 16:9). Also in John's vocabulary, fear, worship, and repent are almost interchangeable [BNTC]. This represents the final turning to God of the Jewish nation [ICC, Ld], after the full number of the Gentiles has been saved (see Romans 9:25, 26) [ICC]. Other Scriptures where this phrase seems to point to repentance are: Joshua 7:19; Isaiah 42:12; 1 Peter 2:12 [Ld]. This is the only place in Revelation where people turn to God following a penalizing judgment. Revelation 16:9 states that the people 'did not repent and give him glory', implying that giving glory to God was an outcome of repentance [WBC].

2. It does not indicate conversion but is merely an acknowledgment of God's power [Lns, NIC, NIGTC, Wal]. Fear compels them to acknowledge that Christ, not the Antichrist, is the true Lord, but this falls short of turning to God to save them [NIC].

QUESTION—How are the nouns related in the genitive construction τῷ θεῷ τοῦ οὐρανοῦ 'to the God of Heaven'?

'The God of Heaven' is 'the God who lives in Heaven' or 'the God who rules from Heaven' [TH]. This is an OT term that distinguishes God from the many heathen gods [EC].

DISCOURSE UNIT: 11:14–19 [ICC, Ld, Lns, NIGTC]. The topic is the seventh trumpet.

11:14 **The second woe passed-away; behold the third woe comes quickly.**

QUESTION—What is indicated by this verse?

It indicates that, following a parenthetical section of 10:1–1:13, the third woe is about to begin [Alf, NIC, NIGTC, NTC, Sw, TH], with the blowing of the seventh trumpet [NTC]. The second woe, as seen after the sixth trumpet is blown, occurred in 9:13–21 [Alf, NIGTC, TH].

DISCOURSE UNIT: 11:15–16:21 [WBC]. The topic is the seventh trumpet and the seven bowls.

DISCOURSE UNIT: 11:15–19 [Alf, BNTC, EC, GNT, NIC, NTC, Sw, TNTC, WBC; CEV, KJV, NAB, NET, NIV, NLT, NRSV, TEV]. The topic is the seventh trumpet.

11:15 And the seventh angel trumpeted; and there-were loud voices in heaven saying, "The kingdom[a] of the world became our Lord's and his Christ's,[b]

TEXT—Instead of the singular ἐγένετο ἡ βασιλεία 'the kingdom...has become' some manuscripts have the plural ἐγένοντο αἱ βασιλεῖαι 'the kingdoms...have become'. GNT does not mention this alternative; ἐγένοντο αἱ βασιλεῖαι 'the kingdoms...have become' is followed by KJV.

LEXICON—a. βασιλεία (LN 37.64): 'kingdom' [BAGD, EC, WBC; all versions except REB, TEV, TNT], 'kingship' [Lns, TH], 'sovereignty (of/over)' [BNTC, TH, TNTC; REB, TNT], 'power to rule over' [TH; TEV], 'reign' [LN, Lns], 'rule' [LN, Wal], 'dominion' [TH]. See this word also at 1:6.

b. Χριστός (LN 53.82, 93.387) (BAGD 1. p. 887): 'Christ' [BAGD, BNTC, EC, LN (53.82, 93.387), Lns; KJV, NAB, NET, NIV, NLT, REB], 'Messiah' [BAGD, LN (53.82), WBC; NRSV, TEV, TNT], 'Anointed One' [BAGD], 'Chosen One' [TH; CEV]. Χριστός literally means, 'the one who has been anointed' [LN (53.82)].

QUESTION—Whose voices were heard saying this?

1. They were probably the voices of angels [NIC, TH, TNTC]. It is the voices of angels since they could call God 'Lord' whereas believers would call Christ 'Lord' [NIC].
2. They were probably the voices of the believers in Heaven (see 7:9 and 19:1 and 6) [NIGTC].
3. They were the voices of angels and believers together [EC, Lns].
4. They were the voices of the four Living Beings and the angels [Alf].
5. They were the voices of the Living Beings or the Cherubim [ICC].

QUESTION—To whom does the term ὁ κύριος ἡμῶν 'our Lord' refer?

It refers to God the Father [EC, Ld, Lns, NIC, NIGTC, Sw, TNTC, WBC].

QUESTION—Does the phrase, ὁ κύριος ἡμῶν 'our Lord', include all believers, or only a select group?

It includes all believers [TH].

QUESTION—How are the nouns related in the genitive construction Χριστοῦ αὐτοῦ 'his Christ'?

He (God) chose Christ to be the Savior of the world [TH].

QUESTION—What is the significance of the aorist tense of ἐγένετο '(the kingdom of the world) became'?

It is a past tense used to indicate a future [Ld]. It looks at the event as being as certain as though it were an accomplished fact already [TNTC]. The event is being celebrated as though it had already occurred [ICC].

QUESTION—What is the relationship between the seventh trumpet and the third woe?
   The seventh trumpet contains the third woe which is the seven bowls of 16:1–21 [EC, Ld, Wal]. The seventh trumpet is the third woe. It is woe to the enemies of God for it announces the final victory of God's kingdom over the world's kingdom [BNTC, NIGTC]. The woe is the wrath of God as seen in 11:18 [BNTC].

and he-will-reign[a] forever-and-ever."[b]
LEXICON—a. fut. act. indic. of βασιλεύω (LN 37.22) (BAGD 1.b.γ. p. 136): 'to reign' [BNTC, EC, LN, Lns, WBC; all versions except CEV, TEV, TNT], 'to rule' [BAGD; CEV, TEV, TNT], 'to control completely' [LN]. See this word also at 5:10.
   b. εἰς τοὺς αἰῶνας τῶν αἰώνων (See this word at 1:18): 'forever and ever' [BNTC, EC, WBC; all versions except REB], 'forever' [REB], 'for the eons of the eons' [Lns].
QUESTION—Who is the antecedent to the pronoun in βασιλεύσει 'he will reign'?
   1. It refers to God [Ld, Lns, NIGTC, Sw, TH, WBC]: God will reign. Verses 16 and 17 show that God is intended here [NIGTC]. Christ will share in God's everlasting rule [NIGTC].
   2. It refers to Christ [Wal]: Christ will reign.
   3. It refers to both God and Christ [EC, NIC]. The singular 'he will rule' occurs because of the unity of their joint sovereignty [EC]. The reign of Christ and God, as an inseparable entity, is in mind [NIC].
   4. It refers first to the millennial reign of Christ (21:9–22:2; 20:4–6), but this becomes the reign of God (21:1–4; 22:3–5). But in reality, the two kingdoms are one [ICC].

11:16 And the twenty four elders [the-ones] before God sitting on their thrones fell on their faces and they-worshiped God
TEXT—Some manuscripts do not include οἱ 'the-ones' before ἐνώπιον 'before'. GNT includes this word but puts it in brackets, indicating doubt about including it.
QUESTION—Where are these twenty-four elders referred to before?
   They are referred to at 4:4 and 4:10 [EC, TH, WBC]. They are referred to in 7:11 [EC, NIC].
QUESTION—What does ἔπεσαν ἐπὶ τὰ πρόσωπα αὐτῶν 'fell on their faces' signify?
   It signifies that they prostrated themselves [NIC, Sw, TH, TNTC, WBC]. It signifies that they knelt down [CEV]. See this Question also at 7:11.

11:17 saying, "We-thank[a] you, Lord God the Almighty,[b] the-one being and the-one who-was,
TEXT—Some manuscripts include καί 'and' after ἦν 'he was'. Others include the phrase καὶ ὁ ἐρχόμενος 'and the one coming' in the same place. GNT

does not include either of these alternatives with a B decision, indicating that the text is almost certain. The reading, 'and the one coming', is included by KJV.

LEXICON—a. pres. act. indic. of εὐχαριστέω (LN 33.349) (BAGD 2. p. 328): 'to thank' [BNTC, EC, LN, Lns, WBC; CEV, TEV, TNT], 'to give thanks to' [KJV, NET, NIV, NLT, NRSV, REB], 'to praise' [NAB], 'to render/return thanks' [BAGD]. Ἐυχαριστέω indicates to express appreciation for some benefit [LN].

b. παντοκράτωρ (See this word at 1:8): 'Almighty' [EC, Lns, WBC; all versions except CEV, NET, REB], 'All-Powerful' [CEV, NET], 'sovereign over all' [REB], 'Omnipotent' [BNTC].

QUESTION—Where is the phrase ὁ ὢν καὶ ὁ ἦν 'the one being and the one who was' discussed previously?

It is discussed at 1:4.

QUESTION—Why is there a reference to God's 'being' and 'having been' but no third reference to his coming?

There is no reference to God's coming because that time has arrived with this verse [EC, ICC, NIC, NTC, TNTC].

because you-have-taken[a] your great power[b] and reigned.[c]

LEXICON—a. perf. act. indic. of λαμβάνω (See this word at 3:11): 'to take' [EC, Lns; NET, NIV, NRSV, TEV, TNT], 'to assume' [BNTC; NAB, NLT, REB], 'to take to oneself' [KJV], 'to receive' [WBC], 'to use' [CEV]. The perfect tense indicates that God has taken power in a permanent way [TNTC].

b. δύναμις (See this word at 1:16): 'power' [BNTC, EC, Lns; all versions], 'authority' [WBC]. Δύναμις here indicates both the authority to do something as well as the ability to carry it out [Wal].

c. aorist act. indic. of βασιλεύω (BAGD I.b.α., 2., p. 136): 'to reign' [EC, Lns, WBC; KJV, NET, NIV, NLT, NRSV, TNT], 'to rule' [BAGD; CEV, TEV], 'to be/become king' [BAGD], 'to obtain royal power' [BAGD]. This verb is also translated as a noun: 'reign' [BNTC; NAB, REB]. The aorist tense is inceptive here indicating 'to begin to (reign)' [BNTC, EC, ICC, Ld, Lns, NIC, NTC, TH, TNTC, WBC; CEV, NAB, NET, NIV, NLT, REB, TEV]. See this word also at 5:10.

QUESTION—What relationship is indicated by ὅτι 'because'?

It indicates that this clause is the reason for the praise of the elders [EC, WBC]: we thank you *because* you have taken your great power and reigned.

QUESTION—What is indicated by the phrase εἴληφας τὴν δύναμίν σου τὴν μεγάλην 'you have taken your great power'?

It indicates that God has exercised or used his great power [TH]. It indicates the final triumph of God over the powers of evil [ICC, Ld, Lns, NIC, NIGTC, Sw, TNTC]. The Millennial Reign of Christ on earth is implied (see 20:4–6; 21:9–22:2) [ICC].

11:18 **And the nations were-angry,[a] but/and/because your anger[b] came**
LEXICON—a. aorist pass. (deponent = act.) indic. of ὀργίζομαι (LN 88.174)
(BAGD p. 579): 'to be angry' [BAGD, LN; KJV, NIV, NLT], 'to get angry' [CEV], 'to be enraged' [EC, WBC; NET, TNT], 'to be filled with rage' [TEV], 'to rage' [NRSV], 'to rage in anger' [NAB], 'to rise in wrath' [BNTC; REB], 'to be wroth' [Lns], 'to be full of anger, to be furious' [LN].

b. ὀργή (LN 38.10): 'anger' [TEV], 'wrath' [BNTC, EC, Lns, WBC; KJV, NET, NIV, NLT, NRSV], 'day of wrath' [NAB, REB, TNT], 'punishment' [LN]. The phrase ἦλθεν ἡ ὀοργή σου 'your anger came' is translated 'you got angry' [CEV]. See this word also at 6:16.

QUESTION—Who are τὰ ἔθνη 'the nations'?
They are the Gentiles or heathen who are hostile to God [TH].
QUESTION—What is the sense of καί 'and' here?
  1. It has a contrastive sense [BNTC, TH, WBC; NAB, NET, NLT, NRSV, REB, TNT]: but.
  2. It has a conjoining sense [EC, Lns; KJV, NIV]: and.
  3. It has a causal sense [TEV]: because.

and the time[a] of-the dead to-be-judged[b] and to-give the reward[c] to-your servants the prophets and to-the saints[d] and to-the-ones fearing[e] your name, the small and the great,
LEXICON—a. καιρός (See this word at 1:3): 'time' [BNTC, EC, WBC; all versions except NAB], 'moment' [NAB], 'season' [Lns]. Καιρός has the sense of appropriate time, opportunity, or occasion [EC, NIC, TH, TNTC].

b. aorist pass. indic. of κρίνω (See this word at 6:10): 'to be judged' [BNTC, EC, Lns, WBC; CEV, KJV, NET, REB, TEV]. The passive voice is also rendered actively: 'to judge' [NAB, NLT, TNT]. This verb is also translated as a participle: 'judging' [NIV, NRSV].

c. μισθός (LN **38.14**, 57.173) (BAGD 2.a. p. 523): 'reward' [BAGD, EC, **LN** (38.14), Lns; KJV, NET, REB], 'pay, wages' [LN (57.173)], 'recompense' [LN (38.14)]. The phrase δουναῖ τὸ μιστόν 'to give the reward' is translated 'to reward' [BNTC, WBC; all versions except KJV, NET, REB].

d. οἱ ἅγιοι (See this word at 5:8): 'saints' [EC, Lns; KJV, NET, NIV, NRSV], 'holy ones' [NAB], 'God's people' [BNTC, WBC; CEV, REB, TEV, TNT], 'God's holy people' [NLT].

e. pres. mid. (deponent = act.) participle of φοβέομαι (LN 53.58, 87.14) (BAGD 2.a. p. 863): 'to fear' [BAGD, BNTC, EC, LN (87.14), Lns; KJV, NLT, NRSV, TNT], 'to honor' [CEV, REB], 'to revere' [WBC; NAB, NET], 'to reverence' [BAGD, LN (53.57); NIV], 'to have reverence for' [BAGD; TEV], 'to have respect for' [BAGD], 'to show great respect/reverence for' [LN (87.14)], 'to worship' [LN (53.57)]. Φοβέομαι indicates a profound respect or awe for God that approaches fear [LN]. See this word also at 1:17.

QUESTION—How many of the following infinitives does the word καιρός 'time' govern?

The word 'time' governs the following three infinitives: κριθῆναι 'to be judged', δοῦναι 'to give (reward)', and διαφθεῖραι 'to destroy' [Lns, Sw]: the time to be judged, the time to give reward and the time to destroy.

QUESTION—What judgment may be referred to here?

The great white throne judgment depicted in 20:11–5 is being referred to [BNTC, NIC, NIGTC, TH]. The judgment portrayed in the seven bowls depicted in 15:5ff. is being referred to [NTC].

QUESTION—How many groups of people are indicated in this verse?

1. There are two groups: your servants the prophets and also the saints [BNTC, EC, Ld, Lns, NIC, TH]. The clause, 'those who fear your name', modifies 'the saints' [BNTC, EC, Lns, TH]: the saints, even to those who fear your name. The clause, 'those who fear your name, the small and the great', further defines both prophets and saints [Ld, NIC]. The phrase, 'the great and the small', further defines 'those who fear your name' (see Psalms 115:13) [Lns]. The phrase 'the great and the small', further defines 'the saints' [BNTC]. The Greek word καί before the words, 'those who fear your name', can also be translated 'even' [Ld]: *even* those who fear your name.

2. There are three groups: your servants the prophets, the saints, and also those who fear your name [Alf, ICC, Sw, TNTC]. It is possible that the final class includes and further defines the first two [TNTC]. The groups, 'the saints and those who fear your name', refer to Jewish Christians and Gentile Christians [ICC]. All three together refer to the entire Church [Alf]. The group, 'those who fear your name', refers to Jewish proselytes [Sw].

3. There is only one group: all of these designations refer to the whole Church [NIGTC].

QUESTION—What does it mean 'to fear God's name'?

It means to fear or respect God [TH; NAB, TEV].

and to destroy[a] the-ones destroying[b] the earth."

LEXICON—a. pres. act. infin. of διαφθείρω (LN **20.40**): 'to destroy' [BAGD, BNTC, EC, **LN**, Lns; all versions], 'to ruin utterly' [WBC], 'to destroy utterly' [LN]. Διαφθείρω is used here in a literal sense of physical destruction [WBC]. See this word also at 8:9.

b. pres. act. participle of διαφθείρω (LN 20.40, **88.266**): 'to destroy' [Lns; all versions except NAB, NLT], 'to cause destruction' [NLT], 'to lay waste' [NAB], 'to ruin' [BAGD, **LN** (88.266), WBC], 'to deprave' [LN (20.40, 88.266)], 'to cause to be depraved' [**LN** (88.266)], 'to pervert, to cause the moral ruin of' [LN (88.266)]. This verb is also translated as a noun: 'destroyer' [BNTC, EC]. Διαφθείρω has the figurative sense of perverting morality [WBC]. Here it has the double sense of physical destruction as well as the perversion of morality [Sw]. See this word also at 8:9.

QUESTION—What does the term γῆ 'earth' indicate here?

It is a figure of metonymy in which the earth is named for the people who live in it [TH, WBC].

DISCOURSE UNIT: 11:19–12:17 [WBC]. The topic is the woman, the child and the dragon.

11:19 And the temple^a of-God in heaven was opened and the ark^b of-the covenant^c of-him was-seen in his temple,

TEXT—Some manuscripts do not include the definite article ὁ 'the', before ἐν 'in', changing the meaning from 'the temple of God in heaven was opened', to 'the temple of God was opened in heaven'. GNT does not mention this alternative. It is omitted by KJV.

LEXICON—a. ναός (See this word at 3:12): 'temple' [BNTC, EC, WBC; all versions except REB, TNT], 'sanctuary' [Lns; REB, TNT]. It refers to the heavenly sanctuary [BAGD].

b. κιβωτός (LN **6.139**) (BAGD 2. p. 432): 'ark' [BAGD, BNTC, EC, Lns, WBC; all versions except CEV, TEV], 'box' [**LN**; TEV], 'chest, coffer' [LN]. The phrase ἡ κιβωτὸς τῆς διαθήκης 'the ark of the covenant' is translated 'the sacred chest' [CEV], 'the Covenant Box' [TEV].

c. διαθήκη (LN 34.44, 57.124) (BAGD 3. p. 183): 'covenant' [BAGD, BNTC, EC, LN (34.44), Lns, WBC; all versions except CEV, KJV], 'testament' [LN (57.124); KJV], 'pact' [LN (34.44)], 'will' [LN (57.124)], not explicit [CEV]. A διαθήκη is an agreement between two parties that details the benefits and responsibilities of each party [LN (34.44)]. This is not a mutual pact between equals, but a one-sided promise on God's part [Lns].

QUESTION—How are the nouns related in the genitive construction ἡ κιβωτὸς τῆς διαθήκης 'the ark of the covenant'?

The ark belongs to the covenant [Lns]. The ark was a wooden box in which were the two stone tablets of the ten commandments [TH] and it was a symbol of God's presence and agreement with his people [CEV].

QUESTION—In the phrase ἡ κιβωτὸς τῆς διαθήκης αὐτοῦ 'the ark of the covenant of him', does αὐτοῦ 'of him', modify only 'covenant', or the whole phrase, 'the ark of the covenant'?

1. It modifies only 'covenant' [BNTC, EC; KJV, NAB, NET, NIV, NLT, NRSV, REB, TNT]: the ark of *his* covenant.
2. It modifies the whole phrase, 'the ark of the covenant' [WBC]: *his* ark of the covenant. In the OT the phrase, 'the ark of God' or 'the ark of Yahweh' occurs 82 times while the phrases 'the ark of the covenant of Yahweh' and 'the ark of the covenant of God' occur 30 times. In these, the word 'covenant' seems to modify 'ark'. It seems best therefore to take

the phrase, 'the ark of the covenant' as a unit here and have 'his' modify the phrase as a whole [WBC].

QUESTION—Which ark is referred to and what does it symbolize?

It refers to the ark of the covenant that is in heaven, the prototype for the one on earth [BNTC, EC, ICC, NTC, TNTC, WBC]. It symbolizes the presence of God [BNTC, EC, Ld, NIC, TNTC]. It symbolizes God's dependability to be kind to his own people and to avenge their enemies [Alf]. It symbolizes the covenant between God and His people [ICC]. It symbolizes God's dependability to keep his covenant [NIC].

QUESTION—Which temple is being referred to here, the heavenly one or the earthly one?

It refers to the temple of God in Heaven [TH]. It specifically refers to the holy of holies of the temple [BNTC, ICC].

QUESTION—What does the scene of the ark in the open temple symbolize?

It symbolizes that in the final realization of God's purposes, the presence of God is available to people [Ld]. It symbolizes that the way into God's presence stands wide open (see Hebrews 10:19) [TNTC]. It symbolizes God's presence with his people and judgment on his enemies [WBC]. It symbolizes that God will keep fully his covenant promises to his people [Ld, NTC]. It symbolizes that God will keep his promises to his own people and will destroy their enemies [NIC].

and there were flashes-of-lightning and sounds and peals-of-thunder and (an) earthquake and great hail.

QUESTION—Where are similar features of nature discussed?

Flashes of lightning, sounds and peals of thunder are discussed at 4:5; 8:5, 7 [TH].

QUESTION—What is indicated by this clause?

It indicates that God will immediately execute judgment on the earth [Wal]. It is an indicator of God's final judgment [WBC]. These five phenomena symbolize the all-powerful strength of God against his enemies [Lns]. They express the power and majesty of God's presence [Ld].

www.ingramcontent.com/pod-product-compliance
Lightning Source LLC
Chambersburg PA
CBHW072148290426
44111CB00012B/2007